02

STRONGER
THAN
CUSTOM

Yearlings Diane Bracy, Dianne Louise Stoddard, Rebecca Ambrose Blythe, and Kelly Lynn Zachgo of F Company, First Regiment, United States Corps of Cadets, pose in their Full Dress Gray uniforms in 1977. Illustration by Pamela Lenck Bradford. Copyright © 2001 by Pamela Lenck Bradford.

STRONGER
THAN
CUSTOM

★ ★ ★ ★

West Point and
the Admission of Women

LANCE JANDA

Foreword by Lieutenant Colonel Donna Alesch Newell

PRAEGER

Westport, Connecticut
London

Library of Congress Cataloging-in-Publication Data

Janda, Lance.
    Stronger than custom : West Point and the admission of women / Lance Janda ;
foreword by Donna Alesch Newell.
        p. cm.
    Includes bibliographical references and index.
    ISBN 0–275–97113–9 (alk. paper)
    1. United States Military Academy—Admission.   2. United States Corps of
Cadets—Membership.   3. Women military cadets—United States.   I. Title.
U410.Q1 J35 2002
355'.0071'173—dc21   2001021168

British Library Cataloguing in Publication Data is available.

Library of Congress Catalog Card Number: 2001021168
ISBN: 0–275–97113–9

First published in 2002

Praeger Publishers, 88 Post Road West, Westport, CT 06881
An imprint of Greenwood Publishing Group, Inc.
www.praeger.com

Printed in the United States of America

The paper used in this book complies with the
Permanent Paper Standard issued by the National
Information Standards Organization (Z39.48–1984).

10 9 8 7 6 5 4 3 2

For my parents, Robert Lawrence and Virginia Kay Janda,

who are also stronger than custom.

Contents

A photo essay follows chapter 4

Foreword

I enlisted in the Army in 1975 primarily because the Army offered me a chance to earn money for college while also gaining valuable workforce experience. My enlistment was a shock to my friends, and to a certain degree, even myself. My only prior involvement with anything or anyone related to the military was wearing a POW bracelet for an Air Force officer from my hometown who was captured and imprisoned in North Vietnam. Maybe the tremendous sense of pride I felt in that man's noble accomplishments left me wanting more when we celebrated his release from captivity.

Shortly after I entered the Army, I was called to my company commander's office at Fort Gordon, Georgia, along with the other women undergoing training and asked if I was interested in attending West Point. My response was "What's West Point?" I was from Albuquerque, New Mexico, and completely ignorant about the United States Military Academy. My commander answered that West Point was "the Army's College." Because I had entered the Army as a stepping stone to higher education, I was thrilled at the chance to attend "the Army's College." Six months later I discovered that "the Army's College" wasn't quite the same thing as the University of New Mexico.

My mother immigrated in 1949 to the United States from Ireland and she instilled several important concepts in me. One was that I should give something back to our wonderful country for the opportunities it had given me. Another was that in the United States, if you work hard, you can achieve anything. While preparing to attend West Point I worked hard, I trained physically, and I studied intently. I was ready—or so I thought, prior to R-day for the Class of 1980.

What I was completely unprepared for was the overall level of animosity I encountered in those early days at West Point.

I didn't understand why such intense antagonism was being directed at me purely because I was a woman. I was bright, motivated, personable, and athletic, and had already willingly and proudly embraced the possibility of giving up my life for my country. I was naive enough to believe that, once our nation's civilian leadership made a decision, our military professionals would act upon that decision—well—professionally. The reality, as Lance Janda's book explains in depth, was something quite different.

To put it mildly, I encountered very immature, clearly prejudicial behavior from a variety of individuals assigned at West Point as staff and faculty—the individuals who were supposedly setting a professional example for cadets. I could cope with the opposing beliefs, behavior, and viewpoints of my fellow cadets by attributing these to ignorance and immaturity. Cadets with a negative attitude—like the squad leader during Cadet Basic Training who made bets with my male classmates on how many women would fall out of a road march—just motivated me to prove them wrong. I felt profoundly betrayed when the so-called military professionals were more antagonistic, often in very insidious and covert ways, than my fellow cadets.

Luckily, I had the support and counsel of my parents and some very wise friends who helped me to understand that the antagonism was not directed at me personally. But even with this understanding, the "class action" animosity hurt. My method to counter the hurt was to adopt an artificial persona. I called it my "perfect female cadet" role. If Academy Awards for acting had been handed out at graduation along with diplomas, I'd have received one. That role served a useful purpose in that it got me through the four years, by all outward appearances, unscathed. The truth was so different. The person residing within my body who graduated from West Point can be best described as an egg—tough exterior, mush on the inside.

I am profoundly thankful that my lieutenant days were in a unit that welcomed me as a soldier who just happened to be a woman. The contentious atmosphere that existed between the sexes at West Point was nonexistent in that first Army assignment. This allowed my battered ego to revert, in a relatively short period of time, back to the healthy one that had arrived at West Point's front gate in July 1976. Each subsequent Army assignment found me evaluated on my performance rather than my gender. I have now experienced twenty-plus years of hard work, personal sacrifice, and supportive command climates that I would repeat in a heartbeat.

By a strange twist of fate, I arrived at West Point just about twenty years to the day after I arrived to be a cadet, with a bit more rank on my shoulders, and was assigned to the Office of the Commandant of Cadets. As I observed R-day for the class of 2000, I took heart in the profound change in atmosphere from what I experienced twenty years earlier. The new cadets reported to the CADET in the Red Sash—not the MAN in the Red Sash. Women cadre were assigned to all levels within the chain of command. Women cadets had long hair and didn't think twice about being with other women cadets out and around the cadet area. I remember wishing that each of my woman classmates could share this scene with me. What I observed twenty years after women first entered the Corps of Cadets was what we thought was possible between men and women at West Point—capable, dynamic, motivated young leaders, standing side by side, working with each other to accomplish a mission without a theme of animosity underscoring the proceedings.

My mom taught me to believe in the best of people. I believe that the majority of the Army and West Point leaders while I was a cadet were more interested in our success than our failure. Sadly, the wounds caused by the minority were not often visible to the outside observer and made for a variety of different strategies to heal those wounds once we graduated.

Lance's book uncovers very interesting facts about the trials and tribulations, hurdles and plateaus of injecting women into the "Long Gray Line." It tells of the conflict between our nation's civilian and military leadership over the role of women in the armed forces. It tells of a proud and renowned institution facing an unwanted change—and how the Academy implemented that change. It gives the perspectives of both the antagonists and protagonists on the subject of women at West Point. Most importantly, it tells the story of what a determined and courageous group of women encountered when they reported to the United States Military Academy on July 7, 1976.

Like what the IBMs and the Bell Telephones and other huge American corporations have encountered, the United States Army of the 1970s was an organization undergoing change in order to be relevant to the nation in the aftermath of Vietnam. The transition to an All Volunteer Army after the end of the draft required a significantly different personnel strategy to ensure a high quality fighting force. And women proved willing and able to step up to the call to defend our nation, ultimately becoming an integral part of the world's best Army. But was the Army of the 1970s ready to mainstream women? The seemingly unanimous opposition within the Army toward including women at the military academy seemed to answer "no" to this question. Though not an imperative for promotion to the highest ranks, a West Point degree is universally regarded as the mark of a career professional, providing officers with a network of fellow graduates with which to traverse the vagaries of the military hierarchy. Dubbed "America's Power Fraternity" by K. Bruce Galloway and Robert B. Johnson, Jr., West Point provides the Army with young leaders of courage, character, and integrity. Why would the Army not want its women officers to be imbued with these same traits?

The simple answer was that the Army did want women officers of courage, character, and integrity. But these same women officers, by Army policy, were not going to be combat arms officers, and the predominant thrust of West Point's training program was combat-oriented. So why put women through an expensive program of training and instruction when they were not going to become combat leaders?

Because, in October 1975, the nation's elected civilian leadership voted to allow women the opportunity.

West Point is the oldest of the nation's service academies, with alumni who have played a significant role in every important national event since its founding in 1802. West Point is a place that, in 1976, we women described as "174 years of tradition untouched by progress." West Point—the Army's college—is unlike any other college experience in the world.

Lieutenant Colonel Donna Alesch Newell, United States Army

United States Military Academy Class of 1980

Preface

More than 200 people participated in the writing of this book, which is my way of expressing the age-old truism that no one really writes alone. They included graduates of the United States Military Academy (USMA), active and retired Army officers, former and current members of the USMA faculty and staff, and a wide assortment of colleagues, librarians, archivists, mentors, family, and personal friends. Their willingness to enthusiastically join in my efforts, and to lend guidance to what at times was a passionately disorganized endeavor, spelled the difference between a work that evolved into a book and one whose fate might have involved gathering dust in the recesses of my office. I can never really repay the debt I owe these people or explain how much it meant when they provided encouragement or shared their memories with me over drinks or a meal I was seldom allowed to buy for myself. Their generosity and friendship made this project profoundly fulfilling on both a personal and a professional level, and I am privileged to be able to thank them here.

In academia, my thanks go to the University of Oklahoma's (OU) Graduate College for funding portions of my research, and to the OU Humanities Council for providing a grant that allowed me to travel to West Point. Within the Department of History at OU I am indebted to Professors Robert L. Griswold, H. Wayne Morgan, David W. Levy, and Ben Keppel for reading and commenting on drafts of the work in progress and to Professor Paul A. Gilje, who first suggested I combine my interests in military and women's history many years ago. At Cameron University I owe a huge debt of gratitude to Debbie Crossland and the staff of the Academic Research Support Center for producing transcripts of dozens of interviews I recorded with West Point graduates. Thanks also go to Cherri Randall, who restored my faith in English majors via a critical and enormously helpful reading of the text, to Tessa Craig, Secretary in the Department of Sociology and Criminal Justice, whose command of Word Perfect salvaged my sanity several times, and to my colleague Doug Catterall, who helped me negotiate the world of Latin, Ovid, and Virgil. Grateful appreciation also goes to Dr. Lionel Tiger, Charles Darwin Professor of Anthropology at Rutgers University. He kindly shared his thoughts and current research with an outsider whose knowledge of anthropology, biology, and physiology may best be described as "limited," and became an important influence on my thinking during the final stages of my work.

At the United States Military Academy, I am deeply thankful to Dr. Stephen B. Grove, the official West Point historian, to his assistant Patricia Mohler, to Alecia Mauldin of the West Point Archives, and to Alan C. Aimone in the Special Collections section of the Omar Bradley Library. Dr. Grove was my professional host at the Academy on two occasions, guiding me through a wealth of primary documents and providing critical background information on the admission of women to West Point. He and Ms. Mohler assisted me in gaining access to many of the exit interviews conducted with the women of the West Point Class of 1980 and answered my endless e-mail requests for often obscure bits of information. Dr. Grove responded graciously and informatively to those inquiries for more than five years and rose above any professional obligations by reviewing the manuscript, offering material for consideration that I had overlooked, and producing a wealth of useful suggestions and constructive criticisms. He was, in fact, my single most important resource during the research and writing of this book, and it is no exaggeration at all to say I could not have written it without him. Ms. Mauldin performed speedy miracles while satisfying my requests for photographs to accompany the text and deserves extra appreciation for keeping the wheels of a sometimes ponderous bureaucracy moving on my behalf. Mr. Aimone helped me make sense of the considerable resources of the West Point library and even let me stay with him after closing one night when the amount of material I needed to review and the number of hours left in my stay at West Point were in mighty conflict.

Within the Academy's Class of 1980 I am obliged to everyone who spoke with me formally or informally about his or her experience as a cadet and to all who so generously shared their photographs, journals, letters, and mementos. Those who were especially helpful include Marty J. Eaton, Nancy L. Gucwa, Karen J. Hobson, Lieutenant Colonel David G. Jesmer, Susan P. Kellett, Kathleen Silvia, Doris A. Turner, William K. Wray, Danna Maller, Lieutenant Colonel Anne W. MacDonald, Major David Grosso, and Robin R. Carrington. Lieutenant Colonel Kelly Lynch deserves special mention and my heartfelt thanks for sharing her scrapbook, identifying classmates in photographs, kindly reviewing the manuscript, and for being supportive from the very beginning. Debra Johnson carefully and thoughtfully reviewed and edited the work as well, along with Sally Johnson and Joan M. Gerth, and each was instrumental in shaping the final version of the manuscript. Joan also sent pictures of training at Camp Buckner, and made sure that I became the first kid on my block to proudly own a bumper sticker that reads,

The United States Military Academy
WEST POINT
established 1802
CO-ED SINCE 1976

I am also profoundly indebted to Lieutenant Colonel Donna Alesch Newell, who reviewed the manuscript, offered answers to my questions and enthusiasm for my plans, and helped me contact a number of her classmates during the course of my research. Her professional and cheerful demeanor came to symbolize to me all that is admirable about West Point and the Army, and for that reason I asked her to write the foreword. She generously said yes to that request, and I am very grateful.

Beyond the Class of 1980, other West Pointers were also a source of encouragement and insight. They passed me around the network of former graduates, offered invaluable opinions and background information in an effort to keep a civilian writing about military matters out of trouble, and generally spurred me onward. Among those who were particularly helpful were General William A. Knowlton (Ret.), Colonel Robert P. Johnson (Ret.), General Andrew J. Goodpaster (Ret.), Lieutenant General Sidney B. Berry (Ret.), Robert C. Lang IV, the staff of the Gerald R. Ford Presidential Library, Dr. William L. Wilson, and filmmaker Joan Jordan. John M. Anderson patiently edited every chapter when the work was young and was a rich source of friendship, support, and internet expertise almost from the very beginning.

In professional circles, I thank the editors at Longman Press for allowing me to quote passages from a chapter entitled "A Simple Matter of Equality: The Admission of Women to West Point," which I wrote for inclusion in *A Soldier and a Woman: Sexual Integration in the Military*, which was edited by Gerard J. DeGroot and Corinna Peniston-Bird. At Praeger, Heather Staines, Frank Saunders, and the rest of the staff earned my warm praise by taking a chance on me and tolerating my endless questions and requests for just a little more time. They made publishing very enjoyable, which colleagues tell me is a very rare thing indeed. I could not have asked for a better experience than I have had with them.

The same may be said of my relationship with Pamela L. Bradford, who drew the wonderful illustrations that accompany and give greater life to the text. They are an evocative lense through which to study life at West Point and a compelling visceral reminder of the qualities that make the Academy such a singularly unique institution in American life. How Pam brought such understanding and emotion to simple sketches is beyond me, but I am gratified beyond words that she did.

On a legal note, the terms "West Point," "United States Military Academy," and "USMA" are licensed trademarks owned by the Department of Defense, and the views and opinions expressed in this book are mine alone. They do not necessarily represent the views of the Department of Defense or any of its components, though of course I think they should!

Within personal circles, I offer my humble appreciation for a lifetime of love and support to my parents, Robert and Kay Janda, and for timeless friendship and excellent editing to Xan E. Blake, Russell S. Post, and James T. LaPlant. Each of them does a fine job of helping me edit and improve my life as well as my work, and I can hardly imagine writing another chapter in my life without them. Naturally, any errors of fact or interpretation that slipped by such a wonderful group of professional and personal supporters are truly mine alone.

Finally, I thank my lovely wife Sarah, who graciously and patiently assisted me at every step and on every level in the completion of this work. In addition to serving as a gifted editor and colleague, she is a welcome reminder that life and work are not the same. It is with her that my sun rises and sets.

Sources

One of the great joys of doing primary research in the recent American past is the abundance of source material. As every modern historian knows, however, that abundance can also be a handicap. At a certain point the sheer weight of material becomes a daunting challenge. This is certainly true for anyone researching the role of women in the armed forces of the United States and for studies of West Point in particular.

Yet another challenge is objectivity. Women arrived as cadets at West Point just over twenty-five years ago, which in historical terms is less than the blink of an eye. My own perceptions of the America of the 1970s, vague as they are, may color my recreation of the past and challenge the collective memory of persons with either stronger recollections or more dogmatic views than my own. Writing about recent events is also particularly difficult because reaching definite conclusions is so fraught with risk (hence the historian's cliché, often heard during my research, that "history stops when you were born," because an aloof, long-term perspective is difficult to find in the recent past). Some of the first women graduates of the Academy are still in the Army, for example, so assessing with finality what their admission really meant for them or the institution is tempting and yet still problematic at this juncture.

Balanced against those concerns are what Arthur M. Schlesinger, Jr. called the "compensating advantages of writing so soon—in particular, the opportunity to consult those who took part in great events and thus to rescue information which might otherwise elude the written record."[1] The "consultations" for this work primarily involved interviews with participants in the admission of women to West Point, and these oral histories pose a unique set of risk and reward all their own. When they are included in the mix of data, sources, and interpretation for any project, the historian risks both bafflement at the variety of accounts of the same event and the haunting knowledge his or her work may have consequences for persons whose reputations, memories, and even careers are bound up in conclusions reached at a comfortable distance from actual events. This is not to say modern history cannot be done with judicious accuracy and compassion, only that it carries with it greater risks than the study of persons long dead or events barely remembered. It is for this reason I chose at the outset of my research to refer anonymously to almost everyone who shared his or her memories and insights about West Point with me.

I conducted 111 formal interviews with United States Military Academy (USMA) graduates and present or former members of the Academy faculty and staff. Sixty-four involved members of the Class of 1980, including twenty-seven women and thirty-nine men. Other interviews involved women who entered the Academy with the class in 1976 but left prior to graduation, former cadets, and others who were in some way involved with the preparations to admit women or could provide background on Academy life. Interviewees were promised confidentiality except for General Andrew J. Goodpaster (Ret.), General William A. Knowlton (Ret.), Lieutenant General Sidney B. Berry (Ret.), and Lieutenant General Harold G. Moore, Jr. (Ret.). Each of these retired officers is too well known in the public record to be treated anonymously, and each reviewed and approved transcripts of his interviews. Neither those transcripts or the tapes of the remaining interviews are available to the public at this time.

The anonymity of the interviews is admittedly a problem, both for the flow of the narrative and for those who might follow up on my research. It was necessary, however, in order to encourage former cadets, especially those still in the Army, to consent to discuss their past with an outsider. I do not pretend they told me everything, but I am certain the invaluable assistance the interviewees provided was made possible in many cases only by my assurances that names would never be discussed in print. I could have invented names for everyone, but that seemed artificial and overly contrived. Members of the Class of 1980 will probably have limited success in figuring out who said what in the pages of this book, and that seems fair because the story is their own. No one else needs to know. My conclusions rest both on their accounts of events at West Point and on relevant documents and secondary sources which can be verified by other historians. From a scholarly perspective, then, the identities of interviewees are unimportant. What they said is enormously important, of course, but their identity is a matter of curiosity and little more, and in that way I hope anonymity protects the individuals without unduly hampering the work.

Academy documents came from the office of Dr. Stephen B. Grove, the United States Military Academy Historian, and from the Special Collections Section of the USMA Library. Documents in the historian's office are part of the material amassed at the order of the West Point Superintendent beginning in 1976. They were assembled to provide records for an official history of efforts directed toward the admission and integration of women and as a defense against anticipated legal attacks. Sent over time from all parts of the Academy to the Office of the Director of Institutional Research, the documents eventually found a home in the office of the USMA Historian. I have provided the name and date of each document referenced in the narrative and retained copies of everything I noted.

Other sources include informal interviews, letters, e-mail correspondence, and exit interviews conducted by members of the West Point staff with the women of the Class of 1980. All sources are abbreviated in the endnotes as follows:

EI	Exit interview conducted with women in the Class of 1980 in April and May of that year by Dr. Stephen Grove, USMA Historian, and Major Irene Evanekovich of the Superintendent's staff. Tapes and transcripts of these interviews are the property of the Academy and the individuals involved. I obtained permission from a number of women to review their transcripts during a research trip to West Point in 1996.
ETA	Electronic mail sent to the author.
GRF	Material from the Gerald R. Ford Presidential Library
IWA	Formal interview with the author on tape.
IWA, author's notes	A non-taped interview with comments taken down by hand.
LTA	Letter sent to the author.
USMA Files	Documents in the USMA Historian's office.

While I made every effort to remain true to the facts as they were presented to me and to be as fair as possible to all concerned, I am acutely aware of the limitations inherent in writing history. C.V. Wedgewood addressed the most compelling problem when she wrote that "history is lived forward but it is written in retrospect. We know the end before we consider the beginning and we can never wholly recapture what it was like to know the beginning only."[2] Finished works often convey final, authoritative conclusions rather than the more murky but honest realization that recreating the past is more art than science, and it would be better if historians followed the humble approach to which Ezra Pound alluded many years ago:

> And even I can remember
> A day when the historians left blanks in their writings,
> I mean for things they didn't know.[3]

I have left no blanks in my writing, but I do confess this work is hardly all-knowing or perfectly complete. It represents, however, a dedicated effort to be as precise and empathetic as possible. Any errors of fact or interpretation, either committed or implied, are solely mine.

NOTES

1. Arthur M. Schlesinger, Jr., *The Crisis of the Old Order: 1919–1933* (Boston: Houghton Mifflin Company, 1957), p. ix.

2. C. V. Wedgewood, *William the Silent* (New York: W. W. Norton, 1967), p. 35.

3. Ezra Pound, *Draft of XXX Cantos*, quoted in *The Oxford Dictionary of Literary Quotations*, edited by Peter Kemp (New York: Oxford University Press, 1997), p. 104.

Introduction

When Congress established the United States Military Academy on the banks of the Hudson River in 1802, no one realized West Point might eventually become an agent of social change or dramatically alter the place of women in the American armed forces. Thomas Jefferson and other proponents of the Academy saw it as a potential source of trained officers for a nation striving to expand on a continental scale, as a place where the Army could train engineers and artillery experts who would form a regular cadre in time of war. In the century and a half that followed its creation the Academy performed this mission with admirable success, producing officers who won American wars and helped explore and develop the United States at an astonishing pace. So great was West Point's success that Congress created the United States Naval Academy in 1845, and the United States Air Force Academy in 1954, so that every branch of the armed forces would benefit from having an institution dedicated solely to producing career officers. By the latter half of the twentieth century these academies were among the premier officer training institutions in the world, recognized as places where combat leaders were forged and prepared for future greatness.

Yet the service academies admitted only men, in obeisance to a pervasive assumption that men alone could lead and fight in combat. By the 1970s, however, almost all assumptions about women were under intense pressure on a national scale, and the rapid pace of cultural change led Congress to use the military, and ultimately the academies, to offer greater opportunities to American women. One step in that process came when Congress opened federal service academies to women in 1976, a historic first which supporters believed would advance the cause of equality. None of the proponents of this change saw themselves as taking a decisive step toward fundamentally altering the role of American women in the military, but they did just that. This revolutionary event *was* a critical step toward placing women in direct combat positions, and toward expanding the importance of military women to the point where the armed services could not go to war without them. The military and opponents of greater opportunity for women foresaw some of these developments and fought valiantly to stop them. They ultimately failed, though their resistance did shape the debate to the point that supporters of dropping the gender barrier shied away from discussing the full implications of their actions. By focusing exclusively on equality they allowed a historic opportunity to fully debate the role of women in the armed forces slip away even as they paved the way for greater inclusion of women in America's service academies than ever before.

This is one among many ways to begin assessing the magnitude of the change undergone by the Academy and the Corps of Cadets when women were admitted to West Point. Fully comprehending this change is difficult, however, especially for outsiders who have nothing in their daily lives comparable to the immersion in tradition and the military ethos which life as a West Point cadet represents. At a distance of more than two decades from the event itself, we also struggle for perspective, too often taking historical events for granted and assuming the invisible Hand of Providence lay behind inevitable social evolutions whose drama is diminished by the passage of time. Yet real men and women confronted the daunting task of breaking 174 years of all-male tradition in 1976, and their most formidable barriers were as difficult to see as they were to overcome. After all, an academy whose graduates include officers who discovered the source of the Mississippi River and helped engineer the Panama Canal was certainly capable of *physically* preparing to accommodate the arrival of women.[1] Overcoming the mental, emotional, and psychological barriers, however, posed a more fundamental challenge. Shaped by socialization, culture, and tradition, young cadets with often limited perceptions of women's capabilities were forced to confront and defy traditional assumptions about gender roles, and those assumptions were not easily overcome. Part of the wonder of the transformation that did occur at West Point is the manner in which a proudly paternalistic hierarchy like the Army assumed a leading role in the expansion of opportunities for women in American society. Bound as they were by almost two centuries of American custom, and linked to codes of gender exclusivity in organized warfare extending as far into the past as recorded history allows, West Point and the Army struggled to adjust to the idea that women should be accepted as cadets and officers on an equal basis. The journey was difficult, occasionally traumatic, and hardly complete when the first women graduated from West Point in 1980.

To study the odyssey those women endured, and to examine the Army's efforts to integrate women at the United States Military Academy as a whole, is to examine in microcosm the entire spectrum of issues raised by furthering opportunities for women in the military. It is to see through a lens refracted by time the certainty that for the Army, gender is more problematic than any other single issue, including race. Ironically, the federal government forced the Army to confront racial discrimination over a generation before mainstream society became engaged in the modern Civil Rights movement, just as it placed the military at the forefront in the quest to expand opportunities for women during the 1970s. That historic pattern, within which Americans have consistently asked a defiant and historically conservative military to lead society in revamping our cultural assumptions concerning race and gender, is interesting indeed and one on which the study of women at West Point can shed considerable light. For while the Army has been extraordinarily successful over the long term in battling racial injustice, efforts to eradicate racism pale before the challenge of integrating women into the society of warriors. Rather than diminishing the very real and persistent problem of racism within the ranks, such a statement emphasizes the extraordinary difficulty West Point and the Army faced when ordered to broaden opportunities for women. Those efforts took a giant stride forward when Congress opened the service academies to both sexes in 1976, and they continue to expand to this day.[2]

Studying the admission of women to West Point is also a very practical way of assessing the schism in American society over how we define what it means to be a man or a woman, and of asking whether biology, physiology, or anthropology should shape the relentless push of American culture for absolute equality at any cost. It is to ask whether as a nation we have confused equity with equality, and whether we have mistaken the principle of equality of opportunity with that of equality of achievement. These issues are especially important in the military, for "they dramatize in such heightened fashion the schisms that rend society as a whole," and in that way tell us almost as much about American society at large as they do about the armed forces.[3]

The arrival of women at West Point is also an important chapter in the larger story of the increasingly important role women have played in the armed forces since the end of the draft and the creation of the All Volunteer Force in 1973. Studying their story is a useful way to explore the essence of a citizen's relationship to the armed forces, for asking if anyone has a *right* to enlist, whether the military is so different in form and function from civilian institutions that traditional concerns over equity should not apply, and if a society rife with sexism can fairly expect the military to conquer problems of harassment and violence against women which plague civilian life. Fundamentally, such a study illuminates the question of whether the armed forces are an appropriate place for "social engineering" or whether they should be expected to do anything besides win our wars.

Such research also deepens our understanding of how institutions respond to the challenge of social change, how they adapt to new realities while striving to protect their essential traditions. It can provide greater insight into how we as a culture view the human body, assigning talents and limitations to other human beings based on their sex alone, and help explain the dynamics of change in previously single-sex environments.

Perhaps most important for our own era, an analysis of what happened when women entered the "warrior culture" at West Point holds the promise of illuminating the complexities of breaking down the monopoly men have historically held over organized, state-sanctioned warfare. It is to see male culture, and particularly male warrior culture, under the stress and strain of expanding to include women. In almost every culture there are places or institutions where women may not go or participate, and in Western countries few male-centered organizations have cultivated greater deliberate exclusivity over their affairs than the military. Such organizations usually concede gender ground only when forced and often do so in controlled ways which preserve *some* inner sanctum where men still rule. Certainly this is true of West Point, of the Army, and of the military in general, and understanding how and why such cultures often choose to resist the inclusion of women may inform our sense of whether they should be forced to open their ranks. If they should, then works in this field can help us plan how best to broaden the warrior culture without destroying it in the process.

Some assessment of what went right and wrong at West Point during those first hesitant years of experimentation and evolution can also highlight the triumphs and tribulations of the Academy's Class of 1980, the first to include women graduates. More than any other cadets, members of that class bore the brunt of assimilating women into the Long Gray Line. Their successes as well as their failures deserve study and recognition and provide lessons for other military institutions struggling with gender integration in our own time. As events during the last few years at The Citadel and the Virginia Military Institute have demonstrated, sex-integration within a military environment is a difficult process. Pundits hovering about those institutions would do well to remember that West Point and the other service academies admitted women more than two decades ago, and the lessons learned at the Academy should have been studied more carefully by those who followed in their wake.

Beyond institutional and class experiences, the 119 women who arrived to break down the gender walls at West Point deserve special notice. Sixty-two of those women eventually graduated, each one a pioneer in a great drama of uncertain outcome. Most suffered a litany of gender-specific abuses while cadets, and those who endured to receive commissions as officers in the United States Army did so in triumph. Their story deserves telling both for its own sake, and because the individual experiences of the first women cadets have much to teach us. They illuminate the myriad shades of gray inherent in asking men and women to live, train, sleep, and coexist within a structured hierarchy for extended lengths of time, and bring to light the difficulties the Army has faced addressing these issues. Many of those difficulties are so fundamental, so deeply rooted in culture, physiology, and biology that they may never be fully resolved. As a host of alarming incidents in recent years demonstrate, the tendency to harass and resent women remains a powerful predisposition within the armed forces, one that confronts women at West Point and throughout the military on a daily basis.

Most of all, their stories highlight the entrenched resistance that confronted the first women cadets and that often frustrated the best efforts of Army officers to make integration work. With the power of West Point and the Army to command obedience, with a code of law wholly outside more lenient civilian jurisprudence, and with a determined plan of integration designed and implemented by officers generally committed to making the admission of women a success, the Academy still faced a variety of hurdles and controversies between 1976 and 1980. Women cadets endured the full spectrum of sexism, from verbal harassment to physical attacks, from persecution in the classroom to sexual assault in the barracks. Though the majority of men at West Point did not commit overtly hostile acts, and while the climate at the Academy today is much improved, it remains true that some of those problems remain with West Point and the Army to this day, more than twenty-five years after women first entered the Academy. To understand that simple truth is to confront how deeply ingrained gender assumptions are within our culture, how biological and physiological differences between men and women really do have consequences, and to recognize how long the military has struggled to find roles for women acceptable to society as a whole. Ultimately, it is to realize the fundamental source of sexism and harassment and violence against women is not rooted exclusively in the military. Those problems pervade society; they belong to us. They *are* us. In that sense, the story of the arrival of women at West Point also illuminates the real progress the Army has made in addressing larger cultural problems within its ranks, and perhaps helps us to discern how much longer and farther the journey toward a more fully equitable and efficient society will take us.

Such a journey may not end in our lifetime, or even that of our children. But if the first chapter of a story matters as much as the conclusion and if accomplishments matter as much as mistakes and grievous wrongs, then some assessment of what the men and women at West Point endured and conquered is in order. One measure of the triumph they shared, and what it means for America, can be gleaned through an exchange I witnessed between a father, his daughter, and a stranger on July 2, 1996. Sitting on a bench beneath the statue of Dwight D. Eisenhower at West Point, the father and his little girl silently watched as over 1,100 New Cadets assembled facing The Plain, the historic parade ground where cadets have marched since 1802. Under a brilliant blue sky softened by the receding evening sun, the cadets assembled in formation by company for the striking of the colors before dinner. The little girl's gaze shifted between the cadets, her feet, and her father. A woman transfixed by the fear and tension on the faces of the New Cadets, as well as by the pageantry of the simple ceremony, sat silently behind them. The father turned to make eye contact, smiled, and said, "This sure brings back memories."

"Did you go to school here?" the woman asked.

"Oh, no. But I was in the Army."

Interested by their conversation, the daughter looked up at the woman and said, "Did *you* go to school here?"

The woman smiled at the eager young eyes. "No," she said. "But you can."

Intrigued, the girl listened and watched with growing interest as the woman pointed out some of the young women standing silently at attention among the ranks of the Army's future leaders. Most impressive of all to the child was the fact a woman was actually *in command* of all the New Cadets. She watched the rest of the ceremony in silence, her demeanor transformed through the simple recognition that women were an important part of the panorama on The Plain, that she too might one day walk in the Long Gray Line. Her gaze no longer wavered. Instead, it remained fixed on the *women* of the United States Corps of Cadets.

Cynics will say the story smacks of sentimentalism, and it does. Yet there are insights to be gained as well. None of the adults present for this exchange came of age in a time when women were permitted to attend the United States Military Academy. The little girl will. That fact is significant for West Point, for the Army, and for all of us as Americans. It is what the story that follows is all about.

NOTES

1. Second Lieutenant James Allen, USMA Class of 1829, discovered the source of the Mississippi River in 1833. The building of the Panama Canal was directed by MG George Washington Goethals, USMA Class of 1880.

2. For a discussion of the Army's efforts to confront racism, see Charles C. Moskos and John Sibley Butler, *All That We Can Be: Black Leadership and Racial Integration the Army Way* (New York: Basic Books, 1996). See also William P. Vaugh's excellent examination of the racism faced by the first black cadets at West Point in "West Point and the First Negro Cadet," *Military Affairs* 35, No. 3 (October 1971): 100–2.

3. Richard Rayner, "Women as Warriors," *New York Times Magazine*, June 22, 1997, 27.

STRONGER
THAN
CUSTOM

The Cadet Color Guard leading a parade on The Plain at West Point. Illustration by Pamela Lenck Bradford. Copyright © 2001 by Pamela Lenck Bradford.

Prologue

Suffice it to repeat that, with the exception of their disparate roles in the physical acts of procreation, childbearing and nursing, nothing has ever been more characteristic of the relationship between men and women than men's unwillingness to allow women to take part in war and combat. One suspects that, should they ever be faced with such a choice, men might very well give up women before they give up war.

—Martin Van Creveld[1]

Sunsets come slowly at West Point, as if golden shafts of light dread leaving the hallowed grounds of the fortress on the Hudson. They linger, reluctantly pulling away from the river as El Sol descends westward behind the mountains, leaving long shadows in their wake. Beams recede past the timeless statues of George S. Patton and Dwight D. Eisenhower, shower through the barracks windows of a thousand cadets, and dance across the weathered visages of Sylvanus Thayer and Douglas MacArthur standing eternal watch over The Plain. Rays glint from the peak of Battle Monument and retreat painfully from the shaded sanctuary of the post cemetery. Like the rearguard of a withdrawing column, one last glittering sliver of light pauses atop the mountains to the west. Desperate to stave off nightfall, it darts brilliantly through the stained glass of the Cadet Chapel, glides across the dusk-shrouded ruins of Fort Putnam, and kindles the clouding eyes of an Old Grad lost in memory along Trophy Point. In an instant, the shimmering brightness is gone, abandoning the United States Military Academy to sable night, yet promising to lead the minions of Apollo back from the east in the morning.

It has been that way as long as anyone can remember, and as long as there have been people to stand on The Plain at West Point and notice. The sun rises across the majestic river and sets behind tree-covered mountains, and in summer, as it has every year since 1802, the United States Military Academy receives a new class of cadets.

One such class arrived on July 7, 1976. One thousand five hundred and nineteen strong, it represented every state in the Union, several foreign countries, and the promise of a generation eager to take its place in the Long Gray Line.[2] During a summer when the nation celebrated its bicentennial and struggled to erase the memory of Vietnam, their celebration included a personal commitment to public service.

Gathering in Michie Stadium, many New Cadets were accompanied by friends and family during their official welcome from Academy officials.[3] They were told what to expect from life at West Point and encouraged to keep a sense of humor during the weeks ahead. Finally it came time for separation. New Cadets went one way, family and friends went another. Young men and women hugged their families, gathered their belongings, and were gone. It was a moment of extraordinary poignancy. Parents wanted it to linger; their children wanted it to end. One group fought back tears and faced a tour of the Academy and a long drive home to a world less full than before. The other stood on the threshold of admission to the society of warriors, at the beginning of the most challenging journey of their lives.

All too quickly the moment vanished. New Cadets moved from a world with precious few rites of passage to one with a dazzling array of hurdles, each linking them more closely to the Corps of Cadets. They left behind a civilian world of individuality where little was expected, failure was commonplace, and the emphasis was on choice, to join a military world where the group mattered most, a great deal was expected, failure was unthinkable, and the emphasis was on obligation.

After several hours and a bewildering array of in-processing formalities including haircuts, uniform issue, and instruction in the timeless art of the military salute, New Cadets formed up for the afternoon parade which signaled the beginning of Cadet Basic Training. Known as "Beast Barracks," the training consisted of a six-week program of instruction focusing on physical fitness, military protocol, and weapons proficiency designed to prepare New Cadets for the rigors of Academy life. The Cadet Captain in charge of the first half of this training period was a first classman traditionally known and feared as the "King of Beast." In July of 1976 his name was Kenneth Franklin Miller.

As the Cadet Training Battalion Commander, Miller led the New Cadets and their company commanders onto the historic Plain at West Point. After taking their oath to "support the Constitution of the United States, and bear true allegiance to the National Government . . . ," the New Cadets formed by company behind the famous "Hellcats," the drum and bugle detachment of the United States Military Academy Band. After aligning their ranks, they began to pass in review before the spectators gathered in the surrounding bleachers to celebrate their first steps on the long road to graduation.[4]

The Hellcats, smartly in step and immaculately attired in Army dress blues, passed first playing the "West Point March." Behind them came the Academy color guard carrying the Stars and Stripes and the colors of the United States Army. Atop the Army's flag were battle streamers commemorating the 168 campaigns and major engagements fought by the Army since the American Revolution. Saratoga mingled with the Argonne, Gettysburg with Normandy and Bataan, and Chosin Reservoir with the Ia Drang Valley. Behind the colors came the New Cadets, arranged into eight companies and struggling to maintain their newly-received places in the Long Gray Line.

Parents and friends strained to recognize their New Cadet in the sea of identical uniforms and closely cropped hair. They cheered en masse as the long column passed in review, letting out isolated bursts of joy when a solemn face became suddenly familiar. They hardly noticed the ragged marching, the awkward attempts to keep in step, or the stressful grimaces settling across the faces of their loved ones. Caught up in the emotion of the moment, they would have forgiven these incongruities anyway. After all, their willing young soldiers were neophytes, not the disciplined formations of precision marchers that would astound crowds at weekend parades in the fall.

In many ways, this rite of passage resembled so many others in the Academy's long history. It represented the first step in a metamorphosis through which civilians became soldiers, young people shouldered the burden of citizenship, and West Point unobtrusively accepted another class of young people and began preparing them for careers in the service of their country.

And yet, at the same time, a very different and new air surrounded the Class of 1980. In the midst of the long column passing the reviewing stands were New Cadets who subtly stood out amongst their peers. Their hair was slightly longer, and something about each one seemed vaguely out of place, out of kilter with the sternly masculine surroundings. Those amongst the crowd who peered closely discerned there were *women*, 119 to be exact, in the midst of the unbroken ranks turning and marching toward Washington Hall and the cadet barracks. The Class of 1980 was breaking new ground at West Point, and quietly, very quietly, Army patriarchy began to crack.

The Long Gray Line marched on.

NOTES

1. Martin Van Creveld, "Why Men Fight," in Lawrence Freedman, ed., *War* (London: Oxford University Press, 1994), pp. 88–89.

2. A handful of foreign cadets are admitted to West Point each year and educated at taxpayer expense. President José Maria Figueres of Costa Rica, for example, was a member of the Class of 1979.

3. Home to Army football, the stadium bears the name of First Lieutenant Dennis Mahan Michie, USMA Class of 1892, who captained the very first West Point team.

4. The United States Military Academy Band is the oldest Army unit at West Point and the oldest military band in continuous service in the United States.

1

★ ★ ★ ★

"The Corps Has"

Maybe you could find one woman in 10,000 who could lead in combat, but
she would be a freak, and the Military Academy is not being run for freaks.
—General William Westmoreland[1]

Watching the president climb into his waiting helicopter, Lieutenant General
Sidney Bryan Berry felt decidedly uneasy—for Gerald Ford traveled with more
than his usual entourage on the way back to Washington; he was taking a West
Point tradition along with him.

The president had come to the United States Military Academy on June 4,
1975 to be the featured speaker at graduation ceremonies for the Corps of Cadets.[2] Berry, the Academy's fiftieth superintendent, listened as the president
began by ceremoniously granting amnesty to all cadets for any minor infractions
of regulations, ending with a simple phrase the accumulated punishment tours
and demerits of the previous months.[3] He told the graduates assembled at Michie
Stadium that the "traditions of West Point run throughout our history. . . . And
now you accept that inheritance, carrying with you not only the traditions of
West Point but the hopes of your countrymen." The president warned that the
"battle of freedom" would never be over, that the "will of America will always
be tested," and that Academy graduates would serve in a dangerous world in
which the United States faced a greater variety of potential enemies than ever
before. In such times, the president intoned, Army officers who epitomized the
West Point virtues of duty, honor, country, were more important than ever to
the future of the republic. It was a timeless message, one made especially rel-

evant by the recent fall of Saigon in April and the seizure and subsequent recapture of the *S.S. Mayaguez* in May. In closing, Ford reminded the audience that "freedom is never free," and his remarks were warmly received.[4]

Following his address, the 862 cadets of the Class of 1975, each wearing the academy's famous full dress gray over white uniform, strode across the giant stage to receive diploma covers and handshakes. Pictures were taken, graduates beamed, and family members swelled with pride. Then came the moment which every cadet dreamed about, the cathartic, triumphant moment made forever meaningful by four years of arduous struggle and anticipation. They were dismissed. The graduates paused for a heartbeat, then erupted in war yells and flung their hats high into the New York sky. As handshakes and bear hugs were exchanged, and as children from the crowd scrambled for cadet hats to take home as souvenirs, another West Point rite of passage was complete. The one hundred seventy-third academy class passed from the secure, isolated environs of West Point into the Army as second lieutenants.[5]

Afterward, Ford climbed into Berry's sedan for the journey back to The Plain, the historic Academy parade ground where an army helicopter waited to take him back to Air Force One. The superintendent joined him for the ride, planning to enjoy a few private moments with his Commander-in-Chief as well as to discuss one of the more volatile issues facing the Academy. For several years, Congress had discussed opening the nation's service academies to women, and on May 20, the House had finally acted. In a 303–96 vote, representatives called for the Army, Navy, and Air Force academies to admit women in 1976.[6] With Senate action pending, and with the president's position in doubt, Berry planned to lobby against further action on the measure. In his view women had no place at West Point, which he believed existed primarily to develop future combat leaders for the Army. That exclusivity was what made the United States Military Academy unique, what had given it purpose for almost two centuries. Women were barred from direct combat duty, and the idea that they should one day join combat units struck Berry, along with most senior army officers, as anathema. It was, they reasoned, a threat to the cohesiveness, morale, and combat effectiveness of every unit in the army; and therefore women had no place in the Long Gray Line.[7]

In the course of their conversation, however, Ford dropped a bombshell. The admission of women was a "political inevitability," he said, adding that Berry "could expect within a very short time, days perhaps, for Congress to legislate the admission of women to the service academies. . . ."[8] There would be no more debate.

When made public, the news struck Army leaders as both ill-conceived and ill-timed, for it came on the heels of one of the most turbulent periods in the Army's history, a time when even the geographic isolation of West Point could not protect the Academy from convulsive changes sweeping American society. On every front, social, political, military, and economic, the nation experienced galvanic shocks. No institution suffered more than the Army, which was riddled with problems in the wake of the debacle in Vietnam. Drug abuse, discipline problems, officer corruption, and low morale plagued the ranks. The quality of many soldiers was appallingly low, and Congress seemed intent on ignoring decades of experience by returning to an all volunteer force and opening the services to more women than ever before. Though the Army has suffered many traumatic periods when public support waned and the quality of troops was abysmal, the 1970s were as difficult a time to be a professional soldier as any in American history. Even West Point suffered an array of internal and external crises, each leading inexorably towards Sidney Berry's dramatic conversation with the President. How much more, he may have wondered, could the Army and West Point withstand?

Beyond Thayer Gate, the dividing line between the ordered world of the Academy and the hustle-bustle of civilian life, America as a whole had indeed been in turmoil. The 1960s had given birth to a rejuvenated civil rights movement, to calls for equal rights for women, to a war on poverty led by an increasingly activist federal government, and to a war in Southeast Asia which ultimately proved the most divisive of all. Riots and violence seemed endemic, especially in college towns, where children of the generation that survived the Great Depression and defeated totalitarianism rejected the world their parents had given them. The most militant despised the materialism, the greed, and the blind patriotism they believed led America into quagmires like Vietnam. They bitterly attacked military involvement in Southeast Asia, racism at home, and often characterized the armed services as a Praetorian Guard for a right-wing establishment rather than an instrument of the American people. Controversy reigned over a wide variety of social and foreign policy issues, and the old morality was slipping away. Young people especially embraced the move toward casual sex, a more widespread use of drugs, and an increasingly caustic and disdainful approach toward authority.[9]

West Point and the Army tried to steer clear of the domestic tumult and remain, as Douglas MacArthur had urged, "serene, calm, aloof," while the great issues of the day were debated by those who had not chosen to serve the profession of arms.[10] Yet it was difficult. Tainted by the increasingly bitter war in Vietnam, the Army became a focal point for the media, for opponents of the war, for those who attacked the draft, and for critics who denounced the increasingly large share of national resources pouring into Southeast Asia rather than remaining in the United States. Rather than seeing the military as suffering the consequences of misguided national policy, they often identified the armed services as a prime *source* of the nation's ills, particularly the war in Vietnam. They forgot, as Samuel J. Bayard told West Point cadets in 1854, "that according to the history of other republics, the people were always corrupted, before the army became dangerous."[11]

Volunteers for military service became increasingly hard to find, and as thousands of middle class young men evaded the draft by staying in college, joining the Reserves, or enlisting in the National Guard, Army standards were lowered to the breaking point.[12] Drug use, desertion, and discipline problems grew to frightening levels. With dissatisfaction over the war growing exponentially during the 1960s, even West Point began struggling to find qualified candidates. Traditionally swamped with applicants following World War II, West Point was a magnet for thousands of young people willing to accept a term of enlistment as an officer in exchange for a free education and a place of honor in the Long Gray Line. The Academy was the equivalent of an Ivy League university, a place where cadets took more courses than were required at Harvard, to which, as the Corps liked to say, a West Point man might have gone. Qualified candidates were normally turned away in droves. In 1972, however, with the Army withdrawing from Vietnam and opposition to the war well-entrenched, West Point received so few applications for admission that *every* qualified candidate was accepted and vacancies were common.[13]

Just as upsetting, and just as clear an indicator of the growing disdain in American society for a military career, was the fact West Point graduates were resigning from the Army in record numbers. Graduates became eligible to leave the service between four and five years after graduation, but traditionally the overwhelming majority chose to stay in the Army. The war class of 1950, for example, lost only eleven percent of its members at the five year mark. In contrast, one-third of the class of 1966 left after five years, and members of the Academy's faculty were leaving as well. When thirty-three instructors resigned in eighteen months the *New York Times* took notice, and the Army became so concerned that the Academy was suffering some sort of general malaise it commissioned a special study to examine the phenomenon.[14]

The malaise it suffered was due to the war in Vietnam. The conflict cast a palpable shroud over the Army, and soon the darkness hung over the Academy as well. Servants of a society which increasingly considered the war a wasteful mistake and military service the province of fools, cadets and faculty sometimes found it difficult to stay optimistic or enthusiastic about their careers. Even after 1968, when the number of American troops in Southeast Asia began to steadily decline, West Point graduates continued to deploy overseas and enter fighting that Americans found increasingly pointless. Some graduates of the class of 1969, for example, left the Academy in May, attended advanced training during the summer, deployed to Vietnam in the fall, and were killed and back at West Point to be buried by grieving cadets before Christmas. Year after year, from 1965 onward, the cycle continued unabated, with young men leaving the Academy in the prime of their lives only to return home in flag-draped coffins. The persistence of death among young cadets born into a culture already ambivalent about military service, and increasingly antagonistic toward involvement in Vietnam, made it difficult for some to justify the sacrifice. It also did nothing for morale, particularly since so many knew their fate might also lead to the hallowed grounds of the Academy cemetery.[15]

In such an environment, and with dissent beyond the Academy exploding into violence on college campuses across the country, it is little wonder that many of the young men at West Point felt estranged from their generation and sensed the gap between the American people and their army growing wider.[16] At commencement exercises in 1970, Vice President Spiro Agnew contrasted the steadfast loyalty to the nation shown by West Point graduates with the behavior of those who he said, "glamorize the criminal misfits of society while our best men die in Asian rice paddies to preserve the freedoms those misfits abuse."[17] His sentiments were echoed by another cadet who expressed his dismay with those attacking the military by saying, "It makes you wonder why the hell you should go risk your neck for those kinds of people."[18]

Worse than estranged, some also felt hated. Just as military personnel returning from Vietnam often met scorn, ridicule, and the ubiquitous protester willing to spit on any uniform, so cadets faced growing resentment among civilians. Some began wearing wigs on leave, changing into civilian clothes when off post, and donning their uniforms only when absolutely required.[19] This represented a dramatic change, for during much of American history the distinctive gray cadet uniform was a common sight in the airports and train stations of New York. Cadets typically found the uniform a magnet for positive attention, and often an invaluable attraction for young women and their parents. It was also commonly a ticket to free drinks in bars, discounted hotel rooms, and bargain prices at some of New York City's most exclusive restaurants. Yet by the early 1970s some cadets were afraid to wear their uniforms in public, especially in the Northeast, California, and Washington, D.C. Those who traveled to the Midwest or South on leave were usually lionized as heroes, but even in conservative parts of the country they were likely to encounter quiet opposition to their perceived role in the U.S. war machine. Whether through aloof former friends, snide comments uttered just out of earshot, or open criticism, cadets were forced to confront the awkward fact that many of their fellow citizens no longer respected those who served their country in uniform.[20]

The Academy also faced a series of wrenching changes and crises during the late 1960s and early 1970s, and by the summer of 1975 the cumulative effect was to make the venerable institution seem a medieval citadel under siege. Congress launched this wave of change in 1964, when it passed legislation authorizing the Corps of Cadets to gradually double in size; more than 4,400 cadets were attending West Point by 1972. This frustrated some Army officers and Old Grads, who feared accepting a significantly larger number of cadets would require a lowering of standards.[21] Their fears seemed confirmed by the steady decline of mean College Board scores for entering plebes, which fell from 654 to 624 on the verbal exam and from 581 to 554 in math between 1966 and 1972. Yet this decline was a national phenomenon. Mean scores for *all* students taking SAT exams during the same period fell from 467 to 443 in verbal and from 495 to 481 in math. The news might have been encouraging, for it showed that even in a time of academic decline the Academy continued to attract cadets who were far above the civilian norm scholastically.[22] But few in the Army saw or spread the word. Instead, most saw a larger and more impersonal Corps in which it was impossible for cadets to know everyone in their class, much less everyone at the Academy, and it concerned them deeply. Coupled with the general disdain for the military felt by the population at large and the worsening situation in Vietnam, the larger size of each entering class seemed symbolic of a society and an Academy out of touch with their roots.

In 1969, the Army abolished "bracing," ending a time-honored tradition of disciplining (or intimidating and abusing) fourth-year cadets, who were known as "plebes" in the distinctive argot of the Academy.[23] Bracing was an exaggerated form of attention in which cadets stood with chests thrust out and stomachs sucked in while forcing their chins down as far as possible, creating wrinkles below the jaw. For decades, plebes were required to brace on command, and while relatively safe from the demands of senior officers while in class, they were vulnerable everywhere else. Some upperclassmen organized wrinkle-counting contests to determine which plebes were most military in their bearing, and because bracing also involved ramrod straight necks and lower backs, there were other criteria to consider as well. If an upperclassman demanded a plebe brace against a wall, for example, and could fit his hands between the wall and a plebe's body, then the plebe suffered. Common punishments included being forced to brace for extended periods, or "sweat" dimes and quarters by remaining at attention against a wall long enough to make the coins stick with perspiration to the wall when the cadet stepped away.[24] The practice had no military importance, though it was deeply rooted in Academy tradition. Because generations of cadets had endured this often abused tactic for teaching military bearing and proper posture, many older graduates became convinced the ban on bracing indicated the Academy was going "soft."[25]

In the fall of 1969, the epidemic of campus antiwar protests reached West Point, when approximately two hundred Vassar students arrived from Poughkeepsie on "Moratorium Day" to distribute flowers and persuade members of the Long Gray Line to abandon their military careers. They left after a few hours of fruitless debates with cadets, many of whom nourished a strong impish streak when dealing with protesters. One told the Vassar girls he had to leave in order to attend "poison gas class," while others politely accepted flowers and proceeded to eat them.[26] There were other, less well-known incidents as well. During a weekend parade the following spring, a protester jumped a barrier and ran onto the Academy parade field, known for decades simply as "The Plain." The man went straight for the color guard, in an apparent attempt to grab the American flag. A cadet marching behind the colors unshouldered his rifle, struck the man in the face with the butt, and resumed marching as Military Police dragged the protester's unconscious body away.[27] Though such encounters were relatively rare at West Point, each confrontation reinforced the budding sense that the Academy and all it stood for were somehow out of step with mainstream America.

The following year, West Point reeled from serious controversy when Major General Samuel W. Koster resigned as superintendent. Koster commanded the

23rd (Americal) Division in Vietnam at the time of the My Lai massacre and
was being investigated for his role in the ensuing cover-up.[28] Rather than bring
discredit to the Academy, Koster walked into Washington Hall on March 17,
1970, and delivered a stunning address to cadets assembled for lunch. He was
resigning. Speaking from the "Poop Deck," a stone balcony above the cadet
dining area, Koster referred to the Academy creed of "Duty, Honor, Country,"
and pledged to remain faithful to those values, just as he had as a cadet in the
Class of 1942. In a parting shot at the powers that were, he added, "Don't let
the bastards grind you down," and for ninety seconds the cadets stood and
cheered. When the cheering stopped, however, the grim reality of a West
Pointer's involvement in a gruesome massacre and cover-up began to set in, and
the ensuing investigations and shock following the superintendent's departure
tarnished the Academy in ways no attack from the outside ever could.[29]

Beyond West Point there was also tarnish on the Army as a whole. It seemed
that the fabric of the service was being torn asunder, and officers were appalled
at the declining quality of American soldiers worldwide.[30] Poorly educated and
unmotivated recruits, low morale, racial strife, and a general dissatisfaction with
the Army dramatically affected discipline around the world, especially in units
whose veteran leaders were transferred to combat units in Vietnam. This was
especially true in southern Germany, where the American Seventh Army was
progressively drained of strong leaders at the troop level and became notorious
as a breeding ground for drug abuse, violence, and a severe lack of respect for
authority. Race riots among U.S. troops were common, as was flagrant use of
heroin, hashish, and a wide variety of other illegal substances.[31] Discipline all
but disappeared in some units; and in others, a frightening pattern of violence
toward German civilians developed. Muggings, rapes, and even murders were
numerous by the early 1970s, and some American officers feared for their own
safety when entering enlisted barracks.[32] While criminal problems were less
common at West Point, the Academy shared in the simmering racial and social
tensions of the day because the violence and tensions of American society at
large were eventually present at every major Army installation in the world.[33]

In Vietnam, the collapse of leadership and discipline could also be seen in
the number of "combat refusals," "fraggings," and desertions in U.S. units. A
combat refusal occurred when members of a unit refused, often temporarily, to
follow orders they considered ill-advised.[34] The refusals sometimes came under
fire, and were usually explained by enlisted personnel as their only defense
against incompetent officers. Fraggings were assaults by U.S. soldiers on each
other, typically involving an enlisted soldier using a grenade to wound or kill
an officer he considered a threat to himself or the unit. Between 1969 and 1972,
eighty-six American soldiers were killed and 714 wounded in incidents *officially*
blamed on other U.S. troops. How many fraggings happened in combat only to
be blamed on hostile fire or accident will never be known. Ultimately, a growing
number of soldiers chose the traditional method for evading military service and
voted with their feet to leave the Army behind. Desertions increased from 1967

through 1971, when 73.4 out of every 1,000 soldiers left their unit without permission.[35]

Discipline and morale problems also plagued units stationed in the United States. Soldiers published underground newspapers protesting service life and the war in Vietnam at a number of installations, giving them titles like *About Face*, *Fed Up!* and *Last Harass*.[36] In Fayetteville, North Carolina, home of Fort Bragg and the Army's elite 82nd Airborne Division, military related crime became so rampant that residents called it "FayetteNam." Drug abuse and violent crime were commonplace, especially rape, because thousands of young women lived alone in military towns during times of war. With their husbands overseas, they were targets for military men who found it all too easy to discover where they lived.[37] This was in stark contrast to life in Army towns before and immediately after World War II, when crime was low and the greater problems of civilian society rarely intruded. Although many U.S. units had few problems with criminal behavior and most officers resisted the temptation to join their soldiers at "FTA" parties, this pattern of events was deeply disturbing to Army officers.[38] Many were so disheartened by the alarming trends that they resigned. Those officers that remained in the service faced daunting problems, especially since the Army found itself in the midst of losing a major war for the first time in American history. Spirits sank to a low ebb.[39]

In America, the growing tolerance of drug use, so prevalent among GIs in Germany and on domestic college campuses, slowly found its way to the service academies, where a combined sixty cases of drug abuse were reported within three years. Most involved marijuana, and in fairness it should be noted that in comparison to civilian schools the number of cases was strikingly low, as cases of criminal behavior at the academies usually were. Yet the rising use of drugs among cadets concerned West Point officials, who feared their institution was gradually losing touch with all but the vices of mainstream life. In a culture which at once scorned both military virtues and the appearance of civilian social ills in military ranks, it was hard to know how to make West Point vital to ordinary Americans again. It was harder still to cling to traditional compasses at a time when nothing was sacrosanct, when *everything* seemed subject to criticism and change.[40]

For the next several years, change came to the Academy at a frantic pace. In 1973, Secretary of Defense Melvin Laird ordered an end to compulsory chapel at West Point, after a series of court challenges made it clear that the rule violated the First Amendment's separation of church and state. Attendance at Protestant chapel dropped by two-thirds and by half for Catholic Mass, leaving traditionalists shaking their heads in disbelief.[41] In the spring, Cadet James Pelosi gained national attention by graduating after enduring "The Silence" for over a year and a half. The Silence was a severe punishment handed down by the Cadet Honor Committee, and normally reserved for cadets suspected of violating the honor code who were either not proven guilty or deemed inadequately punished by the Academy.[42] Suspected of cheating on an exam, Pelosi denied the charge but was convicted by the Honor Committee, which recommended his expulsion. Following an investigation, the Academy overturned the conviction, so the committee resorted to its own brand of justice and subjected Pelosi to The Silence.[43] Pelosi found himself ignored and harassed by other cadets, who spoke to him only on official Academy business. He ate alone, slept alone, and studied alone for nineteen months; though a few cadets bucked the system and secretly supported him, the case provoked widespread criticism of West Point.[44] When the Honor Committee officially did away with The Silence later in the year, another harsh but traditional aspect of Academy life was gone.

American policy makers eliminated another hallowed institution in 1973, when they ended the longest continuous draft in U.S. history. A hallmark of American culture since 1940, the draft was replaced by the All Volunteer Force (AVF), which supporters argued would be a more efficient, more equitable means for providing for the common defense.[45] Those supporters cited the findings of the Presidential Gates Commission, which reported to Richard M. Nixon in 1971 that an all volunteer force represented the best alternative to the draft in the post-Vietnam era. Nixon followed their recommendation and ended the draft soon after the Paris Peace Accords were signed in 1973. Public disenchantment with the draft and the unpopular war in Vietnam were factors in the decision, which concerned both the Army and many liberals. Left wing critics feared the military would become dominated by soldiers who were predominantly poor and/or black and that the armed forces would lose the leavening influence of civilians.[46] The Army saw the end of the draft as political maneuvering at their expense, and felt that having the AVF "forced on them by the president precisely at the moment they were held in the lowest esteem by their country . . . [was] a bitter betrayal."[47] Officers commanded units often composed of undertrained, underequipped, poorly motivated soldiers, yet they were still charged with defending the free world against a wide array of threats, especially from the Soviet Union. Many feared the AVF would fail to produce quality soldiers in sufficient numbers to meet the needs of the armed services and would create a force comprised mainly of the poor, those with limited education, and minorities who would enjoy little popular support among mainstream Americans.[48]

As Americans began adjusting to the AVF and the end of U.S. military involvement in Vietnam, they struggled to adjust to the idea that the United States had finally lost a war. Whether it was lost by the military or politicians in Washington and whether it should have been fought at all were questions which promised much rancor and precious little clarity in the years following the American withdrawal. What was abundantly clear was that the war badly shattered the American army. The shock, dismay, and bewilderment of Army officers in the aftermath of Vietnam are impossible to overstate, particularly since so many senior officers came of age during and after World War II, when the United States emerged as the predominant military power on the planet. That peasants in a distant, underdeveloped country could wage war successfully against such a nation and such an army astonished the world, and challenged the once blind faith many soldiers and citizens had in the armed forces. As James Fallows wrote, "Whatever damage the war in Vietnam did to the self-confidence and certainty of the nation, it did that much, squared, to the professional soldier."[49] Though America as a whole reeled from the Vietnam experience, the Army lay quivering in shambles, and by 1975 seemed to have lost the trust of the American people. In a Lou Harris poll taken in July of that year, respondents were asked if they had confidence in the military, and only twenty-nine percent said yes.[50]

The damage within the Army permeated every level of command. In addition to his final report on the My Lai incident, Lieutenant General William R. Peers submitted a memorandum to General William Westmoreland, then Chief of Staff of the Army. Peers argued that grave problems engulfed the officer corps, that a climate existed where the honesty and integrity of many officers could not be counted upon.[51] Deeply troubled by the report, Westmoreland ordered the Army War College to conduct a study of the professional attitudes and leadership capabilities of Army officers. Entitled the "Study on Military Professionalism," the report echoed much of what Peers had implied, blaming careerism and a host of other internal factors for the decline in officer integrity. Westmoreland classified the study, and it never reached a broad audience.[52] However, those general officers who did plumb the depths of the War College report could not have been pleased with the continuing decline in what was, after all, supposed to be the finest army in the world.

During the early 1970s a growing number of attacks also surfaced in the press; within a few years, the Army had lost the aura of precision and integrity it maintained in the years following World War II. "The Pentagon Papers" began the avalanche of criticism when they debuted in 1971, and there followed a steady stream of articles and books chronicling the corruption and demise of the Army officer corps. Many were written by current or former officers, and a number garnered national attention. Lieutenant Colonel Edward King's *The Death of an Army*, Colonel David H. Hackworth's article, "Soldier's Disgust," and Major Josiah Bunting's *The Lionheads* were released in 1972, making public the Army's agony.[53] Disgust with the Army's decline was so widespread by then that the criticism should have come as no surprise, yet career officers and the general public were shocked that high-ranking men would attack the Army with such vehemence.

In the same year, K. Bruce Galloway and Robert B. Johnson, Jr. published a blistering attack on West Point entitled *West Point: America's Power Fraternity*. They presented the work as an "attempt to cut away the fairy tales and present a critical look at one of the most powerful and oppressive institutions in the country, a 'school' that professes to train 'defenders of freedom' but instead hammers out an elitist group of automatons who are prisoners of their education and afraid of the very concept they are supposed to defend."[54] Galloway and Johnson argued that the Academy existed as a breeding ground for narrow-minded elitists who, because they rose to positions of power within the Army and the national government, were ultimately threats to America and responsible for the debacle in Vietnam. More examinations of the Academy followed, including *School for Soldiers: West Point and the Profession of Arms* by Joseph Ellis and Robert Moore in 1974, and a variety of other books and articles which, while avoiding the pointed critiques of Galloway and Johnson, generally argued that West Point needed serious reform.

For those with a sense of history, these problems were nothing new. Prior to World War II, the American people traditionally held great disdain for the military and, except in times of dire emergency, even for West Point. Calls to close the Military Academy were commonplace throughout the nineteenth and early twentieth centuries.[55] Davy Crockett demanded that the Academy be shut down in 1830, arguing on the floor of Congress that West Point's curriculum was "effeminate and pedantic" and castigating the institution for "spawning a military aristocracy."[56] Alden Partridge, President of Norwich University, echoed his concerns in 1841 when he called West Point a "public charity school," a "nursery of aristocracy . . . calculated to form military pedants and military dandies."[57] Public pressure on the Academy rose and fell in accordance with the politics of the day and in tandem with pressure on the Army itself. Before and after the Civil War, the Army was often poorly supported and critically attacked by the public, and discipline and morale suffered proportionately. Even drug abuse could be commonplace, as it was in the Army during the battle for control of the Great Plains following the Civil War. In the 1860s and 1870s drug addiction and desertion were endemic, which meant that in the long run the problems faced by the Army during the 1970s were nothing new.[58]

Yet few officers were willing or able to take the long view. Most matured in the post World War II era, when the military was generally held in high esteem, and only a handful understood the period had been a fluke. One who did was General William A. Knowlton, who succeeded Koster as superintendent in 1970. As he put it, "We've been living in a kind of aberrated period since World War II. We've been misled by the general high standing of the military in a society that's always been ambivalent about the military." Such historical ambivalence was the norm, he argued, and ignorance of this historical condition accounted for the shock experienced by the generation which endured the Second World War when younger Americans found their enthusiasm for militarism and overseas entanglements waning during the 1960s. As he said, "Our traditionally strong antimilitary elements have been so sublimated that the people who have come of age in this period, and who have not gone back and looked at history, thought this atmosphere of esteem was the norm in American history."[59] That fact, even for those who took time to read Knowlton's comments, offered little comfort for those who loved the Army or for those who resisted the clamor to close or modify West Point. Every superintendent struggled to balance an enduring reverence for tradition with the vital need for the Academy to keep pace with an evolving society. But the challenge was monumental and not always clearly defined except in hindsight. Knowlton was eventually sued more often than any superintendent in the Academy's history, as more and more cadets turned to the courts to redress their grievances with the system. Upon his arrival at West Point in 1970, he was appalled by the mood of the officers on the Academy staff and faculty, saying, "There was a tendency to cry doom and gloom and to consider that West Point was in the approximate state of Rome when the vandals climbed the last contour line of the inner city."[60] Within four years, Knowlton felt that pressure himself. It became so acute, he told Sidney Berry, who replaced him as superintendent in July 1974, that he felt like "the commander of a stockade surrounded by attacking Indians."[61] He might have been speaking for almost every officer in the Army.

The litany of disquieting news continued. In August of 1974, President Richard M. Nixon resigned in disgrace as the Watergate cover-up destroyed both his administration and the faith Americans once had in government. More change came to West Point in 1975, when the number of mandatory drills for cadets was reduced by one third to allow more time for study. Many of the Academy's Old Grads, those who lived in a "gray haze" which brooked no allowance for change, voiced considerable outrage.[62] And in April, just before graduation and the arrival of President Ford, North Vietnamese troops overran South Vietnam, capturing Saigon and validating the conviction in American minds that U.S. involvement in Southeast Asia had been a tragic, losing proposition.

In May, after testifying before Congress and lobbying to prevent the admission of women to the Academy, Sidney Berry learned that they were indeed coming to West Point. Their arrival would have been opposed at any point in the Academy's history and resisted by cadets at any time. No single-gender institution becomes coeducational easily.[63] No one expected a patriarchal, conservative, traditional institution to leap willingly into the vanguard of social change. For the Academy, which embraced the warrior cult dominated for centuries by men, however, the news was especially difficult to accept. For 173 years, almost as long as the United States had existed, the United States Military Academy at West Point was *omnes viri*—all male—and no one knew what bringing women into the Corps of Cadets would do to morale, discipline, or the Spartan environment advocates maintained was so crucial to preparing cadets for battle. Why, the critics soon thundered, did women belong at West Point?

The answer was that women belonged at West Point because the United States had changed a great deal by the mid-1970s, and the push for greater opportunity and equality for women in every segment of American life could not be contained. Their admission was part of a larger social revolution which sought to redefine the roles women, and ultimately men, could play in American culture. Outside West Point, beyond the stoic Hudson River and the gray, Gothic omnipresence of Academy buildings, the political forces intent on expanding opportunities for women were in full stride by the early 1970s. Congress, ever sensitive to public opinion, answered the clarion call issued by a resurgent feminist movement during the 1960s and passed the Equal Rights Amendment

(ERA) in 1972.[64] Though the amendment fell three states short of ratification and did not become part of the Constitution, the high tide of 1972 convinced many Americans that even more radical advances were in store. During the ERA debate, and immediately after its passage, members of Congress even suggested women should be admitted to the various service academies, each of which had always barred them from admission. Those who did so foreshadowed the opening of the service academies to women in 1975, an act which, despite the claims of those who would blame various women's groups, can be traced to Congress alone.

For unlike so many other advances for women, the push to demolish the exclusive male hold on American service academies was not driven by mainstream feminists. They saw sexism in the military as far less important than issues like equal pay and sexual harassment in the civilian workplace because those latter issues affected the majority of women. As Representative Bella Abzug of New York said when the admission of women to America's service academies was debated in 1975, "I do not regard women in the military as my first priority. . . ."[65] Abzug and other feminists were also divided as to whether military women were liberal-minded reformers attacking patriarchy or sell-outs to a male-dominated institution that practiced violence and often exploited women. In philosophical terms, the question was whether emancipation and equal access were the same thing and whether women fighting to enter all-male societal enclaves eventually risked imitating the groups they joined. This debate was never concluded among many feminists, and rather than pushing for the academies to open their doors to women most were silent on the issue until debate began in Congress. Even then, they offered only limited support, lest they play into the hands of conservatives like Phyllis Schlafly who saw feminists as angry women who really wanted to be men.

As the founder of "STOP ERA" in 1972 and publisher of *The Phyllis Schlafly Report*, Schlafly struck many feminists as an especially dangerous opponent because of her intense lobbying and organizational skills. She characterized feminists as "a bunch of bitter women seeking a constitutional cure for their personal problems" and directed an attack aimed at capitalizing on the fears of more conservative Americans that eventually helped defeat ERA at the state level.[66] Most importantly, she focused on the impact the ERA might have on the role of women in the military, arguing that passage of the ERA would force women to register for the draft and serve in combat. At a time when Americans still reeled over images from the Vietnam War and with Schlafly's followers giving signs to children at protests which read, "Please don't send my mommy to war," public opinion soon turned against the ERA for good.[67]

With Schlafly hammering on the issue of women in combat and winning, most feminists were reluctant to make military women's issues any sort of priority when it came to lobbying. They also steered clear of military issues tied to women because they were desperate to convince more conservative Americans they were still "feminine," and going against the fiercely patriarchal military threatened to undermine that goal. Instead, ordinary American citizens and their representatives pushed for the admission of women to the service academies, not because they saw it as a step toward placing women in combat, but simply because it seemed fair.

Although Senator Dennis Chavez (D-New Mexico) called for the creation of a "West Point for Women" in 1954, the chain of events leading toward Congressional legislation admitting women actually began in the early 1960s when Representative Robert B. Duncan (D-Oregon) nominated a woman to the Academy.[68] The Army rejected the nomination, and the issue remained moot until 1972, when New York Republican Senator Jacob K. Javits nominated a woman to the U.S. Naval Academy only a week after the ERA passed Congress.[69] Javits also co-authored a resolution with Representative Jack H. McDonald (R-Michigan) calling for an end to gender discrimination at the service academies. Though the Senate passed the resolution it quickly died in the House, and the matter did not come before Congress again until 1973, when Representative Pierre S. du Pont IV (R-Delaware) introduced the first bill mandating the admission of women. At the same time, California Representatives Jerome Waldie and Don Edwards, both Democrats, nominated women to the Air Force and Naval Academies and sued Secretary of Defense James Schlesinger on behalf of their nominees, moving the campaign into the courts.[70]

In December 1973, the Senate passed by voice vote an amendment to the Armed Forces Enlisted Personnel Bonus Revision Act, stipulating that women could not be declared ineligible for admission to the academies based on gender alone. Senators Javits, William D. Hathaway (D-Maine), Mike Mansfield (D-Montana), Strom Thurmond (R-South Carolina), and John C. Stennis (D-Mississippi), who chaired the Senate Armed Services Committee, cosponsored the amendment. With strong support in the Senate, the measure seemed certain to pass through Congress. Instead, it was dropped by the House Armed Services Committee in a narrow 18–16 vote. Representative Samuel Stratton (D-New York), who supported the admission of women, argued that the Senate amendment had very little to do with the purpose of the Bonus Revision Act and was therefore not germane. It had to be considered separately, after hearings on the admission of women were held in the House that summer.[71]

The hearings were held during May, June, and July of 1974 and saw the armed services close ranks to present a determined, unified front against advocates of coeducation at America's military academies. The Secretaries of the Army, Air Force, and Navy each testified against the admission of women, as did each of the three academy superintendents. Department of Defense General Counsel Martin Hoffman joined them, along with the Deputy Assistant Secretary of Defense for Military Personnel, Lieutenant General Leo Benade; the Vice Chief of Naval Operations, Admiral Worth H. Bagley; Air Force Chief of Staff, General George Brown; Army Vice Chief of Staff, General Fred Weyand; and Jacqueline Cochran, who directed the Women Airforce Service Pilots (WASPs) during World War II.[72] The number of witnesses, to say nothing of their high rank and prestige, said volumes about the seriousness with which the military establishment opposed the idea of opening academy doors to women.

Cochran argued, "[A] woman's primary function in life is to get married, maintain a home and raise a family. . . . [W]omen are nuts if they want to go into combat." Men, she suggested, *had* to go into combat. When asked why, she responded, "Because they are men and we don't have to do it because we are women." Though Cochran's experience as a test pilot testified to the ability of women to perform military duty if called upon, she argued passionately that women had no business at any of the academies. Women might be called upon in time of emergency, she argued, but they should never serve in combat and never attend the military academies.[73]

Military witnesses were more subdued in tone, though still deeply passionate. Howard "Bo" Callaway, Secretary of the Army and a West Point Class of 1949 graduate, dominated the presentation. He spoke against the admission of women to all the service academies in general and protested their possible inclusion in the Corps of Cadets in particular. Along with Generals Knowlton and Weyand, he argued that the presence of women would dilute the "Spartan atmosphere" of the Academy, lowering standards and dulling the combat-oriented training that made West Point so vital. The Army could hardly be accused of sexism, he continued, because women were eligible to become officers through Officer Candidate School (OCS) and Reserve Officer Training Corps (ROTC) programs where the majority of officers received their commissions. This logic carried with it the implication that women posed no threat to ROTC or OCS training precisely because they were inferior to the program of commissioning at the Academy. As Ward Just wrote, "The Army is as hierarchical as the church and as class-conscious and snobbish as Great Britain, West Point its Eton and the Army War College its Oxford."[74] Such elitism prevailed among many West Point graduates, some of whom genuinely considered themselves superior to officers who never wore an Academy ring.

Callaway further argued that officers graduating from West Point were vital to the Army because they received four years of total immersion in a military environment, advanced leadership training, and after graduation were far more likely to enter one of the Army's combat arms than an ROTC or OCS graduate. He feared creating "two West Points," one for men who would enter combat units and one for women who could never serve in the front lines.[75] In the long run, Callaway's arguments became the bedrock of opposition to the presence of women cadets at West Point and were supported by many West Pointers long after women were actually admitted. These opponents of the admission of women argued there *had* to be a place where professional soldiers learned the tools of their vocation in a demanding, unforgiving environment which cultivated the talents of those few who might one day lead the nation's armies in a time of crisis. They noted that West Pointers had dominated senior leadership positions in every major American conflict since at least the Civil War, proving the invaluable asset of a hard core of dedicated career officers even when their absolute numbers were relatively small. In short, they passionately insisted that in wartime those officers with the most rigorous, demanding training were most likely to serve their country with distinction. And as everyone seemed to agree, West Point had proven itself as a forge for combat leaders time and time again.[76]

The combat-oriented mission of the Academy was merely implied, rather than directly stated, however, and critics had long argued that since many Academy graduates entered noncombat oriented branches of the Army there existed no justifiable reason to keep women from competing for admission to the finest school in the service. This argument, said Callaway, missed the point entirely. Law students might not practice law and medical students might not practice medicine, he pointed out, but that hardly negated the need for special schools to produce lawyers and doctors. West Point was a specialized school, he continued, and its graduates formed a core of highly trained officers to which the rest of the Army looked for leadership, especially in times of crisis. He closed by alluding to the accomplishments of generations of West Point graduates and inserted into the record Douglas MacArthur's stirring 1962 speech entitled "Duty, Honor, Country."[77]

Proponents of the legislation included seven members of the House, representatives of several women's groups, the American Civil Liberties Union, and Army Lieutenant Colonel Grace King, who appeared as an individual rather than a military witness. Rooted in her experience as an Army officer, King presented testimony that was the most powerful and concise. She argued the critical issues were whether women would have the same freedom of choice as men within the military and whether the nation could afford to ignore a "pool of talent and intelligence more critically needed than ever." Since ROTC and OCS courses admitted women, she suggested the Army clearly belived that those programs were "good enough for women, but not good enough for men." King also pointed out that West Pointers had an advantage in competing for promotions. Thirty-nine percent of recently promoted brigadier generals were Academy grads, she noted, though only nine percent of all Army officers attended West Point. Those figures indicated women suffered serious professional disadvantages, according to King, because they could only compete for the restricted number of noncombat officer slots within the Army.[78]

The most vocal supporter was Representative Stratton, who blasted military objections and suggested no real argument existed for keeping women out of America's service academies. "I do not regard the official Department of Defense report on our bill . . . as a serious document or even as worthy of what should regularly and predictably be the intellectual level of the Department of Defense," he said. "They have no official arguments, only excuses."[79] Stratton further argued that the bulk of opposition to women in the service academies stemmed from "inertia and resistance to change." He pointed out that 162 graduates of the West Point class of 1973 received commissions into noncombat branches of the Army, and suggested, "[T]he services need qualified women today more than the women need the service academies." For him, the combat-

oriented mission of West Point served as a smokescreen, as did arguments related to morale, cost, spartan living conditions, and Academy discipline, which
he called "Mickey Mouse." "These are the sophomoric, Neanderthal traditional
practices that still apply at West Point ...," he said, and "there is no excuse
for these practices in the military academies anyway."[80]

The hearings produced no report, though they did allow all parties involved
to air their points of view. No further Congressional action took place until
Stratton outflanked the military with a bit of legislative forced-marching in the
spring of 1975. In the past, chairmen of the Military Personnel Subcommittee
had kept legislation aimed at opening the service academies to women pinned
down within the committee. Stratton bypassed the committee quagmire by
amending a military appropriations bill and bringing the issue to the floor of
the House of Representatives. This amendment called for the academies to admit
women in 1976, and passed 303–96 after a short debate.[81] Congress seemed
intent on breaking down the gender walls at America's service academies, including West Point.

Prior to its passage, the amendment triggered a short but vigorous debate on
the House floor. Stratton summarized his support for women at the academies
by arguing, "It is just a simple matter of equality." He warned that opponents
of his amendment would suggest that the academies trained officers exclusively
for combat, that if women were allowed to attend the academies then they should
be allowed to serve in combat situations. Stratton preempted these arguments
by saying it was clearly not true that academy graduates only went into combat
and that the issue of women in combat was a 'red herring.' He suggested that
the question of whether women should serve in combat could be addressed later,
that it had nothing to do with admitting them to any of the service academies.[82]

Stratton was supported by a number of representatives, each of whom placed
equality at the forefront of their reasons for supporting the admission of women
to the service academies. Representative Duncan said, "It has never been right"
that women in the armed forces were excluded from, "those institutions in the
military which have trained the cream of the military." Pierre du Pont argued,
"Discrimination based upon sex is clearly wrong," and that it was unfair to ask
American women to support with their tax dollars institutions which barred their
admission. He said it was "ridiculous, wasteful, and anachronistic to maintain
that the best officer training our Nation has to offer should be limited to men
only," and argued, "The only way we can take advantage of the most talented
young women is to open the service academies to them."[83]

Ironically, few members of Congress saw the impending change as revolutionary. It represented a simple question of equity to most, of extending another
excellent educational opportunity to women for a career that through ROTC and
OCS each of the armed services approved.[84] The majority did not see the move
as a step toward a greater sharing of power over state-sanctioned violence between men and women and thus failed to appreciate how, in the long run, the
issue of women in combat might one day be finessed by the presence of women

at the service academies. What actually was being debated was large indeed, involving as it did the question of what kind of society best suited both the military and the nation and how much opportunity should or should not be tied to a person's sex. These issues, however, were too controversial and abstract for most politicians. Instead, they focused on the issue of equity on a small scale, taking whatever political and social gain they could from supporting the opening of the academies to women and moving onward. They believed they could allow women to wear Academy rings and undergo weapons and leadership training while still somehow keeping them safe once fighting began, that pushing equality of opportunity did not ultimately have to mean sharing equality of responsibility or risk.

One who did fear the connection between the Stratton amendment and the future role of American women in combat was G. V. "Sonny" Montgomery, a Democrat from Mississippi. He echoed the military position that the admission of women was tied inextricably with whether Americans were willing to commit their daughters to battle. "I am concerned that if we have the adoption of this amendment, this really is a foot in the door of putting women into combat," he said. Montgomery was joined by others who suggested it was "nonsense to say that all distinctions based on sex amount to invidious discrimination," that opening the academies to women would allow men incapable of combat duty to apply for admission, and that women would inevitably drag down physical performance standards.[85]

Despite vigorous debate, however, neither supporters nor opponents of admitting women to America's service academies seem to have believed women would ever really serve in combat. Proponents dismissed the possibility for fear it would derail their efforts to promote equality, while detractors dismissed it as a potential disaster inseparable from the question of breaking down academy gender walls. In the end, both sides were wrong. Congress *did* separate the question of academy admission from the question of whether women should serve in combat, and the opening of the academies *did* play a role in putting women into combat situations in the future.

For Sidney Berry, all this legislative maneuvering and counter-maneuvering, all the debate on the advantages and disadvantages of having women at West Point, and all the soul-searching of the last decade over the course the Army and America were taking was a moot point. Like other senior officers in the Army, he viewed changes at West Point in the same way that Edmund Burke once spoke of any dramatic restructuring of the English government. It should be undertaken, Burke wrote, only with "pious awe and trembling solicitude."[86] Berry had taken that message to Congress and the president and had come up short. Now those same elected officials had spoken, and women were on their way.

So after seeing the president off following graduation ceremonies on June 4, 1975, Berry walked slowly towards his home in Quarters 100 at the edge of The Plain. Completed in 1820, the Superintendent's official residence was the second oldest building on the post and home to a pantheon of American heroes that included Robert E. Lee and Douglas MacArthur. All around him the routine of Academy life smoothly continued, and Berry paused to take in once again what Geoffrey Perret described as the "severe beauty" of West Point, "redolent of order, discipline, and purpose."[87]

As he turned to ascend the steps leading into the house, Berry contemplated the future of the Academy. So much had happened already. So much had been endured. Ironically, the greatest change of all still lay ahead. There would be much to do, much to consider, and much to explain to cadets, faculty, staff, and graduates. The last group would be the most difficult to win over, and he knew what they would say: *"The Corps has . . . ."* The phrase was part of Academy lore, uttered by alumni each time a tradition, significant or otherwise, changed at West Point, and the unspoken remainder of the sentence was *"gone to hell."* Most grads muttered the saying to each other with sly smiles, recognizing that they idolized an Academy which existed only in the cherished memories of their youth. West Point had to evolve and the majority knew that, though they could argue with utter conviction and furious resolve about how *much* should be altered, or how fast. When profound change came it was too much for some to bear. They snarled, *"The Corps has . . . ,"* reproached the unthinking, uncaring, ignorant civilian powers of the land with a vengeance, and yearned for a time when America and West Point were more pure. *"Reduced drill? No mandatory chapel? No bracing?"* they would ask incredulously. And the answer was, *"The Corps has . . ."* *"Women at West Point?"* they would grimace. *"THE CORPS HAS!"*

Sooner or later every significant social ill, every noticeable trend, every current of dissent or cultural change appeared at West Point; like the Army, it reflected the society from which cadets and soldiers sprang. Though the Academy cultivated an aura of unwavering dedication to timeless principles, the myth of an institution that never changed vanished slowly in the handful of years preceding President Ford's arrival at West Point. It was a weak myth, to be sure, shattered time and again throughout American history, but one the Academy faithful too easily believed and too quickly reconsecrated. Like the Army, the Academy was shaken by an unpopular war, sweeping social evolution, and a populace which rediscovered its historic antipathy for the military. Even for an American icon founded in 1802, one which weathered the Civil War and two world wars in less than a century, the experience was searing.[88]

NOTES

1. *Family Weekly*, September 25, 1976.

2. The president traditionally appears at graduation ceremonies for each of the military service academies (the United States Military Academy at West Point, New York, the U.S. Naval Academy in Annapolis, Maryland, and the U.S. Air Force Academy in Colorado Springs, Colorado) once every four years. These are the three major service

academies, with West Point often referred to simply as the Military Academy. The federal government also operates the U.S. Coast Guard and U.S. Merchant Marine academies, located in New London, Connecticut, and Kingston, Rhode Island, respectively. Though they train officers for possible military service they are not part of the Department of Defense, falling instead under the auspices of the Department of Transportation (Coast Guard) and Department of Commerce (Merchant Marine).

3. Ford clung to hallowed tradition here as well, and his actions met with hearty cheers from the Corps of Cadets. The tradition dates to the Revolutionary War. Upon hearing news of the defeat of British forces at Yorktown in 1781, the garrison commander at West Point became so overjoyed he emptied the stockade to allow prisoners to join in the riotous celebrations. Since then it has been customary for visiting Presidents to extend similar immunities to members of the Corps, and high ranking foreign dignitaries sometimes (usually with the encouragement of cadets who write to them prior to their arrival) ask the superintendent for the power to grant some sort of amnesty themselves.

4. Government Printing Office, *Public Papers of the Presidents of the United States: Gerald R. Ford—Book I: June 1 to July 17, 1975* (Washington, D.C.: Government Printing Office, 1977), pp. 769–773. North Vietnamese troops captured Saigon, the capital of South Vietnam, on April 15th. Cambodian naval forces seized the *Mayaguez* and its American crew on May 12th. When negotiation failed to free the ship and crew, Ford ordered American forces to recapture them two days later. Under cover of naval air strikes a landing party of U.S. Marines accomplished the task, suffering twenty-one dead and more than seventy wounded. See "Ford's Rescue Operation," *Newsweek*, May 26, 1975, p. 16.

5. The United States Military Academy educates a portion of the Army officers commissioned as second lieutenants every year. The others come from the enlisted ranks of the Army and attend Officer Candidate School (OCS) or from Reserve Officer Training Corps (ROTC) programs at civilian universities.

6. Judith Hicks Stiehm, *Bring Me Men and Women: Mandated Change at the U.S. Air Force Academy* (Berkeley: University of California Press, 1981), p. 10.

7. LTG Sidney B. Berry, interview with the author (IWA), 10–24–95, p. 4.

8. Ibid., pp. 4, 6.

9. The breakdown of traditional institutions during the sixties has been well documented. See Todd Gitlin, *The Sixties: Years of Hope, Days of Rage* (New York: Bantam Books, 1987); Paul Boyer, *Promises to Keep: The United States Since World War II* (Lexington, Mass.: D.C. Heath and Co., 1995); Thomas Powers, *Vietnam: The War at Home* (Boston: G. K. Hall and Co., 1984); and Jim F. Heath, *Decade of Disillusionment: The Kennedy-Johnson Years* (Bloomington: Indiana University Press, 1975).

10. MacArthur's words come from his last public address, delivered at West Point on May 12, 1962. See William Safire, ed., *Lend Me Your Ears: Great Speeches in History* (New York: W.W. Norton and Company, 1992), p. 77.

11. The Honorable Samuel J. Bayard, "Address Delivered Before the Graduating Class of Cadets, June 16, 1854" (Camden: Office of the *Camden Democrat*, 1854), p. 3.

12. See Lawrence M. Baskir and William A. Strauss, *Chance and Circumstance: The Draft, the War and the Vietnam Generation* (New York: Vintage Books, 1978), especially Part II.

13. Rick Atkinson, *The Long Gray Line* (Boston: Houghton Mifflin Company, 1989), p. 319. Of the hundreds of secondary works on the Academy, Atkinson's book is in a league by itself. It is virtually required reading for West Point graduates.

14. See Robert Leider, "Why They Leave: Resignations from the USMA Class of 1966" (Washington, D.C.: Department of the Army, July 1970); Morris Janowitz, *The Professional Soldier* (New York: The Free Press, 1971); Thomas Fleming, *West Point: The Men and Times of the United States Military Academy* (New York: William Morrow, 1969); and Seymour Hersh, *New York Times* June 25, 1972. Many of the resignations were administrative. Barred by law from sending regular officers to law school, the Army staffed West Point's Law Department with ROTC officers. Usually fresh out of law school, these officers voluntarily served for three years, as opposed to the two years expected of draftees. When they left the Army they were listed administratively as resigning from positions as instructors at West Point. They were neither Academy graduates nor long term members of the faculty, however, and most never intended to serve beyond the three year commitment. Press accounts of an exodus by West Point faculty were thus overblown, though they contributed to the widespread feeling that the Academy was in trouble. See GEN William A. Knowlton, IWA, 11-28-95, p. 12.

15. IWA, 9-16-96, author's notes. According to USMA Historian Dr. Stephen Grove, 273 Academy graduates were killed in Vietnam.

16. Some critics fear the gap between soldiers and civilians has widened again. See Thomas E. Ricks, *Making the Corps* (New York: Scribner, 1997).

17. Thomas Fleming, "West Point Cadets Now Say 'Why, Sir?' " *New York Times Magazine*, July 5, 1970, p. 15.

18. Ibid., p. 17.

19. James Kitfield, *Prodigal Soldiers: How the Generation of Vietnam Revolutionized the American Style of War* (New York: Simon and Schuster, 1995), p. 141.

20. Fleming, "West Point Cadets Now Say 'Why, Sir?' " p. 15, 17.

21. Expanding was the pet project of MG William C. Westmoreland, who served as USMA Superintendent from 1960–63. Congress approved the plans in 1964, allowing the Corps of Cadets a maximum strength of 4,417. To house and support them Congress also called for an immense program of construction, including new barracks, housing for additional faculty, and renovations to existing facilities. See Theodore J. Crackel, *The Illustrated History of West Point* (New York: Harry N. Abrams, Publishers, 1991), pp. 263–65, 275. One reason Westmoreland wanted to expand the Corps was to make it approximately the same size as the Brigade of Midshipmen at the U.S. Naval Academy, thereby helping Army coaches recruit more effectively in their timeless quest to defeat the hated "Middies" in football.

22. See *Pointer View*, May 31, 1974, p. 1, and ETA from Amy Roberts Darlington, Archivist/Information Specialist, Corporate Communications and Library Services, Educational Testing Service, 7-18-2000, p. 1.

23. Atkinson, *The Long Gray Line*, p. 403. West Point cadets are classified according to the Academy's Fourth Class System; fourth year cadets, the equivalent of freshmen at a civilian university, are known as "Plebes," third year cadets (sophomores) are "Yearlings," those in their second (junior) year are "Cows," and first year cadets (seniors) are called "Firsties." "Plebe" comes from the Latin word "plebian," which referred to the lowest class of citizen in ancient Rome. "Yearling" refers to being one year old (as in having finished plebe year), and the term was probably borrowed from the agricultural community. "Cow" is shrouded in Academy lore, but may have come from the furlough cadets traditionally took between their second and third year at West Point. Until the modern era, that was the very *first* leave granted to cadets, and legend has it that their behavior off post and upon their return was so wild that plebes were warned they should

fear the day "when the cows come home." "Firsties" refers to those cadets who are in their final year in the Fourth Class System and therefore hold all senior cadet leadership positions and are responsible for running the Corps of Cadets on a daily basis. ETA, 6-12-2000, p. 1.

24. IWA, 1-15-97, author's notes.

25. By virtue of their numbers, their positions of power in the military, government, and business communities, and their often steadfast loyalty and commitment, West Point graduates are enormously influential on the Academy. They traditionally despise *any* sort of change at West Point, and both cadets and faculty often refer to them as "D.O.G.s," which is short for "Disgruntled Old Grads."

26. Atkinson, *The Long Gray Line*, p. 319, and Fleming, "West Point Cadets Now Say, 'Why, Sir?' " pp. 18, 20. Humorists in the Corps also pointed out that Orange County, California, was home to Disneyland; Orange County, Florida, was home to Disney World; and Orange County, New York, was home to the United States Military Academy.

27. IWA, 1-21-97, author's notes. A similar event took place during the Armed Forces Parade in New York City during the fall of 1968.

28. On March 16, 1968, the 1st Platoon of Charlie Company, 1st Battalion, 20th Infantry, assaulted a village known as My Lai 4 in the Quang Ngai region of South Vietnam. Commanded by 1st Lieutenant William Calley, the platoon massacred approximately 500 civilians, including many women and children. Though the circumstances of the attack remain clouded, what is certain is that some Army officers attempted to cover up the incident. Others investigated and court-martialed many of the perpetrators after news of the massacre reached the press in the spring of 1969. See James S. Olson and Randy Roberts, eds., *My Lai: A Brief History with Documents* (New York: Bedford Books, 1998).

29. Atkinson, *The Long Gray Line*, pp. 319–20. On the following day, upperclassmen ordered the entire Corps to march past Koster's residence at "eyes right" in a gesture of support. Some cadets who questioned whether the superintendent deserved such an honor kept their eyes straight ahead in quiet protest, and Koster was eventually demoted to Brigadier General as a result of the My Lai investigation.

30. Upwards of one-fourth of Army recruits in the early 1970s were high school dropouts. See Kitfield, *Prodigal Soldiers*, p. 127.

31. A 1971 Army survey indicated over 50 percent of troops stationed in Vietnam had used marijuana during the previous 12 months. Thirty percent had used some other sort of psychedelic drug, 32 percent had used stimulants, and over 25 percent used depressants or narcotics. The numbers were marginally lower among soldiers stationed in Europe and the Continental U.S., but alarming just the same. See Richard A. Gabriel and Paul L. Savage, *Crisis in Command: Mismanagement in the Army* (New York: Hill and Wang, 1978), p. 184.

32. Atkinson, *The Long Gray Line*, pp. 366–67, 371–74. See also Daniel J. Nelson, *A History of U.S. Forces in Germany* (Boulder, Col.: Westview Press, 1987), pp. 104–27; William L. Hauser, *America's Army in Crisis* (Baltimore: The Johns Hopkins University Press, 1973), pp. 73–124; George H. Walton, *The Tarnished Shield: A Report on Today's Army* (New York: Dodd, Mead, 1973); Haynes Johnson and George C. Wilson, *Army in Anguish* (New York: Pocket Books, 1972); and Gabriel and Savage, *Crisis in Command*. Racially motivated riots were widespread in Korea as well. See Kitfield, *Prodigal Soldiers*, pp. 125–26.

33. For most of the Academy's history, the number of black cadets was excruciatingly small—only 18 graduated between 1889 and 1947—and racism remained endemic. By the late 1960s, there were enough black cadets to form a sizeable minority, but it took time for the Academy and the overwhelmingly white Corps of Cadets to adjust. See Crackel, *The Illustrated History of West Point*, p. 284.

34. "Combat refusal" was a polite way of describing an action which, in other wars, might have been called a mutiny.

35. Gabriel and Savage, *Crisis in Command*, pp. 37–43, 45, 183. There is no historical precedent for the number of fraggings or combat refusals during Vietnam. Modern military units usually experience the phenomena only during periods of extended, severe combat. Yet in Vietnam the number of incidents *increased* during the late 1960s and early 1970s, a time when the total number of casualties from hostile action *declined*. Many fraggings even took place outside the combat zone, often when troops were on leave. In comparison to the mutinies suffered by the French Army in 1917 or those of the Royal Navy at the close of the eighteenth century, the American army broke down under "minimal stress." See Gabriel and Savage, *Crisis in Command*, p. 37.

36. Howard Zinn, *A People's History of the United States: 1492–Present*, rev. and updated ed. (New York: Harper Collins, 1995), p. 485.

37. Atkinson, *The Long Gray Line*, pp. 310–11.

38. FTA stands for "Fuck the Army."

39. These problems took well over a decade to correct, and it was not until the late 1980s that the military could claim real success in improving discipline, raising standards, and dramatically reducing drug use. A West Pointer who graduated in 1979 summed up the chaos of the era by saying he was shocked to find that instead of entering the Army of Sergeant Rock (a comic book hero) he had enlisted in the Army described in Norman Mailer's *The Naked and the Dead*. IWA, 2-18-98, author's notes.

40. "A Decade in the News," *The Pointer* 56, No. 4 (January 1980): 6. Though strictly forbidden, alcohol was no stranger to the Academy, but officials viewed it with much less suspicion than newer drugs like marijuana, LSD, and heroin.

41. Atkinson, *The Long Gray Line*, p. 407.

42. It was also used informally as a means of driving unwanted cadets from the Corps. Many of the first black cadets, for example, were silenced by whites.

43. For a full account of the incident as well as evidence Pelosi may have been guilty, see Ellis and Moore, *School For Soldiers*, pp. 268–69. Their evidence is supported by General William A. Knowlton, who served as Superintendent at West Point during the episode. He argues Pelosi was clearly guilty. During the Academy investigation however, the Deputy Commandant, who oversaw the work of the Cadet Honor Committee judging Pelosi, sent a note to his adjutant ordering him to "expedite" processing of the case. The adjutant then mistakenly included copies of the note in packets detailing the investigation which went out to the Honor Committee, and Pelosi's attorney argued the note proved the Academy's chain of command had ordered him convicted. With the appearance of impropriety too damning to ignore, Knowlton allowed Pelosi to remain a cadet rather than risk a court fight the Academy was likely to lose. GEN William A. Knowlton, IWA, 11-28-95, pp. 7–8.

44. *The Pointer* 56, No. 4: 6. See also "The Silencing," *Newsweek*, June 18, 1973, p. 42, and "An End to Silence," *Time*, June 18, 1973, pp. 24–25. Pelosi lost 26 pounds during the ordeal, and was one of the few cadets to endure The Silence without resigning.

45. Conscription for World War II began in 1940 and ended in 1947 following the

surrender of Germany and Japan. It was resumed in 1948 because of Cold War tensions with the Soviet Union.

46. Baskir and Strauss, *Chance and Circumstance*, p. 237.

47. Kitfield, *Prodigal Soldiers*, pp. 134, 145.

48. Ibid., 134, 149.

49. James Fallows, *National Defense* (New York: Random House, 1981), p. 120.

50. Zinn, *A People's History of the United States*, pp. 544–45. In contrast, 62 percent of Americans indicated they were confident in the military when the same poll was taken in 1966.

51. See LTG William R. Peers, *Report of the Department of the Army Review of the Preliminary Investigations into the My Lai Incident*, 2 vols. (Washington: Government Printing Office, March 14, 1970).

52. See "Study on Military Professionalism" (Carlisle Barracks, Pennsylvania: United States Army War College Study for the Army Chief of Staff, June 30, 1970); Cinncinatus, *Self-Destruction: The Disintegration and Decay of the United States Army During the Vietnam Era* (New York: W. W. Norton and Company, 1981), pp. 129–31; and Fallows, *National Defense*, pp. 120–21.

53. See Josiah Bunting, *The Lionheads* (New York: George Braziller, Inc., 1972); Edward King, *The Death of the Army: A Pre-Mortem* (New York: Saturday Review Press, 1972); and David H. Hackworth, "Soldier's Disgust," *Harper's Magazine*, July, 1972, pp. 74–78. Bunting was a Virginia Military Institute (VMI) graduate; he later became Superintendent of VMI and presided over the admission of women into that historically all-male military institution in 1997.

54. K. Bruce Galloway and Robert Bowie Johnson, Jr., *West Point: America's Power Fraternity* (New York: Simon and Schuster, 1973), p. 21.

55. See Stephen E. Ambrose, *Duty, Honor, Country: A History of West Point* (Baltimore: Johns Hopkins University Press, 1966); and Thomas Fleming, *West Point: The Men and Times of the United States Military Academy* (New York: William Morrow, 1969).

56. George Pappas, "What if the Academy Had Been Abolished in 1830?," *Assembly*, May 1995, p. 12.

57. John J. Lenney, *Caste System in the American Army: A Study of the Corps of Engineers and Their West Point System* (New York: Greenburg Publishers, 1949), p. 113.

58. See Walton, *The Tarnished Shield*; and Russell F. Weigley, *History of the United States Army* (Bloomington: Indiana University Press, 1984).

59. Fleming, "West Point Cadets Now Say, 'Why, Sir?' " p. 20.

60. Ellis and Moore, *School for Soldiers*, p. 281.

61. Atkinson, *The Long Gray Line*, p. 396. Adding insult to injury, the West Point football team went 0–10 in 1973. It was the worst season in Academy history, punctuated by a 51–0 thrashing at the hands of the rival Naval Academy, and a far cry from the days when Army routinely competed for the national championship. See Crackel, *The Illustrated History of West Point*, p. 292.

62. Atkinson, *The Long Gray Line*, p. 403.

63. "Gender" refers to the social construction of specific roles for men and women, while "sex" refers to the biological fact of being male or female. Gender is thus malleable and specific to historical time and place, while sex is permanent. Within this text, gender and sex are closely intertwined, for when West Point admitted women it also of necessity challenged traditional notions of the proper place of men and women in society. For an

excellent discussion of the use of the term gender and the varied meanings ascribed to it, see Joan W. Scott, "Gender: A Useful Category of Historical Analysis," in *Coming to Terms: Feminism, Theory, Politics*, edited by Elizabeth Weed (New York: Routledge, Chapman and Hall, Inc., 1989), pp. 81–100.

64. Randy Shilts, *Conduct Unbecoming: Lesbians and Gays in the U.S. Military, Vietnam to the Persian Gulf* (New York: St. Martin's Press, 1993), p. 161.

65. U.S. Congress, House, Amendment Offered by Mr. Stratton, 94th Cong., 1st sess., 20 May 1975, *Congressional Record* 121: 15455.

66. Edith Mayo and Jerry K. Frye, "The ERA: Postmortem of a Failure in Political Communication," in *Rights of Passage: The Past and Future of ERA*, edited by Joan Hoff Wilson (Bloomington: Indiana University Press, 1986), p. 85.

67. Jane J. Mansbridge, *Why We Lost the ERA* (Chicago: University of Chicago Press, 1986), chapters 7 and 8.

68. "Senator Chavez Seeks Establishment of Women's Armed Services Academy," *Army Navy Air Force Journal*, February 26, 1955, p. 754, Stiehm, *Bring Me Men and Women*, p. 11.

69. Applicants to each service academy required nomination before their application for admission could be screened. In the 1970s, West Point cadets could be nominated by the Vice President, members of Congress, Congressional Delegates from Washington D.C., the Virgin Islands, and Guam, the Governors of Puerto Rico, the Panama Canal Zone and American Samoa, or the Department of the Army, which could offer admission to enlisted members of the Regular Army, National Guard, or Reserves, children of Medal of Honor recipients, honor graduates of ROTC programs, children of career military personnel, and a small number of foreign students. Nominating officials were allowed to name ten candidates for each of their vacancies. See Major William G. Tobin, Memorandum for the Director of Military Personnel Management, "Admission Process for Women at USMA," August 29, 1975.

70. Stiehm, *Bring Me Men and Women*, pp. 11–13.

71. Ibid., p. 14.

72. Jacqueline Cochran was an extraordinarily experienced pilot who logged more than 15,000 hours in flight, directed the training of women pilots during the war, flew experimental planes as a test pilot, and ferried virtually every type of American military aircraft between U.S. bases and England. Her life seemed to validate the claims of those who advocated a larger role for women in the military, yet she maintained a steadfast opposition to expanded opportunities for women in the armed forces, especially women in combat, as long as she lived.

73. U.S. Congress, House, Committee on Armed Services, Subcommittee No. 2, *Hearings on H.R. 9832, To Eliminate Discrimination Based on Sex*, Statement of Miss Jacqueline Cochran, 93rd Cong., 2nd sess., 1974, pp. 254–64.

74. Ward Just, "Introduction," in *About Face: The Odyssey of an American Warrior*, David H. Hackworth and Julie Sherman. (New York: Simon and Schuster, 1989), p. 14.

75. U.S. Congress, House, Committee on Armed Services, Subcommittee No. 2, *Hearings on H.R. 9832*, Statement of Howard H. Callaway, Secretary of the Army, pp. 160–165. The debate continues within the military to this day, though it takes place privately because most personnel fear criticism of national policy regarding women in the armed forces will place their careers in peril.

76. West Pointers have served in senior command positions in every major American war since 1861. A short list of the most famous would include Ulysses Grant, Robert E.

Lee (Civil War), John J. Pershing (World War I), Dwight D. Eisenhower, Douglas Mac-Arthur, Omar Bradley, and George S. Patton (World War II), Matthew B. Ridgway (Korean War), William Westmoreland and Creighton Abrams (Vietnam), and Norman Schwarzkopf (Desert Storm). Critics argue such lists say as much about the "old boy" network among West Pointers as they do about the fighting prowess of Academy graduates.

77. U.S. Congress, House, *Hearings on H.R. 9832*, Statement by Callaway, pp. 160–65.

78. U.S. Congress, House, Committee on Armed Services, Subcommittee No. 2, *Hearings on H.R. 9832*. Statement of LTC Grace M. King, U.S. Army Reserve, pp. 226–37. The problem endures even today, for officers without combat experience are second class citizens in the Army.

79. U.S. Congress, House Committee Armed Services, Subcommittee No. 2, *Hearings on H.R. 9832*. Statement of Samuel S. Stratton, Representative from New York, p. 35.

80. Ibid., pp. 36–39.

81. Stiehm, *Bring Me Men and Women*, pp. 36–37. Federal courts exerted pressure as well. After suing Secretary of Defense James Schlesinger on behalf of female constituents who wanted to attend the Air Force and Naval Academies, California representatives Jerome Waldie and Don Edwards were defeated in U.S. District Court. They won a reversal in the U.S. Court of Appeals, however, and looked forward to a new and full trial of their case on its merits in November 1974. Given the tenor of the times, and the questionable constitutionality of the academies' position, the courts might have forced open the academies' doors by 1976 even without Congressional action. When Congress opened them in 1975, the case became moot.

82. *Congressional Record*, 94th Cong., 1st sess., House, 1975 p. 15449.

83. Ibid, pp. 15450–51.

84. Stiehm, *Bring Me Men and Women*, p. 2.

85. *Congressional Record*, 1975, pp. 15452–54.

86. Edmund Burke, "Reflections on the French Revolution," in *Western Political Heritage*, edited by William Elliott and Neil McDonald (New York: Prentice Hall, 1955), p. 684.

87. Geoffrey Perret, *Old Soldiers Never Die: The Life of Douglas MacArthur* (New York: Random House, 1996), p. 584.

88. Founded in 1802, West Point is the oldest of the American service academies. The Naval Academy dates to 1845, the Coast Guard Academy to 1876, and the Air Force Academy to 1954. See John Lovell, *Neither Athens Nor Sparta? The American Service Academies in Transition* (Bloomington, Ind.: Indiana University Press, 1979), p. 312.

2

★ ★ ★ ★

"A Measure of Our Maturity"

To one who knows nothing of its practical benefits, military training for a girl sounds like a huge joke. . . . But one who has experienced the advantages of this training has a very different story to tell. . . .
—Cadet Elsie F. Fay, Fairfield Seminary and Military College, 1896[1]

In the wake of President Ford's visit, West Point sprang into action with the determination of an army preparing for invasion, for against their will and despite their warnings, Academy leaders were compelled to address a social experiment without precedent in American history. Legions of captains, majors, and colonels on the Academy staff began preparing action plans, conducting studies, and fanning out all over the country to find out exactly what women could and could not do and how the regular Army fared as it also dealt with increasing the number of women on active duty. Yet they were not the first to tackle the problem. Planners quietly began determining the changes required to admit women almost three years prior to Ford's visit, and by 1975 Academy plans were well advanced.

Conceived during the American Revolution and created during the presidency of Thomas Jefferson, the Academy had been run for 173 years exclusively by and for men. Now West Pointers knew the change so many had dreaded and opposed had become more than merely civilian threat or nightmare. It was actually going to happen, almost 200 years to the day after America declared itself free from Great Britain by issuing a Declaration of Independence which proclaimed that "all men are created equal." By 1976, Congress wanted that spirit of equality to envelop West Point and include women as well.

Those most familiar with the Academy may have known that the "warrior society" at West Point was hardly a stranger to women.[2] The first members of the Corps of Invalids, which the Continental Congress established in 1777 to provide for wounded veterans still capable of limited duty, included Margaret Corbin. Struck by British grapeshot in 1776 while fighting alongside her mortally wounded husband in defense of Fort Washington, Corbin joined the Invalid Corps at West Point and remained there for many years. She drew a pension from Congress, could swill grog and curse better than the most scurrilous soldier, and remained a coarse figure in the nearby town of Buttermilk Falls until her death.[3] Deborah Sampson, who left a life of teaching and farming to join the Continental Army in 1782, briefly joined Corbin at West Point. Sampson cropped her hair, donned male clothing, and served in the West Point garrison. Fighting Tories below the Highlands, she was wounded twice, receiving a saber slash to the head and a musket ball in one thigh. As a West Point graduate who later became both a noted historian and an Academy Superintendent put it, "One gets the impression that she was a better 'man' than most of the recruits reporting to Washington's army in the twilight years of the War of Independence."[4]

Outside the realm of warriors but still an integral part of Academy life during the middle of the nineteenth century were the famous Warner sisters. Anna and Susan Warner offered Sunday school classes, Bible instruction, and music recitals for cadets in their home on Constitution Island, just across the Hudson from West Point. Since the Academy was isolated from the outside world and because the Warner sisters were charming hostesses, cadets competed for the coveted opportunity to row over and visit the women on Sundays. Susan achieved global fame as the author of *Wide Wide World*, a sentimental melodrama revolving around Ellen Montgomery, who survives a series of emotional challenges en route to conquering her passions and her will.[5] The book was spectacularly successful and joined *Uncle Tom's Cabin* as one of the most popular books published in the United States during the nineteenth century. Anna achieved her own fame by writing a number of famous hymns, including "Jesus Loves Me," and together the sisters wrote more then eighty-five works. They also developed a tremendous loyalty to West Point over the years and made arrangements to turn both Constitution Island and their prized Gilbert Stuart portrait of George Washington over to the Academy before they died.[6]

At the turn of the century, cadet editors of *The Howitzer*, the Academy yearbook, added their own contribution to the history of women at West Point. In a drawing labeled "The Cadet Adjutant Class of 2000," artist and cadet George B. Comly of the Class of 1900 portrayed a young woman dressed in cadet gray, complete with tarbucket hat, dress sword, and tails.[7] Comly drew her in a very dignified, military pose, with collar-length hair that was both uncommon among women of his era and a reasonably accurate prediction of the length allowed

the first women to attend the Academy in 1976. Rather than comical or traditionally feminine, Comly's female cadet wore a uniform identical to those worn
by men with the exception of a knee-length skirt disarmingly short by standards
of the time, women's shoes with heels, and spats. No comment accompanies
the portrait, though it takes little imagination to picture young cadets in 1900
contemplating the great changes the twentieth century would bring, reflecting
on changes in the Corps during the previous ninety-eight years of Academy life,
and concluding amid guffaws and general laughter that by the year 2000, West
Point would change so much it would admit women. They were more prescient
than they could ever know and only twenty-four years off the mark.[8]

Charles Dana Gibson provided yet another image of West Point women in
1909. Internationally famous for his drawings of elegantly beautiful women
(whose distinctively recognizable features garnered them the name "Gibson
Girls"), Gibson was also a subtle critic of the limited roles women were allowed
to play in turn-of-the-century America. Though he often drew men and women
in romantic and luxurious surroundings for romance novels, he also portrayed
women playing football, serving in the military, and acting as ministers. These
roles were unheard of for women in the early twentieth century, as was the
notion that one day women might attend West Point. Gibson alluded to what
seemed a farcical possibility when he painted a portrait entitled "A Woman as
West Point Cadet" for the cover of an Army-Navy football game program in
1909. Rather than portray her as cheerleader or debutante, Gibson put her in
cadet gray, a subtle if unintended harbinger of things to come.

In an article published fifty-five years later, Colonel Elvin R. Heiberg joined
the cadets of 1900 in predicting the Academy would admit women by the year
2000, though the USMA Professor of Mechanics was more openly tongue-in-
cheek than his predecessors. Women at West Point, he suggested, would officially be called "Codettes" and live in separate barracks on Constitution Island,
well-removed from the men of the Corps. A graduate in the class of 1926,
Heiberg saw an Academy where women would gain admission after passing
"rigid screen tests administered by a panel of Broadway talent scouts who perform this task as a public service." Women cadets could join a glee club known
as "The Gray Canaries," or try out for their own gymnastic team, "The Black
Knighties." Unofficially known as "Dolls," they would dress in gray berets and
skirts, handle "all cheerleading and mule-riding chores," provide "Rockettes"
who performed during half-time at Army football games, and dance partners on
a roster basis for male members of the Corps. Though Heiberg noted the introduction of women "added immeasurably to the esprit of the whole garrison"
and "the after-Taps rallies are overwhelming successes," there were some problems. In this futuristic Academy, he noted, officials found it necessary to "dis-
band the Sailing Club, and to make all canoes and other boats 'off limits' to
cadets," no doubt to keep the men from making secret trips to visit women
cadets living across the Hudson on Constitution Island.[9]

Beyond futuristic predictions, other women played their part in cadet life and legends. Athena, the Greek goddess of war and wisdom, held a coveted place among women residing at the Academy, and her helmet formed a portion of the West Point coat of arms.[10] Joan of Arc appeared in a magnificent mural in Washington Hall, towering above generation after generation of cadets as they took their meals. And in one of the most colorful yet least well-known legends of the Corps, world renowned ballerina Fanny Elssler is said to have danced the famously provocative Cracovienne[11] by moonlight for a party of cadets at their summer encampment in 1840.[12]

Unlike the women of legends and myths, the wives and daughters of the faculty, staff, and garrison actually lived nearby from the beginning, adding color to the often repetitious, dull routine of Academy life. They were not the most important women in cadet lives; that distinction usually belonged to girlfriends back home or young women brought in by the Academy from schools around New York for regular cadet hops during the academic year. Vassar, Wellesley, and nearby Ladycliff College students joined women from other schools and even working-class girls from New York City to attend these hops, where they could dance in Cullum Hall with uniformed "knights" in white gloves, take moonlit walks along the Hudson, or simply indulge romantic fantasy in a storybook setting with young men touted as "gentlemen." Women were as integral a part of cadet lore as Academy trivia and tales of conquest as necessary for a young cadet seeking the acceptance of his brothers-in-arms as performing well on obstacle courses, in strategy and tactics classes, or in marksmanship. The greater the risk with women, the more glorious the triumph, and virtually every cadet knew or at least heard of someone who covertly brought a woman into the barracks, or even into formation dressed as a member of the Corps of Cadets.[13] Pregnant girlfriends were hardly uncommon, though the Academy tried to cover up evidence of cadet parenthood whenever possible. Cadets were, after all, supposed to be gentlemen, and because they were forbidden to marry while members of the Corps, any questions related to paternity carried with them the threat of expulsion. Year after year the number of marriages immediately following graduation added to a legend and cliché rooted in fact. Not all the weddings were tied to pregnancy of course, but onlookers joked every May that many of the children in the crowds assembled to watch graduation parades came to see their daddies.[14]

Yet none of these women, important though they were to the Academy and to the lives of individual cadets, were full-fledged members of the Long Gray Line. The distinction held enormous importance. Women were fought over, they were pursued, and their presence on Academy grounds gave cause for celebration and excitement, but they were *not* part of "what may well be regarded as the most significant of the world's officer-training institutions."[15] In fact, no institution dedicated to training professional military officers anywhere in the world admitted women, and the challenge facing Lieutenant General Sidney Berry and his staff was to find a way to make gender integration work with no precedent to guide them.[16]

They began by referring to studies already completed by the Academy. Hardly immune to the growing demand for gender equality in American society, West Pointers began seriously contemplating what impact the admission of women might have on the Academy as early as the late 1960s. When the Equal Rights Amendment (ERA) passed Congress in 1972, it seemed destined for quick ratification, and many officers feared that a strict interpretation would require the Army to open the Academy to both sexes and drop the restrictions that kept women out of front-line combat units.[17] Joined by the Department of the Army and the Department of Defense, West Point strongly opposed any such changes. Lieutenant General William Knowlton, who served as Superintendent during the early 1970s, summed up the Academy's position before Congress in 1974. He argued admitting women would "seriously detract from the Academy's mission" which "was to provide the nucleus for the Regular Army's combat officers."[18] Although this argument formed the foundation of military antagonism toward opening all of the service academies to women, there were other concerns as well.[19] Some officers suggested women would drop out at higher rates than men, while others insisted an Academy education was too expensive to provide to a future officer barred from duty in combat. There were also those who believed that women would ruin the esprit de corps of the academies, and demolish the time-honored all-male environment.[20] The bedrock issue, however, one which cut through all others and endured the longest, revolved around combat.

At West Point it formed the nucleus of opposition to the admission of women as early as 1972. In a handwritten memo regarding women at the Academy, the Deputy Commandant of Cadets wrote, "[M]y feeling is that we should come out with an 'over my dead body' approach to girls at West Point. The more we act like we can do it," he said, "the more likely we are to be told to do it. I believe we should hang our hat on 'this society is not prepared to accept women as combat leaders yet.' "[21] The admission of women was thus very much on the minds of the senior officers at West Point, who ordered contingency planning for integrating women into the Academy begun the same year.[22] While these plans provoked thoughtful debate and long-range considerations of what gender-integration might mean at West Point, they were formed in a spirit of damage control akin to that expressed by the Army Chief of Staff for Personnel when considering expanding the roles played by women in the Army prior to World War II. "The purpose of this study," he wrote in 1941, "is to permit the organization of a women's force along the lines which meet with War Department approval, so that when it is forced upon us, as it undoubtedly will be, we shall be able to run it our way."[23]

In Annapolis and Colorado Springs, the Naval and Air Force academies were operating in the shadow of the ERA as well, and moving forward with studies of their own. A 1972 West Point memo on the subject indicated the depth of their preparations, stating, "The position of the Navy is that they will admit women when the Equal Rights Amendment is ratified. The position of the Air Force remains that they are developing contingency plans for entrance in the summer of 75."[24] Passage of the ERA thus pushed all the academies into motion; despite their public protests, they were quietly preparing for the admission of women at the request of senior officers in the Pentagon. As one officer concluded in September 1972, "There is definite high level interest in the plans."[25]

Within the Army, specific preparations began that very month, when USMA staffers developed initial contingency plans to admit between twenty and fifty women at West Point "in response to recent DCSPER [Deputy Chief of Staff for Personnel] guidance . . ." from the Department of the Army. Planners completed these first plans in December.[26] Although a clear indication the Army considered the admission of women to West Point a possibility, these early studies should be kept in perspective. They were short-term efforts designed to present alternatives in a worst-case scenario where women were actually thrust upon the Academy, not detailed schemes which considered the arrival of women on the banks of the Hudson as very likely. Like plans for a war with Great Britain which the Army dutifully prepared during the 1930s, the plans for the admission of women to West Point represented an institution going through the motions, and doing what was necessary to be ready on paper while harboring a faith that somehow the nightmare would never really come to pass.[27]

In January 1973, the Army ordered further study of the entrance of women into the Academy,[28] and by spring West Point developed a formal operations plan for their admission known as Operations Plan 1973 (OPLAN-73).[29] Formulated on the assumption that West Point would have twenty months to prepare for the arrival of women cadets, planners pushed for an initial entry group of between thirty and fifty women. They feared a single woman, or even a small group, "will receive publicity and attention far beyond that desired for their appropriate or expected development as individual members of a cadet class." With remarkable foresight, one planner said the attention would "further segregate the female cadets from their male classmates . . . could destroy the group's involvement with their class, and ultimately affect their development of class unity and spirit. . . ."[30]

Discussion continued at the Academy over the next year, and in November 1974, Colonel Gerald W. Medsger submitted a memorandum for the Superintendent entitled "Four Issues Implied by the Admission of Women to USMA." In a wide-ranging essay, Medsger, who served as the Director of Institutional Research, argued that the Academy would ultimately be "ordered to admit women for the sake of equal opportunity" and "that the course of integrating females can go well or badly depending upon how it is handled." He suggested that the Academy "take a fresh look at its mission" in the light of the issues raised by the possible inclusion of women in the corps of cadets. Those issues included the traits "most desired in female cadets," the question of how to manage publicity, the implications of "lower or different standards," the number of women to be admitted, and how their "special needs would be cared for." Medsger called for further research by the Academy, pushed for strict equality in training whenever possible, and noted women would "face special problems not faced by males because of the stress of being integrators, and because of their unique physiology."[31] He also suggested that if "the nation needs female soldiers who are temporarily more aggressive, the girls could be administered small doses of testosterone to make them 'biologically' equal to males in the potential for aggressiveness." This remark, in the midst of an otherwise well-argued and researched essay, indicates the related fear many officers had that women were simply not aggressive enough for combat. The Academy never gave serious consideration to the suggestion, though it says volumes about the uncertainty of many officers as they pondered the myriad issues raised by the notion of ending male dominance at West Point.[32]

The essay received the attention of Lieutenant Colonel John J. Cook, Jr., a member of the Commandant's staff who prepared a critical review for the Academy. He echoed the position that women should not be admitted because "USMA has the specialized mission of producing leaders who are prepared for leadership in ground combat." He added, "Unless we can continue to accomplish this mission better than less expensive preparatory institutions, the justification for Academy existence will disappear."[33] Cook also suggested the Academy forego extensive studies, because "too detailed and too complete a plan could take on a self-fulfilling character." He reiterated the importance of demanding physical training and a single-track system for cadets if women were admitted, noting, "The implications for military training are that women would be carefully managed and that certain positions and tasks, obviously beyond their capabilities, would not be assigned." Rather than special treatment, Cook explained how this merging of abilities and responsibilities actually mirrored what occurred when men entered the Army as well. "One should not consider this to be exceptional treatment," he said. "The same consideration is currently afforded all male soldiers in all stages of training and particularly in the [military occupational specialty] MOS-selection process."[34] Finally, Cook called for women to receive combat training alongside men. Whether they eventually became involved in a combat situation or not, he argued that all officers needed exposure to combat training so they could better support soldiers in the front lines. Officers had to be able to empathize with infantry soldiers and appreciate their "unique difficulties," he said, adding, "An officer who has never been miserable, who has never been challenged by a tough and demanding training program . . . is shortchanging the soldier he supports."[35]

By the spring of 1975, even before Gerald Ford's visit, there were those within West Point who watched with considerable alarm the growing political momentum to admit women gathering in Congress. They knew the Academy might soon lose the fight to prevent the admission of women cadets, but they hoped that resistance among senior Army leaders and civilians in the Department of Defense would prevent such a calamity. Even Lieutenant General Berry put his faith in the confidence of officials in Washington, who said privately that Congress was not really serious about sending women to the Academy. As he later wrote, "Right down to the day in May 1975 that Congressman Stratton took the issue to the floor of the House of Representatives, the senior people in Washington seemed confident that Congress would maintain the service academies as male institutions."[36] The contingency plans existed, he said later, "but nobody thought we would ever have to use them. . . ."[37]

When the decisive House vote came on May 20, 1975, Academy officials were thus taken by surprise, but they dutifully and swiftly dusted off their contingency plans and prepared for the arrival of women cadets. In a memorandum dated the following day, the Academy Chief of Staff delivered "planning guidance for the admission of female cadets to the Military Academy." Under the heading "Assumptions," Colonel James H. Tormey suggested that women would be admitted on a "deliberate" as opposed to a "crash" basis. They would be admitted, educated, and trained in the same manner as men, though it was "anticipated that there will be some deviations to avoid an unreasonable demand upon female cadets." Tormey concluded his list of assumptions by suggesting "there will be 30 female cadets entering with the Class of 1980" and by detailing planning responsibility to the Deputy Chief of Staff for Operations (DCSOPS), who was to have a detailed draft OPLAN submitted by June 20, 1975.[38] Tormey would not have acted without the Superintendent's orders, indicating Berry was moving forward with specific plans even before his memorable conversation with the President on June 4. After the House vote, everyone at West Point realized the political battle had probably ended.

Ironically, on May 20, the very day of the momentous House vote and a day *before* the distribution of Tormey's memorandum, Berry issued a memorandum of his own for the record entitled, "Thoughts on the Admission of Women to the United States Military Academy." Encapsulating the major arguments against admitting women as cadets, Berry reiterated the primacy of land combat to the Army's mission and pointed out that "no modern country in the world . . . as a matter of policy permits its women to participate in ground combat." He argued that Academy training was "austere" and "disciplined," to say nothing of physically demanding. Male cadets were able to follow a "single track" in training, generating a "shared common experience" that provided cadets with "a unity, cohesiveness, spirit and military ethos that has been the essence of West Point for 173 years." The Superintendent called for studies to examine the effects women might have on battlefield effectiveness, and suggested women would forever change the West Point environment because different physical standards would have to be established for them. He argued that greater societal discussion regarding the consequences of making women combat soldiers was necessary and succinctly summed up the Army's position in this regard when he wrote, "Those who would admit women to the Military Academy should first openly and clearly decide that women should and will be combat soldier-leaders."[39] Berry emphasized the connection between West Point and combat by quoting General Accounting Office figures stating that 98.1 percent of West Point's graduates had served in combat assignments. He hoped that "any decision on this issue will be made thoughtfully, analytically, responsibly and with a view toward enhancing the wartime battle effectiveness of the nation's land combat forces." Perhaps with the conviction that change loomed close at hand, he closed by pledging that the Academy would "do its best to make the change work smoothly and effectively" if necessary.[40]

Although the word "combat" did not appear in the West Point mission statement, the importance of the association many officers held between the Academy and leadership of combat units cannot be overestimated.[41] Most graduates did enter the combat arms initially, though never in numbers as large as the Academy preferred. During the post World War II era a few bypassed the combat arms to attend medical school, and those who physically could not serve in a combat unit often accepted commissions in support branches of the Army.[42] Ironically, the Army may have damaged its own case by classifying units as "combat" oriented in the first place. *Every* Army unit was actually a potential combat unit, depending on how a given battle developed. Rear-echelon troops have been either overrun by enemy forces or thrown into front line positions and ordered to fight as infantry on numerous occasions in the Army's history. Though the best-known example is when cooks and clerks were rushed to the front as riflemen during the Battle of the Bulge in 1944, there are others from the more recent past. In 1993, "armorers, cooks, ammo handlers, and communications specialists" from Task Force Ranger were thrown into an emergency relief convoy sent into a vicious firefight in Mogadishu to rescue stranded American forces during a deployment to Somalia.[43]

Still, status and rank within the Army have always depended on rigid distinctions between those who have served in combat units during wartime and those who have not, and virtually every army and tribe in the world make the distinction an imperative delineator between those who should lead and those who must follow. Warriors become the supreme chiefs and generals, honored in song and story, and hold places of honor at social functions. West Point's orientation toward combat was thus a matter of considerable pride, not just professional *raison d'etre*. Hence the confusing and often misleading separation of units into combat, combat support, combat service support, and so forth. The gray areas between each category were considerable, and politically it became easy for Congress to fit women into them. This was especially true once it became clear that even by Army definitions most soldiers supported combat troops rather than fighting with them. Because a sizeable portion of West Point graduates were also deployed in rear-echelon assignments, there were those within the Department of the Army who shared the belief that the combat argument against women at the Academy was flawed.[44]

The most notable was Paul D. Phillips, Acting Assistant Secretary of the Army for Manpower and Reserve Affairs. In March 1974 he separated all active duty senior officers who were West Point graduates into groups by years of service and branch. Phillips concluded, "[T]he (combat arms) argument is a weak one since we seem to average less than 70 percent in CA over the years, less than 75 percent in the first 5 years, and about 80 percent . . . for the 1973 class."[45] Phillips excluded generals from the combat arms branch, leading the Secretary of the Army to add a handwritten comment suggesting the statistics were invalid. Yet the numbers are compelling, for even with generals included, the number of active duty West Pointers in combat branches was well below 75 percent.[46] While impressive in its own right, and a credit to the combat-oriented mission of the Academy, the percentage implied that a fourth of every graduating class at West Point could be open to cadets who did not have to serve in the combat arms. Even though Phillips's report did not reach a general audience, the statistics were available to members of Congress.[47] Most of them looked at the Army's position, which suggested that every West Pointer served in a combat unit, and they knew better. They were not persuaded by arguments that Academy graduates were each *potential* combat leaders and moved to integrate the academies over the collective objections of the Department of Defense.[48]

After Berry released his memo for the record in May, West Point continued to work on comprehensive plans to admit women. On May 30, Lieutenant Colonel Thomas P. Garigan submitted his own memorandum dealing with the public affairs impact the admission of women would have on West Point. He noted that press interest would be especially high when women first arrived and that "invasion by the news media, if not carefully controlled, will be highly disrupting. . . ." Garigan also suggested the "giddying effect of intense notoriety on a young person can lead to inadvertent statements . . . which could be embarrassing both to the Military Academy and . . . to the individual." He closed by calling for the staff, faculty, cadets, and alumni to be thoroughly informed, and suggested "a fast implementation [of plans to admit women] might be preferable to a slow implementation because the life-span of high press interest would be short."[49]

Though much planning occurred prior to President Ford's arrival on June 4, the pace accelerated after his departure. A week later, the Secretary of the Army flew to West Point for a briefing on the admission of women. By then officials were committed to a one track system with "minimum essential, responsible and sensible changes taking into consideration physiological differences in females" and no changes at all to the Academy's academic program.[50] They agreed to keep identical admission standards, substituted women's self-defense courses for the boxing and wrestling courses taken by male cadets, and planned a new Physical Aptitude Examination (PAE) for women because scaling the men's test had proved impractical.[51]

Ironically, the push by West Point to establish differing physical standards for men and women was not forced on the Army by Congress. In fact, Academy leaders decided physiological differences demanded different physical standards for men and women so they would be fair, or equitable. This is not what authors of the legislation opening West Point to women wanted. As Representative Stratton said on the floor of Congress in 1975, "Mr. Chairman, I do not want any special concessions for women. I think they should be required to follow the same program, they should be required to meet the same standards . . ."[52] Yet in meetings with Congress during the summer of 1975, Academy concerns over whether women could meet the existing physical standards led to a change in the wording of the eventual legislation opening the academies to women. Rather than calling for equal standards, as the Stratton amendment had done, P.L. 94–106 adopted language proposed by West Point when it mandated that, "academic and other relevant standards required for appointment, admission, training, graduation, and commissioning of female individuals shall be the same as those required for male individuals, except for those *minimum essential adjustments in such standards required because of physiological differences between male and female individuals. . . .*" (emphasis added).[53]

In the decades following Congressional opening of the service academies to women, the single most controversial issue at each was different physical performance standards for men and women. Male Cadets and Midshipmen resented being held to a different benchmark for their performance and often blamed civilian officials for forcing academy doors open to women. Yet the military brought different standards upon itself, because of the fear that women would not graduate in sufficient numbers if the existing male standards were applied. There was no thought to whether the standards themselves needed modification. Did upper body strength and running times really equate with combat prowess or leadership skill? Despite assumptions, no one really knew; by not considering these questions the military joined Congress in missing a golden opportunity to consider the real potential of women in the armed forces. They also let slip away the chance to explain the differences between equity and equality throughout the military, and neither American society nor the military has effectively confronted them since.

Once it became clear that different physical standards would be adopted, the problem of convincing male cadets that women were working as hard as men became obvious. As an evaluation team reported in July 1975, orientation of USMA staff and cadets "should emphasize that men and women in this Army are paid the same. In those areas of physical training where physiology may dictate *different* efforts, it will not dictate *less* effort."[54] Over time many members of the Academy staff did emphasize this fact to cadets, though it too often fell on deaf ears.

Just as West Point prepared for Congressional action well in advance, so did the other service academies. They worked closely with each other to coordinate planning, though each took different approaches to the integration of women. For example, both the Naval and Air Force academies planned to admit more women than USMA, and while West Point and the Naval Academy planned to place women together as roommates in otherwise integrated barracks, the Air Force Academy began with segregated housing. One novel and entirely successful Air Force approach included the use of active duty female lieutenants as surrogate "upperclasswomen" during the first two years of integration.[55] These women gave new female cadets role models and valuable leadership support and forced upperclassmen to accept women cadets as equals more quickly. This prevented them from relishing their role as the last all-male classes at the Air Force Academy and seems to have diminished much of the sexism that women at the other academies faced in the late 1970s.[56]

In July, Brigadier General Walter F. Ulmer, Commandant of Cadets, submitted a memorandum for the record detailing his impressions of the Reserve Officer Training Corps (ROTC) Basic Camp at Fort Knox, Kentucky. Women had been part of Army ROTC training since 1973, and Ulmer hoped to assess what women could fairly be expected to accomplish in military training. His memo anticipated many of the obstacles that women at West Point faced in the future. "A perception of fairness" in standards and requirements was essential, he said, as was the proper fitting of uniforms and equipment. Women needed "greater pre-camp physical conditioning" and "special training in voice projection." They objected to "being singled out individually or as a group because of their sex, and object specifically to being used openly as an example which males should surpass." Women who are "competent and fair" could be accepted by both men and women, and the young ROTC officers he talked with believed they could "subordinate their emotions" and not allow personal relationships between the sexes to interfere with "their sense of duty." Ulmer also remarked that women were more highly motivated, "often more proficient than male cadets," and "discernibly more perceptive and articulate." He also commented ominously, "Women as a minority create attitudes among males which are remarkably similar to the attitudes of whites during early periods of our racial integration efforts."[57] This was the most accurate of his insights, one that foreshadowed many of the difficulties women at the Academy would face in the years to come.

In August, the Army's Deputy Chief of Staff for Personnel, Lieutenant General Harold G. Moore, Jr., organized a conference on the admission of women at West Point which attracted representatives of major Army commands that trained women around the world, as well as LTG Berry and an officer from the United States Military Academy Preparatory School (USMAPS) at Fort Monmouth, New Jersey.[58] Again, the attendees were able to accurately predict problems the Academy would face in the future. The commander of the ROTC Camp at Fort Knox noted women were generally rated lower than men in leadership and suspected "there was a backlash effect by men who resented attention women received." Other attendees noted that women needed to be "cautioned on food intake or they will gain weight," that "perception of both men and women on substitute training is very important," and that more women than men were injured during basic training. Brigadier General Mary Clarke, Director of the Women's Army Corps, argued cadets would follow the lead of USMA staff and faculty, while another officer commented she "was surprised at the extreme West Point Cadet resentment to women cadets" she noticed during her visit.[59]

Virtually everyone agreed that challenging standards and cooperation were vital to making integration at USMA successful. In the midst of this general agreement, however, were the unprecedented and unpredictable details, and discussion of them revealed the depths to which integration would change West Point in the long run. First, the director of the Academy's physical education program commented that in order to keep women in their program the Los Angeles Police Academy had "let standards for all graduates slip," and he feared a similar pattern would emerge at West Point. Second, an officer urged the Academy to establish a historical record of the admission of women, and plans eventually called for that job to be handled by West Point's Director of Institutional Research.[60] Finally, Moore suggested notifying Academy alumni of preparations for the arrival of women cadets on October 18, 1975, during the Army homecoming game, provided the legislation had actually passed Congress.[61]

In the long run these issues surfaced again and again in discussions over the admission of women at West Point. The debate over physical standards, whether they slipped, stayed the same, or improved, began as soon as women were actually admitted. Over the years standards rose considerably, though women generally did not perform on the same levels as men. Creating an institutional history served the interests of historians and the Army in the event of anticipated legal attacks on the Academy. Fears of legal assaults by men claiming discrimination because they were held to higher physical standards than women and eligible for combat duty never materialized. The historical documents compiled by the Academy, however, most notably the *Project Athena* reports, became an invaluable resource for scholars studying gender integration. The decision to notify the alumni that preparations had been ongoing for several years ultimately angered some graduates, who felt they should have received greater knowledge of the impending change beforehand.[62]

August also saw the completion of research by the West Point Department of Physical Education into the physiological differences between men and women. Based on studies done at both the Academy and Army bases around the country, the department found significant differences between men and women that might warrant "modifications" in the USMA physical entrance exam and training programs for women. Dr. James A. Peterson authored the report detailing departmental findings and generally found that "men perform far better than women in activities which require strength, speed, and power." Reasons for the difference in performance included the fact that women "have less bone mass, less muscle component, but more fat than men . . . ," that men "have a higher center of gravity, different pelvic structure, wider shoulders, narrower hips, longer legs, and greater ventilation capacity." The study concluded that "men have a greater potential for endurance that cannot be matched by women," mainly because of differences in cardio-respiratory factors like blood-oxygen levels and heart size. At "submaximal work levels," Peterson noted, "women have to work much harder to accomplish the same amount of work," are "always operating at a level closer to their maximum than men and will reach exhaustion sooner." Last, he found that women generally had less tolerance to heat than men, so that under higher levels of heat they worked relatively harder than men to accomplish similar amounts of work.[63] This research formed the foundation for subsequent establishment of physical performance standards and a starting point for periodic re-evaluation of the performance of women. Peterson called for continued study because evidence suggested women were only beginning to reach their physiological and athletic potential.[64]

Differing physical standards for men and women cadets eventually proved one of the most persistent sources of complaint among men at West Point, and officers had reason to anticipate others long before official studies warned them of disturbing trends among the Academy staff, faculty, and cadets in 1976. In a study of the Army's military police school, which admitted women in 1974, Wayne B. Nicoll noted that women attending the school were victims of the "rumor mill." In the eyes of their male classmates, "They are either prostitutes or lesbians," and men constantly harassed women with "wisecracks" which, Nicoll said, reflected "a cynicism and general non-acceptance of the women as their equals."[65] Further research confirmed that similar cynicism and nonacceptance of women existed at West Point.

By September, the mountain of assembled information finally emerged as the operations plan that governed the admission of women to the Academy. Known as Operations Plan (OPLAN) 75–1, it covered everything from haircuts and military training to new construction and admission policies to make the integration of women cadets a success. Calling for the full integration of women into the Corps of Cadets, the plan provided that women take self-defense classes and women's gymnastics rather than boxing, wrestling, and men's gymnastics, and that they participate in all athletic activities except combative contact sports. Female cadets were scheduled for inclusion in as many companies as possible depending on the number of quality applicants and in numbers sufficient to provide a support network for women in each company.[66] Major renovations and additions to existing facilities included the construction of women's lavatories and showers, as well as special laundry equipment.[67] Two of the most important distinctions from the regulations governing male cadets were in women's uniforms and the regulations governing the length of their hair. Specific plans were not included in OPLAN 75–1, but the plan did make clear that women would have different uniforms and be allowed to wear their hair longer than their male counterparts.[68]

With the completion of OPLAN 75–1, the Academy moved from formulating policy to the implementation and fine tuning of existing plans. There remained the tasks of informing the extremely active and influential alumni, educating male cadets, seeking outstanding women for admission in July 1976, and bringing qualified enlisted women into the USMAPS in January. During the almost three years prior to passage of legislation opening West Point to women, however, there was much that had already been accomplished. While strongly opposing their admission on the grounds it would hinder the Academy's mission of training officers who could serve in combat, staff officers had quietly assessed what an Academy that included women cadets would be like. They knew the first women would face resentment from male cadets and enormous attention from the press, feared higher attrition rates among women cadets, and believed in as much uniform training as possible. Ultimately their concern centered on finding ways to ensure West Point's effectiveness in training future Army officers, to maintain the institution's almost mythical reputation as a forge for leaders, and to guarantee its survival and relevance within American life regardless of which way the political or social winds blew. By the time Gerald Ford finally signed Public Law 94–106 on October 7, 1975, Academy preparations made the event anticlimactic for almost everyone.[69]

For the men of the Corps of Cadets, however, the event itself was anything but anticlimactic. They received word of President Ford's signature on October 8 during lunch in Washington Hall. The news emanated from the "poop deck," the large wooden balcony which dominated the mess hall, from which MacArthur gave his famous "Duty, Honor, Country," speech in 1962. For a moment the cadets were silent; then, as a 1979 graduate recalls, there were groans and curses as a pervasive feeling of disgust swept the Corps. Some upperclassmen even broke regulations by standing up and leaving the mess hall early as a sign of protest.[70] Though subtle, the cadet response proved indicative of cadet feelings in the fall of 1975 and a dark omen of the reception awaiting women the following summer.

Getting the word out to potential women cadets, alumni, and the young men of West Point became a priority for Academy leaders as soon as President Ford signed the legislation and the Army could lift the thin veil of secrecy surrounding preparation for the admission of women. Between October 1975 and the arrival of women in July 1976, the Academy rushed to attract women candidates, control rumors, fully explain future policy to male cadets, and deal with occasionally severe criticism from former graduates.

Informing potential female candidates constituted a special concern because of the shortened period of admissions. Planners anticipated an attrition rate for women of fifty-eight percent the first year, and believed forty Army slots would exist for women graduates of USMA in 1980. That meant that at least ninety-five women needed to be admitted in 1976, which in turn meant that approximately 1,000 applicants were necessary in order to assure high quality in the first class including women.[71] With no recruiting program for women in place and no tradition in American society of young women considering appointment to the Academy, the challenge seemed daunting. The Academy expected a shortfall in women candidates and feared that many would fail the physical aptitude exams. These concerns led West Point toward active recruitment of Army enlisted women to round out applicants in the first class.[72] To ensure that members of Congress were also aware of their opportunity to seek out and nominate women, General Berry wrote a letter on November 25 to members of both the Senate and the House of Representatives asking for their assistance.[73]

To reach potential applicants, West Point blanketed the press with announcements regarding plans to admit women to the Academy and produced an information booklet especially for women candidates. The booklet answered general questions about the admission of women and explained how they would be integrated into the Corps of Cadets, proclaiming, "West Point is offering you a chance to be a very special woman, an extraordinary woman." While cadet life would be "taxing," it promised women cadets that "one day you will emerge from the Academy a very confident young woman, ready to take your place in professional life: to lead men and women in our nation's defense."[74]

Soon the Academy began reaching out to male cadets, many of whom were both misinformed and suffering a barrage of questions from family and friends wanting to know what changes were in store for the Academy. Briefings on the admission of women to West Point started on November 11, in sessions that quickly became known as "Stump the Stars" because generals Berry and Ulmer appeared uncomfortable answering cadet questions. Cadets zeroed in on any perceived or actual differences in planned policies for men and women and often inquired into the divergent standards for hair length. One cadet suggested that since standards for men and women were going to be the same, he should be allowed to wear his hair shoulder length, just like the women. Ulmer said that would not be permitted; when the cadet asked why, the Commandant's patience snapped and he barked, "Because I say so!" The Corps cheered his display of authoritarianism, but it reflected the anxiety of everyone at the Academy.[75]

In December, cadets published a special edition of their newspaper devoted to the arrival of women at West Point. *The Pointer* published photographs of model Jane Thacker modeling proposed uniforms for women cadets and said the purpose of the special edition was "the elimination of a wildly absurd 'rumor control' presently clutching the Corps." While predicting cadets "will be briefed nearly to death concerning the entrance of women cadets in the summer of 1976 . . . ," the paper presented the arrival of women as a positive step. It outlined what the Academy had done to prepare, discussed physiological differences between the sexes, outlined what daily life for female cadets would be like, and argued, "The success of the program is a measure of our maturity. Let's do it right."[76]

To notify the alumni, General Berry sent letters to all living graduates and published an open letter in the December 1975 issue of *Assembly* magazine detailing preparations for the admission of women. After noting the Army's consistent opposition to the admission of women, Berry told graduates the issue was moot. "Women are coming to West Point," he said. "The orders have been issued." Berry outlined the minimum adjustments that would be made for training women, argued West Point had always been a changing institution, and suggested an integrated Academy represented "a good preparation for life in the Army and, generally, in American society." He closed by asking for support and understanding from everyone connected to West Point as the Academy "undertakes its most significant change since 1802."[77]

Some graduates rallied to the superintendent's side, writing letters of support and sometimes even condolence. "I have shown your letter . . . with great pride, to civilian friends. . . . Nothing could better inform them of the great excellence of the Military Academy," said one graduate.[78] Another told Berry, "[T]hese times call for a steady pilot at the wheel, and you are the man. So hang in there . . . the corps will survive as it has many vicissitudes in the past."[79]

Others were not so kind. "I do not intend to support the Academy in the future either financially or otherwise," said a retired Brigadier General. "If there is anything I will support now, it is the legislation to eliminate the service academies since they have been relegated to nothing more than coeducational trade schools. . . ."[80] Another angry graduate shared his feelings in a letter to a West Point admissions officer. "I am violently and unalterably opposed to females attending West Point," he roared. "In my view it is an act on the part of an ultra liberal Congress to destroy the greatest military institution in the world."[81] One woman echoed these sentiments when she wrote to Senator Barry Goldwater in June 1975 pleading with him to block the rider opening West Point to women. Fearing a two track system would emerge, she suggested a separate facility for women and noted with alarm the inability of Congress to alter the natural order. "There has been, in the history of the world, only one successful female combat officer," she concluded. "That was Jeanne D'Arc, and she was a Saint. Also she did not menstrate [sic]." The author closed by arguing, "Nature did not design women to be men, and even the honorable [C]ongress and Senate of the United States cannot repeal the laws of nature."[82] The letter joined countless others to Berry, members of Congress, and even the President opposing the admission of women. No less a figure than Matthew B. Ridgway suggested to Gerald Ford that opening the service academies to women would "prove to be an ill-considered action inimical to the best interests of the nation."[83]

In the end, most graduates opposed opening West Point's doors to female cadets because they shared the Army's belief that the combat-oriented nature of the institution would be diminished. It can be argued they were simply tied to tradition and an image of the Academy lingering from their own days as cadets, but there is no denying their conviction or passion. Even the Superintendent opposed the arrival of women privately, though as a professional officer he publicly committed himself to making the change a success. He summed up his unique situation well in a letter to a former member of the Academy staff. "It now appears certain that Congress will direct women to be admitted to West Point as members of the Class of 1980," he said. "I believe that this decision is unsound, illogical, irresponsible, and wrong. Yet, paradoxically, my responsibility as Superintendent of the United States Military Academy will be to implement the decision."[84] Almost every Old Grad had trouble accepting the new order at West Point.

As preparations for women continued, the Academy received a presentation dealing with the integration of previously all-male civilian schools, including Yale, Dartmouth, Notre Dame, and Princeton. Prepared by the Air Force Acad-

emy, the most telling evidence researchers assembled concerned the social aspects of integration. The ratio of men to women needed to be equal, they said,
or at a minimum no less than one woman for every three men. When the ratio
of men grew larger than three to one, a variety of problems developed. Women
were often "treated as different . . . regarded as inferior . . . socially rejected by
males (not dated), and excluded from male clubs." Some women attempted to
"make more friends than normal, possibly to gain a part of the power base" and
in such an environment women "need an unusual sense of self-order to maintain
their self-respect."[85] The research also found "strong pockets of resistance from
male students and alumni" and concluded that male faculty members often embarrassed women by trying too hard to make them comfortable or asking them
for the "female point of view" in class.[86] Though it cannot be known for certain
who saw the presentation, it is clear that many officers at the Academy knew
potential problems were brewing.[87]

Some officers were concerned about "male-oriented language usage and
slang" and wondered what might become of Academy songs, sayings, and
traditions. Cadets routinely called their roommates "wives," opened doors for
women, and featured pictures of women in *The Pointer*. Whether they would
have to change their language and look forward to "pinups" of men in future
issues of *The Pointer* was anyone's guess.[88] On a more profound level there
were other concerns. General Berry noted in November of 1975 that in the initial
transition period for women there might be frustrations the Academy "will just
have to live with."[89] In February 1976, fears that the first women might resign
or fail en masse led the Assistant DCSPER in Washington to conclude there
was "no mandate from DA (Department of the Army) to keep women here,"
no "quota for tokenism," and that DA would back the Academy if the women
all failed.[90] In many ways these fears reflect apprehension in the face of a new
and untried situation, and the depth of Academy planning reflects the commitment of planners to make integration work as well as possible. Still, an undercurrent of powerlessness pervades some of the documents, as if planners felt
that while there were many things they could influence, there were also a number
of others over which they had no power at all.

In fact, they had ample reason to expect difficulties well before the first female
cadets arrived. Research at the U.S. Military Academy Preparatory School in
the spring of 1976 clearly demonstrated that some male cadets bitterly resented
the presence of female cadets within their ranks and were more than willing to
harass women as often as possible. In a revealing document written for West
Point's senior leadership, Dr. Nora Scott Kinzer, a research scientist with the
U.S. Army Research Institute for the Behavioral and Social Sciences, detailed
her visit to USMA and USMAPS in March 1976. Women entered USMAPS in
January 1976 to prepare for entry into West Point in the summer, and Kinzer
noted that many of their problems could be traced to "undue and constant press
coverage" and their entry in the middle of the USMAPS school year. "Women
now resent the intrusion on their privacy," she said, and "male students are quite

annoyed that they are not interviewed and that so much attention is focused on women cadets." The women interviewed were sometimes subject to "crank/hate mail," and she urged caution in allowing the press access to women at West Point.[91]

More alarming to Kinzer, however, was the clear harassment of women at the USMA Prep School. As a result of the press coverage, she reported that "*some* male cadets are harassing the women candidates." The harassment took "relatively innocuous forms such as, firecrackers thrown into the barracks area, barking at the women, throwing dog-biscuits into the dorm area, imitating the 'WAC' [Women's Army Corps] cadence," as well as "leaving a mess table whenever a woman sits down, sweeping dust on women candidates' shoes, and stealing the women's dorm cleaning supplies."[92] While "seemingly innocent," Kinzer argued that the pranks "represent deep underlying hostility against the women," who "do not report incidents because they don't want to generate further hostility, or appear too sensitive, or weak." She pointed out that if the women were "black males or Jewish or Spanish . . . the 'pranks' would not be tolerated" and that women could not fight back in the same manner as men because "fisticuffs" to solve personality differences was not an option. While USMA and USMAPS policy statements indicated women would be treated the same as their male counterparts, "the fact is that these women are pioneers, different, darlings of the mass media and in many respects guinea-pigs in a social-educational experiment."[93] Kinzer also raised the question of where training would lead. "While cadet training is predicated on the idea of training boys to be men," she wrote, "no one has addressed the problems of whether or not USMA training will turn women cadets into men." Under the pressure of the male-oriented training regime, she noted, "The USMAPS women cadets resent the fact that they are acting like men (e.g. swearing, yelling, and becoming tough and vindictive)."[94] Kinzer's remarks made it clear that just as young men entering West Point often had sharply defined notions of what it meant to be a man, young women had culturally induced visions of what it meant to be a woman. As it turned out, neither sex was always comfortable when the lines demarcating what each perceived to be gender-acceptable behavior were blurred.

Kinzer closed by calling for firm ground rules at USMA making clear a policy that brooked no tolerance of teasing or harassment of women cadets, just as the Academy refused to tolerate "racial and ethnic slurs against male minority members."[95] This certainly would have been in keeping with the Academy's efforts to reduce hazing, eliminate discrimination, and promote positive leadership; in the short run, the Academy failed to take such measures. Army officers could have stopped much of the harassment of women at West Point by taking these steps early, and Kinzer insightfully noted that such behavior would have been eliminated had the targets been members of a religious or racial minority. Yet Academy officials allowed the teasing and harassment to continue, and the pattern of behavior Kinzer noticed at USMAPS reappeared at West Point.

Why the abuse was allowed to continue is unclear. General Berry was not listed as a recipient of Kinzer's report, and it is uncertain how much of the Academy's senior leadership actually read through her conclusions and recommendations. Perhaps leaders feared greater intervention on behalf of women would further alienate them from their male classmates. In any event, responsible officers in positions of authority had the opportunity to either eliminate or at least mitigate the harassment of women that was to plague West Point in the late 1970s, and they allowed it to slip away. The Academy had good reason to be apprehensive.

Apprehension turned to alarm in March, though not from anything related to the admission of women. Instead, the Academy was thrust into the midst of the worst honor scandal in West Point history. Coming as it did on the threshold of the arrival of women, at a time when the Academy sought to separate itself from memories of Vietnam and the turmoil of the early 1970s, the scandal could not have occurred at a worse time. While there is no "good" time for scandal, the ensuing uproar over West Point's Honor Code became a crisis upon which Academy officials focused for months.

The scandal involved a required course for all cadets called Electrical Engineering 304, or simply "Juice." Widely hated and generally considered an "exercise in 'spec and dump,' which in cadet lingo meant 'memorize and forget,' " the class pushed many cadets to the limits of their mathematical prowess.[96] Trouble began in early March, when over eight hundred Cows (Juniors) from the Class of 1977 took a take-home exam worth five percent of their grade. The exam contained explicit instructions that cadets were not to receive help of any kind, and was due two weeks later. When the exams were turned in, one guilt-stricken cadet scrawled at the top of his exam, "I have received assistance on this paper." Instructors impounded all the exams for review and found "evidence of collusion on a huge scale."[97]

Over the next several months the scandal grew to alarming proportions. Virtually every company in the Corps counted on its roster a cadet accused of cheating, and eventually well over a hundred resigned or were expelled. *Time* ran a cover story on June 7 showing a cadet raising one hand to take an oath while he hid the other behind his back and crossed his fingers. National press coverage became alarmingly intense, particularly when many reports argued cheating was rampant at the Academy, that the Cadet Honor Committee "fixed" investigations to protect friends, and that the Honor Code itself was out of date. Although the Academy survived the ensuing investigations by blue ribbon panels and many expelled cadets were allowed to return after a year's absence, the scandal left a stain on West Point for a long time.[98]

For many graduates, this stain overshadowed the threat women represented to West Point. For if women threatened the essence of the Academy, the implication that the Honor Code resembled an anachronistic joke posed a danger to its very survival. West Pointers, after all, believed that the Academy graduated the very finest Army officers in the world. Much of the justification for this belief came from their conviction that living for four years according to the principles of the Honor Code developed superior character in cadets and that character in the long run was the hallmark of the best Army leaders. They argued that Aristotle had correctly asserted that character was habit. It was "the daily choice of right or wrong," a "moral quality which grows to maturity in peace and is not suddenly developed on the outbreak of war."[99] Such beliefs carried with them the implicit assumption that if West Point stopped producing leaders of sufficient character, it would become a glorified trade school with no claim to superiority over ROTC programs at civilian universities or the Army's own Officer Candidate School. At that point, according to the purists, it would no longer have a reason for being or a means of justifying the considerable expense endured by taxpayers for its support. Graduates thus reacted with alarm and horror to news of the scandal, seeing in it the seeds of the Academy's possible destruction.

As press coverage of the scandal slowly dimmed, West Point approached the day women actually arrived on the historic post. By June 23, the Academy had received more than 13,000 applications for admission in 1976. Women accounted for 867 of the applicants, and 631 of them received nominations. Of those ultimately accepting the offer to join the Long Gray Line, 120 were women and 1,446 were men. With Reception Day (R-Day) scheduled for early July, Academy leaders had little to do but wait and hope their plans would work.[100]

Just before R-Day, West Point joined the rest of America in celebrating the 200th anniversary of the signing of the Declaration of Independence. July 4 began inauspiciously with a mock military disaster, when the Academy's British Army liaison officer staged a prank on his American hosts by raising the Union Jack above the ruins of Fort Putnam at dawn.[101] Yet despite this brief and comical British "occupation," preparations for a massive celebration continued. As one of the nation's showcase institutions, the Academy planned an enormous fireworks display along the banks of the Hudson to commemorate American independence, and Academy officials looked forward to a relaxing evening that might take everyone's mind off the previous months of anxiety and controversy. But as thousands of spectators watched, one skyrocket after another sputtered and tumbled to the ground in a shower of sparks. With the crowd waiting anxiously, investigating technicians discovered the entire collection of fireworks had become damp. Nothing exploded. There would be no tumultuous pyrotechnics, no fitting celebration of 200 years of independence. As word spread of the disaster, "some of the Academy brass found the fiasco amusing. Given the way the Bicentennial year had gone thus far, they told one another, the debacle seemed only fitting."[102]

The first women cadets arrived three days later.

NOTES

1. Susan Finlay Watkins, "It Is No Longer a Matter of Comment to See a Body of Young Ladies Under Military Training," *Assembly* 39, No. 1 (June 1980): 6.

2. John Keegan, *Fields of Battle: The Wars for North America* (New York: Alfred A. Knopf, 1996), p. 147.

3. Dave Richard Palmer, *The River and the Rock: The History of Fortress West Point, 1775–1783* (West Point: Association of Graduates, in association with Hippocrene Books, 1991), p. 308. The Corps of Invalids also tutored young officer candidates for military service, just as the Academy would after 1802. Buttermilk Falls is today known as Highland Falls. Corbin's remains were moved to the West Point cemetery in 1926.

4. Ibid., p. 342. The abysmal quality of recruits in 1782 led Lieutenant Colonel Ebenezer Huntington to claim women were more spirited than his men. He suggested hiring several to recruit other women to fight for the Continental Army, arguing they would help recruit better men as well.

5. First published in 1852, *Wide Wide World* followed a fairly conventional yet enormously popular nineteenth century plot. Women who repressed their natural desires and immersed themselves in marriage and service to others were portrayed as the most noble embodiment of humanity, and *Wide Wide World* is such an archetype for the period that Jane Tompkins called it the "Ur text of the nineteenth century."

6. Jane Green, *Powder, Paper and Lace: An Anecdotal Herstory of Women at West Point* (Charlottesville, Virginia: Priority Press, 1988), pp. 1–4. Stuart's portrait was used in the design of the one dollar bill.

7. Cadet Comly served as an instructor in the USMA Drawing Department between 1903 and 1907, as military aide de camp to President Woodrow Wilson, and as a Professor of Military Science at Penn State University. He died in 1931. See Stephen R. Grove, USMA Historian, ETA, 10-11-2000, p. 1.

8. See *The Howitzer: Annual of the United States Military Academy*, 1900, p. 18, for the original of Comly's portrait.

9. Elvin R. Heiberg, "West Point in the Year 2000," *Assembly* (Winter 1964): 11–12. A feminist student of literature would have a field day with Heiberg's article. Though he clearly intended his remarks to be humorous, they say a great deal about traditional stereotypes of women in the 1960s. The references to "mule-riding" and "Black Knighties" stem from the Army mascot, a mule, and the name of Army sports teams, the Black Knights.

10. The original Academy coat of arms was designed by USMA professors in 1898, and included an emblem comprised of the helmet of Pallas Athena over a Greek sword.

11. According to Professor Julia Stalder of the University of Oklahoma's School of Dance, Elssler became one of five world famous ballerinas during the Romantic Era of ballet. Dr. Louis Veron, director of the Paris Opera, called her "the pagan," a reference to her voluptuous, fiery style, and Elssler took the United States by storm during a two-year tour which included a stop at West Point. ETA, 6-5-1998, p. 1.

12. Kenneth Rapp, "The Legend of Fanny Elssler's Pirouette by Moonlight," *Dance Magazine*, July 1975, pp. 41–42. In the nineteenth and early twentieth centuries, summer training for cadets included an extended period bivouacking near The Plain. This "Summer encampment" involved a relaxed training schedule and an assortment of cadet balls and social activities. Of dubious military value, it was eagerly anticipated by most members of the Corps as a welcome departure from the rigors of the academic year.

13. See Rick Atkinson, *The Long Gray Line* (Boston: Houghton Mifflin Company, 1989), p. 45, for a typical story of a young woman who dressed as a member of the Corps and attended formation. Such antics required the cooperation, or at least the indulgence of cadets beyond the intrepid soul who conned his girlfriend into dressing as

a cadet in the first place. They usually occurred in cadet companies which had a reputation for being less stringent in their enforcement of regulations.

14. IWA, 4-2-96, author's notes.

15. John Keegan, *The Mask of Command* (London: Jonathan Cape: 1987), p. 177.

16. Ironically, West Point women were not the first to be recruited to a military school which stressed discipline and academics. Among the first in the United States were the women who attended Fairfield Seminary and Military College in the 1890s. Located in Fairfield, New York, the school modeled itself after West Point and served as a preparatory school for both sexes. See Watkins, "It Is No Longer a Matter of Comment," pp. 6–7.

17. The shadow cast by the passage of ERA cannot be over-estimated. In his final report to Congress in 1973, Secretary of Defense Melvin R. Laird said, "Because of the impending ratification of the Constitutional Amendment concerning women, I believe that necessary funds should be promptly provided by Congress for facilities at the Service Academies so that qualified women can be enrolled." See Melvin R. Laird, *Final Report to the Congress of Secretary of Defense Melvin R. Laird Before the House Armed Services Committee*, Congressional Records, January 8, 1973, p. 74.

18. Quoted in MAJ Alan G. Vitters and Dr. Nora Scott Kinzer, *Report of the Admission of Women to the U.S. Military Academy (Project Athena I)* (West Point: United States Military Academy Department of Behavioral Sciences and Leadership, September 2, 1977), pp. 5–6.

19. The rationale was based both on tradition and possible legal defense. As Secretary of the Army Howard H. Callaway noted, "My lawyers continue to stress our best argument in court or in Congress is the combat orientation of the Academy." See Howard H. Callaway, Memorandum for the Assistant Secretary of Defense, "Service Academies' Admission Policies," January 12, 1974, USMA files.

20. The cost of a West Point education was widely disputed. The Government Accounting Office estimated the cost of educating each cadet in the Class of 1975 at $101,654, while the Academy reported per cadet costs as $89,976. See MAJ Tobin, Information Paper, "Cost to Graduate Cadet," September 2, 1975, USMA files. Whatever the real costs, they were considerable and historically have fueled critics who argue the Academy is too expensive to justify.

21. COL Burke W. Lee to BG Philip R. Feir, December 18, 1972, USMA files. See also LTC Cline, "Women at USMA: Position Paper," January 27, 1975; and BG R. D. Stevenson, "Admission of Women to USMA," December 30, 1974, also in USMA files.

22. See Commandant of Cadets, "Contingency Planning for the Admission of Female Nominees to the Corps of Cadets, September 27, 1972," USMA files.

23. Cited in Major General Jeanne Holm (Ret.), *Women in the Military: An Unfinished Revolution* (Novato, California: Presidio Press, 1989; rev. ed., 1992), p. 22.

24. LTC Kermit N. Henninger, Memorandum for Record, untitled, September 8, 1972, p. 1, USMA files.

25. Ibid.

26. BG T. H. Tackaberry, Memorandum for Deputy Chief of Staff for Personnel, "Contingency Plan for Women at the Military Academy," September 18, 1972, USMA files.

27. For an overview of the Army and Navy's Joint Plan Red, which detailed American contingency planning for a war with Great Britain in 1931, see Thaddeus Holt,

"Joint Plan Red," *MHQ: The Quarterly Journal of Military History* 1, No. 1 (Autumn 1988): 49–55.

28. See LTG Bernard W. Rogers, Memorandum for All ODCSPER Directors, "Utilization of Women in the Army," January 18, 1973, p. 2, USMA files.

29. See Headquarters, United States Military Academy, "USMA OPLAN-73-1 Admission of Female Cadets," January 2, 1973, USMA files. The plan was clearly an outline. Officials did not want to spend too much time or too many resources on an issue that might go away, and they feared bringing women cadets on themselves if word escaped they were actually planning how to accommodate them. OPLAN-73-1 was classified "For Official Use Only," and only 100 copies were produced.

30. MAJ Turner D. Griffin, Memorandum for Chief of Staff, March 23, 1973, USMA files. Given the experience of Shannon Faulkner at The Citadel in 1996, Griffin appears to have been clairvoyant. He also accurately predicted the problems press coverage would cause the first women cadets at West Point between 1976 and 1980.

31. COL Gerald W. Medsger, Memorandum for the Superintendent, "Four Issues Implied by the Admission of Women to USMA," November 20, 1974, USMA files. Medsger referred often to research conducted by various police departments in the United States. Many were integrating women more fully during the 1970s and faced similar questions regarding acceptance patterns by men in traditionally male environments, weapons training, and hand to hand combat.

32. COL Medsger, "Four Issues," p. 5, USMA files. An officer reviewing the remark noted, "The proposal to administer testosterone to female cadets in order to increase their aggressiveness is absurd. By extension of the same logic, the football team could gulp uppers before a game, the Corps tranquilized by downers to achieve orderly rallies, and the Dean authorized to issue No-Doz to cadets who have difficulty staying awake in class." See LTC John J. Cook, Jr. to DCSOPS, "Memorandum Concerning Female Admissions," December 17, 1974, USMA files, p. 4.

33. LTC Cook, "Memorandum Concerning Female Admissions," p. 1. It is an insightful comment, for generations of critics have pointed out an Academy education is far more expensive to the Federal Government than ROTC programs or OCS. Further, over the last 20 years the domination of the Army's upper echelons by West Pointers has decreased dramatically, leaving some to conclude other sources of officer commissioning are better bargains for the money.

34. Ibid., p. 2. "MOS" stands for military occupational speciality, and in civilian terms it describes a soldier's job. The remark is telling, for the most persistent complaint among male cadets and some officers after women were admitted was that differing physical standards for men and women were unfair.

35. Ibid., p. 3. See also COL Manley E. Rogers, "Memorandum Concerning Female Admissions," December 18, 1974, USMA files. Rogers argued, "USMA should not continue to assume a 'head in the sand posture' . . . [because] It does appear that women will ultimately be allowed to enter one or more of the service academies." He also suggested the example of Tufts University represented "a starting point from which to plan the future integration of women into the West Point community." At Tufts, women enrolled in an independent college within the coeducational university.

36. LTG Berry to COL E.H.B., July 3, 1975, p. 1, USMA files.

37. "Address by Lieutenant General Sidney B. Berry, Superintendent, United States Military Academy, Before the Defense Advisory Committee on Women in the Services," November 16, 1976, p. 6, USMA files.

38. COL James H. Tormey, Memorandum dated May 21, 1975, USMA files. The memo is also classified "For Official Use Only."

39. MG Sidney B. Berry, Memorandum for Record, "Thoughts on the Admission of Women to the United States Military Academy," May 20, 1975, pp. 2–3, USMA files. Most members of Congress never equated admitting women to the service academies with putting them directly into combat. Instead, they focused on equity. In the long run, however, by finessing the issue they implicitly opened the door to accepting women in direct combat positions. The West Point administration did adopt different physical standards for men and women, though they refrained from calling the arrangement a "two track" system. The phrase was useful in trying to influence members of Congress prior to passage of the legislation opening the academies to women, but detrimental to West Point's image afterwards. Adjusted physical standards for women were characterized as "equivalent."

40. Ibid., p. 4. The 98.1 percent figure is interesting. It included combat *assignments* as opposed to combat branches of the Army, meaning a captain who visited the front for a day while serving with a public relations unit could be counted. The example is extreme; to be fair, the numbers undoubtedly included officers assigned to noncombat arms who were later temporarily attached to combat units. Yet even generously interpreted the figure is misleading and far too high to be an accurate indicator of the percentage of officers who led troops in combat. Berry considered resigning to protest the admission of women but later decided against it. See Atkinson, *The Long Gray Line*, p. 408.

41. The West Point mission statement was as follows: "The mission of the United States Military Academy is to instruct and train the Corps of Cadets so that each graduate should have the qualities and attributes essential to his progressive and continuing development throughout a career as an officer of the Regular Army." See *Bugle Notes*, vol. 68 (West Point: United States Military Academy, 1976), p. 4. It has since been modified slightly to be gender neutral.

42. Cadets unable to serve in combat branches for physical reasons generally injured themselves at the Academy, often as members of Corps athletic squads. The terms used to group different Army branches have changed over the years, making comparison difficult for the non-initiated. In brief, the Infantry, Armor, Air Defense, and Field Artillery branches are generally expected to be closest to the enemy. Engineers, Signal Corps, Military Police, and Military Intelligence personnel often move between rear areas and the front. The rest of the branches, everything from Quartermaster to Judge Advocate General, are normally in rear areas. In truth, no soldier is completely safe in wartime, but these distinctions serve as a basis for discussion.

43. See Mark Bowden, *Black Hawk Down: A Story of Modern War* (New York: Atlantic Monthly Press, 1999), pp. 147, 161. The Americans involved in the Mogadishu battle were members of elite Special Forces units and Army Rangers and did not fit the traditional image of rear-echelon troops. Their experience is analogous, however, because those troops assigned to noncombat-oriented positions did not regularly train for or expect combat assignments.

44. In the post-World War II era, the Academy maintained that only in two periods, from 1945 to 1950 and 1964 to 1968, were some graduates commissioned in noncombat arms. Beginning in 1968, one percent of each class was allowed to go to medical school, a policy which ended in 1977 but was later restored. In 1969 the Academy began allowing cadets physically disqualified from combat duty to commission into noncombat

branches. In short, the policy varied greatly over time. Academy officials maintained only a small portion of graduates ever entered noncombat arms, but it really came down to how one defined "combat." See Herman R. Stoudt, Memorandum for Assistant Secretary of Defense, "Admission of Women at the Military Academy," April 12, 1974, pp. 1–2, USMA files.

45. Paul D. Phillips, Memorandum to COL Dyke, "USMA Graduates in Combat Arms Branches," March 13, 1974, USMA files.

46. Phillips listed 9,324 graduates on active duty, with 6,222, or 67 percent in combat branches. Not knowing how many generals were in combat branches in 1974, I added *every* officer Phillips counted in branch groups one and two who could *possibly* have been a general (those with between 21 and 35 years of service) to the total serving in combat arms. Even with this egregious overcounting, I reached a total of 6,780, or 73 percent in combat arms, proving the accuracy of Phillip's conclusions.

47. Congress also had results of a Government Accounting Office (GAO) study completed in 1974 which reviewed 102 randomly chosen service records of USMA graduates to determine the percentage of assignments which were combat or combat related. In results cross-checked by Army officers (including a LTC named John Shalikashvili who later became Chairman of the Joint Chiefs of Staff), the study found 50 percent of the officers' assignments were combat or combat related. See MG Harold G. Moore, Jr., Memorandum for Deputy Chief of Staff for Personnel, "Attendance of Women at the United States Military Academy," November 8, 1974, pp. 1–2, USMA files.

48. There were those within the Army who agreed. BG L. Gordon Hill, Jr., wrote, "[T]here is also no prohibition to the admission of women in the mission of West Point. The commissioning of officers to lead in battle is only an implied and derived mission." See BG L. Gordon Hill, Jr., Memorandum for Headquarters, Department of the Army (DAPE-ZA), "The Admission of Women to the United States Military Academy," undated, USMA files.

49. LTC Thomas P. Garigan, Memorandum for Record, "Public Affairs Impact of Women Admission to the U.S. Military Academy," May 30, 1975, pp. 1–2. Garigan served as the Academy's Public Affairs Officer, and his observations were astute. The press did disrupt training for women cadets, and some women eventually uttered innocent comments in interviews which caused them problems with their male peers. In 1974, Garigan recommended that if women were admitted, the press be barred from women cadets after "limited access during the first days of New Cadet Barracks." See LTC Garigan, Memorandum Concerning Female Admissions, December 11, 1974, p. 1, USMA files.

50. LTC Kermit M. Henninger, Memorandum for Record, "Meeting with SA: Admission of Women to USMA," June 11, 1975, p. 1, USMA files. No changes to the academic program were ever considered. The idea of making minimum essential changes based on physiological differences between men and women became part of the final legislation passed in October 1975.

51. Ibid. Admission to the Academy was based on college board scores, leadership potential, athletic ability, and a score based on a standardized PAE. Early study showed women could not pass the male PAE in sufficient numbers, so a new one was created.

52. *Congressional Record*, 1975, p. 15449.

53. Judith Hicks Stiehm, *Bring Me Men and Women: Mandated Change at the U.S. Air Force Academy* (Berkeley: University of California Press, 1981), p. 10.

54. CPT Anna M. Young, CPT Barbara J. Yost, and SSG Hazel M. Luxford, Mem-

orandum for the Deputy Commandant, "Women's Evaluation Team—Preliminary Comments," July 14, 1975, p. 5, USMA files.

55. LTG Sidney B. Berry, Memorandum for Record, "Air Force Academy Planning for Admission of Women Cadets," July 17, 1975, pp. 1–2, USMA files. Fifteen surrogate upperclass women were initially assigned to the Air Force Academy. See Holm, *Women in the Military* p. 310.

56. The United States Merchant Marine Academy admitted women in 1974 and became a starting point for all of the service academies in their planning for the admission of female cadets. Though not affected by the service academy legislation pending in Congress in 1975, Coast Guard leaders sensed they would be next and voluntarily chose to admit women to the United States Coast Guard Academy in 1976.

57. BG Walter F. Ulmer, Memorandum for Record, "Notes from Visit to ROTC Basic Camp at Fort Knox, 16–17 July 1975," July 18, 1975, pp. 1–2, USMA files.

58. MAJ William G. Tobin, Memorandum for Record, USMA In-Process Planning Conference, "September 4, 1975, USMA files. USMAPS accepts enlisted candidates for the Military Academy who need further academic or physical preparation prior to being fully qualified for admission. The school formed when programs in each Army area were consolidated at Stewart Air Force Base, New York in 1946. USMAPS moved to Fort Belvoir, Virginia, in 1946, and to Fort Monmouth in 1975.

59. Ibid., pp. 5–8, 9–11. The depth of discussion is illuminating, as it highlights the conviction among senior Army leaders that Congressional action opening the academies to women was inevitable.

60. Documents from throughout the Academy were stored in Office of Institutional Research files for several years and later moved to the USMA Historian's office.

61. MAJ Tobin, "USMA In-Process Planning Conference," pp. 8, 12, 13, USMA files.

62. See E.H.B. to LTG Berry, June 8, 1975, USMA files.

63. BG Walter F. Ulmer, Memorandum for Superintendent, United States Military Academy, "Physiological Differences Between Men and Women," August 18, 1975, abstract summary, USMA files. The memo is attached to the paper by Peterson, whose research was instrumental in convincing Congress to insert language allowing minimal differences in standards for men and women that reflected physiological differences between the sexes.

64. Peterson was right. Physical performance standards for women are much higher today than in 1976.

65. Wayne B. Nicoll, "Women in the Military Police Corps: Sexist Attitudes at the U.S. Army Military Police School," Winter Quarter 1975, USMA files, pp. 12–13. Nicoll prepared the paper for a college political science class, but neither his work nor the accompanying letter mentions the name of the university.

66. Department of the Army, United States Military Academy, "OPLAN 75–1: Admission of Women Cadets," September 15, 1975, USMA files, p. a–vi–1. The United States Corps of Cadets consisted of a brigade composed of four regiments containing three battalions each. Battalions contained three companies, and plans called for between four and twelve companies to receive women in 1976. One battalion in each regiment was to receive women each year through 1979, when every company would finally be integrated.

67. Engineers estimated the cost of required renovations/construction at $437,900. See Department of the Army, USMA, "OPLAN 75–1," p. j–6. The actual costs reached approximately $1.8 million by 1980. See Dr. Stephen B. Grove, Memorandum for Mr.

David T. Simpson, Director, Resource Management, United States Military Academy, "Facility Modification/Start-up Costs to Admit Women to USMA," October 18, 1995, USMA files.

68. Department of the Army, USMA, "OPLAN 75–1," pp. a–vii–1, c–I–1. The plan also sidestepped the question of pregnancy, stating the matter was "under revision and would be published at a later date." See p. I–I–1.

69. Though not subject to the legislation ordering the admission of women to America's service academies, the U.S. Coast Guard Academy voluntarily announced in August of 1975 that it too would admit women in 1976. See John Lovell, *Neither Athens Nor Sparta? The American Service Academies in Transition* (Bloomington, Ind.: Indiana University Press, 1979), p. 313.

70. IWA, February 18, 1998, author's notes.

71. LTG Harold Moore, Memorandum through Chief of Staff, United States Army, for the Secretary of the Army, "Number of Women to be Admitted to the Military Academy," November 17, 1975, USMA files, pp. 1–2. Attrition for men averaged 30.9 percent between 1802 and 1975. See MAJ Tobin, Information Paper, "USMA Attrition," September 2, 1975, USMA files, pp. 1–2. LTG Moore reached the higher figure for women by assuming their attrition rate during Plebe year would be the same as for women during their initial year at the U.S. Merchant Marine Academy (33 percent). Assuming attrition for women would remain in the same proportion to that of men over their last three years as cadets as he was assuming for Plebe year, Moore concluded that 25 percent of the remaining women would leave by graduation. (Attrition for men during the last three years at West Point was known to be 15 percent) Combining 25 percent and 33 percent equaled 58 percent. It was a best-guess type of methodology, but remarkably close to the 52 percent of women in the class of 1980 who actually left.

72. LTC Darrell G. Houston, Memorandum for Deputy Commandant of Cadets, "Admission of Women to West Point," pp. 1–3, USMA files.

73. LTG Sidney B. Berry to Members of the United States Congress, November 25, 1975, USMA files. Many needed no prodding from Berry. The chance to nominate one of the first women to attend any of the service academies was commonly seen as an excellent political and public relations move.

74. United States Military Academy Booklet entitled "Information for Women Candidates," undated, p. 5, USMA files.

75. COL Joseph T. Griffin, "Briefings to Cadets on Women's Admission: Nov.–Dec. Schedule," November 6, 1975, USMA files. See also Theodore J. Crackel, *The Illustrated History of West Point* (New York: Harry N. Abrams, Inc., 1991), p. 286.

76. *The Pointer*, Supplement 52, No. 4, December 1975, pp. 5, 11. Cadets endured countless briefings regarding the admission of women, a fact many resented and may have taken out on women when they arrived. *The Pointer* issue was decidedly informative and upbeat, though it should be remembered that Academy officers oversaw the paper's publication. It may have represented the views of many cadets, but not of all of them.

77. *Assembly*, December 1975, inside front cover.

78. A.H. to LTG Berry, November 29, 1975, USMA files.

79. J.L.R., Jr., to LTG Berry, October 20, 1975, USMA files.

80. A.J.G. to LTG Berry, no date, USMA files.

81. J.R.R. to Captain P.P.H., September 8, 1975, USMA files.

82. Letter to The Honorable Barry Goldwater, June 18, 1975, author's name removed, USMA files.

83. M. B. Ridgway to President Gerald Ford, June 9, 1975, USMA files.

84. LTG Sidney B. Berry to COL E.H.B., July 3, 1975, p. 3, USMA files.

85. "Integration of Females Into Previously All Male Universities," a collection of transparencies from the United States Air Force Academy, USMA files, p. 5.

86. Ibid., p. 6. The evidence demonstrates how often male responses to breakdowns in traditionally all-male groups assume familiar patterns. Women at West Point experienced each of the phenomena described in the presentation. The trend, therefore, crosses occupation and age and may be shared by men in general. See Lionel Tiger, *Men in Groups* (New York: Random House, 1969), for an anthropologist's view of the problem.

87. For insight into what breaking gender-barriers meant in the Ivy League, see Janet Lever and Pepper Schwartz, *Women at Yale: Liberating a College Campus* (New York: The Bobbs-Merrill Company, Inc., 1971).

88. LTC Thomas P. Garigan, "Orientation Program, Admission of Women to West Point," February 27, 1976, USMA files.

89. LTC Hugh E. Henson, Jr., Memorandum for Record, "Secretary of the Army Comments During Briefing on Admission of Women to West Point, 17 October 1975," October 20, 1975, p. 3, USMA files. The Secretary of the Army noted concerns about educating the Corps of Cadets and indicated that those problems would probably have to be lived with as well. See LTC Leonard P. Wishart III, Memorandum for Record, "Admission of Women to USMA, October 23, 1975, p. 3, USMA files.

90. LTC Donald H. Cline, Memorandum for Record, "After-Action Report, Women's Admission Update Briefing, 28 Jan 76," February 10, 1976, p. 3, USMA files.

91. Nora Scott Kinzer, Memorandum for Record, "Report on Trip to USMA and USMA Prep School," March 16, 1976, pp. 1–2, USMA files. The same pattern developed at West Point.

92. Ibid., p. 3.

93. Ibid.

94. Ibid.

95. Ibid.

96. Atkinson, *The Long Gray Line*, p. 397.

97. Ibid.

98. Ibid., pp. 394–417. There had been previous cheating scandals at West Point, most notably one in the 1950s involving the Academy football team. Cheating was also commonplace during the nineteenth century, to the point that when George Armstrong Custer was caught searching for exam answers in an instructor's desk he was still allowed to remain a cadet. In the twentieth century, however, the Honor Code was codified during the superintendency of Douglas MacArthur and became holy writ. It reads, "A Cadet will not lie, cheat, or steal, nor tolerate those who do." Evidence that the Honor Code was in peril thus became a dire threat to the very thing that made the Academy unique— the inculcation of character—and West Point leaders reacted accordingly.

99. Lord Moran, *The Anatomy of Courage* (Boston: Houghton Mifflin Company, 1967), p. 160.

100. MAJ Robert B. Cato, Memorandum for Record, "Comparison of Admissions Status: Classes of '78, '79, and '80," USMA files. The number of applicants for the Class of 1980 was considerably higher than for the two preceding classes, which received just over 10,000 applications each. One woman who accepted an offer of admission was medically disqualified, so that 119 women eventually entered West Point on R-Day. In comparison, the Naval Academy admitted 80 and the Air Force Academy accepted 123.

See Randy Shilts, *Conduct Unbecoming: Lesbians and Gays in the U.S. Military: Vietnam to the Persian Gulf* (New York: St. Martin's Press, 1993), p. 267.

101. Keegan, *Fields of Battle*, p. 139. The British occupied Constitution Island briefly in the fall of 1777, only to withdraw when news of their defeat at Saratoga reached them in October. The grounds were fortified the following year and thereafter remained in American hands. Fort Putnam became part of the fortifications and is today restored and open to the public. See Sidney Forman, *West Point: A History of the United States Military Academy* (New York: Columbia University Press, 1950), p. 9.

102. Atkinson, *The Long Gray Line*, p. 404.

3

★ ★ ★ ★

"A Higher Calling"

Then, if we are to set women to the same tasks as men, we must teach them the same things. They must have the same two branches of training for mind and body and also be taught the art of war, and they must receive the same treatment.

—Plato, *The Republic*[1]

In the fall of 1975, in countless living and dining rooms across America, in barracks and college dormitories, the news that West Point was opening its doors to women began affecting lives beyond the Academy. Walter Cronkite announced the news to the nation on October 7, while newspapers and radio programs followed suit the next day. Over the succeeding weeks, word passed between family members and friends, from officers to enlisted personnel and from counselors to high school students.

West Point played an active role in the process, encouraging continual press coverage, contacting candidates by mail, and going to great lengths to recruit as many women applicants as possible. With less than eight months between the passage of legislation and the arrival of the first women cadets on July 7, 1976, West Point faced the daunting prospect of seeking enough qualified women to allow selection of the best possible candidates, to avoid the appearance of tokenism, and to provide the first women with a peer support group that could conquer West Point's demanding regimen and help them graduate. Confronting what an Academy report later called "an event without precedent in the history of the Western world,"[2] the Army sought to identify young women with the characteristics necessary for successful careers and encourage them to apply. Working within a society and culture that seldom encouraged women to enlist and had never before offered them admission to the nation's service academies, the Army faced a formidable challenge. The challenge was particularly acute because no professional military academy or army in the annals of history provided a relevant model. As John Keegan wrote, "Warfare is, nevertheless, the one human activity from which women, with the most insignificant exceptions, have always and everywhere stood apart." It is, he said, an "entirely masculine activity;"[3] and while such a statement is perhaps an over-generalization, it remains true that in 1976 the United States Military Academy ventured into a revolutionary new era accompanied only by the other American service academies. Their task was truly daunting.

Like West Point, the young women whom the Academy ultimately admitted with the class of 1980 also faced a series of challenges and hurdles to overcome. They had to answer for themselves the question of why they wanted to go into a lions' den of 4,000 men, why they desired a West Point education or an Army career. They had to persuade dubious family and friends that the hazards of battering down walls of convention dating to the administration of Thomas Jefferson would really be worth it. Finally, the women had to obtain admission, which meant meeting both physical and academic standards designed to weed out all but the most fit and being nominated by a member of Congress, the President, or the Department of the Army. Male cadets in the Class of 1980 followed an identical process, but Academy officials knew how to recruit them, and they knew why most young men came to West Point. In return, young men had almost two centuries of legends, myths, and facts to use in determining why they wanted to join the Long Gray Line. When it came to understanding why women might want to attend the Academy, everyone—including many of the women themselves—was groping in the dark.

The West Point Office of Admissions sprang into action as soon as President Ford signed Public Law 94–106. Even as the ink from his pen dried, the Academy reviewed applications from candidates and found that over 7,000 men had already applied for admission in the class of 1980. They also found files on forty-five women, most of whom had applied in anticipation of the change in federal law. To boost this number, West Point sent out letters to 18,643 high school counselors informing them of the opportunities available to young women on the banks of the Hudson and encouraging them to refer qualified candidates to the Academy.[4]

Officials also contacted 2,000 women who had applied for Reserve Officer Training Corps (ROTC) scholarships in 1974 and 1975, appealed to women already in ROTC programs around the country, and enlisted the aid of the American College Testing (ACT) Program in identifying 2,200 young women who scored well on the mathematics portion of the widely given ACT college entrance exam.[5] These initiatives supplemented Army bulletins issued to all major commands ordering officers to examine their units for qualified enlisted women, and demonstrate West Point's willingness to explore every known source of qualified candidates.

Like their male counterparts, women chose to pursue educations at West Point for a variety of reasons. Most were conservative, came from middle class families in which finding money for college posed a major concern, and were intrigued by the unique challenges offered by the Academy. Very few considered the recently ended war in Vietnam or the scandals that plagued West Point during the early 1970s in their decision-making process, and most were only lukewarm toward military careers. Many were captivated by the Academy's aura, however, and all were tempted by the prospect of receiving an excellent education at taxpayer expense, a guaranteed career opportunity, and a salary during their years as cadets. Yet these are generalizations. In truth, the 119 women who entered West Point in 1976 did so for very individual reasons.

One former cadet was a senior in college when she discovered that West Point was opening to women. Unsure of what career path to follow, she found the prospect of four years at West Point more appealing than pursuing years of graduate work, and after talking with her professors, decided to apply. She preferred attending the Air Force Academy, but her Congressman only had a nomination available for West Point. The reality of pursuing a military career never fully entered her mind; what mattered most was the challenge and putting off real life for a little while longer.[6]

Another who applied after several years of college confessed to wanting an Academy education for "all the wrong reasons." Having spent three years in a college ROTC program, she realized her service commitment would begin as soon as she graduated. If she attended the Academy, however, the ROTC service obligation would be waived. West Point graduates were obligated to five years active duty after graduation and a lesser term if they resigned following the first day of their junior (Cow) year.[7] Cadets leaving *before* that time walked away without obligation. She could therefore receive three years of college through ROTC, two years at West Point, and then resign with five years of college credit paid for by taxpayers and owe the Army nothing.[8] The two free years offered a convenient rationale for others as well, regardless of their sex. Those who were uncertain about military life or West Point often decided to give the Academy a try because they knew they could leave early without being trapped.[9] That seemed like a deal too good to pass up.[10]

Other women went for more traditional reasons. One remembered hearing about the opportunities for women at the nation's service academies in December of 1975. Listening to the radio while driving with her father, she heard news concerning women at West Point and the idea of applying suddenly made enormous sense. She was thinking about ROTC anyway, had been told by Texas A&M that women were not allowed in the Aggie Corps band, and knew a great deal about the Academy because her father was a West Point man. Combined with the opportunity to pursue an excellent education, the news made her decision easy.[11] Another cadet applied along with other women at her high school after meeting with an officer recruiting for West Point,[12] while one of her future West Point classmates graduated in the last all-female class at a Catholic high school before moving on to break down the sexual barrier at the Academy.[13] For these and countless other reasons, women wanted to go to West Point. And whatever their initial reasons for applying, many women saw the Academy as a unique challenge and a way out of "the hometown trap," or became cadets because their hopes for an education at Wellesley, Smith, or other prestigious schools were impossible for academic or financial reasons.[14]

Still others applied on a lark. As a young freshman at the University of Nebraska, one woman found herself sitting with a group of friends reading the university newspaper. Someone discovered an article about the opening of the service academies to women. They laughed at the prospect of one of their group applying, then agreed to draw straws to see who it would be. The woman, a promising pre-med student, drew the short straw and applied for admission in the fall of 1975. Less than a year later she stood on The Plain at West Point as a New Cadet and member of the Class of 1980.[15]

Many of the young women who applied for admission came from progressive environments which actively encouraged the participation of women in every aspect of American life. When Congress passed Title IX legislation calling for greater emphasis on female sports in the early 1970s, for example, the male seniors on a high school soccer team in the Midwest responded by volunteering to teach interested girls how to play. One of the women who responded to their call eventually lettered in soccer and sought a place at the Academy because she thought it would be a "great outdoor adventure."[16] She ultimately found herself in a company of "evil, vicious people" at West Point, and discovered the place of women in the Army much more controversial than the place of women in sports in the Midwest.[17]

In the midst of that controversy stood the ubiquitous American press, and many women who applied to West Point found themselves overwhelmed by attention and publicity from the start. Newspaper, radio, and even television stories quickly created a momentum to attend the Academy that spread to friends and family members, and few could resist it for long. "As soon as I got the nomination," said one cadet, "the newspapers and radio station came to my house. The newspapers built it up so big I couldn't have backed out if I'd wanted to."[18] In many instances women learned they had been accepted to West Point from the governor of their state or from members of Congress who called them personally.[19] Politicians often notified the local press before they contacted the women themselves. In turn, the press notified candidates and barraged them with questions before they received official confirmation from the Academy.[20] Some women benefitted from this early experience and learned to "avoid the press at all costs," but for most that lesson came only with time at West Point.[21]

The limelight too often proved intoxicating for a young person. One Cadet said she was "swept away"[22] by the attention, and all were surprised and often overwhelmed by the pictures in the paper, the stories on radio and television, and their newfound prominence among teachers, friends, and family members. Most became hometown heroines, especially in smaller towns where cadets were featured on the front page of the paper and celebrated as native daughters of the entire community.[23] One woman remembers playing softball just prior to her departure for West Point. As she was batting the umpire asked over and over about the Academy and why she was going.[24] Everyone wanted to share or at least understand the accomplishment. Pride and prestige became a communicable phenomenon, easily acquired by parents stopped on streets or in supermarkets by their friends and asked, "How is your West Point daughter?"[25]

Members of Congress were often part of the pressure as well. When a midwestern woman learned of her admission, she informed her representative that she planned to decline. Her plans included medical school and a career as a doctor; spending four years at West Point and five more in the Army looked like a detour. Infuriated, the congressman then called personally to let her know he traded a representative from Delaware for the slot he wanted to give to her. Besides, he insisted, if she failed to go then her state would have no woman at West Point. After receiving assurances she could go to medical school (which the congressman had no power to give) via West Point, the young woman relented.[26]

In addition to forces exerted by the press and/or Congress, some young women received tremendous pressure to attend West Point from their parents. One woman's mother and father learned of the changes at West Point and did much of the admissions paperwork for her. Although she had no interest in either the Army or the Academy, the applicant went along with her parents because she believed she would never be admitted. When West Point informed her she could join the class of 1980 she balked, flatly informing her parents she had no desire to attend. They responded by informing her there would be no financial assistance from them for college if she refused to go, and in the end she saw no alternative but to yield to their wishes.[27]

Other parents used the lure of a West Point degree to more constructive ends. One cadet's mother voiced frustration at her daughter's desire to become a carpenter instead of attending college. When West Point announced plans to admit women, she remembered that at one time her daughter had decried the lack of opportunity for women at the Academy. "Put your money where your mouth is," the mother insisted. "It's open now, so apply." Taking the challenge, the daughter applied to West Point and nowhere else.[28] As she put it later, "If I hadn't gotten accepted . . . I would have gone into carpentry. All or nothing."[29] She was accepted and thereafter pursued a very successful career in the Army, traveling all over the world and living in several foreign countries.

In the Army, enlisted women usually found their decision to apply to West Point also influenced by parental figures, though in their cases officers rather than family members often played a decisive influence. One woman's company commander encouraged her to apply, did the paperwork personally, and hand-carried it around for proper signatures to make sure it received the necessary approvals.[30] Another woman discovered her commander started the admissions process without checking with her first. Though uninterested in West Point, she eventually went because she felt she owed it to her commanding officer for taking such an active interest in her career.[31]

Those who applied from the ranks of the Army often entered the United States Military Academy Preparatory School at Fort Monmouth, New Jersey, where they received training in mathematics and English to prepare them for the rigors of the West Point curriculum. Most women entered in January 1976 and took an abbreviated six-month course of instruction. The normal pattern was for USMAPS cadets to attend classes for a year, and male cadets were hardly pleased with the attention, accelerated admissions, or different physical standards which were applied to women.[32] When men realized that the accelerated admissions schedule meant women also entered USMAPS with automatic privileges that male cadets were denied during the first six months of their enrollment, their frustration magnified considerably. Most may have realized the decision to bring women in as equals with established male students was "fair" in the sense they were slated to graduate from USMAPS at the same time as their male peers, yet it hardly endeared female cadets to men who had fought several months for the privileges associated with being close to entering West Point.[33] Ultimately, trapped as it was between the passage of legislation in October 1975 and the legal requirement to admit women in July 1976, the Military Academy had no choice but to rush women through USMAPS as soon as possible. That fact hardly mattered to many men, however, and resentment at the "poop school" foreshadowed the resistance men later demonstrated at West Point.[34]

As the rush to admit women into USMAPS as well as West Point grew throughout the spring of 1976, female cadets found themselves both the victims and the beneficiaries of the accelerated timetable for admission. Men often began applying for admission during the fall of their junior year in high school and worked towards admission for years. Driven by the relentless calendar, however, the Academy admitted some women in a matter of weeks. One woman saw a magazine article in March 1976, applied and visited West Point in April, was admitted in May, and took her place alongside the rest of the class of 1980 on Reception Day (R-Day) in July. A southern belle whose boyfriend expressed considerable dismay at her sudden urge to attend West Point, she shocked her friends and pleased her parents in a span of time no male cadet could ever hope to match.[35] That fact was hardly her fault, for the Academy faced a situation unique in its 174 year history. No woman is on record as asking for special treatment from the Academy, but those who received it faced resentment from many men just the same.

One of the most unusual routes to the Academy was taken by a woman who applied as a "second thought" in January 1976. With little history of athletic prowess, she had trouble with the Physical Aptitude Examination administered by West Point and took it twice before passing. Still considered a marginal candidate, she eventually earned admission and later became adept at a variety of physical performance measures during a long and distinguished Army career. Interestingly, she learned later that one of the reasons she was admitted had been her looks. Rumor had it some Academy officials complained there were "all these women who look like men" and West Point needed "women who look like women."[36] Sexism may thus have worked ironically to her benefit and helped gain her admission prior to R-Day, though it certainly became a daunting obstacle afterwards.

Others also applied as a second thought or out of curiosity rather than any burning desire to attend West Point. One received a postcard from the Academy on the basis of her ACT scores and returned the postage-paid reply card requesting more information without much thought. "If I'd had to put a stamp on it I probably never would have gone," she said.[37] Rather than being committed to the notion of becoming soldiers, many women applied for admission and even entered out of a sense of inquisitiveness. Like many men, some later found a real devotion to the Army and to the Academy which endured all their lives.[38]

One of the women who later found that sense of devotion began her journey toward West Point on the island of Malta, where her English parents lived and her father served in the Royal Navy. Shortly after her birth, the family moved back to England, where they lived until deciding to sail around the world in 1966. Leaving England and the Royal Navy behind in a forty-foot yacht refurbished with their own hands, they traveled for three years before stopping in St. Lucia in 1969. During their stay, mother and daughter went ashore while the father agreed to take out a group of sightseers on a fishing expedition to raise money. While he was gone a terrible hurricane descended on the Caribbean island, and neither the father, the yacht, nor the tour group were ever seen again. With virtually all their worldly possessions gone, the mother worked for six months as a receptionist at a local hotel to save enough money to move with her daughter to New York to live with her sister. Landing at John F. Kennedy Airport with $100, the mother searched for work at once, and finally was hired as a receptionist for a doctor in Elmsford, New York. As the years went by, her daughter excelled at nearby Alexander Hamilton High School and took an after-school job as well. When she neared graduation she realized the family had no money to pay for a college education, a dilemma which seemed insoluble until her guidance counselor mentioned that the United States Military Academy had recently begun accepting female cadets. Pooling their resources, mother and daughter used their savings to pay an attorney who helped them become naturalized citizens, and Congressman Peter A. Peyser (R-New York) held open a nomination slot long enough for the daughter to earn it and join the rest of her classmates on R-Day in 1976.[39] Her journey hardly represents the typical process by which young women became cadets at West Point, but it does stand as a memorable example of the poignant tapestry Congress began to weave when it opened the United States Military Academy to women in 1976.

For others who contributed to that tapestry, the process of gaining admission to West Point had a very subtle way of incrementally creating a sense of commitment toward attending the Academy. It simply took so much work to be accepted that some candidates resolved to go even before they were admitted in order to justify the effort. There were physical and medical exams, the arduous battle to acquire congressional nominations, the attention from family, friends, and the press, and the tense waiting as an often rushed bureaucracy at West Point struggled to keep up with demands for decisions.[40]

At the Academy the most controversial and difficult problem for staffers during the admissions process lay in determining how to make the male Physical Aptitude Exam (PAE) fairly measure and challenge the very different physiology of women. The exam was "used to predict the potential of entering candidates to successfully complete the physical aspects of USMA training," and involved throwing a basketball from a kneeling position, performing a standing long-jump, running a timed shuttle between two lines for a distance of 300 yards, and doing pull-ups. West Point leaders had no established performance criteria for women, however, and knew from experience with women in basic training units that few women could do any pull-ups at all. In tests conducted by Army researchers few women could do one, and less than one-tenth of one percent could do the six which classified male candidates as physically marginal.[41] The data indicated a pressing need for a new measurement, and Academy officials chose the flexed arm hang. Previously used by the Army in basic training for women, the test involved hanging with both hands with the chin over the bar for a measured period of time.[42] Researchers insisted it was as challenging for women as pull-ups were for men, but many male cadets and officers were never convinced.

West Point also scaled the times and distances in the other activities on the basis of data accumulated in Project 60, a research program conducted to gauge the performance of young women in activities demanded by the Academy curriculum.[43] Based on results of the research, West Point issued PAE scoring guidelines for women that were significantly lower than those for men. Women who scored 250 or better were in the "A" Zone, while men had to score 450 or better to receive similar status.[44] The guidelines reflected physiological differences as well as sociological realities, but were hardly conducive to creating a sense of equality among men who faced the PAE with equal trepidation.

As the Class of 1980 took shape, it became clear that many women were generally far below their male classmates in height, weight, and physical aptitude as measured by West Point standards. Opinion polls showed that most cadets were comfortable with the Academy's doctrine of "approximately equal with few exceptions" policy regarding cadet standards, but a sizeable minority of men wanted identical treatment with no exceptions.[45] This rift over standards on selected physical performance measures became one of the most significant and controversial issues among those who criticized the presence of women at West Point.[46]

Unaware of the controversy their impending arrival had already created, several women candidates visited the Academy prior to their arrival as cadets, particularly if they lived relatively close to New York. Most were struck by the stern beauty of the Academy's Gothic buildings and the "majestic" grandeur of the valley and hills that inspired the entire Hudson River School of painting.[47] It was "awe inspiring" and "beautiful," even "idealistic," a place where the most jaded citizen could get "caught up in the myths" that have surrounded the Academy since the Revolution.[48] Visitors stayed in the historic Hotel Thayer and walked among the red and white oaks, the giant sycamores, and the dogwoods standing near The Plain. A symbol of rebirth, regeneration, and Easter, the dogwoods were joined by white pines, Virginia creepers, and a prodigious assortment of wildlife including deer, raccoons, and a variety of birds.[49] The juxtaposition of an institution dedicated to the study of war and the training of combat leaders nestled amidst such stunning natural beauty struck many who visited West Point, as it did Charles Dickens during a visit in the nineteenth century. "In this beautiful place," he wrote, "the fairest among the fair and lovely Highlands of the North River, shut in by deep green heights and ruined forts . . . is the Military School of America." Dickens described the Academy as "hemmed in, all round with memories of Washington, and events of the revolutionary war . . . ," and standing "along a glittering path of sunlit water, with here and there a skiff, whose white sail often bends on some new tack as sudden flaws of wind come down upon her from the gullies in the hills. . . ." West Point, he said, "could not stand on more appropriate ground, and any ground more beautiful can hardly be."[50]

Beyond the beauty of the surroundings, some women who visited during the spring of 1976 discerned the subtle rumblings of men who did not want women among them as peers. They encountered the often adolescent male culture of the Academy in the mess hall, where bratwursts were known as "donkey dicks" and cadets often bluntly encouraged women to pursue an education elsewhere.[51] One cadet recalled a conversation in Washington Hall: "Just as I was swallowing my last forkful of blueberry pie," she wrote, "a tall cadet sitting across from me leaned over the table and said, 'Excuse me, miss, but why do you want to come here?' " Putting her fork down, the young woman answered, "Because I want to become the best Army officer I can be." The cadet answered, "That's fine, but couldn't you do it someplace else?"[52]

Another woman encountered resistance as well, though in more muted form. As she waited with other applicants at West Point for an escort to show her around the grounds, a cadet walked in and asked for volunteers to accompany him. When none of the men seated around her spoke up, she raised her hand to go. Alarm spread across the cadet's face and he exclaimed, "Oh no! I can't take you!" He took one of the men instead, and soon another cadet came into the room. Rather than ask for volunteers, however, he asked for her by name and explained he had volunteered to be her escort because he was one of the few men who supported the admission of women to the Academy. Most of the men, he said, were against it. The ingrained male culture within the Corps of Cadets became even more evident when she entered the mess hall to the sounds of catcalls, whistles, and shouts from cadets.[53] Women who visited were also warned to get rid of their long hair, which was very much in fashion during the 1970s. "You gotta cut that when you get here!" the men shouted.[54] One woman who visited the mess hall felt like "a freak at a freak show" and sensed hostility from the men everywhere she looked.[55] Her apprehension was echoed by a future classmate, whose escort told her bluntly that if he ever saw her again he would do everything he could to run her out of the Academy. As fate would have it, he was a leader in her Cadet Basic Training company the following summer.[56] This sort of open disdain for women cadets grew increasingly widespread in 1976, and cadets were able to harass women visitors because the oversight offered by commissioned officers remained very limited. Under what the Academy called the Fourth Class System, the Corps of Cadets largely regulated and oversaw itself. While cadets were seldom completely unsupervised, the system made it relatively easy for cadets to escape close observation and harass visitors or ultimately female cadets when an opportunity presented itself.

Outside the Academy there were also men working more subtly to discourage women from applying to or attending West Point, from angry fathers to jealous boyfriends to dismissive counselors or teachers. One Army doctor made a clearly effective effort when he told the daughter of a West Point graduate she could never make it physically as a member of the Corps of Cadets. Ironically, she would have been a member of the Class of 1980 had she been admitted but she chose not to apply in large measure as a result of her doctor's warnings. She later married a member of another West Point class; in hindsight her husband, knowing his wife had the physical ability to become a cadet, wondered if the doctor's talk was simply a "male's ploy to keep another female out?"[57]

Others heard through the grapevine that they would be unwelcome, or encountered cadets in their home towns who shared the unhappy news with them. One woman saw the West Point Glee Club perform and managed to talk with some of the cadets. They were clearly unhappy about the change made by Congress and dreaded the arrival of women at the Academy.[58] Many men waited for years to attend West Point and had watched reruns of television shows like "The West Point Story" with young stars Clint Eastwood and Leonard Nimoy, as well as a host of Hollywood epics about the Long Gray Line.[59] Some women saw those cultural icons too, but prior to 1975 they had no reason to believe they could relate or aspire to them. In contrast, men usually shared preconceptions, myths, and hopes about what the Academy would be like, and none of those visions included the presence of women. The adjustment period promised to be difficult for everyone, a fact either lost or only dimly perceived by most of the women who went to West Point in 1976.

By far the most common appeal of West Point for young women, just as for young men, was the price. The allure of free tuition, room and board, plus a salary and an excellent opportunity at a career, seemed too good to ignore, especially for those who came from large families with limited finances. "The price was right," said one graduate, while another pointed out that as the fourth of five kids she had to find her own money for college.[60] One woman put the financial draw of the Academy in more matter-of-fact terms by calling her admission the "best scholarship offer" she received.[61]

Most cadets mentioned the "challenge" of West Point in interviews, with one arguing it gave focus and direction to her life.[62] Some also pointed to a commitment to the military or society, to a sense of duty to America. As one woman who entered the Academy with a year of college under her belt put it, "I felt I really owed something to society."[63] Another cadet reflected this attitude, saying, "I didn't come here just to get an education and to be a cadet. It was more than that," she said. "I know, you can call it loyalty or just wanting to give something back. Something like this is really hard to put your finger on but it's just sort of a higher calling or something."[64]

A few also came from patriotic families in which a parent or sibling had served in the military or been killed fighting in Vietnam, while a fraction had relatives who attended or had been stationed at West Point.[65] For them, a military career seemed appealing for a variety of reasons, and some had joined ROTC units or applied to West Point even before women were formally admitted.[66] One applied because she dreamed of one day becoming the American ambassador to the Soviet Union and thought an Army career would prepare her for leadership and geopolitical challenges on a global scale.[67]

Most women enjoyed the support of their family and friends, though parents sometimes voiced concerns relating to combat, to the distance of West Point from home, or about the challenge inherent in living among more than 4,000 men who were generally appalled by the prospect of women joining the Corps of Cadets. Even parents who disagreed with the idea of opening the service academies to women often found it impossible not to support their daughters. As one father put it, "I'm opposed to women going to the military academies . . . but if they're going to admit women I might as well have my daughter there."[68]

A few women faced lingering resentment from those who carried a hatred of the military dating to the Vietnam War. As a teacher told one future cadet, "You're too much of a lady to go to West Point."[69] Friends sometimes expressed amazement that anyone would give up summer vacation and the perks of a civilian college to have her hair cut and join a restrictive and stressful military environment.[70] Having matured in a society that stressed individual rights and liberties, they had trouble understanding why their women friends would abandon so many of those rights and liberties to be soldiers.

None of the women who chose to enter the Academy that summer in 1976 were really shaped by the end of the Vietnam War or the turmoil at West Point during the 1970s. They usually knew of these events, but only in the disinterested and superficial way most people know about events that do not immediately concern them. One woman heard a reference to the honor scandal during a final exam at the University of Tennessee. A teaching assistant monitoring the test by walking between rows of students called out, "No cheating here. This

isn't West Point."[71] Still, most women took the attitude that "those things happen" regarding the honor scandal, and only their time as cadets provided any
sense of perspective on how the scandal and even the war in Vietnam really did
affect them at the Academy. Prior to their arrival, they simply could not have
known.[72]

Much of what is statistically known about the first women at West Point stems
from the work of Academy researchers participating in "Project Athena."[73] The
project began in December 1975 as an effort to compile an institutional history
and database for the admission of women, and eventually became a four volume
series assessing how effectively West Point dealt with the assimilation of women
into the Academy. Researchers found women in the class of 1980 generally did
better in high school than their male peers, though the purposeful search by
West Point for women with high ACT scores, ROTC experience, and prior
enlisted service influenced that finding.[74] Men and women were generally similar
in their motivations for attending the Academy and in their background, and
those differences that did exist were usually associated with culture. Men, for
example, were more likely to participate in sports and to have tried to gain
admission to other service academies prior to attending West Point.[75] Not sur-
prisingly, over half the men of the class of 1980, and almost half the women,
had fathers who served at least one tour in a branch of the military.

It is interesting to note that Athena researchers played down the importance
of differences in physical performance between men and women. "Without a
'job analysis' which justified a preference for certain traits in West Point graduates," they argued, "there is no logical basis for preferring physical aptitude
over mental aptitude in a candidate."[76] It was a remark utterly foreign to most
graduates of West Point, for in the Army leadership and physical prowess were
seen as interrelated. What Athena analysts recognized was that the Army had
no hard and fast scientific reasons for preferring certain physical characteristics
in cadets. What it had instead were deeply held beliefs about what made leaders
successful in combat situations, and those beliefs were as rooted in the peculi-
arities of history and the male-dominated culture of the Army as they were in
practical battlefield experience.

In fact, the emphasis on physical prowess was a decidedly twentieth century
phenomenon, not a tradition that dated to the early days of either the Army or
West Point. It stemmed primarily from World War II, when the generation of
young men that survived the Great Depression were drafted into the Army.
Millions suffered the lingering effects of urban and rural poverty, including
malnutrition and severe weight loss, and often scored badly on Army intelligence tests because their formal education was limited. Those men with the
lowest scores were usually assigned to combat units, especially the infantry,
while those mastering the exams found themselves in technical fields like the
Air Corps or administration. In other words, men who came from more affluent
backgrounds who were physically fit and well-educated were the least likely to
receive assignments to the most important units in the Army—those that did

the fighting. This deeply flawed system meant that men who were poorly educated and in poor physical condition flooded combat units; to counter the
alarming trend, the Army instituted physical qualifications for infantry units, and
eventually for every other branch as well. Given the overwhelming number of
men in the American Army during World War II, it is no surprise that the
qualifications were male-oriented. They emphasized upper body strength, including pull-ups and push-ups, and combative sports like football. The standards
paid no attention whatsoever to skills in which women excel, such as sit-ups
and swimming, nor to characteristic female strengths, such as tolerance of pain
and the ability to endure food and water shortages. Most importantly, they were
not intended to represent a list of prerequisite characteristics for soldiers going
into combat.[77] They were meant to get soldiers in shape and grew out of the
unique circumstances of the World War II/Great Depression Era. Unfortunately,
by the 1970s these male-oriented physical standards were embedded deeply
within Army culture, and the idea of changing them for all soldiers or cadets
to accommodate women seemed unthinkable. It should have been no more unthinkable than the idea of instituting such standards in the first place, but it was.

What was *not* unthinkable to Academy officials was the idea that West Point
needed to attract women who wanted to serve their country. As the information
booklet sent to prospective female candidates explained, "West Point is embarking on a new chapter in its history of service to the country—the education
of women as well as men officers for the United States Army." It proclaimed,
"The Academy and the Army offer remarkable opportunities for meaningful
service and personal satisfaction. West Point is resolved to challenge all cadets
to their best efforts and to graduate quality young leaders for the Army."[78] When
all the attention from the press faded away, when the clamor of proud family
and friends quieted down, that remained the West Point mission in essence. For
good or ill, few women fully understood that mission when they arrived at the
Academy; like their male peers, they soon learned the meaning of the mission
in earnest.

The greatest paradox surrounding the 119 women who arrived at West Point
on July 7, 1976, is that they were overwhelmingly traditional young women
assuming decidedly nontraditional roles. Like most young people they were
often self-absorbed, and many failed to appreciate the enormity of the journey
on which they were embarking. Those who stayed four years as cadets and
served at least the minimum five years on active duty were explicitly promising
the Army nine years of their lives. For those who were eighteen years old that
was half-again as much time as they had been alive, and few considered that
profound truth in any meaningful way prior to taking the oath as cadets on R-
Day.[79] Rather than dreams of martial glory or the desire for a military career or
a West Point ring, the majority of women, just like the men, went to West Point
because it seemed to be in their best interests to do so. They did not go to ruin
or change the institution, to create a "trailblazer atmosphere" for the women's
rights movement, or to find husbands as some male cadets feared.[80] Most had

no idea how disturbing their arrival at West Point would be to cadets and officials of the Academy. They were "too young and naive to know"; while they knew their admission was unpopular in many circles, most had faith they would be accepted by their fellow cadets rather quickly.[81] As one put it when asked how she thought male cadets would respond to the arrival of women, "Once they see we can do it, I think they'll accept us."[82] After all, most had never confronted blatant discrimination or bias before, and they generally came from climates where they were accustomed to success and acceptance. West Point proved to be more difficult than any of them could have imagined.

NOTES

1. Plato, *The Republic of Plato*, trans. Francis MacDonald Cornford (New York: Oxford University Press, 1968), p. 149.

2. Alan G. Vitters and Nora Scott Kinzer, *Report of the Admission of Women to the United States Military Academy, Project Athena I* (West Point: BS & L, June 1978), p. 137. Western military academies similar to West Point include St. Cyr in France, Sandhurst in England, and both the Royal Military College and the College Royale Militaire at St. Jean in Canada.

3. John Keegan, *A History of Warfare* (New York: Alfred A. Knopf, 1993), p. 76.

4. Theodore J. Crackel, *The Illustrated History of West Point* (New York: Harry N. Abrams Inc., 1991), p. 286, and Vitters and Kinzer, *Project Athena I*, p. 15.

5. Vitters and Kinzer, *Project Athena I*, p. 19. West Point's curriculum emphasized mathematics and engineering courses, an emphasis traceable to the Academy's original mission of graduating trained engineers. The curriculum also reflected a widely held Army conviction that math and science courses were the best means of teaching decisive, analytical thought. High scores in math on the ACT were historically an excellent predictor of success for male cadets, and West Point used ACT scores to select desirable women cadets as well.

6. Interview with the author (IWA), 3-10-96, side A. Others were initially attracted to the Air Force Academy as well, only to end up for a variety of reasons at West Point. See EI, no date, p. 2; IWA, 12-12-95, and 3-10-96, side A.

7. Academy graduates were obligated to a term of service from the early nineteenth century onward; in 1897, Congress passed laws stipulating that West Point graduates serve a minimum of four years on active duty. Since then the obligation has been modified many times. See Geoffrey Perrett, *Old Soldiers Never Die: The Life of Douglas MacArthur* (New York: Random House, 1996), p. 30, and ETA, 6-8-2000, p. 4.

8. IWA, 4-2-96, side A. The tactic was used periodically during the Vietnam War by men trying to avoid service overseas. In this case, the Academy won the woman over, and she ultimately enjoyed a long and successful Army career.

9. IWA, 2-4-96, and 11-28-95, both side A.

10. It was good for West Point, too. The Army had no reason to want soldiers in an all-volunteer army who did not want to serve and certainly had no need for the negative press that would inevitably surround former cadets who complained of military entrapment.

11. IWA, 1-22-96, side A.

12. IWA, 2-28-96, side A. West Point has officers assigned to various regions of the country to coordinate the recruiting and admission of potential candidates, and in 1975 and 1976 was assisted by the Department of the Army, which encouraged regular Army recruiters to seek out young women who seemed likely to succeed at the Academy.

13. EI, 5-8-80, p. 3.

14. EI, no date, pp. 2–3; IWA, 7-28-96, 7-19-96, 12-12-95, and 7-19-96, all side A.

15. IWA, 3-18-96, side A.

16. IWA, 6-20-00, side A.

17. IWA, 6-20-00, side A.

18. Helen Rogan, *Mixed Company: Women in the Modern Army* (Boston: Beacon Press, 1982), p. 193.

19. IWA, 2-29-96, and 7-28-96, both side A.

20. EI, 5-6-80, p. 1.

21. IWA, 7-28-96, side A.

22. IWA, 2-29-96, side A.

23. IWA, 3-6-96, side A.

24. Ibid.

25. Ibid. It could also be a source of jealousy for brothers and sisters and was felt by men who chose an Academy education as well. One member of the Class of 1979 described the reaction in other people when he announced his admission this way: "When I mentioned it [West Point] I got this immediate *glow*." IWA, 2-18-98, author's notes.

26. IWA, 3-18-96, side A. Members of Congress often trade nomination slots if they receive a large batch of qualified applicants, or if they wish to nominate someone but already have their allotted number of cadets in attendance at the service academies.

27. IWA, 3-11-96, side A.

28. IWA, 5-13-96, side A.

29. EI, 5-5-80, p. 2. There were other cadets who applied only to West Point as well. See EI, 5-7-80, p.1.

30. IWA, 3-26-96, side A.

31. IWA, 4-4-96, side A.

32. Ibid.; and EI, 5-8-80, p. 2.

33. IWA, 3-26-96, side A.

34. At West Point, cadets describe required bits of knowledge as "poop"; hence the USMAPS was called the poop school, for it prepared cadets for life at the Academy. Like their male peers, women "prepsters" were generally better prepared for the military side of Academy life than their classmates who came from civilian environments, and had a better sense of the resistance to women at West Point as well. IWA, 3-26-96, side A. Bitterness over the speed of women's admissions plagued men at West Point too. IWA, 4-13-96, side A.

35. IWA, 4-4-96, side A.

36. IWA, 7-28-96, side A.

37. IWA, 2-16-96, side A.

38. IWA, 2-29-96, side A.

39. ETA, 7-26-2000, pp. 1–2.

40. IWA, 2-29-96, side A. Many women in the class of 1980 were "additional appointments," meaning they were appointed by the Department of the Army to bring the Corps of Cadets up to desired strength. Though discretionary, the Army gave these

appointments to some women because so many members of Congress had already allocated all of their own nominations prior to passage of legislation opening the academies to women in 1975.

41. The question of whether doing pull-ups is vital for soldiers or simply part of male culture was not addressed at the time.

42. Vitters and Kinzer, *Project Athena I*, pp. 15–16. Some women indicated they never did the flexed arm hang at West Point; they attempted pull-ups the first day and that was it. LTA, 4-4-2000, p. 3.

43. Ibid., p. 13.

44. Ibid., pp. 17–18. The complete table read, A Zone—Men 450, Women 250; B Zone—Men 400–449, Women 200–249; C Zone (marginal)—Men below 400, Women below 200.

45. Ibid., p. 31.

46. The rift remains among some cadets to this day. As one 1980 graduate explained, "I just cannot and never will understand why many men don't understand there are physiological differences between men and women which affect what they are physically capable of doing, no matter what effort is involved." ETA, 6-12-2000, p. 2.

47. IWA, 3-6-96, side A.

48. IWA, 7-19-96, 2-16-96, and 5-13-96, all side A.

49. Much of the wildlife is practically tame. During one visit to West Point, I arrived at 4 a.m. on The Plain to contemplate the Academy in the mystical quiet of early morning. Bathed in moonlight and surrounding the statue of Eisenhower were a half-dozen whitetail deer. Most were asleep and seemed undisturbed by my approach. I sat nearby and peacefully watched the Academy slumber. It was a moment of profound grace, one made interesting by the mingling of nature, human beings, and war, a mix common on the peninsula of West Point for almost two centuries. The real irony, however, is that while the Academy is dedicated to the study of war, it is also an institution which reveres order. Thus, the deer were probably safer surrounded by soldiers and guns than they might have been anywhere else in North America.

50. Charles Dickens, *American Notes* (Boston: Dana Estes and Company, 18?), p. 317.

51. IWA, 2-16-96, side A.

52. Carol Barkalow, with Andrea Raab, *In the Men's House: An Inside Account of Life in the Army by One of West Point's First Female Graduates* (New York: Berkeley Books, 1992), p. 9.

53. IWA, 11-28-95, side A.

54. Group IWA, 5-19-96, side A.

55. IWA, 2-5-96, side A.

56. EI, 5-9-80, p. 6.

57. ETA, 9-24-96, p. 9.

58. IWA, 7-19-96, side A.

59. Atkinson, *The Long Gray Line*, p. 27. "The West Point Story" aired from October 1956 until July 1958 on both CBS and ABC. Among the eventually famous guest stars besides Nimoy and Eastwood was Barbara Eden, who later achieved prominence in the series "I Dream of Jeanie." See Alex McNeil, *Total Television: A Comprehensive Guide to Programming from 1948 to 1980* (New York: Penguin Books, 1980), p. 767.

60. IWA, 2-5-96, side A, and 3-6-96, side A. Almost every interviewee mentioned the free tuition at West Point as a factor in her decision to attend, and many came from

large families. See IWA 2-16-96, 3-12-96, 4-4-96, 7-28-96, 2-4-96, and 7-19-96, all side A.

61. LTA, 9-2-96.

62. IWA, 2-27-96, side A. Others mentioned the challenge as well. IWA, 9-10-96, side A.

63. Ibid., and EI, 4-30-80, p. 1.

64. EI, 5-6-80, p. 3.

65. Group IWA, 5-19-96, side A.

66. IWA, 4-10-96, and 4-23-96, side A.

67. IWA, 4-23-96, side A.

68. IWA, 7-28-96, side A.

69. IWA, 2-16-96, side A.

70. IWA, 3-12-96, side A.

71. IWA, 2-27-96, side A.

72. IWA, 2-5-96, side A.

73. The project was originally known as *Project Assimilate*.

74. Vitters and Kinzer, *Project Athena I*, p. 36.

75. Ibid., p. 31. Title IX legislation opening more high school and college programs to women had barely taken effect in 1976.

76. Ibid., pp. 34 and 36.

77. D'Ann Campbell, "Servicewomen and the Academies: The Football Cordon and Pep Rally as a Case Study of the Status of Female Cadets at the United States Military Academy," *Minerva: Quarterly Report on Women and the Military* 13, No. 1 (Spring 1995): 3–4.

78. United States Military Academy, "Information for Women Cadets" (West Point booklet dated November 1975), p. 17.

79. IWA, 3-26-97, author's notes.

80. Group IWA, 5-19-96, side A, and EI, 5-6-80, p. 2. One woman emphasized that those few who did go to West Point to meet men or find a husband didn't last long as cadets. See EI, 5-6-80, p. 2.

81. IWA, 2-5-96, side A.

82. *Potomac News*, April 9, 1976, p. A-2.

4

★ ★ ★ ★

"The Little Things"

Now, for the purpose of producing a woman fit to be a Guardian, we shall not have one education for men and another for women, precisely because the nature to be taken in hand is the same.

—Plato, *The Republic*[1]

July 7, 1976, dawned gray and humid, with intermittent rain showers adding dampness to an already dreary day. The weather seemed to reflect the mood of the Academy as it solemnly pushed through daunting change, and it suited the apprehensive demeanor of New Cadets confronting an intimidating watershed in their own lives.

Change swept the outside world as well. At the Academy, the admission of women was the most tangible sign of the greater social revolutions beyond the Hudson River Valley and a clear indication that women were seizing more national and international attention than ever before. In 1974, an unprecedented eighteen women were elected to the U.S. House of Representatives, while 130 were chosen by voters to serve in state legislatures nationwide.[2] Barbara Walters broke new ground by becoming the first woman to earn more than a million dollars a year as a network anchor, and Nadia Comaneci dazzled the world on her way to gold medals in gymnastics at the 1976 Summer Olympics in Montreal. And though unrelated to the admission of women to West Point in any way, it is worth noting that Cliff Richard released a single called "Devil Woman" in July which went gold almost overnight. One suspects it may have been popular with many male cadets that summer of 1976.[3]

No music greeted the Class of 1980 as they arrived at the Academy, however. Instead, as more than 1,000 young men and a handful of young women hesitantly approached West Point, they slowly crossed the threshold between civilian life and the myth-shrouded career of a cadet. The first day of their odyssey was officially known as "Reception Day," though cadets referred to it as simply "R-Day." Between 7 and 10 a.m., New Cadets arrived with their loved ones at Michie Stadium, pausing briefly to meet with Academy officials who told them what to expect as cadets. In short order, parents and friends left for tours of West Point, while their New Cadets caught buses to the Central Gymnasium for in-processing. Though utterly formulaic and well planned, the ritual proved emotional just the same for the young men and women who said goodbye to their loved ones and the life they knew in order to enter the strange and unknown fold of the Academy.

The rite of passage also carried with it considerable emotional symbolism for the cadet cadre and officials of West Point. Most of them could recognize themselves in the uncertain faces maneuvering through in-processing stations, for at one time the majority had also been New Cadets cautiously seeking acceptance in an unfamiliar world. The Class of 1980 did more than trigger hallowed or frightful memories, however, for their arrival signaled the beginning of a new era at West Point, one that the institution did not seek for itself. Indeed, to some Academy faithful, the Class of 1980 seemed to threaten the very institution they were solemnly entering. There were, after all, women among the New Cadets that July in 1976, and they added an upsetting dimension for every graduate who believed gender integration epitomized a step towards weakness and a loss of tradition. As Rick Atkinson wrote, "Had a company of Martians suddenly appeared on the Plain in dress gray and tarbuckets, there would have been no greater sense of invasion and outrage than was provoked by the arrival of ten dozen American females."[4] Academy leaders fell back on advance planning as well as time-honored ritual to cope on R-Day, so that despite their uncertainty it unfolded almost identically to the many others endured by New Cadets at West Point throughout history.

As soon as the New Cadets were out of sight of their loved ones, clutching the one bag or suitcase permitted by the Academy, the yelling began. One woman reacted by thinking, "Well, I guess my parents have already left, so it's too late to quit."[5] The yelling came from members of the upperclass, who were the real leaders of the Corps of Cadets as well as the trainers and enforcers of what was known as the Fourth Class System, and it began the long process of introducing the New Cadets to military life. As the buses discharged their passengers at the gymnasium, New Cadets moved through a variety of stations inside. They were "stripped, examined, and fitted with new clothing—white T-shirts, black gym shorts, black knee-socks, and oxfords."[6] Women received crew-necked shirts while men retained the old v-neck variety, and all New Cadets received both green and yellow tags pinned to their shorts which included lists of where they had been, what they had been issued, and where they needed to go next. They dropped off their luggage and money, were measured by Academy tailors for their uniforms, had their photograph taken while wearing a swimsuit so staffers could judge their posture and overall level of physical fitness, then did pull-ups, acquired shoes, pants, and uniforms, and received the first of many haircuts.[7]

The dominating figure at each of these stations—indeed, the dominating figure of every New Cadet's R-Day experience and of many an Old Grad's memory—was known as "The Man in the Red Sash."[8] Actually, there were many men in the red sash; they were Firsties, seniors who wore the distinctive scarlet sash around their waist to distinguish themselves as the leaders of the Corps. Assisted by third year cadets and Academy staff, these Firsties shepherded the New Cadets through a dehumanizing process meant to shock as much as to educate. R-Day began six weeks of military training known as Cadet Basic Training (CBT). Commonly known as "Beast Barracks," the period introduced New Cadets to military life and the fundamentals of being soldiers.[9] R-Day provided the convulsive shock which began the process and was a day which cadets never forgot. They were taught how to salute, how to march, and issued a wide variety of equipment in a methodical and often hurried manner.

Along the way it quickly became clear that not all New Cadets faced identical treatment. Women, for example, were sent to the barber shop far more often to receive haircuts. This may have resulted in part from confusion over the differing hair regulations for women. While men's hair was cut well above the ears and very short, the rules stipulated that women's hair could not extend beyond the top of their collar nor more than a limited distance in any direction away from their head. Ultimately, however, the additional trips to the barber were a way for men to harass women in a seemingly legitimate manner; because any upperclassman could order a New Cadet to get another trim, there were many women who endured multiple trims that first day. One woman was sent to the barber shop *seven* times.[10]

There were differences in the uniforms too. Women's trousers had no back pockets, for example, ostensibly to make their wider hips appear as slim as possible. This was a practical calamity of the first order, however, for it meant women had no place to carry feminine hygiene articles, which were located two miles from the barracks at the post exchange and difficult to get anyway.[11] Some carried these articles in their hats or socks until pockets were added; others used a small black leather bag with a zipper which the Academy provided to women cadets during Plebe year.[12] Worse, the zippers and buttons on the pants were on the wrong side, and the flimsy plastic zippers broke time and time again.[13] In the long run each of these maladies was cured (new pants appeared as if by magic on July 9), but on R-Day it meant many women marched in the afternoon parade wearing trousers borrowed from male upperclassmen or pants fastened precariously with safety pins.[14]

New Cadets learned the famous "four responses," which were the only acceptable answers to any order or question. They were "Yes, Sir," "No, Sir,"

"No excuse, Sir," and "Sir, I do not understand." They learned to walk at 120 steps per minute, eyes straight ahead, squaring corners, close to the walls, with their arms bent at ninety degree angles, and began to understand they were responsible for following orders immediately, no matter how many were issued at once.[15] Some, especially those who walked in with no idea what to expect, often expressed bitter frustration over why "they [upperclassmen] didn't explain everything," seldom realizing there was method to the madness, that the Academy believed in a system devoted to quickly destroying old habits and painfully creating new ones among cadets.[16]

Perhaps the only New Cadet who escaped the disorienting maelstrom of R-Day was an older woman who took advantage of the system. "I just checked off as many stations as I could on my Green Tag," she explained, "and then hung out in my room and smoked." R-Day, she said, "was a snap, an absolute snap."[17]

For most New Cadets, however, R-Day consisted of a blur of orders, haircuts, processing stations, the Man in the Red Sash, moving into rooms, briefly meeting classmates, eating lunch, and then preparing for the afternoon parade on The Plain. No more rapid or astonishing transformation can be found in the theater of American life. At 10 a.m., more than 1,000 young civilians in distinctive clothes had nervously clutched their meager belongings and said farewell to their loved ones in Michie Stadium. At 5 p.m. those same young men and women emerged from the Academy's historic sally ports with military haircuts and wearing the familiar West Point white over gray uniform. They marched in great columns onto The Plain and assembled in formation behind squad and company commanders who were strangers only hours before, yet who now held power and leverage over their charges most parents would have envied. Thousands of friends and family members filled bleachers fronting the parade ground, searching for their New Cadet in the midst of a sea of utterly similar faces.

Waiting to take the oath of allegiance and begin their journey toward becoming Army officers, the New Cadets listened as they were welcomed to West Point by the Superintendent. He was speaking mainly to the nervous parents in the stands, however, so most spent the time checking their posture, their spacing between other cadets, and their uniform. All these things, utterly unimportant only hours before, already assumed monumental importance in their lives. Then they raised their right hands and took their *sacramentum* as cadets at the United States Military Academy. When the deed was done they passed through the intersection of anticipation and palpable experience, where adolescence began to give grudging ground to experience, and crossed the threshold between myth and reality, between tradition and tangible truth. They were no longer simply teenagers. Instead, they were young people en route to becoming officers charged with the defense of their nation and implicitly challenged with making the admission of the first women at West Point a success. This was history in action—one West Point replacing another.

The cadet journey in 1976 differed considerably from the old days, when New Cadets often arrived individually. They stepped off of trains at the station down by the river or traveled by horse, carriage, or foot to pass through the Academy's main gate. In the 1850s, New Cadets met their First Sergeant amidst a barrage of buttons fired from a brass candlestick loaded with gunpowder; throughout the nineteenth century, there was little formality until training and classes began.[18] Even in the years prior to World War I, a young cadet might have several days or even weeks pass before every member of his class arrived.

Such informality passed away in later years, though the odyssey from civilian to cadet remained essentially the same, involving as it did the timeless exchange of individual autonomy for allegiance to a group; of loyalty to oneself for dedication to duty, honor, and country. The journey drew West Pointers of different eras together, and across the passage of time, throughout the tumult and triumph and sacrifice of American history, helped the United States Military Academy cultivate an aura of unchanging, steadfast dedication to national service. Part of the euduring myth of West Point was that very little had changed since 1802, when Congress established the fledgling institution as a means of providing trained military officers and engineers for an adolescent nation. Even outsiders often found it remarkably easy to slip into nostalgic reverie at the Academy, to believe the romance of the place was static and permanent, somehow well above the pedestrian norms of American life. Yet change *did* periodically come to the Academy, and never was that spirit of evolution more apparent than when the R-Day parade ended and the Class of 1980 returned through their barracks' sally ports for the evening. A new era had begun.

The next morning, with parents and loved ones gone and the press less noticeable than on R-Day, members of the Class of 1980 formally began Beast Barracks. They found West Point an environment famed primate specialist Jane Goodall would have recognized in an instant: a place where primitive, physical battles for supremacy raged among males for leadership of the group. There were rituals to establish hierarchy and a socialization process wholly unacceptable in the outside world beyond other closed male societies like fraternities and secret clubs. This world deliberately intended to break some cadets, and from the Academy's point of view, the sooner the weak ones left the better. Army careers hardly favored those who were soft, especially when they involved combat; immersion in the West Point experience represented the first phase of preparing cadets and future officers for whatever challenges the world might offer. As Arthur M. Schlesinger wrote of Franklin Roosevelt's years at America's most exclusive college prep school: "some—the tougher ones—were braced by their years at Groton even while they suffered under the system. They were strengthened," he said, "by the intellectual training, inspired by the moral purpose, and sent into the world with a high sense of their duties as Christian gentlemen. To survive unhappiness at Groton was to be capable of anything."[19] He could have been describing West Point.

Very quickly, New Cadets learned the primal importance of physical prowess.

It largely determined both the official and unofficial pecking order among cadets regardless of sex, and was measured primarily in terms of rigorous, mandatory runs which were a daily rite of passage and test of power in which personality and intellect hardly mattered. Success in those runs counted as the "only thing that got you accepted," because it indicated physical fitness, and that equaled leadership.[20]

This emphasis on running and physical power, while easily dismissed as unimportant and obsessively macho, made a certain amount of sense at West Point. Every group has rites of passage, tests which potential members must pass to be accepted. For some human groups the rites are cerebral; attorneys must first graduate from law school and then pass the bar exam, doctors must graduate from medical school and become licensed, while professors must earn graduate degrees, research, and write on problems in their field of study. For others, the rites are physical and action oriented. Gang members must show a willingness to commit violence, football players must demonstrate strength, speed, and stamina, and soldiers must show proficiency at marching, shooting, and hand to hand combat. The more exclusive the group, the more challenging the rites. Earning a Ph.D. is more difficult than earning a bachelor's degree, being a neurosurgeon more prestigious than practicing family medicine, and joining an elite combat unit more physically challenging than doing paperwork in an administrative section. West Point made its tests both physical and mental; but, true to military tradition, physical prowess counted the most. Always. No vocation demanded more physically than the society of warriors; as future Army officers charged with winning America's wars, West Pointers historically prided themselves on being especially tough and demanding. Women seemed to threaten that tradition, particularly when they did not have to meet the same physical standards as men.

Yet it became difficult in practice for cadets and the Army to distinguish between standards that were vital for all soldiers to meet and standards which existed merely because they were masculine and within the range of most men. Whether characteristics like upper body strength and speed really mattered for soldiers in either peacetime or war constituted an open intellectual question, but it was a question traditionalists could answer with ease. Those characteristics *did* matter to them, and challenging the primacy of entrenched physical assumptions became a very volatile course of action for many West Pointers. The weight of that tradition meant that men could not simply change the harsh, male-oriented environment of the Academy when confronted with the first women cadets. Just as important, some of them had no intention of even trying to make the system equitable. Male New Cadets did receive physical harassment and hazing, but their female peers faced physical hazing and harassment, sexual harassment, innuendo, and an extraordinarily challenging environment demanding constant struggle through the rites of passage to become Plebes without the promise of ever being fully accepted as members of the Corps. The high-pitched voices of some women were mimicked by the Beast cadre, who often com-

plained that women's voices were unmilitary.[21] Women were routinely barked
at by men, as at USMAPS the previous spring, and the cumulative stress was
palpable for many New Cadets.[22] "The first time I called home all I did was
cry," said one woman.[23] On daily runs, upperclassmen jumped on men who fell
out before the first woman did, and once all the women had been eliminated
the cadence and "Jody" songs became much more sexist and ribald.[24] While a
handful of women tried to accept this pattern stoically because they realized,
"The power they [the upperclass] had over me was the power I gave them,"
most women found Beast the first of many traumatic hurdles to be overcome at
West Point.[25] The Fourth Class System in many ways represented an enormous
rite of initiation. It gave young people tremendous power over each other, however, and thousands of men power over 119 women who often had little understanding of where the privileges of rank stopped for their superiors. For
members of the upperclass who bore the emotional scars of Plebe year themselves and harbored grudges, Beast afforded a cherished opportunity to release
frustration. That fact contributed greatly to a situation in which the conditions
became ripe for women to "catch it."[26]

Beyond stress, with sixteen-hour days full of marching, shooting, and bivouacking, Academy leaders hoped Beast would develop in cadets the "cardinal
military virtues of obedience and loyalty."[27] Beast also introduced New Cadets
to "Plebe Poop," the vast array of miscellaneous Academy knowledge and trivia
upperclassmen demanded Plebes recite on command. Cadets had to know, for
example, of the Administration Building's place in Academy lore as the tallest
all-stone masonry building in the world, that the Federal Silver Depository stood
just outside Washington Gate, and that the shaft of Battle Monument (which
one author called "radically phallic"[28]) represented the largest piece of turned
granite in the Western Hemisphere.[29] At a moment's notice a Plebe might be
asked to bark out the cadet definition of leather, which ran: "If the fresh skin
of an animal, cleaned and divested of all hair, fat, and other extraneous matter,
be immersed in a dilute solution of tannic acid, a chemical combination ensues;
the gelatinous tissue of the skin is converted into a non-putresible substance,
impervious to and insoluble in water; this sir, is leather."[30]

They had to know that Lusk Reservoir contained seventy-eight million gallons
when water flowed over the spillway, that 340 lights adorned Cullum Hall, and
were responsible for reciting the condition of the "cow." "How is the cow?" an
upperclassman would demand. The Plebe would answer: "Sir, she walks, she
talks, she's full of chalk, the lacteal fluid extracted from the female of the bovine
species is highly prolific to the nth degree."[31] No practical military application
existed for this kind of memorization. Instead, it endured exclusively to give
Plebes more tasks which demanded their time, their energy, and their immersion
in the culture of West Point. Even more important, it forcefully demonstrated
to each of them that when orders were given, they were to be followed immediately. Period.

As Beast continued, even neophyte New Cadets felt the persistent aftershocks of the spring honor scandal, for they rocked West Point to its foundation. In June, during graduation ceremonies for the Class of 1976, Rabbi Avraham Soltes delivered an invocation referring to the higher ideals sought by West Point and the most idealistic members of the Long Gray Line. "While the world around us condones a cynical disregard of standards and the casual compromise of principle," he prayed, "we have sought, here, to affirm our unflagging faith in the integrity of man's word to his fellow man. . . ."[32] It was a stirring appeal to principle, one that stood in stark contrast to the ugly stain on the Academy's reputation which the scandal represented. Yet the shadows cast by the scandal could not be avoided. More than eighty attorneys representing cadets accused of violating the Honor Code were entrenched in Thayer Hall that summer, suggesting some cadets placed more of their unflagging faith in the courts than in their fellow man.[33]

The investigations created inevitable press interest and an almost constant pressure from higher authorities that led Superintendent Berry to proclaim, "I've never been in more of a combat situation than I am now."[34] Coming from a veteran of combat in both Korea and Vietnam, his remarks said a great deal about the fear the scandal generated in the minds of many graduates, who believed the survival of West Point hung in the balance.

They feared that a gradual decline in standards throughout America was destroying the efficacy of the Honor Code among cadets, and to a point they seemed correct. Investigators found a "cool on honor" subculture at West Point, where roommates and friends cooperated on homework and exams, and the Honor Code too often existed only as a target for ridicule. This went beyond bed-stuffing incidents, when cadets piled clothing under their blankets to simulate their presence while they slipped quietly off post. And it went beyond routine disregard for certain regulations, for cadets recognized a profound difference between breaking a rule and an honor violation. Those who snuck out of the barracks after taps, for example, were breaking a rule, while those who lied committed an honor violation. Between those two extremes existed an almost limitless array of possible pitfalls, many of which became a rich source of discussion and occasionally humorous exchanges among cadets and within Academy lore.[35] These discussions existed ideally to promote a fuller understanding of the limits of ethical behavior, and they served as a constant reminder that some cadets would eventually violate the code and be dismissed from the ranks of the Corps. It was thus no surprise to the Academy or to Old Grads when some cadets were found in violation of the Honor Code in 1976. The surprise lay in the sheer magnitude of the scandal, and it deeply frightened many graduates because it demonstrated that honor violations were not an aberration. They were a consistent fact of life for much of the Corps in the 1970s, and while that sort of generalization marred those cadets who were innocent, it nonetheless held true.[36]

When the honor boards finally concluded their investigations, 152 cadets from the Class of 1977 were dismissed from the Academy with the option to return the following year.[37] This decision frustrated almost everyone. Some cadets believed that many more of their peers were guilty of cheating, while others concluded that the Honor Code lay in such shambles by the late 1970s that almost all of the Corps should have been expelled. Then there were the Old Grads and those who believed honor violations threatened the essence of the Academy and should be punished ruthlessly. They were generally appalled by the notion that expelled cadets could receive the option to return, for it implied that those who violated the Honor Code deserved no greater punishment than waiting an extra year to graduate. The Academy argued that it made little sense to ruin a good cadet's career for a single mistake and that violations of the Honor Code were so pervasive during the scandal that some allowance had to be made for those who were simply caught up in the "cool on honor" subculture. Purists remained unconvinced, and their staunch, strict interpretation of the Honor Code harkened to the view espoused by the 1908 edition of *Bugle Notes*, which stated: "A thief, a liar, and a coward cannot be extenuated in the eyes of the Corps, and it is no part of the function of West Point to become a reformatory of morals."[38] Such a statement reflected the world of the early twentieth century, when West Point expected civilian society to inculcate morals in young people before they entered the Academy. By the 1970s, however, American society had changed, and governmental institutions were being forced to step in to develop morality and ethics among young people themselves, just as they were forced to revamp societal assumptions about race and gender.

As Beast continued, and as the Class of 1977 cadre disappeared from leadership positions to face honor investigations en masse, female cadets found that more than societal assumptions about gender needed reform; the Army needed to revamp the equipment issued to women. Parade sabers and ponchos were too long for some, and regulation Army boots did not always fit properly. On the generally smaller feet of women they rolled too easily, forcing the leather into achilles tendons and heels and therefore risking ankle injuries. Army swimsuits often fit poorly, physical education shorts were too short, and regulation cadet robes were precariously thin. The robes demanded immediate action, because they were transparent when wet and so short they only reached mid-thigh.[39] The Academy responded to all of these problems eventually, and to the robe situation with great speed, bringing in long, thick, terry cloth robes for women within a few weeks. Yet each of these "little things," however understandable in a situation where West Point and the Army were learning as they went along, contributed to a sense of chaos and frustration among some women that never really faded.

Beast Barracks came to an end in the last week of August, when the CBT Regiment returned to West Point in a triumphant march from training at nearby Lake Frederick. Following their arrival, the New Cadets of the Class of 1980 became Plebes and were brought into the fold of the Corps at the annual Acceptance Day Parade, the parade in which they became members of the hive, and began looking forward to the rigors of the academic year.

Soon after, the remainder of the Corps returned from summer leave and training and Plebes transferred from the eight companies which made up the CBT Regiment into all thirty-six companies in the Corps. This process filled the period between the end of Beast Barracks and the beginning of the academic year, and in formal Academy jargon was referred to as "Reorganization Week." The Corps called it "Re-Orgy," and it dramatically changed the nature of the Corps and the daily life of the average Plebe. The reason was simple mathematics. During Beast an average of only one upperclassman lived in the barracks for every ten New Cadets. When Beast ended and the rest of the upperclassmen returned from leave and/or training, the ratio changed to three upperclassmen for every Plebe. Fourth Class cadets who thought upperclassmen were everywhere during Beast thus suffered the daunting realization that for the first time they were genuinely and decisively outnumbered, meaning their odds of being harassed increased considerably. The vast majority of the returning Yearlings, Cows, and Firsties were quick to capitalize on these Plebe fears and began hazing almost immediately.[40] They were often eager to take their first crack at women cadets as well, to locate, talk with, and investigate the most celebrated and despised Plebes in the Academy's history.[41]

During this transition period, some female cadets struggled in vain to find acceptance as soldiers and cadets and to force their male peers to see them as more than just women. For some women, the struggle left many scars. "I had these boots that were too big for my feet," recalled one woman. "I was in my fatigues, . . . and I looked funny. I'm sure I did. I looked like a little toy doll. And all of the Yearlings in the company came out in the hall and started laughing." As she moved toward her room she became increasingly frustrated, because, as she put it, "I wanted to be a soldier. I wanted them to look on me that way. But there was nothing I could do."[42] In the rigidly hierarchical world of West Point, she discovered, Plebe women simply had to bear down and attempt to win over their male peers one cadet at a time.

When Re-Orgy ended, the fully formed Corps stood organized as a Brigade divided into four regiments of three battalions of three companies each, with an authorized strength of 4,417.[43] A Cadet First Captain commanded the Brigade, with Cadet Captains, Lieutenants, Sergeants, and Corporals staffing the chain of command all the way down to the squad level. In turn, the Brigade commander answered to an Academy officer corps which fell under the command of the Superintendent, a three star (Lieutenant) General who had graduated from West Point. A Commandant of Cadets oversaw the military training of cadets, and a Dean of the Academic Board handled academic affairs. Legions of Colonels, Lieutenant Colonels, Majors, and Captains filled the Academy staff and faculty, with some serving as West Point Tactical Officers (TACs). The TACs oversaw individual cadet companies and served as mentors for cadets adjusting to their roles as leaders and future officers.[44] They constituted the primary role models for cadets and were the officers with the most direct responsibility for monitoring cadet behavior in and out of the barracks. And because their style of command influenced the cadets in their charge, TACs had enormous influence over the manner in which Plebes and matters of discipline were treated. Those who took charge and made no allowance for abuse typically oversaw companies in which discipline remained tight and cadets knew exactly how far they could push their authority. Those who made a habit of looking the other way, either because they believed in "tradition" or the concept that West Point needed to be unusually harsh to toughen cadets for careers in the Army, often let senior cadets run wild. TACs in the latter group were a terrible threat to all Plebes, for they sometimes deferred to the law of the jungle and allowed cadet behavior to sink toward the lowest common denominator. While the women of the Class of 1980 did not yet know it, such TACs were a particular threat to them and were one of the reasons that treatment of women varied so much from company to company.

Re-Orgy spread the small number of women at West Point precariously thin and denied them any sort of meaningful support from each other during their first year at the Academy. It also introduced them to the unique identity of each company and regiment within the Corps. Cadets spent the bulk of their time within their companies and drew from them a distinctive identity rooted in Academy lore and tradition. It was therefore a matter of tremendous consequence when Plebes received their company assignments, for their success or failure as cadets depended in large measure on their willingness and ability to blend into their company culture. By fate alone Plebes were cast into companies whose leaders exhibited widely varying talents and styles and whose culture could vary from professionally supportive to anachronistically harsh. Company assignment could thus spell the difference between a challenging yet fulfilling Academy career or an extraordinarily difficult nightmare, and cadets had little control over the process. This fact accounts for the wide variety of experiences among cadets, even those who graduated in the same class. Every regiment and company had unique characteristics, created by the TAC, upperclassmen, and subordinates tied to whatever tradition the unit carried forward from year to year. First Regiment, for example, prided itself on being the toughest at West Point, while Fourth Regiment projected a generally more lenient and laconic image. Each regiment contained companies labeled A through I, and cadets in each company never referred to their company as an island unto itself. The company existed solely as a part of the regiment. A cadet in Company B, Second Regiment, would thus abbreviate his or her home by saying they were in B-2, and each company had songs, chants, or phrases reflecting its character. Laid back I-4, for example, made "Quit the Corps and Join I-4" their battle cry, while the legendary strictness of F-1 garnered the company an obscene unofficial nickname among cadets.

Plebes found the Academy a virtual world, one in which the vocabulary, clothing, and mannerisms were strictly prescribed and entirely alien to civilians. Beds became "bunks," dorm rooms changed to "barracks," cafeterias converted to "mess halls," and so on. The quotidian life of a West Point Plebe meant walking at 120 steps per minute, squaring corners, fretting over uniforms, ducking into latrines to avoid hazing when possible, and being quizzed at meals by upperclassmen intent on exposing gaps in the poop each first year cadet was required to learn. All of them read the *New York Times* to track national and international events, for they were liable for information in daily editions of the paper as well as their normal quota of West Point lore and legend.[45]

Women faced the additional and persistent harassment of being ordered to get extra haircuts, and of trying to satisfy upperclass demands for a flawless "gig line." Gig lines were the lines made by jacket edges and trouser seams on a cadet's body, and regulations demanded they be exactly straight. Male Plebes had to have proper "gigs" too, but the Academy had spent more than a century and a half designing and perfecting uniforms so that they glorified the male physique. On the more rounded figures of many women the gig lines were virtually impossible to keep straight for long, and female uniforms did not always align neatly because the shirt opening, pants opening, belt buckle, and zippers were not all on the same side. They were on men's uniforms, but that seldom bothered upperclassmen, who delighted in nailing women for improper gig lines again and again.[46]

On a much more humorous level, the first female cadets at West Point quickly realized they had an advantage when it came to room inspections because most upperclassmen had no idea how to deal with women's underwear. Female undergarments did not fold into neat squares the way male undergarments did, and they were not always traditionally Army colors like white, beige, or olive. Worse, some men had so little experience with female underwear they became embarrassed when forced to determine whether bras were folded neatly and correctly and whether feminine hygiene articles were correctly displayed. They had no idea, and many did not want to have an idea. A large number dealt with their embarrassment and discomfort by simply refusing to inspect drawers that contained female underwear, and some women seized this advantage and hid candy or other illicit items in tampon boxes or amidst their underwear. Female cadets in one company even ordered the most provocative lingerie possible in order to further embarrass their squad and company commanders.[47]

These humorous distractions hardly mitigated the challenges of West Point for all cadets, however; from the very first day of Beast, some Plebes decided against pursuing an Academy life any further. The steady trickle of resignations continued into the fall, and those who chose to leave the Long Gray Line moved quickly to the Boarders Ward in Eisenhower Barracks (known as the "Quitters's Prison"), lest their contagion spread to others.[48] There was little need for worry, for most cadets drew back at the thought of leaving. The fame, excitement, and expectations associated with attending West Point made it hard to quit, even for those who truly hated their new life. And leaving the Academy seemed more like suicide than dropping out or simply changing schools. Those who said they wanted to go were counseled by other cadets, by the staff and faculty; only if they truly desired to leave were they allowed to depart. When they were gone they were discussed only in the past tense, as if they had died rather than simply left to attend another university.[49]

The grueling physical regime, which included running, exercise, and athletics every single day, meant cadets ate voraciously, and some Plebes lived for desserts especially. One member of the class said he survived Beast by reminding himself over and over again, "They're going to feed me."[50] The Academy prohibited snacking, though packages from home containing food (known as "Boodle") were acceptable so long as cadets ate all of the food on weekends and did not attempt to keep leftovers. Plebes, kept so busy answering questions at meals that they had difficulty eating, found Boodle particularly valuable because they were part of a long tradition of hazing through food-deprivation at West Point. While the deliberate denial of food had faded as a tool of harassment by the 1970s, it held a powerful place in Academy lore and undoubtedly motivated the author of the ancient West Point anthem which read, "Through the lips, O'er the tongue, Down the esophagus, By one lung, Cheer up tummy, Here I come, BOODLE!"[51]

Plebes became familiar with Corps discipline, meted out primarily through a system of demerits known as "quills" and "slugs." Quills were given for minor infractions and derived their name from the fact quill pens were once used to record them. Slugs were for more serious offenses and usually included "punishment tours," which involved walking the North Area between barracks in full dress uniform for a period of hours.[52] Utter silence and discipline dominated these tours, and many a Plebe spent dozens of hours on weekends walking away their transgressions, marching monotonously back and forth with a rifle on their shoulder. Inclement weather never delayed carrying out a punishment tour, and those who accumulated more than 100 hours on the area were known as "Century Men." A handful of rebels, often those who chose to deliberately test the limits of the system or make themselves a legend within their class, even moved on to become "Double Century" cadets. Those who did so tempted the Fates, however, for receiving more than a prescribed number of demerits each month led to a review board and possible expulsion.

In addition to being constantly ready for questions and inspections from upperclassmen and completely prepared for classes, Plebes were also subject to an assortment of mundane duties which kept the Corps functioning. These jobs rotated among Plebes within each company, normally on a weekly basis. Laundry Carriers handled the pickup and delivery of both dirty and clean laundry; Orderlies handled the cleaning of common areas; Mail Carriers delivered newspapers (a copy of the *New York Times* for every cadet every morning), mail, and official Academy correspondence; Linen Carriers dealt with the pickup and delivery of bed linens; and Minute Callers barked out the time remaining prior to every formation which included more than half of the callers' company. To handle unanticipated situations, Company Minutemen stood by to be available on a minute's notice to handle special duties.[53]

In the Mess Hall, designated Plebes served at each table as Gunners and Hot and Cold Beverage Corporals. Beverage Corporals had to know the preferences of everyone at the table, even if wicked upperclassmen indicated their preferences varied according to the day of the week or the dish being served, and then serve beverages accordingly. Dessert Corporals handled and served desserts, and had the stressful responsibility of slicing pies and cakes into equally-sized portions depending on how many cadets at their table wanted to eat. This could be an agonizing endeavor because they had to make accurate slices regardless of how many people were at the table. Above all, they were to avoid marring the icing lest they face the wrath of the table commandant. (The key was to make templates for the number of pieces and to dip the knife into a glass of water to avoid marring the icing on cakes).[54] Those who butchered the job were often required to stand and shout, "SIR, THE DESSERT HAS BEEN RAPED, AND I DID IT!"[55] So it went, day after day, with Plebes eating meals at attention and by the book, sitting erect a fist's distance from the back of their chairs and cutting their food into tiny, bite-sized pieces. The routine relaxed only for those who received "Dear John" letters in the mail. They were often allowed to "fall out," or relax at mess the day the letter arrived.[56]

Besides being arcane and utterly alien when compared with life in the civilian or even the regular Army world, these rituals served to remind Plebes they lived in a world unto itself where nothing functioned as it had in their previous lives. Every ritual, every event, every encounter with an upperclassman created an occasion for pressured decisions and an opportunity for failure. All things being equal, they were opportunities for success as well, but few Plebes saw them that way. The penalties for failure were much greater than the rewards for success, and under the rigorous scrutiny of the upperclass and the grinding dawn to midnight schedule, every Plebe eventually failed at something many, many times. Cadets were under so much stress that some developed rashes or saw their faces break out, and most women stopped menstruating for extended periods. One women became so stressed during Beast that her body froze and she had to be carried on a stretcher to the West Point hospital. The attending psychiatrist said, "Your body is telling your mind what your mind won't accept. You don't want to be here. You might as well go home."[57] Little wonder that when parents or loved ones came to visit the Academy, Plebes were instructed to take a fellow cadet along just to get them out of the barracks and away from the stress for a little while too.[58]

Beyond these routines, running and physical fitness were the most important barometers of where cadets stood in the Academy pecking order, and Plebes quickly learned the paramount role of athletics. Douglas MacArthur formed the foundation for the focus on physical fitness and competition while serving as Superintendent, and penned the famous passage, "Upon the fields of friendly strife are sown the seeds that upon other fields, on other days, will bear the fruits of victory." It was a message the faithful believed at West Point, and every cadet participated in intramural or intercollegiate athletics. "Corps Squads" competed against other schools, while intramural sports pitted company against company in both the fall and spring. They included football, track, soccer, triathalon, flickerball, boxing, wrestling, and many others. The coaches, officials, and senior cadets in every sport were Firsties, so that even in sports upperclassmen were given experience in leadership.[59]

They used that experience primarily on Fourth Classmen, who learned the timeless truth that in the Army and at West Point only the group really mattered, that duty and sacrifice in the very best soldiers came before self. The nineteenth-century writer William Dean Howells noted the distinction between soldiers and civilians during a visit to West Point in 1891, proclaiming, "We civilians talk, we almost talk solely, of our rights, but in the army, it seems that men talk chiefly of their duties, . . . and never of their rights. . . . It seems to correct all the mistaken tendencies of the time before they became soldiers."[60] West Pointers shared such a view, and upperclassmen often took it upon themselves to pass it along to their subordinates.

Plebes also learned of the countless idiosyncracies of the specific and seemingly endless cadet vocabulary. To "smell hell" was to anticipate hazing.[61] "Flamers" were cadets or officers who were hard on Fourth Classmen, who were also known as "Beanheads," "Beaners," and "Smacks." Roommates were "wives," dates were "drags," and the path along the Hudson where cadets could escort guests was known as "Flirtation Walk," or "Flirty." The Brigade was formally known as the United States Corps of Cadets, which abbreviated U.S.C.C., and in cadet lore stood for "Uncle Sam's Community College." Cadets who were perfect in military bearing and knowledge were "STRAC," West Point itself became "Woo Poo," "Hudson High," or the "South Hudson Institute of Technology" (S.H.I.T); high ranking upperclassmen were known as "Striper Dogs," a reference to the large number of rank chevrons on their sleeves.[62]

To balance the demands of Plebe poop, academics, and athletics, there were social activities to keep cadets occupied year round. Seventy-six clubs offered a range of interests for every member of the Corps to pursue during his or her limited free time, and the large number of cadet hops held annually by the Academy meant weekends were often busy as well.[63]

Yet none of the social activities, none of the jargon or tradition, and certainly none of the Plebe poop could compete with the indelible mark made by hazing. An informal institution dominating every Plebe's life, hazing became a reality for most Plebes from their very first day on post. Ironically, such a means of discipline, training, and even tyrannical abuse should not have flourished at West Point, for officially it was neither encouraged nor permitted. Plebes even had to memorize "Schofield's Definition of Discipline," which read in part: "The discipline which makes the soldiers of a free country reliable in battle is not to be gained by harsh or tyrannical treatment. On the contrary, such treatment is far more likely to destroy than to make an army."[64] The phrase sounded good, and in the Regular Army it had meaning. At West Point, however, it usually fell on deaf ears among tradition-conscious upperclassmen.

As a rule, "hazing" referred to abusive or tyrannical behavior on the part of an upperclassman that by design indoctrinated, abused, or humiliated Plebes for no practical military or disciplinary reason. Officially banned, hazing began in 1865 when the Academy raised the upper age limit for admission to twenty-four in order to admit Civil War veterans. Desperate not to be intimidated by older combat-savvy plebes, upperclassmen instituted new forms of hazing to remain firmly in control. This stood in stark contrast to the earliest days of West Point, when Sylvanus Thayer insisted that each cadet behave as a gentleman, but over time hazing became a hallmark of the institution.[65] Hazing eventually carried real weight with everyone, from graduates to members of the Academy staff, and certainly among the ranks of the upper classes. This weight stemmed from the conviction that hazing made cadets strong, and the belief it represented a cohesive force among cadets from one generation to the next. As one writer noted, "Hazing is tolerated by the military authorities at West Point—not infrequently approved, openly or covertly. It is not one whit less binding upon the Academic Board, other military officials and the cadets of the military academy than the enactments of Congress."[66]

Hazing dated to the nineteenth century, when fraternities, the English school system, and other military institutions were also practitioners of the art. Cadets at the Virginia Military Institute required future Army Chief of Staff George C. Marshall to squat over a bayonet until his knees buckled and he fell on the upturned blade, narrowly escaping severe injury. Young men at The Citadel and countless other military academies duplicated his experience, for practitioners believed the practice made cadets tough.[67]

At West Point, the late nineteenth and early twentieth centuries were also eras when hazing became notoriously brutal. Upperclassmen called on more than a hundred different methods of making Plebe life miserable, including scalding steam baths, "dipping (pushups)," "eagling (deep knee bends over broken glass)," forced feeding, paddling, sliding down splinter boards naked, and running a gauntlet of upperclassmen tossing buckets of cold water. Generations of cadets suffered through these and other practices, including a young Douglas MacArthur. Three groups of upperclassmen once forced him to eagle for over an hour until he eventually fainted. The incident left MacArthur convulsing uncontrollably in his tent afterward, but he refused to allow his tent companion to request any assistance.[68] Plebes were sometimes required to address insects as equals, and anyone who protested the system was "called out" and beaten with bare knuckles by the biggest upperclassman in the Corps. This pattern held at a time when the Academy endured in geographic isolation, when cadets had little chance for a reprieve during their years at West Point. They were not allowed to dismount horses beyond The Plain, to go home for Christmas, or to leave the post except for Army–Navy football games and a brief furlough after their Cow year.[69]

By the middle of the twentieth century, the more violent forms of hazing faded from most companies, though a Plebe might still be asked to "swim to Newburgh," which meant balancing on top of the wall separating portions of older cadet rooms and duplicating the motions of a swimmer, or to sweat shadows or coins to the wall.[70] Some upperclassmen continued the practice of denying Plebes enough food, and virtually all practiced some sort of emotional, psychological, or physical harassment. While many graduates eventually applauded the reduction in brutal hazing, there were those who echoed the sentiments of General John J. Pershing, who had served as a notoriously brutal TAC at West Point and defended the spartan environment and training. Pershing even argued the merits of hazing, saying he hoped it would never end at West Point.[71]

While not as abusive as in the "Old Corps," in which upperclassmen sometimes had Plebes warm their toilet seats for them in the morning, hazing remained demanding in 1976.[72] Normally consisting of emotional, psychological, and physical challenges designed to push Plebes to the breaking point, it took on a wide variety of forms, including extra physical training, bracing, the endless recitation of "Plebe poop," and cheap shots during intramural sports.[73] There was also "crawling," in which upperclassmen subjected Plebes to a rapid barrage of questions and insults, and the hated "clothing formations," when Plebes responded to orders demanding they report in formation wearing certain uniforms, only to be given an impossible amount of time to change into another uniform and report to formation yet again.[74] "Magical Mystery Tours" involved seemingly endless recitations of Plebe poop to a never ending array of upperclassmen, who sent Plebes from one upperclassman's room to another to be hazed and run ragged in the process.[75] The ordeal could take hours, and ended only when upperclassmen tired of the proceedings, relented to allow Plebes to perform mandatory duties, or it came time for lights out.[76] "Round Robins" took place when Plebes were forced to move every minute to the next room down the hall; at each stop, upperclassmen would yell at and haze them.[77] Then there were "ski slopes," which required Plebes to put on all their field equipment, including helmet, web gear, rifle, and pack, and march from the barracks to the top of the Academy ski slope several miles away. Once there, the Plebe had to properly display the equipment on the ground, then put it all back on and hike back to the barracks.[78] Upperclassmen occasionally tried to intimidate or test Plebes, as when one Squad leader pointed his dress sword at a Plebe's nose and then thrust it into the wall by the frightened fourth classman's ear to see if he would scare easily.[79] Through these and other practices many Plebes lost the small amount of free time they had in the evenings for study or simple reflection, and they lost it in spite of the official prohibition placed on hazing by the Academy.

Many examples of hazing doubled as practical jokes and could be carried out either in a humorous or a profoundly mean-spirited manner. Cadets who were "Rat-Fucked," for example, returned to their rooms to find their drawers and closets emptied and all of their possessions thrown on the floor. Beds usually were turned over and shorn of their sheets, and in extreme cases doused with some sort of liquid (water or urine were readily available). Conducted mildly, the practice might celebrate a cadet's birthday, and was occasionally called a "whirlwind." Carried out viciously as a kind of punishment, it meant more stress and work for a victimized cadet perhaps already thinking of leaving the Academy. On a more personal level, the phrase also described the practice of stripping cadets and tying them to trees or other solid objects in a public place. One Class of 1980 cadet saw a visiting Air Force Academy cadet stripped and tied to a chair with tape, covered with toilet paper, and placed in the Central Area between the barracks. Again, while never pleasant, such an activity could be carried out by cadets along a wide spectrum of viciousness, depending upon how far they stripped their victims and how long they left them exposed. The same held true for "blanket parties," in which cadets were covered with blankets and jostled around or perhaps beaten by fellow cadets. Done mildly, it was a prank. Done severely, it represented an extreme form of abuse.[80]

For the women of the Class of 1980, hazing often seemed more personal and driven by appearance and gender rather than just tradition. Women who were considered cute or attractive, for example, inevitably suffered the accusation they used their looks to try and minimize hazing or duties. Cadets referred to any success at lessening the arbitrary harshness of cadet life as "getting over," and those who overtly attempted to get over were despised by their peers. Almost all cadets attempted to covertly get over, and those who were the most successful earned the of admiration of their peers because cadets uniformly suffered at least some of the injustices of the West Point system and could understand anyone who honorably tried to beat the system. A thin line existed between overt and covert efforts, however, almost as thin as the line between breaking a rule and violating the Honor Code. Women thus ran the risk of being accused of a cardinal sin simply because a male cadet thought they were attractive. And the allure of a pretty face often led to other harassment as well. Some upperclassmen quickly realized they could only pay attention to (or flirt with) a Plebe woman for an extended period while they were on duty, and that almost always meant more hazing for the woman in question.[81] In that sense physical attractiveness mattered a great deal for women, but usually in a negative way. The most attractive women received greater attention from the upperclass; as every West Pointer knew, attention virtually guaranteed more hazing. Anything, in fact, which made cadets stand out carried with it the certainty of bringing unwanted attention, for at West Point "to be different is to be in trouble."[82] Being unattractive meant being different too, but it seemed to draw less attention, especially if the women concerned was "squared away." In any case, women received far more hazing than their male classmates, regardless of the motives of upperclassmen.[83]

To be fair, attractiveness mattered for men too. No ugly, dumpy young man ever became First Captain, for example, and West Point had regulations barring the admission of cadets who were deemed unattractive. There were minimum and maximum height and weight requirements, and in rare cases applicants could be given medical exclusion for extreme acne scars. Cadets also hazed men who were ugly or overweight. In one instance, after failing to run an overweight male cadet out of the Academy via the Honor Code, upperclassmen began leaving candy bars in his room.[84] Everyone, it turned out, had to look and act within the envelope of what constituted a "proper" cadet. As one graduate put it, "If you don't look the part, you have the silent permission of everyone who does to be intimidated."[85]

And while it is true that looks matter among almost all human groups, at West Point their importance had official sanction. Cadets had to submit photographs of themselves in full body profile wearing swimsuits prior to admission and updated photos when being considered for promotion. The reasoning, according to one graduate, was that good appearance and physical fitness went hand in hand.[86] At West Point, there was actually a measurable correlation between looks and cadet rank, and then between cadet rank and the eventual rank a West Point graduate reached in the Army.[87]

The importance of being attractive was noticeable in the real Army too, where "studs with a little gray and a blaze of medals" often had a far better chance of promotion than even the most talented officers who did not have the right look.[88] While deplorable if taken to an extreme, the phenomenon was hardly different than the more understated but identical pattern among executives of Fortune 500 Companies or stars and starlets in the entertainment industry. Looks matter in American culture and in virtually all human affairs, for as Herman Melville put it, "there is an aesthetic in all things. . . ."[89]

At West Point, however, everything physical mattered, not just looks. While male cadets were certainly horrendous in their treatment of many women, they were not entirely atavistic. Height, weight, and physical performance of all kinds were proof of prowess and leadership. From Sylvanus Thayer's days in the early 1800s for example, right up until 1957, every cadet at West Point received a company assignment based on his height. The tallest cadets were placed in "flanker companies," which got their name from the fact they were usually assigned to the flanks of the Corps when on parade. Shorter cadets found themselves in "runt" companies, which over time became famous for producing the meanest, nastiest cadets and the most brutal hazing rituals.[90] On parade the results were impressive; the height differences between individual cadets were too small to be noticed in individual companies or at a distance, and when assembled en masse the Corps seemed a uniform, inexorable juggernaut. It was beautiful. And while the Corps on parade in the modern era remained imposing and impressive as well, there were many Old Grads who insisted that doing away with the runt and flanker companies had ruined the apparent uniformity that made parades so spectacular. Looks, it seemed, mattered as much for the group as for individuals.

These rituals, traditions, and customs, whether they involved the Corps on parade or the administering of hazing, flourished in part because they relied on the adolescent world of young men, a world which the regulations at West Point easily froze in time. Many women were appalled by the common behavior of male cadets who seemed locked in a fifteen-year-old's time warp. Part of the problem stemmed from the fact that men and women matured at different rates;

the rest came from the Academy itself. By creating an artificial world regulating every aspect of a cadet's life, West Point took away much of the normal peer socialization pattern of choice and consequence that usually regulates human conduct. At the same time, the Academy also gave cadets a level of responsibility with virtually no equivalent in civilian life, and the chasm between the extreme kinds of responsibilities they were granted and the more mundane ones they were denied sometimes became problematic. Upperclassmen might be given the responsibility for a platoon of cadets, for example, and at the same time be denied the freedom to decide when they should return to their barracks at night. The rigidly hierarchical system made these decisions for them; in fact, it made almost all of their decisions, even those of a social nature. It told them when and how to do everything, from when they could eat to what they could wear to what time to go to bed at night and get up in the morning. This artificial world demanded very little emotional growth from cadets, who could survive and even flourish within because it demanded so little choice. A cadet's life required responsibility and discipline, but within the confines of West Point it offered very little freedom. That lack of freedom and the lack of ubiquitous opportunities to make individual decisions and mistakes and then learn from them became the foundation for the notoriously wild behavior of many cadets on leave. Given a measure of freedom, even for a limited period, they rushed to do as much as possible within the allotted time, whether it was drinking, dating, eating, or sleeping. These periods of unbridled freedom were always limited; when they were over, cadets returned to an Academy life in which an understanding of the rules and a willingness to live within them provided good odds of survival and even graduation. In this environment cadets also enjoyed tremendous power over their peers; because so many were young and sometimes very immature, petty individuals, there were bound to be abuses. In a way a European peasant living under divine right monarchy in the Middle Ages would have understood with great clarity, *rank mattered*. Ineptitude or meanness were simply to be endured unless they became so egregious that outside intervention proved necessary.

The worst hazers usually worked in packs like jackals, gaining strength in numbers. As one cadet put it, "They are always in a group. There is never any one-on-one."[91] It had always been that way at the Academy, just as in fraternities, gangs, and other social organizations where some form of abuse formed part of initiation rituals. In fact, hazing represented the fundamental component of initiation in most all-male groups throughout history, especially when those groups committed themselves to some form of violence. The standard elements of initiation included being "separated from the women and being kept in seclusion," being "hazed and humiliated by their elders," and being "compelled to learn masses of arcane wisdom, as well as the proper conduct of ritual and the proper cherishing of myths and traditions of the group."[92] Warriors around the world, be they members of stone-age tribal societies or state-sanctioned armed forces, were as familiar with this process as cadets at West Point. Hazing became less and less acceptable during the twentieth century, when critics argued that it was too brutal and primitive to be of any value, but it endured in a variety of shapes and forms just the same.

Even as hazing declined, especially in Western Europe and the United States, there were those who defended the practice well into the modern era. Rear Admiral James B. Stockdale suffered eight years as a prisoner of war in North Vietnam, and argued after his release that hazing at the United States Naval Academy had helped steel him for the privations and degradations of being a POW. "I came out of prison being very happy about the merits of Plebe year at the Naval Academy," he said, adding, "I hope we do not ever dilute those things. You have to practice being hazed. You have to learn to take a bunch of junk and accept it with a sense of humor."[93] A West Point graduate from the 1940s echoed this attitude succinctly. "We were not guard-house lawyers in my era," he wrote. "And surviving such treatment [hazing] pulled our class together as an entity."[94]

Pulling units together constituted the most powerful positive influence those who defended hazing could point toward. While no one sought to defend abuse, there were those who argued that hazing provided a form of shared adversity and a rite of passage that made people bond together in the face of common enemies. That bond, what military leaders called unit cohesion, became the indispensable and historically proven factor that made the best units fight while others fell to pieces in the cauldron of combat. During the battles around Neuve Chapell in France in 1915, for example, the 2nd Scottish Rifles entered the fighting with over 900 men and emerged from the trenches five days later with less than 150 and only one surviving officer. Yet the unit did not collapse or break down, and John Baynes argued the reason lay in a series of rites of passage which created a loyalty to the unit transcending the fear of personal sacrifice. More than religion, patriotism, or even fear, Baynes believed, shared experiences and a pervasive refusal to let the unit down held the 2nd Scottish Rifles together; on a smaller scale and in less frightening circumstances, West Point tried to use similar rituals to push cadets closer to each other. The theory behind such practices held that "Equality under stress fosters group solidarity . . ." that "the tougher the treatment, the prouder the sense of inclusion," and it seemed justified because historically the proudest, most effective combat units were always those in which membership remained the most difficult to obtain.[95]

There were also those who defended hazing precisely *because* it was unfair, arbitrary, harsh, and degrading, for in those details it reflected life on battlefields. During a dinner at The Citadel, a military college in South Carolina, a retired Army general and West Point graduate told historian John Keegan that in his era the Academy had been so tough and disciplined that little in World War II surprised him. In his view, "when every inch of self . . . has been subjected to the regulation of a higher, institutional will, the individual loses the capacity to protest against the cruelties and unfairness of the battlefield."[96] His views would have struck many educators as abhorrent, especially if they were ignorant of the

calamitous and capricious nature of battle. Among those charged with training
military officers, however, especially if they were products of a system of education that emphasized hazing, they were widely held indeed.

The problem, of course, came when one tried to determine the difference
between hazing that served a purpose and hazing pursued for pure sport, between
calculated rites of passage and mere brutality masquerading as tradition. "One
man's harassment is another man's hurdle to belonging to a unit," according to
General William Knowlton, and the gray area between abuse and more constructive bonding rituals often blurred because rites of passage had a life of their
own at the Academy. They were associated with toughness, with tradition, and
with being "manly," and upperclassmen proved recalcitrant when it came to
doing away with rigors that they had endured as Plebes. Efforts to eradicate
hazing usually met with scorn from those who argued it had to be difficult and
demeaning in order to make cadets tough and from others who enjoyed the
enormous power hazing gave them over fourth year cadets. At West Point the
arrival of women complicated this situation, because it became vital, if sometimes difficult, to determine the difference between harassment aimed at women
because they were Plebes and harassment driven by sexism.[97] For example, if
an upperclassman asked a Plebe, "Do you want to listen to music and hang
around?" and the Plebe said "yes," it meant he or she got to hang by his or her
fingers in the upperclassman's closet while music played on a stereo.[98] That sort
of treatment usually had nothing to do with a cadet's sexuality. Unfortunately,
other kinds of treatment clearly did.

And the most abusive kinds of harassment proved that hazing represented far
more than a process designed to steel individuals for the rigors of combat.
Instead, hazing also served as a tool of social power within the Academy. It
defined those who were in control and those who were not. Ultimately, it also
became a weapon used against those whom cadets collectively wished to run
out, whether they were African American cadets in the nineteenth century or
women in the 1970s. Women received especially high levels of harassment
because they threatened the last and perhaps most important role of hazing at
West Point: defining masculinity and making men. Those cadets at West Point
who saw the process of becoming a man at the Academy threatened by women
reacted almost immediately in powerfully abusive ways to protect their rights
and rituals. They spit on women, punched and kicked them, and called them
derogatory names. Old Grads often refused to return female salutes at Hops or
ceremonial occasions, and some blamed female cadets for the poor performance
of the Army football team.[99] One approached a female cadet inside the West
Point Officer's Club and asked, "What the hell are you doing at West Point?"[100]

A small number of upperclassmen went beyond verbal criticism and deliberately tried to run women out.[101] At a company inspection during Beast Barracks one squad leader howled, "I'm gonna get every one of you fuckin bitches
out of here!"[102] Another upperclassman made similar remarks privately. While
discussing the prospect that female cadets might one day graduate from the

Academy he leaned in and whispered to one woman, "Never. You are never going to graduate from West Point. I am going to make sure of it."[103] One woman in the Class of 1980 found herself called into an upperclassman's room every day for a week so he could explain to her how much men respected West Point, how she was ruining it, and then ask how in good conscience she could possible stay.[104] This routine continued unabated until it was finally stopped by the female cadet's company commander. In another case, a squad leader told the women in his unit that he would not recommend them for formal admission to the Corps at the end of their Plebe year because "God did not make women to be soldiers."[105] And in one regiment, a company commander held regular (and prohibited) formations of all the Plebe women in his unit every morning before reveille for weeks. He did so in order to haze them and to announce his personal intention to run every woman out of his command.[106]

These personal attacks blended with a more general sort of harassment toward female cadets to create an atmosphere in which few women could ever really relax or feel comfortable at West Point. Female cadets who called out "Good morning, Sir" when passing upperclassmen often heard "Good morning, bitch" in return; in one famous exchange, an upperclassman responded, "It's not going to be a good morning until you goddamn bitches get out of here."[107] Women saw sexual slurs on barracks walls, had condoms placed on their bunks, and received vibrators through the mail from male cadets. A few even had dress sabers thrust through their pillows and bed linens, or left shoved through the middle of their mattresses.[108] Others had water balloons, eggs, tomatoes, and condoms full of water thrown at them from barracks windows or into their rooms, or had salt thrown in their beds.[109] If they were considered too feminine men called them "fluffs," while those deemed too masculine were "dykes." Some women tried to blend in by lowering their voices and avoiding makeup, and a few even had "command voice practice down in the locker room."[110] Others starved themselves and became anorexic, because losing their curves made them harder to identify at a distance.[111] Men resented them anyway. They made fun of women for their inferior upper body strength and endurance, their longer hair, and especially resented the attention women received from the Great American Public (GAP), which fawned on them like tourists chasing the "bears at Yellowstone."[112]

Female cadets also endured whistling, name calling, and being patted on the behind by male cadets, and some struggled to deal with upperclassmen entering their rooms without permission.[113] Rumors abounded about how each of the sex-integrated companies in the Corps actually functioned as brothels; in one company, a group of men organized a contest to reduce every woman in the unit to tears at least once.[114] Other upperclassmen used food as a weapon. One refused to allow women to eat at his table in the mess hall until told to do so by the chain of command.[115] Others starved almost all Plebes, to the point that one member of the Academy staff began routinely sneaking them food.[116] Those who could eat often suffered at the hands of upperclassmen who made fun of women that gained weight consuming the Academy's 4,000 calorie a day diet. Those women, they said, had caught the dreaded "Hudson Hip Disease," and a running Academy joke began with the question, "What is the difference between a female cadet and a squad car?" The answer was, "It takes two squad cars to make a roadblock."[117]

Some upperclassmen regularly went into cadet rooms and used their sabers to scratch female shoes and belt buckles. Later, they would return and write up those same cadets because their equipment had become damaged.[118] No doubt this sort of behavior plagued some male cadets as well; in the midst of this litany of various forms of harassment directed against female cadets, it should be remembered that *every* cadet had to deal with harassment of some kind at West Point. Again, the issue is how much and what kind of harassment cadets faced and why the harassment occurred. Viewed that way, there is no question that female cadets as a group endured greater and more vicious harassment than their male peers and that much of the harassment and hazing came not because they were poor cadets, but simply because they were women.

The pressure this harassment created is difficult to fathom because it enveloped many female cadets entirely, leaving very little opportunity to escape for even a brief period. One female cadet who later graduated became so fearful of hazing in the hallways that she urinated in her sink rather than risk an encounter with an upperclassman during a walk to the bathroom.[119] Some male cadets became expert at making derogatory comments about women between themselves in voices deliberately loud enough to be overhead. "She's easy," they would say. "Just think about getting into bed with her." They made comments about women's breasts and buttocks, criticized female cadets en masse, and told individual cadets they were not real women. "If you were a real woman you wouldn't be here," they would say. "I have a real woman at home."[120] Women who wore makeup were "whores," while those who did not wear makeup were judged to be gay.[121] Over the years, some female cadets developed a willingness to stand up to upperclassmen in these situations; in most cases, the male cadets backed down.[122] In the interim, however, the suffering continued, and how many female cadets were driven out of the Corps who might have made fine officers and served their country with distinction will never be known.

On many occasions the harassment even became physical. In a subtle example, male upperclassmen in one company made a habit of running their fingers down the backs of female cadets during inspections to make sure they were wearing bras.[123] In more brazen instances, female cadets were roughly handled by members of the upper classes. "We had girls molested, we had women who were, you know, harassed, we had people physically handled," said one cadet. She later recounted an incident in which a classmate wore a newly issued cadet skirt to a regimental formation before dinner. On the way into the mess hall the regimental commander grabbed her by her skirt, pulled her down some stairs, and then snarled, "Look bitch. If you ever wear this skirt in my formation again I'll have your ass, okay?"[124]

This pattern of harassment grew increasingly distinctive because it targeted cadets on the basis of their sex alone. They were hazed primarily *because they were women*, rather than on the basis of a perceived weakness that might be addressed like physical fitness or personality. In this sense, the first female cadets at West Point had much in common with the first African Americans at the Academy, for both groups were persecuted on the basis of characteristics (race and sex) that could never be changed. Both thus faced harassment with no prospect of winning over the hard core of cadets who committed themselves to persecution. Overweight cadets might get in shape, those whose personalities rubbed their peers the wrong way might improve their people skills or attempt to blend in, but for women and African Americans there existed no hope of redemption save time. The first African American to graduate West Point was Henry Ossian Flipper, Class of 1877, and between his nightmarish cadet years and the 1970s the most virulent forms of racism had vanished. African American cadets faced far fewer institutional or societal hurdles than in the nineteenth and early twentieth centuries; for women, the battle had only just begun.

Some battles took place in the classroom, where a minority of the faculty and staff contributed to the persecution of female cadets by telling inappropriate jokes or singling women out for attention. "What do you call a Plebe swimming class full of women?" asked one instructor. His answer: "The Bay of Pigs."[125] Another faculty member privately told a female cadet to resign because she did not belong at West Point.[126] While most members of the faculty conducted themselves professionally and made no mention of their feelings about the admission of women in class, enough did to make an impression with some women cadets. As one put it, "I truly was shocked at the prejudice—the 'we don't want you here kind of stuff'—from the faculty, [and] from fellow cadets."[127]

Ironically, the admission of women even caused consternation at sporting events, where for the first time female cheerleaders joined the Army's famous 'Rabble Rousers' in zealously promoting Army spirit. Some men welcomed women into the prototypically traditional American role of cheerleader, seeing them as a welcome addition to the historically all-male Rabble Rousers. Others, however, felt the presence of women lessened the martial spirit of football games, made West Point seem too much like regular civilian colleges, and were uncomfortable seeing fellow cadets cast as traditional sex-objects on the sidelines. Rather than finding acceptance in a traditional role, cheerleaders thus found themselves recipients of an odd mixture of hatred, resentment, attraction, and repression all at the same time. They also became visible targets for harassment, as an incident in September of 1976 made clear. Prior to a home football game, members of the Class of 1979 produced a banner showing a male Rabble Rouser holding a female cheerleader over his head. In successive frames he lowered the woman on to his face, while the caption proclaimed, "Rah! Rah! RAW!" Unfurled at a pep rally, the banner almost triggered a riot among frenzied male cadets.[128]

In this environment of harassment and contempt for women there were many men who tried to stem the misogynistic tide. Major George Crocker, the A-1 TAC, promised the women in his company they would be neither "harassed out of the academy" nor "coddled," and along with some other TACs attempted to quietly protect women from undue harassment.[129] Some physical education instructors also attempted to explain the necessity for different physical fitness standards for men and women. One explained it by saying, "Okay, guys, physiologically the women have 40 percent more body fat, so just to make it even, let's give you a seventy-pound weight to carry. They have only 60 percent as much lung capacity, so let's degrade your breathing by making you wear this mask." He pointed out that women "have a little mechanical disadvantage in their hip structure, so we'll put a brace between your legs to make you pigeontoed. Now go run a mile, guys, and see if you can keep up with the women."[130] His stirring appeal to reason unfortunately fell on deaf ears; despite his efforts, a great many female cadets continued to suffer relentless harassment.

Yet there were other men who tried to see that women were treated fairly. TACS often quietly ran interference for female cadets by checking on them under the guise of routine security checks, or handled problems unobtrusively so as not to create more resentment toward women.[131] Some male cadets quietly spoke up when women were being unduly harassed or worked behind the scenes to calm their most bitter and angry peers and encourage them to act more professionally toward female cadets.[132] "There were a lot of our classmates that were very supportive," said one female member of the Class of 1980, and her comments rang true for many members of the upper classes as well.[133] A majority of them never purposely tried to run female cadets out of the United States Military Academy, and whatever their personal feelings, most tried to do their best and be fair.[134] The minority that did not, however, enjoyed great freedom of action either because their superiors looked the other way when they behaved improperly or because very few cadets understood what some women were facing. Male cadets were just as isolated within their companies as females and just as likely to be so immersed in trying to survive the rigors of the Academy that they never really understood what went on outside their squad or company. Certainly there were too many men who deliberately ignored or condoned despicable behavior toward women, and it is no mitigation of the responsibility cadet and Academy leaders had for protecting *every* cadet under their command to say that not all men were to blame for sexual harassment at West Point. It is only to say that blame should be apportioned specifically rather than generally, and that those male cadets who supported their classmates regardless of sex should be as highly praised as those cadets who tried to run women out of the Academy should be rigorously condemned. As one woman put it, "We all knew who the 'good guys' were." They were men who would buck peer pressure to support their female classmates, and in her view were the "real heroes" of the Class of 1980.[135]

It should also be noted that many women found ways to cope with the abuse in the barracks, whether through after-taps conversations with roommates, conversations with friends, or letters to and from family members. One group of women in Fourth Regiment even found themselves able to battle the plots of the men in their company thanks to the design of their barracks. Renovation had placed the women's bathroom on their floor across the hall from their company commander's room, and each night he gathered his platoon leaders to decide which Plebes would receive the bulk of harassment the following day. By positioning themselves in the bathroom and listening in on these conversations, the women could plan in advance how best to keep targeted female cadets as far away from the chain of command as possible. They were not always successful, of course, but even a modest sense of control over one's fate meant a great deal to Plebes at West Point. So did knowing other cadets were looking out for them.

While women in Fourth Regiment and others like them subtly battled (as Plebes always do) the upperclassmen, the resistance to female cadets at West Point became so pervasive in some circles that Class of 1980 men were judged guilty by association. They were blamed for bringing women in with them. "Jesus Christ," an upperclassman would say to a male Plebe, "your class doesn't even average 2.0 balls per cadet!" This disdain made it difficult for men to support women, especially if they were in a company that resented women en masse. Anyone who spoke out openly in support of women in the Class of 1980 usually "caught hell."[136] In this cauldron of peer pressure many men in the Class of 1980 quickly learned to despise women at the Academy. As one reflected years later, "Not having an opinion before I got there, I determined very rapidly that if I had to be for or against it [the admission of women], it was in my best interests in terms of self-preservation to be against."[137]

Like the men of the Class of 1980, female officers at West Point also received a fair amount of disdain or resentment as a result of the admission of women to the Academy. One former staffer said male cadets would cross the street to avoid saluting her and often behaved in a disrespectful manner. She solved the problem by talking it over with the Cadet First Captain. Afterward, she said male cadets would aggressively seek her out to offer up salutes, even when she wore civilian clothes.[138] Everyone, it seemed, had to deal with the repercussions stemming from the admission of women to West Point sooner or later.

In the midst of this resentment, female cadets often received a mixture of protection and harassment by dating upperclassmen, a practice which flourished soon after their arrival in July. Interestingly, the cadet newspaper predicted just such a development even before women were admitted. In an April 1976 issue of *The Pointer*, Cadet Eric Pointe parodied Shakespeare with a brief version of *Romeo and Juliet* in which the star-crossed lovers were cadets. Entitled "Romeo and Juliet and Whiskey Papa," Pointe's rendition followed Romeo and Juliet as they were forced to hide their affections behind regulations and officially sanctioned behavior. The most revealing passage came from the character Benvolio, who decried the attention given to women Plebes by upperclassmen. "There has been a rash outbreak of indiscriminate recognition throughout the Corps" he said. "The few girls in our regiment have been recognized by half the Corps from the three other regiments . . . You know the kind . . . the type that say come to my room to listen to my stereo and have some pizza."[139] It hardly took studies or analysis to conclude there would be dating between men and women cadets, and the Corps quietly recognized that truth long before women cadets even arrived. What it did not publicly acknowledge were the ways in which dating proved to be a far greater liability for some women than for men.

Academy leaders anticipated dating as well, and they attempted to balance the need to preserve professional distance between Plebes and upperclassmen with a recognition that romantic and sexual liaisons were inevitable. They did so by sanctioning romantic relationships only between Plebes, meaning Plebes could date each other but not upperclassmen. In theory, the rule protected Plebes and upperclassmen alike from the pitfalls inherent in a system where military rank and romantic relationships might become intertwined. In practice, the rule proved impossible to enforce uniformly, and it served as a benchmark for acceptable behavior only among those cadets professional enough to impose it meaningfully on themselves.

Even within the rules, however, cadets risked a great deal when they dated each other, with Plebes predictably facing the greatest number of hurdles. Beyond the jealousy of men who were not dating women within the Corps and aside from the distractions of flirting and finding precious time to be alone, Plebes risked harassment from their peers and upperclassmen and faced a variety of rules which made conventional dating impossible. They had no cars, little free time, almost no privacy, and few places to go together where they could be alone. Regulations stipulated that doors to cadet rooms had to be open if men and women were inside, and traffic outside these rooms sometimes increased as curious cadets walked by and glanced inward to see what their neighbors were doing. One TAC even used masking tape on the floor to mark how far cadets should open their door when women in his company entertained men.[140] The risks were magnified if either cadet in a relationship found him- or herself assigned to a company known for despising women, or if they crossed company lines. "God have mercy on those Plebes who crossed the company/ regiment lines to date a female Plebe in a company of woman haters," wrote one cadet, who described how upperclassmen often tried to break up such relationships as soon as possible. Plebes from other regiments seeking their "date" were "run off", and curious upperclassmen often hounded the male in a dating relationship with questions regarding whether "Ms.———was 'putting out'," and argued the Honor Code compelled the Plebe to answer. If the male cadet responded in the affirmative, then he risked more hounding and demands for details.[141] This pattern of inquest increased rather than diminished with time, and male cadets known to have slept with a woman cadet were eventually derisively said to have earned their "Gray Wings."[142] In short, a great deal of abuse often accompanied dating, and cadets of either sex went to great lengths to keep their relationships as secret as possible.

When upperclassmen dated Plebes the dynamic changed considerably, with the seniority and rank of the upperclassman a distinctively different factor influencing the relationship. These relationships faced even greater hurdles than those between Plebes, for they existed in outright defiance of Academy regulations and tradition. In particular, they violated the prohibition on upperclassmen "recognizing" Fourth Classmen. The Academy defined recognition as the "establishment of a personal relationship between an upperclassman and a Fourth Classman on an individual basis," and such relationships were customarily established via a handshake. Historically, recognition occurred between two male cadets, and West Point tightly regulated the practice in order to keep cadets at a comfortable professional distance from their superiors. This distance eased training and helped Plebes adjust to the formality of military life. When women arrived at West Point, Academy leaders hoped the regulations would also serve as a barrier against problems associated with fraternization between the sexes. Traditionally, Fourth Classmen earned recognition by the Corps immediately following the Graduation Parade for the First Class in May or June. This rite of passage signified the termination of a difficult first year and a triumphant milestone in cadet life. It endured as a prominent highlight of Plebe year because it signified to Fourth Classmen their full admission into the Corps as upperclassmen and their place in the society of soldiers.[143]

In theory, the barrier between Plebes and the upperclass remained absolute. In practice, however, it had always been more porous than purists liked to admit. Many upperclassmen recognized Plebes early, especially if they were involved in cadet clubs or on USMA athletic squads with them. Such recognition made practical sense in these cases, because too much formality on a football field or basketball court made teamwork impossible. Even in these instances, however, the Academy had rules to govern cadet life, and early recognition of a Fourth Classman could be tolerated in specific instances provided the Plebe did not serve in the same battalion as the upperclassman. Dating destroyed the principle in theory and in practice, for it became impossible for men and women who were familiar or intimate to play the officially sanctioned roles of senior and subordinate. The limited number of women at West Point, and the fact that not all of them dated upperclassmen, kept male-female recognition fairly limited, but it became a source of friction within the Corps because Plebe women who dated outside their class were seen as "getting over."

Some women in the Class of 1980 minimized the risks of romantic liaison by refusing to date men outside their own class, arguing it caused problems because it broke the fraternal bond between classmates and because the men usually got too protective or jealous. Even perceptions could be damning. Those who were seen alone with a man were subject to dirty looks and the ubiquitous rumor mill; rather than face a gauntlet of suspicion and harassment, some women chose not to date men outside their class under any circumstances.[144]

Even so, dating flourished from the very beginning, despite the fact it involved risk for everyone involved. Men who dated women cadets were often hated by their peers and sometimes harassed by the Academy staff. One male cadet found himself "frozen out" by his TACs once it became clear he and another cadet were dating.[145] Another had friends say to him, "You are an attractive guy. There's nothing wrong with you. Why are you dating a female cadet?"[146] Women risked being labeled "easy", and while all cadets had to deal with the "anxiety, jealousy, and envy" dating produced, the risks for women were always higher.[147] If a woman broke up with an upperclassman, for example, she risked hazing from the upperclassman in question and often from his friends as well.[148]

Those who chose to date sometimes snuck male cadets into their rooms after taps, which put their roommate at risk of punishment and created a number of awkward situations. Female cadets sometimes stumbled over the boyfriend of their roommate in the dark, or lost precious sleep because the lovers in their midst made too much noise. Not all women engaged in such activity, of course, and the consensus among those that graduated is that most women who snuck men into the barracks eventually left the Academy. It should also be remembered that sneaking a member of the opposite sex into the barracks was hardly a new idea in the late 1970s. Male cadets had infrequently brought women on post after taps for years. The risks for male cadets, however, were not the same, and those female cadets who did chance nightly liaisons brought an added dimension of anxiety to themselves and their roommates which few male cadets ever shared.[149]

Those who chose to attempt romantic relationships within the confines of West Point also had to figure out where to meet, and cadets became ingeniously creative in finding places to be alone, especially on weekends. They met at the homes of faculty sponsors, in the library (especially on the upper floors), behind Fort Putnam, and, like generations of cadets before them, in the woods. These outdoor encounters carried with them the risk of being found by other cadets, some of whom snuck into the woods above the Academy to get drunk. One couple under a blanket found themselves surrounded by rowdy cadets one evening and hid for hours until finally deciding to make a run for safety. When challenged by the heretofore unaware group, they pointed out that none of them were supposed to be there, and the moment passed without anyone getting caught. On another occasion, a couple spending the night in the woods found themselves surrounded by fishermen because they camped too close to a pond.[150] And on an evening full of warnings for all would-be lovers of nature, two cadets chose an inopportune spot to consummate their passion in the summer of 1977. Both found themselves covered with poison ivy in their most private regions and suffered largely in silence (amidst the snickering of their classmates) because they could not go to the West Point doctor. An Army physician, after all, would have asked how they got the poison ivy rash; in such a situation, the Honor Code would have forced confessions that promised both demerits and punishment tours writ large.[151] Dating at West Point, it turned out, carried with it all sorts of risk.

Even women who refused to date other cadets were often drawn into the complexities of sexual politics, because refusing the advances of an upperclassman meant risking more hazing. One woman in the Class of 1980, for example, found herself pursued relentlessly by an upperclassman. He asked again and again for dates, and when she politely refused or tried to change the subject he pressed even harder. Eventually he decided she needed proof of his intentions and gave her a copy of the book *Everything You Wanted to Know About Sex But Were Afraid to Ask*. Frustrated and angry, she burned the book in her trash can, only to get slugged for damaging government property because part of the can melted during the fire.[152]

Yet for all the novelty and difficulty inherent in dealing with romantic liaisons, the effort to confine dating within a military environment represented only one of the many battles West Point waged with American culture. Cumulatively, the Academy faced a daunting array of opponents, for it attempted to obliterate everything that delineated one civilian from another. Race, class, education, and ethnicity were all to be overwhelmed by Cadet Gray, by the commitment to Duty, Honor, and Country that transcended the petty divisions of nonmilitary life and which West Pointers made their credo. By and large, West Point enjoyed great success in these battles, just as it did on more traditional military fields of strife. Not always, of course, and not permanently, but over the years the Army and the Academy had consistently turned people into dogfaces, grunts, Plebes, enlisted soldiers, and officers, and the old differences were pushed aside as much as possible. The very best armed forces always knew how to "obliterate the distinction between 'thou' and 'I' in favor of 'we,' " and West Point long ago mastered the process of minimizing those differences among men. Obliterating gender distinctions, however, proved far more difficult.[153]

Those gender distinctions were manifest in physical performance, in dating, in cultural assumptions, and in a variety of Academy regulations specific to women which caused resentment among many male cadets. Men initially had v-neck t-shirts while women had crew neck t-shirts, women ran with the M-16 instead of the standard M-14 because the former was two pounds lighter, and the operating rod springs on M-14s were cut down for women to make it easier for them to open the bolt of the rifle with the side of one hand during the inspection of arms in formation. Each of these changes convinced some cadets that women simply did not and could not measure up, despite the fact no one argued using the side of one hand to pull back the bolt of a rifle would ever make sense in combat. What they did argue was that women seemed to need special treatment, and it angered many men. Most never seemed to realize that some men shortened the springs on their rifles as well, and the story of the shortened springs swiftly spread into the community of West Point graduates and the Army at large as proof women could not make it on their own.[154]

Another constant source of fuel for the animosity so many men at West Point felt toward women cadets came from the incessant attention the press directed toward everything related to women at the Academy. Anything female cadets did seemed to be treated with inordinate fanfare, even if hundreds of male cadets had accomplished the same activities for many years. In an environment where all cadets struggled, the extra praise and publicity showered on women made some male cadets livid. As one woman from the Class of 1980 put it years later, the press coverage "resulted in much of the animosity from our own male class-mates." Ironically, she added, all the glory heaped on women may have made some of the men feel like "second class citizens."[155]

Some men responded by using the press attention as one more excuse for victimizing female cadets, especially when reporters from the *New York Times* took photos of or quoted West Point women in articles. Cadets received a copy of the *Times* every morning, and the proximity of West Point to New York City meant the paper paid far more attention to the USMA than almost any other newspaper in the country. Those two facts conspired to make life more stressful for female cadets, even if they tried to avoid interviews and photographs. One cadet found herself harassed for appearing on the front page of the Sunday *Times*, for example, despite the fact she had eluded a pursuing photographer for several hours. He finally succeeded in taking her picture when regulations dictated she stop to salute the American flag during the playing of the "Star Spangled Banner." It made for a patriotic, poignant moment, but she suffered harassment for a long, long time.[156] Other women found themselves quoted and misquoted in the *Times*, suffering harassment as a result even when the Academy arranged the interview without checking with the cadet in question first. After the publication of one such interview, men in the quoted female cadet's company lined up to urinate on the article.[157]

These behavioral harassments joined with less deliberate but still frustrating reminders that the Academy found itself in uncharted territory when it came to the presence of women at West Point. Among the most frustrating were the changes made to the Full Dress uniform designed for female cadets. The original uniform dated to 1816, when the Secretary of War formally approved new and distinctively gray uniforms at the Military Academy. Legend has it that gray was chosen to honor the performance of American troops under General Winfield Scott at the battles of Chippewa and Lundy's Lane in Upper Canada during the War of 1812, but that legend is most likely a myth. Scott's troops wore gray during those battles because regulation blue uniforms were in short supply, and though they fought well against British regulars, there is no evidence the Army deliberately chose to honor the color of their uniforms. The real attraction of gray was that it was less expensive to produce, and the Secretary of War was probably moved more by economics and less by any sense of martial passion when he chose new uniforms for West Point cadets.[158] In any case, the 1814 battles were symbols of American fighting prowess in the early republic, and cadets were only too happy to claim the new uniforms as a symbol of honor and victory at West Point.[159] Those uniforms remained largely unchanged for men in 1976, with a high collar and forty-four buttons tapered downward from the shoulders toward the waist, and they glorified the male physique. The Academy decided to change the Full Dress uniform for women, however, to make it more feminine.

With the help of Hart, Shaffner, and Marx, a well-regarded men's clothing firm, the Academy invested a great deal of time and effort designing uniforms for women that were similar to those worn by the men but tailored to suit women's bodies. Their most important and misguided decision involved removing the tails from Full Dress uniform jackets because they believed the tails were unflattering on women's wider hips. As every woman knew, however, removing the tails only enhanced what the Academy hoped to conceal, especially when cadets marched in Full Dress jackets and white pants. The only cadets without tails, women were noticeable at a distance even within the vast ranks of the Corps on parade. They quickly became known as "cotton tails" by other cadets and spectators alike.[160]

In the midst of these trials and despite the changes accompanying the arrival of women, life at West Point continued much as it always had. There were classes, calisthenics, Plebe duties, hazing, formations, meals, athletics, parades, homework, and so on until one day largely resembled the next. The sameness of so many days tied cadets to those who had come before them in the Corps, and many Plebes found that in the midst of this maelstrom of activity they slowly began appreciating the daunting richness and depth of the Academy's past. West Point may be "aptly defined as an area of the world that has produced more history than could be consumed locally,"[161] and cadets were often told by faculty members that "Much of the history we teach was made by the people we taught." Indeed, West Point retained a poignancy and power unique among American institutions, for in virtually no other single place did so much of the nation's past come together.[162] The Academy's past formally began with European exploration and settlement of North America and Henry Hudson sailing past West Point in his ship *The Half Moon* on September 14, 1609. By the middle of the seventeenth century Dutch settlements dotted the eastern bank of the great river which bore his name.[163] Among those who lived along the Hudson, "the West Point" distinguished the peninsula on which the Academy eventually grew from what Europeans considered the older, more established areas to the east.[164]

West Point drew significance from the fact it overlooked a place where mountains narrowed the Hudson River and forced it to turn. Those mountains were part of a belt of gneiss and granite rock roughly fifteen miles wide, extending from New England southwest through what became New York, New Jersey, and Pennsylvania, and formed an area known as the Hudson Highlands. The Highlands included deep river gorges, rocky islands, terraces (like the one that became The Plain), and sharp turns in the river where rock held the water back.[165] Those turns, at places like Dunderberg, Anthony's Nose, and West Point, became strategically important by the mid-1700s because they offered occupying armies the promise of controlling traffic on the river. By virtue of the height of the surrounding mountains and the narrowness of the river, West Point tantalized engineers as a place where land forces could effectively block river transportation with artillery batteries and supporting infantry; a month after the first shots of the American Revolution echoed across the village greens at

Lexington and Concord, a Committee of the Second Continental Congress called for the area to be fortified.[166]

Early reports mentioned "Fort Constitution," constructed directly across from West Point on Constitution Island, and soon other fortifications dotted both sides of the river. After the British briefly threatened the area in 1777, patriot forces returned and constructed more permanent forts and defenses which survived the Revolution intact. They included the Great Chain, which American forces dragged out each spring between Constitution Island and the west bank, and Forts Clinton and Putnam, which dominated the river. George Washington moved his headquarters to West Point in 1779 for a brief period, and later called the site the "most important post in America."[167]

In the years following the Revolution, the United States Army shrunk to only eighty men; in 1784, fifty-five of them were stationed at West Point guarding stores and cannon for use in future wars.[168] By 1794, candidates for Army service were taking instruction at the post, which Congress had purchased from Stephen Moore for $11,085 in 1790.[169] George Washington called for the creation of a permanent military academy to train officers for a standing army during this period, even addressing the issue in his last letter on public business before his death.[170] A fiscally conservative federal government ignored his advice for fear of creating an officer caste, and it was not until the political climate changed in 1802 that Congress created the United States Military Academy.[171] President Thomas Jefferson mollified fears of an elite officer class by arguing that Academy graduates would be few in number and that the school would produce engineers rather than aristocrats. Desperate for surveyors and engineers who could help settle the growing American West, Congress relented.

During the nineteenth century, the Academy evolved into the forge which produced the greatest captains of the American Army. Graduates were instrumental in victories during the Mexican War and commanded armies in every American war fought afterward. They also dominated the great engineering projects of the era, and by the twentieth century, West Point honored their exploits with markers and monuments scattered throughout the Academy grounds. One of the most famous places to contemplate their achievements was the post cemetery, where one could walk amid sweet mimosas filtering rays of sunlight through weeping branches and reflect before the resting places of Colonel Edward H. White II, George Armstrong Custer, and Robert Anderson, each of whom graduated from the Academy and found his place on the Army's roster of heroes.[172] It became a place where "Death and beauty intermingle in a cunningly contrived Arcadia, eloquent of the ease with which [West Pointers] fall into romantic communion with the ideals of self-sacrifice and love of country."[173] Outside the cemetery, yet still a part of Academy lore, were Montgomery C. Meigs, Class of 1836, who supervised the building of the National Capitol dome and wings; 1st Lieutenant Thomas E. Selfridge, Class of 1903, the first person killed in a plane crash when his aircraft, piloted by Orville Wright, went down at Fort Myer, Virginia in 1908; Brigadier General Henry M. Robert, Class of 1857, who wrote "Robert's Rules of Order"; and Lieutenant Richard Shea, Class of 1952, who refused a place on the American Olympic Team to join his classmates in Korea. He was killed on Pork Chop Hill, and posthumously awarded the Congressional Medal of Honor.[174]

Amidst the tradition and history, cadets also discovered the traditional strengths inculcated in graduates by the Academy: the patriotism, love of loyalty and honor, and above all the commitment to duty, honor, and country for which West Point was famous. In a country awash in individuality and buckling under the strain of changing societal norms, cadets in the 1970s found the Academy still appealed without reservation or remorse to the unselfish, noble nature of men and women. It remained a place where honesty, integrity, courage, duty, honor, and country were always meant to be more than words. They were tangible benchmarks by which cadets could measure their worth. The cadets who endured were, like Saul on the road to Damascus, forever changed, brought into the true fold by turning all their previous customs on their heads.[175] Cadets found themselves members of a lionized cadre of heroes that included Lee, Grant, Eisenhower, Bradley, MacArthur, and Ridgway. What other route promised talented but unknown teenagers from obscure towns the chance to close ranks with American's paladins?[176] Where else could one feel so noble while so young?

As cadets immersed themselves in academics, the women of the Class of 1980 continued their struggle to endure the extra rigors of life in a predominantly male environment. They were assisted in the fall by the women's basketball team, which drew large crowds of male cadets to games and gained a reputation for tough, gritty play. Basketball, like most sports at the Academy, was devoutly followed and appreciated by cadets.[177] Football endured in an Olympian realm all its own of course, but with the Army team struggling during the mid-1970s the Lady Knights, known to cadets as the "Sugar Smacks," were a sorely needed antidote to the contagion of defeat and a powerful vehicle for gaining some measure of acceptance for women at West Point that first year.

The Academy attempted to assist the first class of women by adding more women faculty and staff members on post, but their efforts were hampered by the limited number of qualified women in the Army and the fact there were no women West Point graduates. Worse, many female cadets perceived the early women officers at West Point as weak and overly masculine, and therefore hardly an inspiration to those seeking assurance there was a place for feminine women with talent to succeed at West Point and within the Army.[178] After an introduction to one especially poor female role model, one cadet feared she would become "destined to be a single overweight woman and wear a funny green uniform."[179]

West Point also attempted to provide women with a vehicle for mutual support and the airing of common problems and grievances. Known as "Corbin Seminars," after the famous Revolutionary War figure, Margaret Corbin, these regular meetings were designed to appeal primarily to cadet women and featured prominent speakers and well-known feminists from around the United States. Eventually, the seminars grew into annual events which representatives from every service academy attended to discuss the progress of sexual integration at their respective institutions. Unfortunately, very few women of the Class of 1980 ever attended the early seminars, because they faced extra harassment and "major ostracization" from men if they did. Worse, the Corbin Seminar was labeled a "communistic organization," and one more example to many cadets of both sexes of special treatment allotted to women.[180] Even when the Academy tried to be supportive, it seemed, the system found a way to keep women apart.

Day by day, the Class of 1980 made its way through the Academy. The seasons changed, and as fall gave way to freezing winter and then to glorious spring, many of the first women endured. By the end of their Plebe year they had gained an appreciation for the rigors of West Point life, and a shocking sense of the depth of the resentment felt toward them by many men at the Academy. Some believed the worst had passed, for traditionally Plebe year represented the hardest period in cadet life. After that came the greater privileges of life as an upperclassman, including rank and opportunities for leadership. Like most assumptions about improving gender relations in those early years, however, these hopes were dashed by the resilience of sexism. Men who were uncertain how far they could push women during that first year had gained a measure of how far they could push the system, how much they could get away with without retribution, and a small number used that knowledge to make Yearling year the hardest and most frightening of all for many women in the Class of 1980.

NOTES

1. Plato, *The Republic of Plato*, trans. Francis MacDonald Cornford (New York: Oxford University Press, 1968), p. 154.

2. Randy Shilts, *Conduct Unbecoming: Lesbians and Gays in the U.S. Military. Vietnam to the Persian Gulf* (New York: St. Martins Press, 1993). p. 197.

3. Norm N. Nite, *Rock On Almanac: The First Four Decades of Rock n' Roll: A Chronology* (New York: Harper and Row, 1989), p. 305.

4. Atkinson, *The Long Gray Line* (Boston: Houghton Mifflin Company, 1989), p. 408.

5. EI, 5-1-80, p. 2.

6. Carol Barkalow with Andrea Raab, *In the Men's House: An Inside Account of Life in the Army by One of West Point's First Female Graduates* (New York: Berkeley Books, 1992), p. 11.

7. Cadet Journal, 7-7-76.

8. When women became Firsties the title was changed to "The Cadet in the Red Sash."

9. New Cadets were "beasts" upon arriving at the Academy because of their ignorance in all things military. Hence the name "Beast Barracks." See Richard C. U'Ren, M.D., *Ivory Fortress: A Psychiatrist Looks at West Point* (Indianapolis: Bobbs-Merrill, 1974), p. 17.

10. Barkalow, *In the Men's House*, p. 12. Many upperclassmen seemed confused as to what the haircut regulations were for women, or how to interpret them. Some women concluded very quickly that "to avoid harassment it was easier just to keep [their] hair very short." ETA, 6-12-2000, p. 1.

11. IWA, 6-9-96, author's notes.

12. ETA, 6-12-2000, p. 1. Some men eventually carried the bags too. LTA, 4-4-2000, p. 2.

13. Helen Rogan, *Mixed Company: Women in the Modern Army* (Boston: Beacon Press, 1982), p. 194.

14. Barkalow, *In the Men's House*, p. 16; and Cadet Journal, 7-9-76.

15. IWA, 3-26-97, author's notes.

16. EI, no date, side A. Stories concerning neophyte New Cadets are plentiful at West Point and a great source of amusement for graduates. Over the years New Cadets have arrived with furniture, golf bags, stereos, cars, and the entire range of adolescent paraphernalia. Some have been so shocked by the military environment they left the Academy within hours of their arrival.

17. IWA, 10-07-96, author's notes.

18. Daughters of the United States Army, West Point Chapter, *West Point: The United States Military Academy* (Charlotte, N.C.: C. Harrison Conroy Co., 1994), p. 37.

19. Arthur M. Schlesinger, Jr., *The Age of Roosevelt: The Crisis of the Old Order, 1919–1933* (Boston: Houghton Mifflin Company, 1957), p. 321.

20. IWA, 7-28-96, author's notes.

21. EI, 5-7-80, p. 4; and IWA, 1-22-96, author's notes.

22. IWA, 1-22-96, author's notes.

23. EI, 5-7-80, p. 4.

24. IWA, 3-26-97, author's notes. Jody songs were sung on marches or runs and involved a call and response between the group and a leader. They were often both sexually oriented and obscene and drew their name from "Jody," the ubiquitous civilian who stole soldiers' girlfriends in times of war. Interestingly, the mafia uses the term "Jody" to describe a man chosen to satisfy the emotional, financial, and sexual needs of an imprisoned mobster's wife. The Jody is usually chosen by the prisoner himself.

25. IWA, 4-2-96, author's notes.

26. Ibid.

27. U'Ren, *Ivory Fortress*, p. 18.

28. Elliott G. Gruner, "Merging Fear and Fantasy: Early Images of Women at West Point." *American Transcendental Quarterly* 7, No. 3 (September 1993): 273.

29. Taylor Hall, the West Point Administration Building, boasts a 160-foot tower. The depository is home to the bulk of America's silver bullion, and Battle Monument honors the 2,230 officers and enlisted men of the Regular Army who died in the Civil War. See USMA, *Bugle Notes*, vol. 68 (West Point: USMA, 1976), pp. 131, 135, and 146.

30. USMA, *Bugle Notes*, p. 188.

31. Ibid. In the mess hall, the "nth" degree was the number of containers of milk remaining at the Plebe's table.

32. *Assembly*, September 1976, p. 21.

33. Atkinson, *The Long Gray Line*, p. 401.

34. Ibid., p. 395. It was a dramatic remark, for Berry was a highly decorated combat veteran with four Silver Stars. A former military assistant to Secretary of Defense Robert

MacNamara, Berry was described as a "fast burner," and was profiled by *Life* in a 1970 article which predicted his eventual ascension to Chief of Staff of the Army.

35. LTA, 9-24-96, p. 3. The classic cadet conundrum was deciding whether it was an honor violation to say "I love you" to a date if, at some later time, the cadet decided he or she was not in love at all. The consensus was that if the cadet meant "I love you" *at the moment* the phrase was uttered, then no honor violation had taken place.

36. A similar scandal took place in 1951, when disdain for the Honor Code resulted in widespread cheating centered around the Army football team. Ninety cadets were expelled, and one player summed up his views on the Honor Code by saying, "I don't give a fuck. I didn't come here for all this honor shit, I came to play football." See David H. Hackworth, *About Face: The Odyssey of an American Warrior* (New York: Simon and Schuster, 1989), p. 217, and IWA, 5-16-97, author's notes.

37. ETA, 7-8-96, author's notes.

38. Quoted in *Assembly*, June 1977, p. 7.

39. LTA, 5-15-96, p. 1.

40. ETA, 9-24-96, p. 9.

41. EI, 5-1-80, 14.

42. EI, no date, pp. 3–4.

43. USMA, *Bugle Notes*, p. 46.

44. U'Ren, *Ivory Fortress*, pp. 1–2. Many of the Colonels at West Point lived on "Colonel's Row," in homes designed by Stanford White which sit on tree-lined streets in the hills above The Plain.

45. IWA, 3-26-97, author's notes.

46. Rogan, *Mixed Company*, p. 194, and ETA, 6-12-2000, p. 2.

47. IWA, 6-20-2000, side B; and IWA, 4-2-96, p. 6.

48. The Boarders Ward was a busy place in 1976. In additon to New Cadets who wanted to leave West Point, Cadets accused of honor violations were housed there pending the outcome of their investigations as well. See Atkinson, *The Long Gray Line*, p. 401.

49. IWA, 3-26-97, author's notes.

50. Ibid.

51. *The Pointer*, September 29, 1923, p. 24.

52. William Manchester, *American Caesar: Douglas MacArthur, 1880–1964* (New York: Dell Publishing Company, 1978), p. 63.

53. United States Military Academy, "The Fourth Class System: 1976–1977" (West Point: USMA, 1976), pp. 7–11.

54. IWA, 3-26-97, author's notes. Resourceful Plebes typically carried the templates in their trouser pockets or inside their caps, and fellow Plebes often either asked for or declined dessert to make the job easier. Also ETA, 6–12-2000, p. 2.

55. Ibid.

56. Ibid.

57. EI, 5-9-80, p. 10.

58. IWA, 3-26-97, author's notes.

59. USMA, *Bugle Notes*, pp. 78–80.

60. William Dean Howells, "Editor's Study," *Harpers's New Monthly Magazine* 82 (January 1891): 317.

61. Rick Atkinson, *The Long Gray Line*, p. 30.

62. The phrase "STRAC" dated to the 1960s, when General Paul D. Adams' Strategic

Army Command (STRAC) mandated performance standards for all Army units. An acronym for perfection, troops also said STRAC stood for "Stupid Troopers Running Around in Circles," or "Scatter, the Russians Are Coming." See Hackworth, *About Face*, pp. 452–53. At West Point, STRAC stood for "Straight, Tough, and Ready Around the Clock." See Barkalow, *In the Men's House*, p. 15; and ETA, 6-12-2000, p. 3.

63. USMA, *Bugle Notes*, pp. 70–74. Activities included language and athletic clubs, a cadet radio station (WKDT), theater, choirs for every chapel on post, a glee club, rifle team, band, and the spirit leading Rabble Rousers. Hops were typically held on Saturday nights and often centered around a special weekend for one of the four classes, such as Ring Weekend (when Firsties received class rings), 500th Night Weekend (when the Cows began the countdown towards graduation), 100th Night Weekend (for Firsties), or graduation.

64. Ibid., p. 39.

65. Jeffrey Simpson, *Officers and Gentlemen: Historic West Point in Photographs* (Tarrytown, N.Y.: Sleepy Hollow Press, 1982), p. 100.

66. John J. Lenney, *Caste System in the American Army: A Study of the Corps of Engineers and Their West Point System* (New York: Greenburg Publishers, 1949), p. 136.

67. Geoffrey Perrett, *Old Soldiers Never Die: The Life of Douglas MacArthur* (New York: Random House, 1996), p. 32. Marshall was scarred for life. The Virginia Military Institute (VMI) and The Citadel are the two most important state-supported four-year military colleges in the United States.

68. Manchester, *American Caesar*, pp. 62–63, and Perrett, *Old Soldiers*, p. 32. MacArthur later testified before Congress during inquiries into hazing at West Point prompted by the death of a cadet.

69. Manchester, *American Caesar*, p. 48. This commitment to isolation ran so deep that when Congress authorized a road to the Academy in 1863, the Superintendent denounced it, saying "It would be ruinous to the morals and discipline of the Corps." See Simpson, *Officers and Gentlemen*, p. 34.

70. IWA, 5-16-97, author's notes. Cadets sweated shadows by standing at attention or bracing against a wall long enough to leave perspiration marks outlining where they stood after stepping away.

71. Perrett, *Old Soldiers*, p. 31.

72. Atkinson, *The Long Gray Line*, p. 42.

73. LTA, 9-24-96, p. 3.

74. Thomas Fleming, "West Point Cadets Now Say, Why, Sir?" *New York Times Magazine*, July 5, 1970, p. 20.

75. IWA, 3-26-97, author's notes.

76. Ibid.

77. EI, no date.

78. EI, April/May 1980, pp. 4–5.

79. Ibid.

80. EI, 5-80, p. 10, and EI, April/May 1980, p. 4.

81. LTA, 9-24-96, p. 4.

82. U'Ren, *Ivory Fortress*, p. 4.

83. LTA, 9-24-96, p. 4.

84. IWA, 2-16-96, p. 24.

85. IWA, 8-8-95, author's notes.

86. IWA, 7-28-96, side A.

87. See Allan Mazur, Julie Mazur, and Caroline Keating, "Military Rank Attainment of a West Point Class: Effects of Cadet's Physical Appearance," *American Journal of Sociology* 90, No. 1(July 1984): 125–50.

88. Hackworth, *About Face* p. 608.

89. Herman Melville, *Moby Dick* (Norwood, Conn.: The Easton Press, 1977), p. 298.

90. Atkinson, *The Long Gray Line*, p. 44, and IWA, 5-16-97, author's notes. By tradition, some companies still use the terms when describing themselves, though today the reference typically refers to the level of discipline in a given unit.

91. EI, 4-22-80, p. 8.

92. Lionel Tiger and Robin Fox, *The Imperial Animal* (New York: Holt, Rinehart, and Winston, 1971), pp. 158–59.

93. Rear Admiral James B. Stockdale, "Experiences as a POW in Vietnam," *Naval War College Review* (January-February 1974): 3.

94. LTA, 1-26-96, p. 1.

95. U'Ren, *Ivory Fortress*, p. 4, and LTA, 2-14-96, pp. 2–3.

96. John Keegan, *Fields of Battle: The Wars for North America* (New York: Alfred A. Knopf, 1996), p. 147.

97. EI, April/May 1980, pp. 5–6, and IWA, 5-16-97, author's notes.

98. IWA, 3-26-97, author's notes.

99. EI, no date, p. 10.

100. EI, 5-80, p. 18.

101. IWA, 5-16-97, author's notes, and EI, 5-8-80, p. 5.

102. IWA, 8-3-00, author's notes.

103. EI, no date, p. 5.

104. EI, 4-17-80, p. 12.

105. EI, April/May 1980, p. 3.

106. IWA, 6-20-00, side A.

107. EI, 5-80, p. 8, and Atkinson, *The Long Gray Line*, p. 411.

108. IWA, 7-11-96, side A.

109. EI, 4-22-80, p. 7, and EI, April/May 1980, p. 4.

110. EI, 5-9-80, p. 12.

111. Group IWA, 5-19-96, author's notes.

112. As one of the nation's premier tourist attractions, West Point is an open post, meaning much of the installation is open to the public. Cadets on parade, in formation near the barracks, or walking between classes are thus at the mercy of tourists and their cameras, and women draw a great deal of attention.

113. EI, 5-9-80, p. 18.

114. Atkinson, *The Long Gray Line*, p. 411, 413.

115. EI, 4-17-80, p. 6.

116. IWA, 7-9-96, side A.

117. IWA, 5-8-00, author's notes.

118. IWA, 6-20-00, side A.

119. IWA, 4-2-96, pp. 18–19.

120. EI, 5-8-80, p. 11.

121. IWA, 6-20-00, side A.

122. EI, 5-8-80, p. 11.

123. IWA, 6-20-00, side A.

124. Ibid.

125. IWA, 2-27-96, p. 7.

126. EI, 5-1-80, p. 20.

127. IWA, 7-11-96, side A.

128. IWA, 2-18-98, author's notes.

129. Atkinson, *The Long Gray Line*, p. 410. Crocker enjoyed a long career in the Army, eventually serving as the commanding general of the 82nd Airborne Division.

130. Ibid., p. 413.

131. EI, 5-7-80, p. 9, and EI, April/May 1980, p. 4.

132. EI, 4-30-80, p. 10.

133. IWA, 5-13-96, p. 9.

134. IWA, 3-11-96, p. 6.

135. IWA, 2-4-96, p. 21.

136. LTA, 9-24-96, p. 5.

137. IWA, 11-8-95, p. 7.

138. Group IWA, 5-19-96, author's notes.

139. Eric Pointe, "Romeo and Juliet and Whiskey Papa," *The Pointer*, April 1976, p. 15. "Whiskey Papa" in Army phonetic code stood for "W.P.," which in turn represented West Point.

140. Atkinson, *The Long Gray Line*, p. 411.

141. LTA, 9-24-96, p. 5.

142. IWA, 11-4-99, author's notes.

143. USMA, *Bugle Notes*, p. 54.

144. IWA, 1-22-96, author's notes.

145. EI, 5-5-80, p. 23.

146. IWA, 4-2-96, p. 12.

147. IWA, 2-18-98, author's notes.

148. One woman remembered a male cadet asking one of her friends for a date. When her friend refused, the male began "hazing her like crazy." See EI, 5–5-80, p. 16.

149. IWA, 4-2-96, author's notes, and IWA, 8-3-00, author's notes.

150. IWA, 4-2-96, pp. 22–23.

151. IWA, 11-8-95, pp. 8–9.

152. IWA, 5-13-96, p. 22.

153. Martin Van Creveld, *The Transformation of War* (New York: The Free Press, 1991), p. 186.

154. IWA, 3-26-97, author's notes. Out of formation and behind closed doors, some women were forced to demonstrate proficiency with the longer springs as well. LTA, 4-4-2000, p. 2.

155. ETA, 4-9-96, p. 1.

156. EI, 5-9-80, p. 24.

157. IWA, 2-16-96, p. 22.

158. Dr. Stephen B. Grove, ETA, 6-8-2000, p. 5.

159. United States Military Academy, "West Point Cadet Uniforms" (West Point: Public Affairs Office Fact Sheet, undated), p. 1.

160. Women's uniforms were eventually made almost identical to those worn by the men, and women in the Class of 1980 are the only cadets ever issued Full Dress Gray coats without tails. Some chose to keep the unique memento after graduation.

161. Russell D. Buhite, *Decisions at Yalta: An Appraisal of Summit Diplomacy* (Wilmington, Del.: Scholarly Resources, Inc., 1986), p. 39. Buhite wrote about Poland, but the phrase befits West Point too.

162. *West Point: A Prospectus and 1991 Admissions Guide* (West Point: USMA, 1991), p. 14.

163. Atkinson, *The Long Gray Line*, p. 15.

164. Augusta A. Berard, *Reminiscences of West Point in the Olden Time* (East Saginaw, Mich.: n.p. 1886), p. 17.

165. Sidney Forman, *West Point: A History of the United States Military Academy* (New York: Columbia University Press, 1994), p. 5.

166. Ibid., p. 7.

167. Ibid., pp. 6, 8, 11–12. Dutch settlers named Constitution Island Martelaer's Rock Island, or Martyr's Rock. Polish patriot Thaddeus Kosciuszko designed most of West Point's fortifications, and added a small garden below The Plain which is preserved.

168. Dave Richard Palmer, *The River and the Rock: The History of Fortress West Point, 1775–1783* (West Point: Association of Graduates, USMA, in association with Hippocrene Books, 1991), pp. 354–56; and George H. Walton, *The Tarnished Shield: A Report on Today's Army* (New York: Dodd/Mead, 1973), p. 7.

169. Palmer, *The River and the Rock*, p. 355; and Forman, *West Point*, p. 4. The West Point area was originally settled through land grants. Moore sold 1,795 acres to be the Federal Government in 1790.

170. Palmer, *The River and the Rock*, p. 357.

171. Forman, *West Point*, p. 18. The Academy was created at a time when western European nations were creating similar institutions. They were influenced by the French Revolution, and sought to place large armies of citizen soldiers under the command of professional officers who were no threat to the political order. See John Keegan, *The Mask of Command* (London: Jonathan Cape, 1987), p. 5.

172. White was the first American astronaut to walk in space; Custer gained notoriety during the Civil War and in wars with Native Americans on the Great Plains, and was killed along with most of his command at the Battle of the Little Bighorn in 1876; Anderson was the first Union hero of the Civil War and the commander of Fort Sumter when Confederate forces bombarded the post in 1861.

173. Keegan, *Fields of Battle*, p. 239. Keegan was actually referring to the British people, but the passage suits West Point well.

174. USMA, *Bugle Notes*, pp. 194–97. Had Shea competed in the Helsinki Olympics with the U.S. team, he would have done so as a long distance runner.

175. A paraphrase of a passage from William Manchester, *Goodbye Darkness, A Memoir of the Pacific War* (Boston: Little, Brown and Company, 1979), p. 353.

176. The roll of West Pointers also included diverse figures such as James McNeil Whistler, Edgar Allan Poe, and Timothy Leary, though none of them graduated. See Atkinson, *The Long Gray Line*, p. 104. Critics often point out that Anastasio Somoza, Jr., the brutal dictator of Nicaragua, graduated with the West Point Class of 1946, proving the Academy's roster of "heroes" is more tarnished than commonly known.

177. West Point had its share of great coaches, too. Both Bobby Knight and Mike Krzyzewski coached for Army during the 1960s and 1970s. See Atkinson, *The Long Gray Line*, p. 90.

178. IWA, 4-4-96, author's notes.

179. IWA, 12-12-95, p. 21.

180. IWA, 2-4-96, p. 7; IWA, 2-28-96, p. 19; and Memorandum entitled "Findings of Major Evanekovich," February 11, 1981, USMA Files.

The United States Military Academy at West Point. Looking south, this 1976 photograph shows the proximity of the Academy to the Hudson River on the left and to the surrounding Highlands of upstate New York. The cadet parade ground (known as "The Plain") is to the right of the baseball diamond, across the sidewalk. Above The Plain is Washington Hall and the cadet barracks, and above them lie the Cadet Chapel and Michie Stadium. USMA Archives.

Lieutenant General Andrew J. Goodpaster, USMA Class of 1939, Superintendent, 1977–1981. USMA Archives.

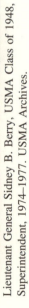

Lieutenant General Sidney B. Berry, USMA Class of 1948, Superintendent, 1974–1977. USMA Archives.

An Academy landmark since 1897, Battle Monument honors the soldiers and officers of the Union Army who died during the Civil War. It contains the largest piece of turned granite in the Western Hemisphere, and stands on Trophy Point, overlooking the Hudson River. Illustration by Pamela Lenck Bradford. Copyright © 2001 by Pamela Lenck Bradford.

Finished in 1910, The Cadet Chapel looms three hundred feet above the Academy parade ground and houses the largest church organ in the world. Illustration by Pamela Lenck Bradford. Copyright © 2001 by Pamela Lenck Bradford.

New Cadets playing softball in front of the Superintendent's home in 1996. Illustration by Pamela Lenck Bradford. Copyright © 2001 by Pamela Lenck Bradford.

Cadet George B. Comly, USMA Class of 1900, drew this picture for *The Howitzer* when he was a Firstie. Comly later taught drawing at West Point and served as a military aide to President Woodrow Wilson. USMA Archives.

"Gotta run, fellas. I have a date with a West Point cadet."

Legendary cartoonist Bill Mauldin characterized the confusion among many men regarding the admission of women to West Point when he published this cartoon in 1976. "Gotta Run Fellas," by Bill Mauldin. Reprinted with special permission from the Chicago Sun-Times, Inc., copyright © 2001.

New Cadets Cheryl Maloney and Ron Miller reporting to Michie Stadium on R-Day, July 7, 1976. USMA Archives.

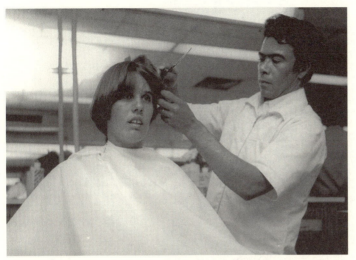

A first female cadet gets the first of many Academy haircuts on R-Day. USMA Archives.

Members of the Class of 1980 taking their oath as New Cadets and joining the Long Gray Line. Donna Sue Alesch (third from the left), Donna Marie Wright (fifth from the left), Kelly Lynn Zachgo (fifth from the right, foreground), Carol Anne Barkalow (second from the right), and Janis Marie Calhoon (first from the right) all graduated. USMA Archives.

Attacking the Indoor Obstacle Course during Beast Barracks. Rita
Annette Null, Class of 1980, is the second cadet. USMA Archives.

Richard A. Wagner Jr., and Greg Arthur Gorzelnik, both USMA Class
of 1977, inspect New Cadet Carol Ann Young of the Class of 1980
during Beast Barracks. Note the differences in the length of their hair.
USMA Archives.

Training at Camp Buckner in the summer of 1977. Joan Marie Zech, Class of 1980, is in the middle, with her left arm across her waist. USMA Archives.

During a parade on The Plain, members of D Company, Second Regiment, pass in review. Jane Hunter Perkins (fifth from the right), and Debra Malvene Lewis (sixth from the right), both USMA Class of 1980, were platoon commanders in D-2. USMA Archives.

The Brigade Staff on graduation day, May 28, 1980. From the left are Paul Rupert Capstick, John Keagy Stoner III, Scott Andrew Snook, Kathleen Mary Gerard, and Vincent Keith Brooks, First Captain. USMA Archives.

Diane Bracy, USMA Class of 1980, at graduation. USMA Archives.

The Class of 1980 experiences their last rite of passage at West Point, the traditional tossing of the caps at graduation. USMA Archives.

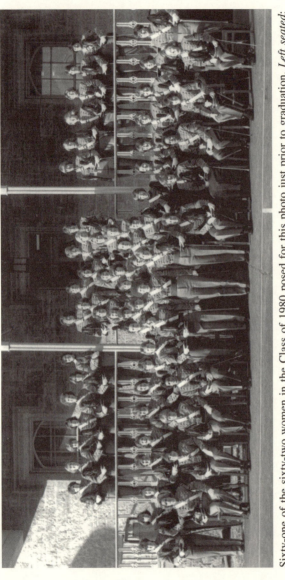

Sixty-one of the sixty-two women in the Class of 1980 posed for this photo just prior to graduation. *Left seated:* J. McEntee, K. Gerard, D. Dawson, J. Dallas. *Right seated:* A. Hollen, C. Young, P. Walker, C. Kirby, A. Muir. *Standing Front:* B. Treharne, D. Wright, J. Harrington, S. Kellett, K. Wheless, J. Perkins, D. Maller, D. Johnson, R. Fennessy, D. Stoddard, J. Smith, S. Reichelt, D. Turner (*in front of the post*), R. Null, B. Benya, M. Flynn, D. Bracey, E. Griffin, C. Stevens. *Standing on the first step:* J. Zech, L. Pfluke, E. O'Connor, T. Tepper. *Standing on the second step:* B. Sheets, S. Moran, K. Cicchini. *Standing on the third step:* K. Wildey, K. Silvia, R. Todd. *Standing on the fourth step:* D. McCarthy, J. Calhoon, C. Barkalow. *Standing on the fifth step:* K. Kelly, A. Hughes, T. Kaseman. *Standing on the sixth step:* S. Nikituk, B. Fiedler, N. Gucwa, D. Alesch. *Left standing back:* M. Nyberg, K. Hinsey, S. Ashworth, B. Blyth, M. Rosinski, D. Lewis, B. Fulton. *Right standing back:* K. Kinzler, A. Fields, A. Colister, K. Zachgo, M. Gridley, V. Martin. USMA Archives.

5

★ ★ ★ ★

"Servants of the People"

You and I have been bequeathed our share of this our country with our
brothers . . . it is not a responsibility we can evade.

—An American girl[1]

As the Class of 1980 made the transition from Plebes to Yearlings and prepared
for summer training at Camp Buckner in 1977, it became abundantly clear how
profoundly the presence of women cadets changed and threatened the way many
men saw West Point. Women seldom changed the Academy in profoundly physical ways, yet they threatened the image male cadets nurtured in their minds
about what it meant to be a cadet, a soldier, and even a man. In hindsight these
images were the real barriers to successful integration of women, for by the end
of Plebe year there remained little question of whether women could handle the
rigors of Academy training or prove their worth in the Army.

What did remain, and what endured in the minds of many officers and cadets
in the years following the admission of women, was the gnawing sense that
women simply did not belong at West Point. Overcoming that sense of uncertainty, which stemmed from deeply rooted cultural and social stereotypes about
women and the role they should play in society, became the most important
battle in the war to fully integrate women at West Point because their arrival
generated profound insecurities among many cadets. For the admission of
women to be successful, men had to overcome these stereotypes and accept
women as peers and colleagues and, in the process, overcome their phobias,
uncertainties, and doubts. They had to deal with cultural messages beyond the

Academy's gates which divided men and women into separate roles based on their sex, the official proclamation within West Point that said women should be treated as equals, and the unofficial word among many cadets that held that the process was a sociological experiment foisted on the military by ignorant civilians. Some cadets and Army officers never reconciled these different messages. Many of those who did found the process troubling, confusing, and sometimes fearful.

One of the first socially constructed assumptions many cadets confronted when they dealt with women involved the unstated but very real emotional and cultural connection between being soldiers and being male in American society. While women were involved in every war in U.S. history and played a role in all human conflicts over time, men still dominated organized warfare in virtually every culture on earth. Whether this dominance stemmed from the physiological differences between men and women or cultural habit, it gave men power over politics, property, business, the law, and the entire spectrum of societal institutions. As Barbara Ehrenreich wrote, "War . . . has for millennia existed in a symbiotic relationship with male domination, both drawing strength from and giving strength to it."[2] Some authors argue that men dominated war making for physical reasons, others that specialized labor was the culprit—someone had to hunt while others guarded infants and children—and over time these roles became gender-specific. Martin Van Creveld suggested the phenomenon, which crosses culture and time throughout human history, may be best understood if viewed as an attempt by men to make up for their inability to have children.[3]

Whatever the reasons, the defining characteristic of this trend is that most societies took as an article of faith the notion that men were responsible for fighting. Language in many cultures reflected this assumption. The "association between 'man' and 'warrior' is," as one author wrote, "so close that in many languages the two terms are interchangeable."[4] This connection had enormous social and political consequences, because warriors often held positions of cultural leadership in addition to their roles as protectors of the tribe. Homer alluded to this fact more than 2,000 years ago in the *Iliad*: "Not unjust it is that our kings hold Lycia, eat the fat hams and drink honey-sweet wine; they prove their right when they fight among the first rank of the Lycians."[5] Vergil followed in Homer's footsteps and echoed this ideal in Roman times when he began *The Aneid* with the line, "I sing of arms and a man . . ."[6] The dominance of men over the waging of war therefore resonated as a theme in the language and literature of the very earliest human civilizations and endured as a foundation of most cultures well into the twentieth century. It was, in fact, the keystone arch of male power and control.

Women and the roles they filled seemed inferior by comparison, because women did not usually participate in organized warfare and as a result held few positions of political leadership in either small tribes or organized nation states throughout most of history. Again, language reflected the pattern. In most societies, and particularly in the West, simply saying a job was "women's work" meant labeling it with "inherently lower social status" and prestige.[7] As William W. Savage, Jr., wrote, the language of masculinity is intensely cultural, composed of a "rhetoric of imagery" which is "inflationary" for men and "subordinating" for women.[8] Any thesaurus reflects Savage's conclusion. Webster's, for example, lists synonyms for "feminine" as including "soft," "delicate," "gentle," "sensitive," "tender," and "shy." In contrast, synonyms for "masculine" are "courageous," "honorable," "virile," and "potent." Thus it is hardly surprising that men in general, and warriors in particular, often attempted to connect themselves to virtues which language indicated were their special province, and in turn to denigrate the contributions of women. Men were said to be strong, to be leaders, and one of the vital proofs of their strength and leadership was their willingness (and even eagerness) to fight other men. Therefore, in Western cultures at large and in military circles in particular, any implied connection between men and women, between the work "real" men did and the culturally subordinate work of women became an insult. As a former West Point commandant said later, there existed a "sense that the Army was tough and physical. But if women can make it, can it [the Army] really be tough?"[9]

These cultural assumptions, preconceptions, and attitudes were passed down over time in the West and held by many Americans even in the latter half of the twentieth century. They largely ignored the vital roles women have played in every conflict in American history but were passionately held in many quarters just the same. Even the fact that women served in large numbers in a variety of military occupations during World War II did little to change them. Women were barred from serving in direct combat positions during the war and generally mustered out of the service as soon as the fighting ended. This meant the experiment of allowing women into previously all-male jobs or occupations did not last long enough to threaten the assumptions of most Americans about gender roles. They could argue that temporary change driven by the needs of the war made sense and that permanent adjustments were unnecessary because women really belonged in more traditional occupations.

This often unstated but very real assumption underpinned even the majority of advances in the field of women's rights during the early twentieth century. Passage of the Nineteenth Amendment in 1918, for example, granted women the right to vote nationwide and stemmed in part from a Congressional commitment to thank women for their service to America during World War I. The service of women in that war, however, as in World War II just over twenty years later, represented a natural extension of women's traditional roles as mothers and wives. They typically served in medical or administrative fields, as cooks and laundry women, and in those rare instances when they broke into predominantly male occupations like manufacturing or repair, the government quickly pointed out that such service would only be for the duration of the war. Because this effort allowed more men to fight at the front, even taking on these jobs was seen as another way that women supported men, not a step toward competing with or replacing them. When the wars ended, women largely returned to the traditional roles assigned to them, and male control of the military and other state-supported institutions allowed to use violence (like police departments) remained extraordinarily resistant to sex integration.

Most importantly, after both world wars Americans reinvented the Hydra-like myth that women were second-class citizens incapable of contributing actively on the battlefield. This occurred even after World War II, when Army research concluded that women were more than capable of serving with distinction in antiaircraft units and that combined male/female units performed better than those comprised exclusively of the same sex.[10] In a nation like the United States where knowledge of the past is infamously poor, the myth reappeared again and again with predictable frequency. The admission of women at West Point broke with this pattern and deeply threatened many men in uniform, because women who served as cadets and officers on an equal basis with men did not fit into any sort of traditional mold. They threatened to break the mold entirely. And by competing with and ultimately replacing men who might have attended West Point in their place they threatened the virtual monopoly men held on the societal role of warrior and soldier.

This American pattern appeared elsewhere in the world as well. Historically, women were allowed to enter the armed forces in most societies only when severe discrepancies in force existed. When the tide of battle shifted or the war ended, women usually found themselves removed from the military for cultural or political reasons and relegated to more traditional, often socially inferior roles. This pattern held in the United States for both World Wars and in Israel prior to and during the 1948 War for Independence. Prior to that war, the Palmach led the Jewish resistance against the British in Palestine. An elite group of volunteers from both sexes that eventually formed the core of the Israeli Defense Force (IDF), the Palmach fought in raids and as a terrorist organization until 1948, when the IDF was formed and the War of Independence with surrounding Arab nations began. At that point women were relegated for cultural reasons to secondary roles in the military as support troops.[11]

The same pattern can be used to assess the expansion of opportunity for women in the American armed forces of the 1970s. With the Cold War raging and the draft at an end, U.S. planners feared a discrepancy in force might exist in the future and called for more women to make up for projected shortfalls in the number of qualified male recruits. The military *wanted* more women. The services *asked* for them. No one expected that these moves would bring women to West Point or ultimately threaten the male monopoly on control of combat units. But they did, and no one at the Academy or in the Army was happy about it. The irony is that the military laid the foundation for the changes its members most despised themselves.

At West Point, assumptions tied to the past about the "proper" role of women as well as men were alive and well among generally conservative male cadets in the 1970s. Women were barred from admission to West Point, barred from direct combat duty, and generally considered physically incapable of combat, and these barriers reinforced the natural tendency of the Academy as a single-sex institution to encourage sexual stereotyping.[12] Even the vernacular of the Academy reflected the distinction between men and women. Cadets who were considered physically weak were "women," "ladies," "fairies," or "pussies," and men who showed effeminate characteristics were often viciously hazed.[13] Plebes found the indignities of their own lives could also be characterized in feminine terms. As Lucian Truscott wrote in a fictional account of West Point life, "Being a Plebe . . . was like being a woman for a year."[14] These messages and cultural assumptions were among the major obstacles women faced in their attempt to gain acceptance and respect within the society of warriors at West Point, and were difficult for them to overcome because they emanated from both inside and outside the Academy's walls. For its part, West Point struggled with overcoming assumptions about women that often came from the institution itself as well as from the Army at large. It also struggled to sell the idea that women could make excellent cadets and officers because women trained as soldiers were the antithesis of the nurturing, domestic role much of society (and certainly most Army men) thought proper for women in the mid 1970s.

Adding to the mix were the biological issues involved, though few in 1976 or after could confront them without being labeled a misogynist, male chauvinist, biological determinist, an apologist for sexism, or worse. On a fundamental level, however, there could be no denial of the physical differences between men and women, and for the first time the Army had to determine whether those differences were truly significant in military terms. Would they prevent women from fulfilling the duties of a West Point cadet or Army officer? Did they preclude the presence of women in combat units? Despite generous assumptions and centuries of tradition, no one could answer these questions with any sort of scientific certainty, and West Point plunged into a vigorous period of research and debate to try and find out.

Traditionalists argued women were unfit physically, psychologically, and physiologically for the hard work of leading soldiers and winning wars. That view faded slowly over time, at least officially, and by the 1990s women empirically proved their physical ability even as they fought for more opportunity to prove themselves in the combat arms.[15] Yet biology, as evidenced by the predictable pattern of interaction between men and women, did have consequences for West Point that caused considerable concern and that demonstrated "how fundamental is the fact of being male or female."[16]

Nowhere in cadet life did that fundamental fact have more impact than in romantic relationships, for cadets who dated each other sometimes influenced the morale and cohesion of entire units. This phenomenon had never before been faced within the Academy. Cadets dated women outside West Point, but those women did not usually threaten the bond between men of the Corps. And one of the fundamental goals of the entire West Point experience had always been to solidify the bonds between men, to develop esprit de corps and a faith in each cadet that other West Pointers would never let them down. Women cadets seemed to threaten the Corps from within, for if men competed for attention from the limited number of female cadets they risked running afoul of other men. The Academy tried to minimize these forces by allowing cadets to date each other but prohibiting Plebes from dating upperclassmen. The latter condition aimed to prevent early recognition of Plebes and any deterioration in the senior-subordinate relationship between members of the Fourth Class and those who outranked them. Cadets, however, broke the rule early and often at West Point, which struggled to manage romantic relationships within a structured, military environment that emphasized the group over individual attachments.

That this pattern developed surprised almost no one, for human beings are fundamentally primates and social animals. Academic discourse often adamantly downplays the importance of biology and distinguishes between the natural and social sciences, implying along the way that "social life, especially among people, is not natural."[17] In practical terms this dichotomy forms the core of the "nature/nurture" debate. Many scientists, for example, would argue that human beings are predisposed to certain kinds of behavior because they are animals and cannot always control their natural instincts to do things like eat, sleep, and reproduce. Taken to an extreme, this logic suggests that human social behavior is also driven by biology or by nature and that human institutions like the military are organized to reflect natural biological laws (e.g., boys will be boys, women cannot fight, etc.). Opposing this belief to varying degrees are those who accept John Locke's notion that human beings are born "tabula rasa." The Latin phrase means "blank slate," and Locke contended that human beings are born with almost no predispositions. What they eventually do and believe is shaped by what they learn from other humans; therefore human behavior is driven primarily, if not exclusively, by culture. Social scientists are often prone to this body of belief, which stands in stark contrast to the view among natural scientists that nature and ultimately biology matter a great deal in determining interaction among all animals, including humans.

At West Point the vital truth that human beings are primates meant cadet men and women pursued sexual liaisons in spite of official regulations to the contrary and that these relationships had tangible consequences for cadet groups as a whole. This should have been no surprise. The surprise, as Lionel Tiger wrote of men and women serving aboard U.S. Navy ships in 1997, "would be if the animals did not chronically seek sexual congress."[18] Yet the tension such behavior sometimes created, between cadets and Academy officials and between those cadets who dated other members of the Corps and those who did not, had implications that the traditionalists blamed on women. After all, they argued, the threat individual romantic relationships posed to group cohesion did not exist before women were admitted to West Point. They too easily forgot that men were equally to blame and that upperclassmen, because they knew the rules best and were in positions of authority, were the most egregiously at fault.

Assigning blame missed the point in any case, which was that sexual relationships within military units presented new problems for the Academy because "[h]ealthy human males respond to healthy human females in predictable, biologically determined, and culturally mediated ways."[19] Those problems were hardly helped by any reliance on models of sexual integration taken from the civilian world, for in that environment men and women typically worked together for forty hours a week. At West Point they lived, ate, trained, and slept in close proximity *seven days* a week. Any comparison between sex and racial integration could also be misleading, because race represented "an unimportant biological category."[20] Race and gender assumptions were enormously influenced by culture, of course, and tremendously significant behaviorally, but in the end, the fact that men and women were attracted to each other sexually had repercussions for the West Point hierarchy and culture which resonated more than racial differences ever could.

In practical terms Academy policies reflected two concurrent notions, one which held men and women were essentially identical and one which recognized their differences. The first argued that for the sake of equity men and women had to have the same opportunities, rewards, and challenges as cadets because they were virtually identical. The second said that when differences did become apparent, when women became pregnant or had difficulty doing pull-ups, for example, those differences would be handled either administratively or with the creation of modified standards for women.[21] Male cadets were therefore told that in principle women would face the same challenges as men, only to find that women did not have to take boxing, run as fast as men, or do pull-ups, and it bothered them immensely. West Point struggled to be fair and reasonable in creating standards, and there was truth in the official pronouncements that women were equally challenged even in those cases where performance standards differed. Yet Academy leaders never effectively conveyed the reasons for these differences to men, nor did they thoroughly explain culturally driven variations like the length to which cadets were allowed to grow their hair. And by rushing to change standards which more women might have met in the long run given proper conditioning, the Academy may have retarded and even delayed the acceptance of female cadets by their male peers.

The driving power of biology even had implications for hazing, for the natural physical attraction between young men and women pre-ordained some cadets to a certain amount of sexual interaction and even harassment. This fact does not condone harassment or severe hazing, but it does reflect the great pressures placed on cadets to subvert what might be called natural instincts in the name of discipline. Very few professionals in any field were asked to discipline themselves in such a manner in the 1970s. Few military officers had ever done it, and almost no professionals in comparable civilian fields (like firefighting and police work) did so either. Women certainly were moving into more and more previously male-dominated fields in that period, but only at West Point and the other service academies did they live and train side by side with men in an environment steeped in male tradition and laden with deeply rooted gender images for men.

Such a climate made friction between some men and women inevitable. While there is no excuse for harassment or hazing, those incidents that did occur were at least in part the responsibility of Congress and the Academy. After all, those institutions asked young people to wage war with what some anthropologists are prepared to call forms of natural and instinctive behavior. As Lionel Tiger wrote, "I am suggesting the creation of a hostile environment is precisely not the responsibility of those who engage in wholly predictable human behavior, but of those who cause them to exist in conditions so fanciful as to constitute somewhat cruel and certainly unusual forms of quotidian existence."[22] Such a view should not mitigate the responsibility of individual male cadets for their actions, but it should serve as an indicator of the depth to which biology mattered among cadets of both sexes. It manifestly served the long term interests of the Academy and the United States to admit women to West Point, even if their admission introduced new problems associated with sexual behavior into the Corps of Cadets. The problems that did arise were significant, however, and were not eased by official doublespeak which proclaimed that a cadet's sex both did and did not matter. Sex *did* matter. It mattered in terms of physical fitness standards, uniforms, and personal appearance, and the Academy struggled to reconcile differing rules and standards with a traditionally military desire for uniformity.

Above all, the Academy found the greatest threat to discipline and cohesiveness in the existence of romantic relationships between cadets. Romance demanded that individuals focus their attention and concern on each other at a time and place where the military ethos held that individuals should focus their attention and concern on the needs of the *group*, whose primacy "is an important theme at West Point."[23] From the Academy's perspective, the jealousy, sexual passions, and flirting attendant with dating were barriers to forging the powerful group bonds which held humans together in combat, and interfered with training at every level.[24] They were an unavoidable hurdle attendant with sex integration, but that hardly made them easy for cadets to overcome, and many in the Army questioned whether the military should or could deal with such shades of sexual gray. After all, group love and individual love were two different matters entirely. At what point, some Army officers asked, would the group love upon which military and especially combat units depend turn into the more indulgent and self-centered kind of exclusive romantic/sexual love that binds individuals together but tears units apart?[25] Or, as General Knowlton once asked, "When does sacred love become profane?"[26] West Point struggled to deal with these questions, to "create a machine designed for violence that is free from violence, from exploitation, from the naked use of power for any personal gain, a machine that permits sexual conduct that doesn't detract from the performance of a unit during an operation."[27] It was a tall order.

Where culture and biology mattered most was in the pervasive idea that some jobs were meant for men only and that formerly all-male fields of endeavor lost prestige when they admitted women. This notion lay deep within some male cadets and formed the foundation for resentment toward many female cadets that had nothing to do with their physical or mental capabilities. Such opposition lay far "deeper than reason and ideology" and is therefore difficult to measure. As a palpable emotion among many men, however, it cannot be denied, and the feeling of resentment came from a larger societal fear among some men that their unique roles in society were threatened.[28] Even by 1970, two years before Congressional passage of the Equal Rights Amendment and a full six years prior to the admission of women to West Point, critics were noting the feeling among many men that social changes were ending the days of gender-specialized jobs. "To the undying astonishment and regret of many men," wrote one, "there are few things in the United States today that American women do not or cannot do."[29] He added, "[I]n America today it is no longer possible for men to affirm their maleness simply in terms of the tasks reserved for their side of the fence."[30]

The threat genuinely resonated within the Academy, where a conservative, male-oriented, hierarchical, and "basically southern" culture thrived among cadets.[31] Moreover, the Academy drew cadets primarily from midsized and smaller towns, not from generally more liberal big cities. Members of the Class of 1975, for example, were predominantly from two-parent homes in moderately sized towns of fifty thousand or less. They were more conservative than students at comparable civilian schools, and research indicated that cadets usually became more conservative during their years at West Point, not less.[32] By any standard, the Academy hardly offered an environment which welcomed change or adjusted to it easily, and when the change involved pushing the envelope of socially constructed gender roles, it is little wonder the Academy rebelled. After all, for the most conservative and hidebound officers and cadets, Camelot could not exist without princesses to be saved and protected, without ladies to fawn on knights and convince them of their nobility. These men derived satisfaction from their perceived role as protectors of women and children, not from the abstract notion they served their fellow citizens. Admitting women into the warrior culture removed them from their pedestal and allowed them the dirty and yet honorable work of protecting the tribe. Men were denied the exclusive role of guardian, however, and on a very visceral level many recoiled at the infringement on their exclusive niche in society.

Of course, protection never really existed as a zero sum game. It could be shared by men and women and extended to everyone. Service and sacrifice were noble virtues regardless of sex, and when pushed amid calm surroundings, most men at West Point probably knew that. Yet their feelings were cultural and not always rational, especially among the largely adolescent Corps of Cadets. They were rooted in socialization, in the formative years of generally conservative young men who usually had definite ideas about what it meant to be a man, a soldier, and a leader long before West Point gave them formal ways of constructing those concepts. In the hyper-macho environment of the Academy, it was an easy thing for young men to become misogynists when it came to women in the military, and it took time for their views to begin to change. The admission of women to West Point represented "the pitting of an ancient and culturally embedded view of what it means to be a warrior against the irresistible force of democracy, in the sense of absolute equality," and for some men the jump in thinking was simply and tragically too great.[33]

Most of all, the presence of female cadets at the Academy forcefully intruded upon an organization that existed and thrived for almost two centuries as an exclusively male institution, and many men resented their arrival on a very fundamental level. This resentment stemmed from cultural forces as well as from a historically very male tendency to form or join groups dominated by men. Around the world and across time, especially among younger men, "[t]he most obvious [general principle] is that at all times and all places men form groups from which they exclude women."[34] This pattern reveals itself particularly among men drawn to violent organizations like the military, where their exclusivity reinforces their power, unique roles, and dominant relationships with other men. As one author wrote, "when men are called up to act together in an all-male activity, particularly a dangerous one, they may affirm their solidarity partly by degrading the male-female bond at the expense of the male-male bond. . . ." The implicit message of such bonding "is that, in some circumstances, no woman is as important to any man as men are to one another."[35] This phenomenon, like the tendency of men to dominate warfare and centers of political and social power, evolved via male dominance of hunting and war over the ages. It inextricably linked culture to biology, for "[w]ar and fighting and the hunt have always been the province of human males, just as the protection of the troop is the business of male primates," and women were kept out of these endeavors because their involvement represented a "potential source of disruption to the unity, loyalty, and trust necessary to comrades in arms."[36]

Certainly no cadet at West Point listed these factors as reasons for opposing the admission of women (though many argued that women had no business being involved in combat), but they were there as a cultural and biological undercurrent just the same. The admission of women to West Point therefore proved a far greater harbinger of change for America than anyone realized in 1976. As part of a larger redistribution of power within society in which women seized greater influence than ever before, it provided a powerful step toward redefining gender roles within the United States. By triggering debate over what it meant culturally and biologically to be male or female and by forcing the armed forces to adapt despite their reluctance, Congress did more than expand opportunities at West Point and the other service academies. It took the first steps toward sending women into combat and fundamentally altering the roles of women within the military.

There was irony in all this, particularly in the institution America chose to lead such mammoth social change. As in 1948, when President Harry Truman desegregated the armed forces well before mainstream society seemed prepared to confront the injustice of segregation along color lines, so it was in the 1970s when the armed forces were asked to lead the way in expanding opportunities for women ahead of mainstream culture and before any other nation in the world had taken similar steps. Congress ordered West Point to accomplish quickly and with a minimum of conflict a social revolution unprecedented in any military Academy in the world. *None* of them admitted women, and it was easy to ask why Congress chose a proud bastion of male dominance and patriarchy to lead the way rather than leaning on the private sector or even state and federal institutions to expand opportunities for women. It was as if changes in the military became a sort of barometer for the kinds of changes society believed were right and just, even if it could not always bring those changes on itself.

The American military, however, could not exist entirely above and aloof from the society from which it sprang; like America at large, it found itself torn between the relentless drive for equality and the need for equity. As an ideal, for example, the principle of equality meant women deserved equal access to West Point. Once there, however, physiological differences between the sexes persuaded Army planners to adjust physical standards for women so they would be fair, or equitable. Yet what seemed "fair" could never really be "equal." These two concepts were easily confused and yet entirely dissimilar, so much so that on many occasions they actually conflicted with each other, as when male cadets flunked physical education tests with times or scores that would have been passing for women. Unfortunately, neither American society nor the Academy ever really confronted this issue directly, with the result that conflicting messages were sent to cadets on a routine basis. They were told that women were to have the exact same training as men, for example, only to find out that the rules regarding the length of their hair, physical fitness standards, and duty assignments were entirely different. Americans seemed unable to reconcile the gap between equality and equity in a way that left everyone feeling comfortable.

Part of the explanation for the government's willingness to tinker with the military is that it could *force* the armed services to drop the color barrier or admit women to the service academies. The rights and liberties guaranteed civilian individuals by the Constitution and Federal statutes did not apply to members of the armed forces, which in practical terms meant private citizens could find more ways to discriminate than a soldier could on active duty. For while soldiers defended freedom and democracy, they did not enjoy them on duty. A separate body of law known as the Uniform Code of Military Justice governed all military personnel, and it made no allowance for dissent. Uncle Sam might be hesitant to make Exxon or General Electric promote greater equality between the sexes for political reasons, but he could force the military to do just about anything. Whether purchasing a certain weapons system, training recruits in a particular way, or even assimilating women into the service academies, the government had greater fiat over the military than over any other segment of American society. That fiat had the added benefit of being constitutionally easy to wield. As Commander-in-Chief, the president could institute sweeping changes without Congressional consent and could do so with little fear of public backlash because the military represented an easy political target. Its constituents were small in number, geographically diverse, and fearful of budget cuts. That meant the president and members of Congress could experiment with the military to score public relations points without fearing severe political retaliation at home, and it meant that the armed forces themselves often had precious little leverage on Capitol Hill. That leverage had to be used both sparingly and wisely, and military lobbyists generally reserved it for the largest weapons contracts rather than for financially less explosive issues like the presence of women in the armed services.

A further explanation is that for America, the armed forces represent what society hopes to be, as opposed to what it is. They are ideally the truest meritocracy, where birth, income, religion, race, and gender are in theory unimportant. Those trivial demarcations between people, it is said, pale in military ethos before the grander ideals of duty, honor, and country, and the American people look to the services for proof anyone can still rise to the top. Hence the focus on generals who once were privates, or Chairmen of the Joint Chiefs of Staff who grew up poor and uneducated in some rural backwater or urban ghetto. Secretary of the Army Martin R. Hoffmann made note of the pattern when he addressed the West Point Class of 1976. "It is remarkable," he said, "how often in the past, when faced with . . . trials and doubts, the nation has found in the Army those ideals, inspirations, and leadership it seeks." Such ideals were visible, according to Hoffmann, "not only in such commanding figures as Washington, Marshall, and Eisenhower, but also in the dedication and integrity of many thousands of soldiers—citizen and professional—who have compiled an enviable record of the nation's trust upheld." The secretary said, "This trust is neither surprising nor suspect. It has survived well because the Army has been an essence, or distillation of the people, a symbol of the nation at its best."[37]

Federal officials have taken advantage of this ideal time and again. When Harry S. Truman concluded that the time and politics were right to begin the fight against racial discrimination, for example, he began by desegregating the armed forces in 1948.[38] It was the government's way of saying, "Here is the way things ought to be, and we expect the rest of the government and society to follow suit." So it followed with furthering opportunities for women in the 1970s and 1980s, and the attempt to minimize discrimination against homosexuals in the military in the early 1990s. The latter effort may have been politically misguided and it certainly failed, but it is no accident President William J. Clinton chose to attempt mandating equal rights for homosexuals in the military before proposing similar legislation that would affect other segments of American society.

Americans, in the form of Congress, also asked the young to lead the way in enforcing new values and modes of behavior when women were admitted to West Point. The military is, after all, predominantly a young person's domain.

To be thirty in the armed forces is to be old, perhaps a veteran with ten or more years of service already looking toward retirement, and the bulk of the soldiers, sailors, airmen, and marines have traditionally been enlisted personnel between eighteen and twenty-five with a high turnover rate. Not even these professionals were chosen to make integration at West Point work. Instead, it fell upon the young (eighteen to twenty-two years old) cadets of the service academies to put aside a culture they inherited and make a revolution succeed. They were shepherded by their elders, of course, but in the end, the success or failure of the integration of women rested primarily on less mature, less experienced shoulders. It should be no surprise that some of them struggled with the transition, for the Academy learned from experience that supposedly more mature, more experienced, and more professional officers had trouble as well.

At West Point, those young men struggling with their perceptions about the role of women in society included cadets who paid their own price for being associated with the admission of women. They were the men of the Class of 1980, and they struggled for recognition in the shadows of the bright lights which history, the press, and the public focused on their female classmates. It is little wonder that some of them felt forgotten and that some joined with older graduates in mourning the loss of traditional West Point life. They did so for a variety of reasons, whether from frustration or envy at the attention focused on women cadets, because they believed the admission of female cadets represented a change for the worse at West Point, or because they sometimes received extra sneers from men in other Academy classes simply because women were among them. Upperclassmen attacking women cadets in general often turned to a man from the Class of 1980 and harangued him for the performance of "YOUR" female classmates, or reminded him that "YOUR" class had ruined the West Point experience. These men also suffered the realization that they could not have the same West Point experience as the men who graduated before them. They often resented women more than other male cadets because the attention from the press and Academy officials affected them directly.[39] They were "catching a lot of shit from the upperclassmen because there were women in the class," and were perhaps influenced by the often bitter Class of 1977 Firsties who led the Corps during their Plebe year.[40] Not all men of the 1980 class felt they were blamed for the presence of women, but most experienced at least some tangible reminders that their class differed from those that had gone before.[41] History forever marked it with distinction, and it became a distinction which more than a few men regretted.

For other men, even those outside the Class of 1980, there were social consequences tied to associating with female cadets, especially when it came to dating. After asking a young cadet woman to a dance, for example, a male cadet accepted a ride from the wives of two Academy officers when he needed to travel from one end of the post to another. In the midst of idle conversation, he casually mentioned that he was dating a female cadet, and the discussion suddenly ceased. The women refused to talk with him for the duration of their journey.[42] Their silence reflected yet another layer of the resistance toward female cadets at West Point, for the wives of Academy graduates, faculty, and staff members sometimes resented the presence of women within the Corps of Cadets even more than their husbands did.

Yet resentment always remained strongest inside the barracks, where many men felt that female cadets successfully bent the rules more often. Women, it was said, often called out "dressing" to keep upperclassmen out of their rooms until they were ready. Men could do that as well, but the consensus among many cadets was that women abused the privilege.[43] Male cadets, they suggested, were far more likely to suffer the indignity of having an upperclassman barge into their room without warning hoping to find items out of place or catch inappropriate behavior. Women were said to use tears to leverage their way out of tough duty, and the men hated it. Much of this criticism reflected deeply rooted, sometimes unconscious antagonism toward women more that it did any sort of widespread truth, and some cadets maintain they never saw a woman cry on duty.[44] It should also be remembered that many male cadets cried as a result of the frustrations and exertions of cadet life, a fact too often ignored or neglected by male members of the Corps. Still, the perception that women were "getting over" remained pervasive, and it became an enduring source of (and an excuse for) hostility towards women cadets that lasted long after the Class of 1980 graduated.

There were other frustrations. Male cadets often resented the unprecedented speed with which the first women were admitted, for it stood in stark contrast to the painstakingly slow process by which they were forced to compete with thousands of other candidates for an excruciatingly limited number of slots at the Academy.[45] They resented the fawning adulation showered on the women as well. The attention came from everywhere at once: from the president, the press, Congress, the Secretary of Defense, the Secretary of the Army, and every tourist on the post. In 1978, Columbia Pictures even made a movie for television titled *Women at West Point*, and the men hated that too. Women "represented a very small portion of the class" of 1980, yet they seemed to garner more notice than the rest of the Academy put together.[46]

Women also seemed to quit too easily, and when they did, the men grumbled mightily about the prized slot that had been wasted on a woman while a more deserving man who could have entered the combat branches of the service had been left at home. "There goes another slot a guy could have had," they said, though one male cadet wrote later in life, "We forgot how many men quit so easily."[47]

Then there were the tiny but seemingly important changes to cadet life which women brought with them. Prior to their arrival, for example, cadets considered it a "big thing for the upperclassmen to saunter to the bathroom with nothing on but a towel over their shoulder," because such posturing separated them from Plebes who by regulation were required to be clothed at all times except in the shower. Once women arrived, the Academy took away that "privilege."[48] Some cadets also lamented the fact that the "admission of women limited the lexicon available to the upperclass when dressing down Plebes," because some cadets (but by no means all) felt compelled to obey orders against swearing in the presence of women.[49] Plebes were barred by regulations from swearing, but for upperclassmen the new reluctance seemed to be yet another small but important denial of a privilege for many men.

Then there were the new privileges bestowed on female cadets. Unlike their male peers, women had window shades in their rooms, which in the long run became both a blessing and a curse.[50] The shades were installed in haste when the Academy realized during Beast Barracks that female cadets were visible through their windows, especially at night. While providing some measure of privacy, however, the shades had the unfortunate effect of identifying which rooms belonged to women to everyone passing by outside the barracks. In that way the shades were bulls-eyes which made life much easier for those who wanted to harass women by attempting to peer inside their windows or throw things at them, and the shades therefore represented a well-intentioned effort by the Academy which made life harder for many women. In the long run, as the rooms rotated among cadets year after year, the rooms became prized havens because the shades allowed cadets regardless of sex to sleep later in the morning without being awakened by the sun.[51] Yet in the short run, they were one more example of what many male cadets saw as preferential treatment for women at West Point. The fact that changes in tradition or physical facilities were neither asked for nor implemented by women did not matter within the Corps, even though it should have. Congress ordered the Academy to admit women. West Point officers ordered changes in tradition, behavior, and physical accommodations, and yet female cadets received the blame. And while many of the changes seem excruciatingly trivial, they had a real effect on the traditionally minded. As William Whyte wrote, "The more exquisite distinctions are, the more important they become."[52]

Above all, many male cadets felt great anger and frustration over the differing physical standards, over the fact women could pass with times and performances for which men would fail. These standards contained within them seldom-questioned, male-oriented standards of leadership. Those standards put a premium on physical prowess, and when physical requirements were modified for women, male cadets had to examine their assumptions about what it meant to be a leader as well. Many were bitter because the arrival of women and the establishment of modified standards for them seemed to tarnish the Academy's elite reputation. As one member of the Class of 1979 wrote, "It was the appearance of weakness that we perceived that women brought to West Point and simple resistance to change that caused us to resent the women."[53]

Men also resented the fact women were put through self-defense courses while they were pushed through mandatory boxing classes. Celebrated at West Point because it demanded a willingness to suffer and inflict actual physical pain on an opponent, boxing seemed to approximate combat in a way no other physical activity could. Instructors said boxing helped identify very early which cadets would fight the hardest when threatened and toughened cadet bodies and psyches to a remarkable degree. Many male cadets feared boxing, however, and endured a series of ritual beatings at the hands of cadets either larger or more skilled than themselves. Given the opportunity, many of them would have jumped at the chance to avoid the training altogether, but it never came. As one man put it, "I wish I could have avoided boxing and wrestling."[54] The differing regulations, the fact that women did not have to box or wrestle, reflected decisions made by the Academy rather than by by female cadets, but they fueled resentment against female cadets just the same.

Perhaps most fundamentally to many male cadets, the admission of women just did not seem to make any *sense*. Why, they asked, admit cadets to an institution dedicated to preparing young leaders for combat if they would never be expected to command troops in battle? The notion seemed to mirror the fanciful notion of a football team investing the time and effort to devise drills and modified standards so that someone who would never be allowed to play in a real game could make the team. Some found it manifestly apparent that Congress had forgotten the purpose for which the United States Military Academy had been created in the first place. In the eyes of purists, West Point did not exist to serve the ends of artists, poets, or musicians, or for philosophers, priests, or social workers. The institution existed solely to train people for combat, to instill in them a willingness to kill and the skills to lead soldiers in battle and to cope with death. Cadets were there to learn how to win wars, whether popular or unpopular, long or short, limited or total, and being *fair* had nothing to do with that sort of training. Fairness, after all, did not exist amidst the random injustice of a battlefield, and cadets railed at the "idiots in Congress and the Courts that made us accept women."[55]

Such resentment grew particularly acute among those men who conceived of West Point as a capstone of masculinity, a place where a young man went to prove his manliness or worth physically, mentally, and emotionally. These young men were usually conservative, with culturally induced conceptions of women that made no allowance for female inclusion in the Long Gray Line. Their views were perpetuated by the regular Army officers of the Academy and by the legions of Old Grads for whom the admission of women represented a lachrymal event.[56] One woman from the Class of 1980 suggested that family heritage influenced the feelings many young men had toward women cadets as well. Referring to male cadets who despised the presence of women, she said, "I think it's just the old 'diehards' that have wanted to come here since they were little because their dads and their grandads and everybody went here." She added, "I can understand that. That's kind of a tough thing, and then they find women are going. It's like the whole thing has just crumbled. . . . When you're brought up with that idea, it's hard to get rid of it."[57]

To fit in, women learned to adopt the West Point style of leadership, and male cadets were confronted with the realization that many women were superb leaders even though they were hardly masculine and often donned "masks of command" which were unfamiliar to them. Even when leadership styles were different, cadets found in the long run that sex had nothing to do with real effectiveness. The best leaders showed themselves to their followers "only through a mask . . . made in such form as will mark him to men of his time and place as the leader they want and need,"[58] and that was true whether the leaders and followers were men, or women. Physical strength, it turned out, did not matter as much as strength of character.

Amidst all of these conscious and unconscious changes and in the fulcrum of peer pressure, tradition, and cadet assumptions about West Point, it required extraordinary maturity and reflection for a male cadet to realize women were not to blame for changes at the Academy. Unfortunately, West Point leaders were not always helpful in this regard. As one cadet said later, "Introspection was never something stressed at West Point. . . ."[59] Women did not break down Thayer Gate or march in angry columns on the Superintendent's quarters to be admitted; Congress had opened West Point to them. Women were not to blame for the attention the press showered on them and could hardly be castigated for occasionally enjoying the limelight. After all, male cadets liked the attention they received, too. Women were not responsible for the differing physical standards and could not be held responsible for the fact the Academy sometimes bent over backwards to accommodate them. They were not to blame for the fact tourists fawned on them and sponsoring families on post competed for the chance to feed them dinner and socialize with them as their "West Point family." Women, it turned out, came to the Academy for the same reasons the men did: they were drawn by the aura, the free tuition, and the chance to serve their country. They were hardly dyed-in-the-wool feminists when they arrived at West Point, and though many were driven to become more active participants in the fight for women's rights by the injustices they endured at the Academy, they were hardly leading rebellions on The Plain. Instead, they wanted to fit in and be accepted, just as the men did. Too few male cadets recognized these truths, however, and in the competitive atmosphere of the Academy, almost all bowed to the forces opposing women at least once.

Some men of the Class of 1980 struggled to reconcile a conviction that women did not belong at the Academy with the admiration and respect they felt for women as individuals. As one said, "When they are an impersonal group of 'women' it's easier to harbor ill will. When those same women become known as individuals that shared many of the same concerns, fears, and hopes that you did it is harder to hold those views."[60] This sort of one-on-one example often proved the only way some men came to change their views, a point made by a woman cadet in 1980. "I think the best way to get through to a male cadet is when he's working right next to female cadets and [they are] pulling [their] end of the load." There was nothing the institution could have done to change the minds of male cadets in advance, she argued, because "[t]hey already have a mind set once they are here . . . ," and in the long run "[t]here's nothing that the organization could have done to change his mind. . . . There's just nothing you can do. Except for the piece-by-piece example."[61] In the end, most men who came to support the integration of women into the Corps were won over in just this manner, one at a time.

From the very beginning of the process, a minority of men never held misogynistic views and chose instead to support the admission of women to the Academy. It should be noted the majority of the Corps of Cadets did not go out of the way to drive women out. If over four thousand men had closed ranks in an attempt to expel barely a hundred women, they would almost certainly have been successful; whatever the faults of many male cadets and the entire West Point system were, that clearly did not happen. Instead, most men were too concerned with their own survival to take the time to systematically harass women. Too many took the occasional cheap verbal shot or engaged in misogynistic banter with their fellow male cadets, but most refrained from stepping beyond these forms of discrimination, especially in private. As one woman put it, the "Corps" personality disapproved of female cadets, but in small groups or one on one the resistance among men was not as bad.[62] A violent minority of men went beyond harassment and engaged in sexual assault and physical intimidation, but the rest grew to accept the presence of women cadets over time, and some men even embraced the arrival of women as a positive good for the Academy.

Those who supported women usually fell into two categories: those who supported women from the first, and those who grew to believe the Army benefitted from the presence of women after witnessing their performance at West Point. One cadet in the latter group opposed the arrival of women prior to Congressional action, then reconsidered because, as he said, "I strongly believed then and do now that I am a servant of the people."[63] After seeing the women of the Class of 1980 in action, his views moved even farther until he argued, "If we're going to have women in the Army, why not make them the best officers we can?"[64] Making them the best, as every grad knew, meant allowing them to attend West Point.

For its part, the Academy generally did the best it could to assimilate women, and most officers dedicated themselves to making the new West Point work regardless of their personal feelings concerning the wisdom of placing women in Cadet Gray. They were groping in the midst of a new and bewildering situation, however, and predestined to make some mistakes. All of this made for wonderful news stories; after the turmoil of the early 1970s and the catastrophe of the honor scandal, the Academy leapt at the opportunity to capitalize on the admission of women as a positive public relations coup. Few cadets were able to see through the smoke of change and realize that their women peers were innocent byproducts of the greater social evolution behind the turmoil. The changes at West Point were manifestly not the responsibility of women; yet because they were there, it was far easier to lash out at them than to howl at abstract enemies like the American people or the distant Congress. Further, because many career officers on the Academy staff and so many of the alumni bitterly and savagely criticized women, it became an easy if ultimately despicable thing for male cadets who were desperate to fit into Academy life to jump on the vehemently antifemale cadet bandwagon.

Ironically, those young men at West Point were critical to making the integration of women any kind of success. For patriarchy to recede, men have always had to change; at West Point, that meant everyone from the Superintendent to the civilian work crews had to accept and become accustomed to seeing women in military leadership roles. They had to believe in their peers as well as the system, and demonstrate a willingness to obey and defend women in all sorts of environments, even when only other men were present. Too few did, and women in subsequent classes were forced to endure many of the privations inflicted on the women of the Class of 1980, but those strides that were made are a testament to the willingness of many cadets and officers to try and adjust their attitudes to the new reality Congress and the Army thrust upon them.

West Point and its all-male tradition thus had a great deal to face when women were admitted in 1976. Culture, history, biology, and tradition intermingled to create myriad obstacles in cadet minds against accepting women at the Academy, and only with time and a great deal of effort were those obstacles overcome. In the process, the old West Point passed away, and it is no paean to patriarchy to note that something unique and profoundly male disappeared in the process. Academy grads felt the loss most keenly, as did many members of the Corps. It took time to realize that a stronger, more beautiful, and perhaps even greater West Point could emerge in the long run.

NOTES

1. "When I Opened the Shutter," *Ladies Home Journal* 34 (August 1917), p. 15.

2. Barbara Ehrenreich, *Blood Rites: Origins and History of the Passions of War* (New York: Metropolitan Books, 1997), p. 237.

3. Martin Van Creveld, *The Transformation of War* (New York: The Free Press, 1991), pp. 181–82.

4. Ibid., p. 183.

5. Homer, *The Iliad*, vol. 12, 309–28, quoted in Alfred S. Bradford, *Some Even Volunteered: The First Wolfhounds Pacify Vietnam* (Westport, Conn.: Praeger, 1994), p. 171.

6. Vergil, *The Aeneid*, trans. and ed. by R. D. Williams (Edinburgh: Thomas Nelson and Sons, 1992), p. 1.

7. Van Creveld, *The Transformation of War*, pp. 182–83.

8. William W. Savage, Jr., *The Cowboy Hero: His Image in American History and Culture* (Norman, Okla.: University of Oklahoma Press, 1979), p. 95.

9. IWA, 5-16-97, author's notes.

10. See D'Ann Campbell, "Women in Combat: The World War II Experience in the United States, Great Britain, Germany, and the Soviet Union," *Journal of Military History* 57 (April 1993): 301–23.

11. Van Creveld, *The Transformation of War*, pp. 183–84. Interestingly, Israel modified the prohibition on women serving in combat so that women could serve as combat pilots and captains of combatant naval vessels in 2000.

12. See Janet Lever and Pepper Schwartz, *Women at Yale: Liberating a College Campus* (Indianapolis: Bobbs-Merrill, 1971), p. 193, for a discussion of the tendency of "monosexual education" to "foster sexual stereotyping."

13. Cadet Stephen M. Bird, for example, committed suicide on New Year's Day, 1919, after being viciously hazed for writing poetry. See Thomas J. Fleming, *West Point: The Men and Times of the United States Military Academy* (New York: William Morrow, 1969), p. 305.

14. Lucian K. Truscott IV, *Dress Gray* (Garden City, New York: Doubleday, 1979), p. 8.

15. Physical fitness standards for women rose throughout the 1980s and 1990s, and studies show most women can perform rigorous physical duties as well as men, provided they are correctly prepared and trained. See "Undermining Old Taboos," *Armed Forces Journal*, May 1996, p. 13.

16. Lionel Tiger and Robin Fox, *The Imperial Animal* (New York: Holt, Rinehart, and Winston, 1971), p. 95.

17. Lionel Tiger, "Durkheim, Sociology, and the Science of Bodies in Conflict" (Paper prepared for the Interdisciplinary Summary Conference Study of War Project, Triangle Institute of Security Studies, June 1997), p. 3.

18. Lionel Tiger, "Are the Harassers in Charge?" *Journal of Contemporary Legal Issues* 8 (Spring 1997): 80.

19. Tiger and Fox, *The Imperial Animal*, p. 96.

20. Tiger, "Durkheim, Sociology, and the Science of Bodies in Conflict," p. 18. It is a compelling argument, for "The legal fiction," as Tiger wrote, "that race and sex are equal and similar categories of equity-risk is the strange and bitter fruit of biological ignorance." Ibid., p. 19.

21. See Ibid., pp. 16–17, for a modern discussion of the phenomenon.

22. Tiger, "Are the Harassers in Charge?" p. 81.

23. Richard C. U'Ren, *Ivory Fortress: A Psychiatrist Looks at West Point* (Indianapolis: Bobbs-Merrill, 1974), p. 3.

24. The problem persisted for a long time. In December of 1997, an 11-member advisory committee appointed by Secretary of Defense William Cohen and led by former Senator Nancy Kassebaum Baker of Kansas "unanimously recommended that the Army, the Navy, and the Air Force significantly roll back the integration of men and women in basic and advanced training." The committee argued gender integration resulted in "less discipline, less unit cohesion and more distraction from the training programs," because recruits and instructors spent too much time dealing with problems tied to sexual interaction, including illicit liaisons and even harassment. See Steven Lee Myers, "To Sex Segregated Training, the Marines Remain Semper Fi," *New York Times*, December 26, 1997, p. A1.

25. Romantic/sexual bonds have been used in the past to pull soldiers together, as when the ancient Greeks deliberately placed male lovers side by side in battle under the assumption they would fight harder for each other. This system was not passed down to modern Western armies, however. In the United States Army, openly homosexual soldiers are barred from serving, and sexual relationships are associated with dissension and discord within small units.

26. LTA, 2-14-96, p. 3.

27. Richard Rayner, "Women as Warriors," *New York Times Magazine*, June 22, 1997, p. 55. Rayner was writing about the Army as a whole, but the sentiment fits West Point as well.

28. Tiger and Fox, *The Imperial Animal*, p. 101.

29. Myron Brenton, *The American Male* (Greenwich, Conn.: Fawcett Publications, 1970), p. 81.

30. Ibid., pp. 81–82. See also Michael Kimmel, *Manhood in America: A Cultural History* (New York: The Free Press, 1997); and E. Anthony Rotundo, *American Manhood: Transformations in Masculinity from the Revolution to the Modern Era* (New York: Basic Books, 1993).

31. U'Ren, *Ivory Fortress*, p. 119.

32. Ibid., pp. 8–10.

33. Rayner, "Women as Warriors," p. 26.

34. Tiger and Fox, *The Imperial Animal*, p. 94.

35. Ibid., p. 93.

36. Ibid., p. 57.

37. "Graduation 1976," *Assembly* 35, No. 2 (September 1976): 20.

38. Truman acted both from principle and from a desire to gain support from African Americans in the 1948 presidential election. With the Democratic Party badly divided over civil rights, Truman needed all the support he could get.

39. The depth of resentment stemming from press attention paid to the women of the Class of 1980 cannot be overestimated. One subtle indication came when the 1980 *Howitzer* was published; in a 27-page pictorial dedicated to the Long Gray Line and the Firsties who would graduate in May 1980, only one photo of a woman appeared, and she was talking to a reporter.

40. LTA, 9-24-96, p. 4. The Class of 1977 was decimated by the cheating scandal during the fall of 1976, and many class members were angry and resentful towards the Academy. As leaders with no memory of women at West Point during their own formative years at the Academy, they were also unlikely to look upon the radical change in gender roles with approval.

41. IWA, 3-26-97, author's notes.

42. EI, 5-5-80, p. 8.

43. One cadet admitted that some women occasionally used this tactic but added that in her experience women sat studying in their undergarments so that they could say "dressing" without violating the honor code. She added that this was "only a desperation tactic used when someone was having a hard time and needed those extra couple of seconds to maintain composure/sanity!" See ETA, 6-21-2000, pp. 1–2.

44. IWA, 3-26-97, author's notes.

45. IWA, 4-13-96, author's notes.

46. LTA, 9-24-96, p. 4.

47. Ibid.

48. ETA, 7-8-96.

49. James Lovell, *Neither Athens Nor Sparta? The American Service Academies in Transition* (Bloomington, Ind.: Indiana University Press, 1979), p. 265.

50. ETA, 7-8-96.

51. IWA, 6-9-96, author's notes.

52. William Whyte, *The Organization Man* (New York: Simon and Schuster, 1956), p. 157.

53. ETA, 7-8-96.

54. ETA, 7-24-96.

55. ETA, 7-8-96.

56. EI, 5-80, p. 17.

57. EI, 5-14-80, p. 16.

58. John Keegan, *The Mask of Command* (London: Jonathan Cape, 1987), p. 11.

59. LTA, 1-18-96.

60. Ibid.

61. EI, no date, p. 12.

62. EI, April/May 1980, p. 14.

63. LTA, 9-24-96, p. 2.

64. Ibid.

6

★ ★ ★ ★

"You Are Here for Your Country"

[T]he bravest are surely those who have the clearest vision of what is before them, glory and danger alike, and yet notwithstanding go out to meet it.
—Thucydides[1]

One of the many ironies of life at West Point is that it varied so much from one cadet to another. Certain broad experiences were common for everyone, but on an individual level some companies were simply better than others, as were some TACs, members of the faculty, and individuals among the upper classes. The ways in which these factors interacted had a great deal of influence on cadet lives, especially for the women of the Class of 1980. They found, for example, that many of the old rules of cadet life hardly applied to them at all. After Plebe year, most cadets were accepted as full-fledged members of the Corps, and the harassment and stress gradually declined as they accumulated rank and power and began focusing on the responsibilities inherent in holding greater authority. While life as a West Point cadet remained extremely demanding, life as a Yearling afforded greater ease and more security than that of the lowly Plebe. Yearlings usually reveled in their newfound freedom, using it over the years to establish a reputation as the wildest pranksters in the Corps. They also usually came to the aid of Plebes, for they were the closest in age, rank, and experience to the new class of cadets which entered on their heels.

Unfortunately, this pattern did not hold for the women of the Class of 1980. They found instead that their Yearling year proved even harder than their baptism by fire as Plebes, for by the fall of 1977 the Corps had polarized, and some men committed themselves to harassing female cadets more than ever before.[2] While the men of the Class of 1980 tried as a rule to help the incoming Plebes, the women, driven by harassment to distance themselves from each other and from the women of the Class of 1981, seemed distant and aloof from their subordinates. This generated resentment toward Class of 1980 women from below that sometimes rivaled the hatred and resentment they suffered from above, and by the end of their Yearling year, many women in the class felt more isolated and threatened than ever.

These feelings grew amidst a sense of continued isolation, for most women did not enjoy the bonding with upperclassmen that usually took place during a cadet's Yearling year. Instead, too many faced resentment from cadets above, below, and equal to them in rank, in companies which operated as virtual islands unto themselves. Each had its own peculiar mores and an often insular approach to training, which meant women could go days on end without seeing another female cadet. As a day-to-day reality, this meant that the five or fewer women assigned to each company in 1977–78 had few peers with whom they could discuss their unique problems, and when attrition inexorably reduced the number of women the problem became even worse. The enormous size of the Corps precluded most cadets from having more than limited contact with anyone outside their company and became a particularly difficult hurdle for the first female cadets at West Point to overcome. Membership in clubs and athletic activities sometimes mitigated this phenomenon because it might involve a blending of cadets from different classes, but it still remained possible for women in the 1980 and 1981 classes, through no fault of their own, to have absolutely no contact with each other.[3] The situation improved gradually as more women arrived each year, but that represented little comfort to the women of the Class of 1980. Plebes, after all, provided no solace for Yearlings, Cows, or Firsties. Thus, in isolation and without sufficent role models, most of the first women of West Point continued to suffer.

Their year as Yearlings began with a surprise in the summer of 1977, when both Superintendent Sidney B. Berry and Commandant Walter F. Ulmer were transferred to other Army posts prior to the end of their expected tours of duty. The "Supe" typically served four years, while the Commandant normally served for three, yet Berry received reassignment after three years and Ulmer after only two. The Army downplayed their removal, which had much to do with the honor scandal and a conviction among some officers that the opposition both Berry and Ulmer had expressed towards the admission of women made the successful integration of female cadets into West Point especially difficult. Most agreed Berry and Ulmer had done their best to make integration work once the order had been given, but some felt their past opposition, well-documented in the press and an article of faith among many male cadets, lingered forcibly in the minds of many West Pointers and could not be overcome without new leadership. Brigadier General John C. Bard replaced Ulmer, while General Andrew J. Goodpaster emerged from retirement as a four star general to take Berry's place in the three star (Lieutenant General) Superintendent's post.

A former aide to President Dwight D. Eisenhower, Goodpaster had served as Supreme Commander of NATO in the early 1970s. Highly regarded in the Army for his academic background and erudition, Goodpaster served as a professor at The Citadel prior to accepting the position of Superintendent at the request of Army Chief of Staff Bernard Rogers in June 1977.[4] Though widely applauded, Goodpaster's assignment spoke volumes about the trouble the old guard saw brewing at West Point, for in the entire history of the Academy no four star general had ever returned from retirement to serve in the three star post as Superintendent.[5] The unprecedented move came at the behest of Army officers and West Point alumni who felt their sacred alma mater, more accurately described as alma *omnia*, was in danger. The Army therefore took what steps it could to address the situation forcefully and, in the jargon of the service, to "drive on." While the honor scandal largely drove their fear, one graduate argued that Goodpaster's arrival did more than send a signal that the Honor Code needed reform. It also had a positive impact on the way West Point faculty members treated women, because many of those who were critics of the admission of women began changing their behavior and attitudes after Berry and Ulmer were "relieved."[6] Perhaps the Army hoped that would happen.

Goodpaster quickly took stock of the resentment towards women at West Point and realized that a great deal of "submerged opposition" needed to be brought out in the open. He attacked it by holding a series of meetings with staff and faculty in which he explained his views on women at the Academy. First, he argued, their arrival represented a positive good for the Army. He reasoned that if women were going to be in the Army there had to be female officers, and they had to have "preparation equal to that of the men." That meant admitting them to West Point and avoiding a separate training regime. After all, he suggested, "we know from past experience that separate but equal is not equal." Further, civilian leaders in Congress had made the decision to admit women; once that decision had been reached, it became time for every officer to "get with it." Finally, Goodpaster said that anyone who could not perform under those conditions could leave West Point. "I will walk with you down to the South Gate," he said, "shake your hand, and send you on your way."[7] The Superintendent's tone began a gradual improvement in the climate for women at West Point, though the gap between official pronouncements and life inside the barracks remained enormous for many years.

As Goodpaster and Bard settled into their positions, the Class of 1980 returned from a brief summer leave to attend Cadet Field Training (CFT) at nearby Camp Buckner. While some believed that resistance and overt harassment might begin to ebb during the second year for women at the Academy, male abuse actually grew considerably worse. To be sure, most men did not participate in sexual harassment on a routine basis. If they had and the majority of more than 4,000 men had decided to drive fewer than 200 women out of the Academy, the position of female cadets would have been untenable. Yet if only ten percent of those same men were adamantly opposed to the presence of women to the point they were willing to openly abuse female cadets, that represented 400 men in positions of authority who could make women's lives miserable. And if only one percent of male cadets were willing to use sexual violence or intimidation to accomplish the same ends, female cadets faced forty men in an enclosed environment who meant them harm. Whether these statistics are indicative of the actual ratios among male cadets is impossible to know, but they are illustrative of a salient point. Whatever the numbers, far too many men took the opportunity to abuse their female peers. For while most cadets were a reflection of America's best and brightest, there were a few who more closely personified societal ills. Such cadets were always present, for even West Point could not attract a representative galaxy of American youth without also garnering a cross section of otherwise intelligent and capable cadets gone morally and ethically astray. Unfortunately, those men who strayed from professional behavior toward bigotry and sexism became bolder in the summer of 1977. They made their presence felt most forcibly at Camp Buckner.

Located at the western edge of the West Point Military Reservation and originally named after Lake Popolopen, Camp Buckner honored General Simon Bolivar Buckner, a former Commandant of Cadets killed on Okinawa in 1945.[8] Utilized every summer for CFT, Buckner provided Third Class cadets with a basic introduction to the combat branches of the Army. Training lasted eight weeks and was divided into segments focusing on infantry, recondo, armor, weapons, land navigation, communications, field artillery, engineers, and air defense artillery. These classes were taught by upperclassmen and occasionally by regular Army soldiers who provided instruction in specialty areas and offered expertise regarding the latest field equipment. In addition, because all cadets at Buckner were upperclassmen, they enjoyed greater opportunities for relaxation than during Plebe year. Cadets could attend hops, participate in a wide variety of athletic activities, and relax by swimming, water skiing, or following other recreational pursuits.[9]

Unfortunately, there also existed much greater opportunity for harassment of women at Buckner than there did within the more closely supervised barracks. Living in sparse wooden buildings or camping in the field that summer of 1977, many resentful male cadets took advantage of their relative isolation to openly discriminate against and attack women on a routine basis, and there were few brakes on their behavior.[10]

Female cadets were especially vulnerable at Buckner because of the housing arrangements. Cadets slept in buildings which had not been modified with private latrines or partitions, which meant that regardless of unit assignment women were housed in a centrally located barracks area rather than with their usual company and an assortment of male peers. In terms of developing cohesion among women cadets this proved a good development. Unfortunately, it also made them very easy targets for men because the huts in which women stayed were a considerable distance from some assembly and training areas. Men harassed women cadets running to distant company areas, and sometimes threw rocks at the women's huts, breaking windows and howling insults even at night.[11] Some male cadets spit on women, made cat-calls, and the physical distance between male and female barracks created communication difficulties that led to women sometimes showing up for drills wearing the wrong uniforms.[12] The daily regime for women quickly became intensely frustrating. One remembers Buckner as a place where it seemed "sometimes almost nonstop that someone was crying."[13]

As training continued it grew increasingly difficult for the cadre to maintain control, and the accumulated hostility of male cadets erupted. One cadet told his sergeant that in a combat situation he would shoot women in the back.[14] Others clapped when women fell out of training runs, and the Jody songs became more wild and sexist.[15] Because the runs were more combat-oriented they involved full field gear on some occasions, including helmet, rifle, pack, fatigues, and combat boots. These runs were a shock to cadets who exercised in shorts and t-shirts during the academic year and were extraordinarily difficult for most women. They struggled with the heavy packs and in particular with regulation Army boots that seldom properly fit the smaller feet of women. As many as half of the women routinely fell out on morning runs, to the accompanying jeers of men who argued that women had no place at West Point. Those same men usually ignored male cadets who fell out with little comment.[16] Women who could not run, after all, proved to many cadets that *all* women were incapable of being soldiers, while men who fell out reflected poorly only on themselves. Emotionally and psychologically the runs became a dreadful ordeal for some women, who felt themselves being slowly ground down by what Ken Kesey called "the Combine," or the system in his novel, *One Flew Over the Cuckoo's Nest*. One woman later described the aftermath of these physically and emotionally demanding runs by saying, "In the women's barracks after the runs, it was a time of consolation, whispering, and quiet. Very little was discussed."[17]

Buckner marked a turning point in which many women realized that sexism lay at the heart of their ill-treatment. Yearlings were not supposed to be treated as badly as Plebes, but when abuses against women continued at Buckner, many women confronted the unpleasant reality that they were hated simply for being female. Paradoxically, most female cadets refused to appeal to the chain of command for help. Most did not want to be "martyrs" or say things were too rough, and deep down each knew that among too many male cadets and officers, "any girl that complains is a bitch, that's it."[18] Even worse, some women argued the Tactical Officers (TACs) did not pay close enough attention to what happened at Buckner, and rather than encouraging women to come forward with any problems they often discouraged them from complaining entirely.[19] On some occasions, reporting incidents to TACs actually resulted in even greater harassment.[20] "You were really signing your own death certificate [if you complained to the TACS]," said one cadet, because word always got back to the subjects of the complaint and they would then increase their hazing "until they broke you."[21]

Though some men were sympathetic from the beginning, others grew to respect women as cadets and leaders only over time.[22] One woman cadet later noted she had "found guys [at West Point] that are just really super people themselves."[23] If men were too helpful, however, they risked bringing the wrath of the angriest cadets on themselves, and most succumbed to the "tremendous lure to play the game—to say the right things" in the presence of those who argued that women had to be expunged from the Corps.[24]

Even well-controlled yet enjoyable cadet activities like swimming were often spoiled at Buckner because some instructors let male cadets relax by ranting about women.[25] All of these factors meant that most Class of 1980 women remembered Buckner as the nadir of their cadet years. "I remember crying a lot more at night by myself at Buckner," said one.[26] Her sentiments were echoed by a classmate who said some of the men "were just incredibly mean," adding, "I think that's when it [harassment] hit an all-time high—out at Buckner."[27] Another said, "I think I cried every night at Camp Buckner," adding that the worst part of the ordeal was "feeling like I didn't belong."[28]

Ill-treatment and resentment of women reached a pinnacle during the five-day introduction to advanced small unit combat and patrolling begun by Brigadier General William C. Westmoreland in 1961 during his tenure as Superintendent. Known as RECONDO, a hybrid of the words "reconnaissance" and "commando," the demanding field exercises emphasized infantry tactics and culminated in a timed challenge involving an outdoor obstacle course and land navigation tests.[29] Those who successfully completed the course in time received a coveted black RECONDO badge, and controversy brewed from the beginning in 1977 because women were allowed more time on the obstacle course than men. When a number of cadets of both sexes were given more than one chance to complete the course in defiance of regulations, some cadets who had already earned their badges stripped them off and burned them in protest. Many men focused on the women who were given second and third chances, arguing they offered proof of preferential treatment by the Academy. At the same time, too many ignored the men who were given extra opportunities to pass the course as well.[30] Though only a small number of male cadets burned their patches, their public disdain enraged many women, symbolizing as it did the frustration and sexism that existed within the Corps.[31] The burning of patches also caused a stir at the Academy because the press quickly reported and often exaggerated the incident.

More importantly, the incidents surrounding RECONDO training in 1977 highlight the difficulties inherent in the manner in which the Academy attempted to successfully integrate women at West Point, and they foreshadowed the eventual elimination of RECONDO in 1981. That elimination came after nineteen years of continuous RECONDO training during CFT and after a ten-year period between 1965 and 1975 when the Superintendent's Annual Report consistently showcased RECONDO as the high point of the Third Class summer.[32] The highly successful program foundered between 1977 and 1981 at least in part because the Academy chose to modify RECONDO standards for women, and in the long run those modified standards created enormous resentment among male cadets. As with other changes, female cadets were not to blame, though there were men in the Corps who thought they were in the late 1970s.

The Academy found it impossible to maintain RECONDO training because it abandoned the concept of equality in terms of physical standards in spite of the fact that West Point planners emphasized "equality" in all aspects of sex-integrated training. OPLAN 75–1, for example, stressed equality from the very beginning.[33] Yet that commitment ran up against the stark fact that in 1977 male cadets performed better than women on the grueling final portion of RECONDO training, a timed physical fitness exam conducted on an obstacle course and known as the Enduro Run. Eighty-nine percent of male cadets passed the run on the first attempt, while only forty-two percent of female cadets did the same. Academy studies found that women did better when paired with men and properly conditioned and that women enjoyed a seventy-three percent pass rate when given a second attempt. Yet by 1979, after two summers in which an average of fifty-eight percent of women cadets failed the Enduro Run, the Academy decided to make changes in standards rather than training. Men were required to complete the run in twenty-seven minutes after 1979, while women were allowed thirty-one minutes.[34]

This change occurred because Academy leaders argued that an average of ninety-seven percent of men passed the Enduro Run over time, indicating a clear need for a higher male standard. Further, they reasoned that the Enduro Run played on physiological differences between men and women, meaning the creation of different standards would be fair, and they concluded by suggesting that making a twenty-seven-minute test the primary discriminator in whether cadets passed or failed a five-day training regime made no sense.[35]

While sound on every level, as indicated by the higher percentage of women who passed the Enduro Run on the first attempt the following year, the imposition of different physical standards in RECONDO training highlighted the differences between the male and female training experiences at West Point and contributed to divisiveness rather than fostering cohesiveness and unity. As Captain David L. Grosso wrote of the changes, reducing the physical standards "simply emphasized and exacerbated the differences between male and female cadets at the Academy and in the end retarded the integration of women into the Corps of Cadets."[36] That retardation proved so divisive that leaders abandoned the entire RECONDO training regime in 1981, giving opponents of the admission of women to West Point one more change in tradition to blame on female cadets.

Perhaps most frustrating is the realization that Academy leaders were trying to do the right thing when they changed the physical standards. They acted in accordance with the idea of "Comparable," or "Equivalent Training," which Brigadier General Walter F. Ulmer, Commandant of Cadets, had outlined in 1976. Equivalent Training, he wrote, could be considered when physiological differences made it clear that women could not perform certain tasks and when Academy leaders developed acceptable modifications that would achieve the desired training results.[37] In short, Ulmer and those who followed his guidelines were attempting to help women survive the West Point environment, and their ideas later evolved into a "Doctrine of Comparable Training" by 1981.[38] What they helped create, however, especially at Buckner and within the RECONDO program, were feelings of intense resentment among male cadets that triggered even greater changes in the training program by Academy leaders. As Lieutenant Colonel Donna A. Newell of the Class of 1980 put it, West Point "opted to change the standard [for the Enduro Run] to make the women's performance appear more successful." Unfortunately, she argued, "In an organization popu- lated by motivated, intelligent, idealistic people, cadets and professional soldiers, this 'smoke and mirrors' move was seen as such and ultimately resulted in a 'corporate backlash' toward the women. . . ." That backlash among cadets and some members of the faculty and staff "appears to have caused the senior USMA leadership to dictate sweeping program changes (doing away with RECONDO altogether, for example) rather than incremental changes."[39]

While too much should not be made of changes to a single cadet training program, and while factors besides the presence of women may have influenced the decision to omit RECONDO training after 1981, the changes made between 1977 and 1981 to CFT are revealing because they show in microcosm the at- tempts by Academy leaders to protect cadet women and maintain a fair per- formance environment. By attempting to promote fairness rather than equality, however, they encouraged divisiveness by emphasizing the differences in female training, and they acted far too soon. Given the considerable strides made in female cadet physical performance over the last twenty years, it is reasonable to presume that women could have eventually met the higher standards if prop- erly trained and prepared. Rather than changing the training, however, West Point changed the standard, a move that Academy leaders made in a variety of other physical fitness realms as well. If the standards had remained the same, it is possible that female cadets might have earned respect among their male coun- terparts for attempting to meet the higher goals. Those that did meet the uniform standards of RECONDO training might have encouraged retention of the pro- gram, which Grosso argues "would have facilitated the integration of women into the United States Corps of Cadets and by extension the United States Army . . ."[40] Given the difficulties women faced in gaining acceptance from their male peers during the late 1970s and early 1980s, it is a pity the Academy did not try this approach.

When the summer of 1977 drew to a close and the Class of 1980 returned to the Academy for their second year, they were stunned to learn that West Point officials had dramatically "shuffled" much of the Corps. Characterized by the periodic reassignment of cadets en masse to different companies and regiments, shuffling broke up cadet cliques and taught the Army's future officers the importance of working with a variety of different people on a recurring basis. The shuffling done prior to the start of the 1977–78 academic year, however, had more than the usual aims in mind, for Academy officials hoped it would ease the integration of women as well. Researchers with Project Athena had concluded that companies which were all-male were the most antagonistic towards women, so the Academy scattered women into almost every cadet company in September. This came as a shock to many cadets, for it represented an abandonment of the original plan to slowly phase women into every cadet company by 1979. The move indicated an effort to break down the entrenched sexism of the Corps and a recognition by the Academy that immediate steps had to be taken to make sex-integration more successful.

While well-intentioned, the shuffling of women in the Class of 1980 had disastrous results for some female cadets. The bonds within individual squads and companies were extremely tight, formed as they were in the shared crucible of Beast and Plebe year. Being a Yearling meant almost nothing in a company which had not seen a new member weather the rigors of Plebe year, and many a victim of the shuffle found themselves outcasts in companies which made no secret of their dislike for the new members. This phenomenon grew exponentially worse when a woman found herself transferred into a company of "women-haters" whose members thought they had another year (or more) before females invaded their ranks.[41] Those whom fortune smiled on were transferred to a "good" company or stayed in their original assignment, and for them the effects of the shuffle were minimal. For those who transferred into companies that were hotbeds of misogyny, however, the shuffle meant one more year of severe harassment and abuse.[42] And all women were forced to confront a new situation in which there were fewer women in every company. That translated into a greater attrition rate because the support network among women weakened and stretched to the breaking point.[43]

Throughout the Academy, the renewed forms of harassment during Yearling year varied from company to company. One general theme was the persecution of homosexuals, for like the Army itself, West Point constituted a notoriously homophobic institution. Cadets known to be homosexuals were expelled, and those who were suspected of homosexual tendencies were often the victims of vicious hazing.[44] In the hunt for lesbians some male cadets even formed an informal "binoculars club" that routinely spied on women through open cadet windows. Besides enjoying the adolescent thrill of spotting women dressing or undressing, members of the club hoped to catch gay women being affectionate with one another.[45] On at least one occasion they were successful, spotting two women embracing each other in their room and immediately reporting the incident to higher authorities. Because the women were barely clothed, they were quickly dismissed from the Academy for getting "caught in the act."[46] Beyond bigotry, the incident demonstrated considerable hypocrisy on the part of cadets, for men were dismissed if suspected of homosexuality as well. "But see," as one woman said, "nobody ever hears about that with the guys," and the expulsion of suspected lesbians affirmed the convictions of those who argued that the women at West Point were all either "whores or lesbians."[47] The assumption became so familiar that some female cadets deliberately wore dresses when off post to avoid being labeled "queer."[48]

There were other signs of abuse as well, signs which told every woman at West Point they were both despised and vulnerable to the misogyny plaguing the Corps. Often the abuse and harassment came with a lewd, adolescent sexual twist. One woman opened a drawer in her room and found her swimsuit balled up and filled with semen.[49] Male cadets yelled "Move out bitch!" through barracks windows at women below them, a civilian janitor was caught stealing women's dirty underwear, and women were exposed to sexism aimed at non-Academy women as well.[50]

One of the most notorious examples was the "Pig Pool," in which a group of cadets contributed money into a pot prior to a Hop or other social event. To win the cash, a cadet had to accompany or engage in sexual acts with the most unattractive woman possible, with results determined by a vote of the group.[51] This demeaning exploitation of women actually stemmed from a game Regular Army soldiers sometimes played with prostitutes, and cadet women occasionally took part in the judging, or at least in the accompanying banter, because it provided a way of being accepted by male cadets and because resistance seemed so futile.[52] What it cost them to see other women treated so maliciously is impossible to know. One female cadet summed up the practice by saying, "I see [it as] more of a subtle, silent aggression against women. . . ."[53]

That aggression could appear even at social functions meant to raise rather than lower morale. At hops, for example, female cadets often dreaded wearing their formal Army dress uniforms while civilian women bussed in from other schools wore "beautiful gowns"[54] and drew the bulk of male cadet attention. "The dances were always heart-breaking," said one female cadet, "because they'd truck in real women for the men. . . ."[55]

Women also found their presence acknowledged in a cartoon strip which appeared for the first time in *The Pointer* during the fall of 1977. Titled "The Adventures of Peter Parsec, Space Cadet," the long running strip focused on the United Space Military Academy, which orbited Earth in the year 2078. Cadets at the academy were led by a beautiful First Captain named "Carrie Sabres," whose confident command of the futuristic Corps stood in stark contrast to the swashbuckling antics of her lowly sidekick, Peter Parsec.[56] Whether artist Mike Conrad intended any sarcasm with this arrangement is unknown, but he seemed to recognize that women were at the Military Academy to stay.

Between the comic strip and the various forms of harassment, women clearly could not hide at West Point. "To move freely in the United States Corps of Cadets, you had to be *anonymous*," wrote one cadet, and anonymity was a condition impossible for women to achieve.[57] Their notoriety and conspicuousness made them noticeable anywhere on post, and as a tragic consequence, many women found themselves vulnerable to sexual assault. They were often isolated in a sea of men within particular companies and at risk particularly in the evenings because the absence of locks on cadet rooms made them accessible targets. Like other forms of abuse, assaults became more common for the Class of 1980 during their Yearling year, a time in which many women experienced the worst harassment of their four years as cadets.

They were not the first to suffer at West Point. The colonial troops who began constructing fortifications at West Point in 1778 called the site "Point Purgatory," a reference to the forbidding climate and terrain and their isolation from settled, more comfortable areas.[58] By 1977, however, some women had reason to think of the Academy as a purgatory of another and much worse kind, for almost all of them characterized their Yearling year as the most difficult in terms of physical, emotional, and sometimes sexual abuse. The spring of 1978 in particular saw a dramatic increase in the number of late night incidents in women's rooms when cadet men appeared uninvited and molested or even assaulted female cadets. The number of occurrences rose noticeably after Eisenhower Hall began serving beer to upperclassmen.[59] "Lots" of uninvited guests began arriving in women's rooms after taps; though some of the encounters were relatively innocent, if still inappropriate, visits by shy men who "just wanted to have a nice talk with a pretty girl" and usually did not get "too out of hand," they were still an additional concern for cadet women.[60] Others involved alcohol, and sleeping women sometimes awakened in the middle of the night to find a male cadet standing silently over them.[61] How many serious incidents actually took place will never be known, for West Point is notably successful at keeping unpleasant episodes out of the public eye. Yet the attacks certainly took place and were a source of anger for many of the women of the 1980 class.

The Academy recognized the danger inherent in asking a few hundred young women to sleep without locks on their doors in the midst of several thousand young men and instituted a policy which barred women from sleeping alone. The policy had widespread implications on weekends, when members of the upper classes often went on leave and departed the post, and women whose roommates departed found themselves forced to move for a night or even two and sleep in a room with a stranger. Most bitterly resented the requirement because no similar policy affected male cadets, and a few defied the requirement and continued to sleep by themselves.[62] Others appealed for a repeal of the policy on the grounds it discriminated against women cadets and by arguing they could protect themselves in the event of trouble.

That at least some of them had reason to be worried is beyond doubt. The Commandant of Cadets in 1978 said that some women from the 1980 class reported a late night visitor known as the "cadet masher," and indicated that "any time the 'cadet masher' has identified himself they have been able to turn him away." The Commandant, however, "did not agree and intended to continue the policy [of barring women from sleeping alone]."[63] Though the reference to the "cadet masher" contained no specific information on the frequency of his visits or the danger he might represent, the Commandant's memo did indicate how serious senior officials at West Point considered the problem of uninvited guests in the rooms of women cadets even before the most severe attacks occurred in the spring of 1978.

One occurred during 100th night activities for the Class of 1978, when a drunken male cadet entered the room of a female Yearling in Fourth Regiment whose roommate had left for the weekend. The woman awoke to find the male cadet assaulting her and escaped only by persuading him that continuing the attack would bring consequences neither of them wanted. When he finally left, the woman almost immediately reported the incident to the chain of command, which responded by giving the male in question 150 demerits and 100 hours marching the area.[64] The punishment seems to have taken him right up to the verge of expulsion and might have been more severe had he continued with the assault any further. This incident is important because it illustrates how effectively the chain of command worked in *some* companies and how the Academy's desire to hide such incidents prevented other cadets from fully appreciating the threat they faced when sleeping alone.

That threat became abundantly clear a few weeks later when "Tiffany Clark," a Yearling in Third Regiment, suffered a serious assault at the hands of her platoon sergeant, a male Firstie in the Class of 1978.[65] Following " 'flag pole leave' to the Golden Rail Bar and Grill in [nearby] Newburgh where alcoholic beverages were consumed," the platoon sergeant returned to West Point and "signed in the company departure book" at 4:15 am on April 16. Shortly afterward, he entered the room of Cadet Clark, "who was sleeping alone in her room" despite Academy regulations ordering women not to do so. Clark was "awakened by Cadet . . . as he stood beside her and placed his hands upon her in a vulgar, demeaning and intimate manner." At first Clark tried to frighten her intruder by moving about as if she were about to awaken. Rather than leave the room, however, her Platoon Sergeant tried to hide behind her desk. She then got out of bed, turned on the lights, and clearly identified her attacker. After ordering him out of her room, Clark attempted to go back to sleep. Still frightened, she moved to the room of two women in another company without awakening them, then returned to her room around 7:00 am and made contact with the Cadet in Charge of Quarters.[66]

For a time the Academy struggled with how to punish the offending male cadet. Though he admitted drinking in Newburgh and entering Clark's room, he denied touching her in any manner, and in the end it was his word against hers.[67] Some members of the administration questioned her version of the incident. They suggested she invented her story for personal reasons, arguing it seemed suspicious because by her own account she did not scream or fight her assailant.[68] Academy officials initially decided to allow the man to receive a diploma but not a commission, yet this struck many cadets as a reward rather than any sort of reprimand or condemnation. Instead of having to serve his term in the Army as an officer, the decision would have allowed him to benefit from four years of free education and walk away. Eventually, in part because of protests made by a delegation of women from the Class of 1980, a review of the case led to the cadet being separated (expelled) without a diploma or a commission.[69] No criminal charges were ever brought against him.

Most women in the Class of 1980 were troubled by the way the Academy handled the incident, by the secrecy surrounding the assault and by the uncertain response of West Point officials.[70] The Commandant, one woman said, talked circles around women who went to talk with him about the incident, and others complained that Clark suffered "terribly" because she had little institutional support and no attorney or representative present in meetings with Academy officials or the attorney of her alleged assailant.[71]

In the aftermath, the Academy went to greater lengths to punish late night visitors. As one cadet indicated, "Since then (the Clark incident), like guys who have done the same thing have really gotten screwed, you know, a hundred hours [of punishment tours] and that kind of thing."[72] Men caught near women's rooms after hours were punished more severely than ever before, and yet the pattern and the severity of the abuse continued.[73] One woman reported a Cow coming into her room during her Yearling year to kiss her while she slept. Later in her cadet career she was forced to knee a male cadet from the Class of 1979 in the groin after he appeared in her room demanding sex in the middle of the night. He retreated, and she never reported the incident.[74]

How far some of those abusive encounters progressed is uncertain, but there certainly exists a possibility that one or more cadets were raped. As one women said in 1980, "I don't really think it (the Clark incident) has been the worst case though."[75] Another added that she was "sure there were people that were raped or attacked."[76]

Despite the notoriety of the Clark case among Academy women and some men, the late night "visits" continued, and the majority were suffered in silence. One cadet estimated that "Maybe fifty percent" of molestation cases were reported, and that the rest went unreported, in part because many of the victims were Plebes who were afraid to say anything.[77] Another cadet answered the question of whether a lot of sexual harassment went unreported by saying, "Yes, ma'am. An awful lot. I know myself that when I was a Yearling guys would come back drunk, and they would come to your room," she said. "And you couldn't report it or you felt stupid. People would say it was just you. The guy wasn't making an advance on you. And having to report it through your chain of command so everyone knows what happened. Where it's just such a 'touchy' issue is often very hard." Instead of reporting incidents, cadets often simply said, "Get out of my room. Leave me alone."[78] Some women maintained that all incidents were reported to "someone," but too often that someone had no connection to senior Academy leaders.[79] One cadet said she knew of two women who were touched at night without reporting it; another indicated she had been touched late at night by an unknown cadet and slept with a broom balanced against her door afterward, while another said the Clark attack constituted one of "numerous" cases she knew of personally.[80] One cadet indicated the attacks continued well beyond Yearling year, with a female Cow in her company fighting off an attack in her room when members of the Class of 1980 were Firsties.[81]

One of the reasons so many of these incidents went unreported is that women were frequently reluctant to announce unpleasant incidents to a male-controlled chain of command that often seemed indifferent to their situation. In such an environment, the victim felt put on trial, just as many rape and assault survivors often feel victimized by a judicial system that publicly describes their traumatic experience and allows attorneys to ridicule them. As one cadet put it, "How many rapes on the outside get reported?"[82] At West Point, the cadet chain of command and TACs were often to blame when this pattern occurred, for they sometimes suggested women provoked improper behavior among the men. This happened in both serious and relatively mild incidents, as when a male cadet threw a condom filled with water at a woman cadet. After reporting the incident the woman involved said, "It appeared to me I was the punished one. I was the one that had to report to such and such tactical officer's office to report to him what happened. And was I *sure* that this actually happened? Wasn't I exaggerating a little bit?"[83] When minor transgressions were handled poorly by Academy officials, women became less likely to report more serious attacks the Army might have dealt with more appropriately. The end result was that at times the most responsible members of the chain of command were in the dark. As one cadet said in 1980, "I don't know if the men realize that all of the women won't say anything."[84]

In the face of so much smoke it is difficult to understand why Academy officials did not take firmer action to quench the sexual assault fires raging in the barracks. One former graduate blamed institutional inertia and denial, as well as a very military tendency to believe that behavior prohibited by orders simply did not take place. In this environment, officials turned blind eyes toward unpleasant information and believed their own reports which said sexual harassment simply did not represent a major problem at West Point.[85] Such denial created a real hesitancy among some officers to follow up orders to see that they were obeyed. Instead, they demonstrated a tendency the Duke of Wellington saw in William Pitt the Younger. He was, the Duke said, "too sanguine. . . . He conceives a project and then imagines it done."[86] So it seemed at the Academy. As Major Nederlander of the West Point staff said in 1980, "Here, for example, they say there will be no more harassment, and leave it at that."[87]

How the Academy could believe reports which downplayed harassment in the wake of the exit interviews conducted with the women of the Class of 1980 is difficult to fathom, especially since the Superintendent's Special Advisor on Women's Issues, Major Irene Evankovich, conducted many of the interviews in which the extent of harassment became perfectly clear. Moreover, given the widespread nature of the abuse, there had to have been TACs and male cadets who were aware of the problem long before Evankovich's interviews, particularly since some cadet men became so concerned about the phenomenon they began standing guard in their company hallways to protect women at night.[88] One member of the Class of 1979 argued the real problem lay with Academy duplicity, that women "exposed the hypocrisy of the institution" and "the Janus-faced nature of many West Point leaders." Those leaders showed a tacit willingness to permit harassment, he said, even while the well-oiled Academy public-relations machine assured everyone concerned that all remained well along the Hudson.[89] In the end the most meaningful changes to protect women were not made until the early 1990s, when locks were finally placed on the doors to all cadet rooms. It was a change that women in the Class of 1980 had called for during exit interviews by a two-to-one margin.[90]

One former staffer indicated that another part of the problem stemmed from the fact Academy leaders simply did not know how to handle the assaults and therefore dealt with them in a punitive fashion and hoped they would simply go away. If a problem did not involve "how many bullets or how much equipment," he said, or some other kind of tangible question that merited an obvious and attainable response, then the military training given West Point's leaders generally did not prepare them to handle issues such as those involving male/female interaction. They therefore convinced themselves the problem would take care of itself.[91]

If the institution deliberately or unconsciously lied to itself, so did some women. A sense of denial pervaded many of them according to some graduates, and many cadets refused to believe the extent of the harassment that took place inside the barracks after the final notes of "Taps" drifted across the sleepless Hudson each evening. After fighting to enter a prestigious and world-famous military institution that attracted some of the finest young people in America, some women tended to blame themselves or their peers rather than the Academy for allowing assaults to take place.[92] "I guess," said one woman, "that, you like to think that the image they portray here is that these are gentlemen, and we don't expect ungentlemanly behavior from them."[93] This chasm between the noble young knights of West Point myth and the crude reality of some male cadet behavior drove women to despair. As one put it, "I've never seen a group of men that were so ungentlemanly-like in my whole life." They put on a good show, she explained, but were "pigs" when no one was looking.[94]

In his seminal novel *Once an Eagle*, Anton Myrer said, "You fight your bravest battles un-applauded and alone." That certainly held true for women at West Point. Everyone knew nights were the most dangerous time of all, for in the early morning most cadets slept and the midnight gropers prowled the halls. Like members of the infantry who have struggled against fear in war zones since time immemorial to make it to sunrise, many women struggled to relax and combat their fears until daybreak. Not all of them fought these battles, but some did, and those encounters strongly indicate that there were men who saw the women as targets rather than comrades-in-arms. All cadets had to fight against their inner fears and the tangible obstacles of academics and physical fitness to stay at the Academy, yet by their second and third years at West Point men seldom feared their fellow cadets. Too many women did.[95]

The assaults and late-night visits were part of a consistent pattern of male aggression against women in the armed forces, for historically "at every step toward their incorporation into the military, women have been met with coarse, mysogynistic resistance—jeers, hazings, and, above all, sexual assaults and harassment aimed at reminding them that, in the most primitive calculus, women are still not predators, but prey."[96] At West Point the hard truth endured that while all cadets were liable for what they did, women cadets were also liable for what they were. Men might be intimidated. They might live each day worrying about failure. But few men were ever in fear for their personal safety. Many women were.

Officially, the Academy admits to no rapes involving cadet women on post between 1976 and 1980 and no hard evidence is known to suggest otherwise.[97] Unofficially, however, and informally, some former cadets and members of the Academy staff and faculty believe rapes took place. "I don't want to remember what happened back then," said one woman who worked as an Academy staffer in the late 1970s, adding, "Everyone was just so scared." She argued TACs and members of the staff knew about the worst incidents and turned a blind eye, and that word seldom reached the public because "[t]hey keep things very quiet . . ." at West Point. "I think there were rapes," she said, "I really do."[98] If so, those rapes were extreme examples of a larger pattern of established harassment carried out by an excruciatingly small minority of the male cadets at West Point, and the ground between individual and institutional responsibility in such cases can become murky indeed. Yet the United States Military Academy is an institution which emphasizes the overwhelming importance of leadership, and one of the first lessons of leadership is that command and responsibility go hand in hand. Surely the powers that were, those cadets and officers responsible for the men and women in their charge, bear some measure of responsibility for whatever infamous acts were perpetrated against those under their command. There should be an upper limit, after all, to what even West Point cadets endure while training to serve their country.

One Academy graduate who served on the West Point staff in the late 1970s and early 1980s echoed this view, saying "horrific things happened" to female cadets, and that an internal USMA study in 1980–81 indicated more than forty female cadets had been groped and/or visited in their rooms by unwanted late-night intruders. Even more frightening to the staffer than the actual report was the reaction he found among the West Point hierarchy. One officer responded to the report by saying, "Oh my God. Thank goodness! I thought it [the number of visits] was more than that!"[99] This evidence must be kept in perspective by noting that the alleged study has yet to be found. If it does exist, however, it would give tangible credence to the overwhelming anecdotal evidence that assaults were a serious problem at West Point during the late 1970s.

In the midst of the harassment, the assaults, and the intimidation, it is interesting to ponder why so many women stayed at the Academy. For some, the
decision to leave or stay became a question of stubbornness and resiliency or a
simple refusal to let their enemies win. Perhaps others found, as Ulysses S.
Grant did, that the virtues of Academy life outweighed the defects. Geoffrey
Perret wrote, "The injustices inherent in the West Point system angered him all
his life, yet Grant could not help his deep attachment to 'the best school in the
world. . . . ' " It was "a place that for all its faults provided an excellent academic
education, a camaraderie among the cadets that led to lifelong friendships, a
competitive system that allowed poor boys to compete on equal terms with the
rich, and, above all, a place where Grant's deepest faith—patriotism—was
taught as the highest virtue a young man could aspire to."[100]

Others struggled on a daily basis with the temptation to leave until they
suddenly found themselves wanting to stay, desiring a military career, and sometimes even loving the austere cadet life at West Point.[101] "By all stretches of
the imagination," said one woman, "it was very clear that I should have left.
But there was just something that held my heart."[102] This indefinable something,
a spirit of sacrifice or patriotism or service, grew increasingly important to many
women who decided to endure the rigors of the Academy, just as it did among
many men. One woman spoke of having some good days and some bad, until
finally, "You're out at a parade and tingles go down your spine when they are
playing 'The Star Spangled Banner' because you are here for your country . . .
not because you're first."[103]

Such idealism certainly never overwhelmed all cadets, and even among those
who felt the mystic pull of West Point it could be a fleeting thing. On most
days, the parades and formations, the endless fealty to form, tradition, and regulations made cadets weary beyond their years. Most were too busy and too
focused on simply getting through the day and surviving to get idealistic about
West Point. The place scared them for for the first few months as cadets, and
after that it became a test of endurance. Almost all cadets mocked any sense of
misty-eyed reverie as suitable only for Old Grads and gung-ho civilians, and
they did so even when the more reflective among them realized they would one
day be Old Grads themselves.

Yet service, sacrifice, and patriotism were an implicit and unavoidable part
of the United States Military Academy, and many cadets came to "love the
discipline and the challenge."[104] More than a few, perhaps even a majority, also
found that when the mood and setting were right they could be overcome with
the palpable *meaning* of service at West Point. Duty. Honor. Country. Each
word resonated with many cadets, animating the shadows cast by the Bradleys
and the Pershings, making them somehow more comforting and less intimidating. The ties that bound cadets to each other, to the Army, and to America were
tangible in such moments, heartfelt and genuinely pure. They enjoyed a "bond
of shared experience no one can match," and a feeling of community apart from
the pedestrian norms of a society outside West Point so seemingly drunk on

egalitarianism it believed in nothing save the self.[105] Those moments could inspire almost anyone for a long, long time. As West Point graduate John Alexander Hottell wrote in his obituary, "I deny that I died FOR anything—not my country, not my Army, not my fellow man, none of these things. I LIVED for these things, and the manner in which I chose to do it involved the very real chance that I would die in the execution of my duties." That chance he understood. "I knew this and accepted it, but my love for West Point and the Army was great enough—and the promise that I would some day be able to serve all the ideals that meant anything to me through it was great enough—for me to accept this possibility as a part of a price which must be paid for all things of great value." He concluded by saying, "If there is nothing worth dying for—in this sense—there is nothing worth living for."[106] It would be an absurd stretch to argue that all cadets or officers shared Hottell's idealism or sense of sacrifice, but no stretch at all to say that cadets required some measure of idealism, patriotism, or sense of duty to endure their struggles at West Point. And whatever their source of inspiration, those cadets who persevered tapped into it just often enough to resist the urge to bolt from the ranks and abandon West Point for civilian life.

Ultimately, many found a timelessness to West Point. A pervasive feeling of strength emanated from the storied granite rocks of the fortress on the Hudson. Even the bronze sentinels standing eternal watch over The Plain seemed humbled by the serenity, the utter conviction which flowed down from the hills and rose up from the mighty river to envelop the ghosts of MacArthur, Eisenhower, Patton, and the rest of the Long Gray Line. West Point was special. Three million visitors a year traveled to the Army's Holy of Holies to attempt to sense that uniqueness, bringing with them a sense of curiosity, admiration, and awe which seldom met with disappointment. Mars, the Roman god of war, would have felt at home there, for the United States Military Academy existed as a Mecca for warriors, for those who sought the profession of arms as a vocation. It pulsated with conviction, with commitment, with purpose. That purpose represented one of the reasons many cadets went there in the first place, because being a cadet gave "one a sense of belonging to something greater than oneself and doing something on a grander scale."[107] Though the Academy could be deliberately anachronistic, that fact sometimes became enough reason to stay by itself. Man or woman, cadets knew they received a sense of accomplishment at West Point they could not receive anywhere else. The Academy honored and urged them to embrace ideals their civilian peers too often seemed to abandon, and it mattered.[108]

Some women, of course, went beyond patriotism and stayed simply because they were stubborn or felt outside pressure to endure. One who had thrown a newspaper route as a young girl, using her brother's name because the paper in her hometown would not hire girls, said she just hated being told no.[109] Others were trapped by the feelings of relatives, either real or perceived, or by the myths and aura that surrounded the Academy. Cadets, after all, never left or transferred from West Point, they *quit*, and many adhered to the idea they should take advantage of what everyone in their lives usually described as a golden opportunity. Many of them feared disappointing loved ones. As one woman said, "There had been so much press coverage, so many people who had invested so much in me that basically I just couldn't let them down."[110]

Yet if loved ones sometimes represented a source of pressure forcing cadets to endure, they were also the supportive influence that allowed cadets to persevere in a positive way. One female cadet received a box of suppositories from her mother during a period of particularly bad treatment from upperclassmen. Inside her mother had penned a note which said, "Tell the upperclassmen to cram these! Love, Mom."[111]

Inside each cadet there also seems to have been a kind of emotional cost versus benefit analysis occurring on a regular basis, and for some cadets, the Academy simply required too much sacrifice to leave. A single day at West Point demanded considerable physical and emotional effort just to endure, much less excel, and the effort cadets made just to survive the system meant they were invested emotionally and psychologically from the very first day. A tremendous bond of shared experience tied them to other cadets in ways few other colleges could match, and even those who left early often remembered their time as cadets as the most intense, most challenging period of their lives. All these forces combined to give even cadets who hated the Academy pause before leaving. Some even said they admired those cadets who actually had the strength to leave, because, "it takes so much courage to resign from here. . . ."[112]

Religion also became a powerful influence on some, providing a sense of faith and courage to endure the many privations of Academy life. As one woman remarked, "the Academy is very religious," and in the numerous chapels on post many cadets found a sense of solace notably lacking inside the barracks.[113] Chapels were also among the very few places at West Point where upperclassmen could not discipline Plebes, and thus provided cadets with tangible forms of relief as well.

Chapels also represented a part of the Academy and even Army history, and they celebrated the achievements of West Point graduates. In that way services were a time when cadets felt drawn closer to West Point even as they sought divine providence and inspiration. The Old Cadet Chapel, for example, dated to 1836 and contained battle flags and plaques commemorating graduates and feats of arms throughout the nineteenth century. Above the altar stood a painting entitled "Peace and War," by Robert Walter Weir, who served as Professor of Drawing at West Point from 1834 to 1876. On the east side of the choir loft hung a plaque which made silent reference to General Benedict Arnold, whose service against the British during the Revolution merited *some* notice, but whose eventual treason led to the posting of the plaque without his name.[114] And below, even while enjoying services, cadets could sit in the famous "sleeping pew" and ponder the fate of the legions of upperclassmen who competed for the opportunity to sleep there in the nineteenth century. They did so because a pillar blocked any clear view of the pew from the pulpit, and many an upperclassman may have slept more there than inside the barracks.

This sense of history, of tradition, found even more dramatic expression in the Gothic Cadet Chapel, completed in 1910, which towered over the Academy grounds from a perch 300 feet above The Plain. Inside the chapel hung regimental flags and banners from the Civil War, the Spanish-American War, and the Philippine Insurrection, and stained glass windows commemorating every graduating class between 1802 and 1976 adorned both sides of the 200-foot long nave.[115] Twelve bells weighing more than seven tons hung in the bell tower, along with a carillon consisting of 122 miniature bronze bell units whose peels could be heard for miles.[116] Finally, services were given a passionate power by the largest church organ in the world, which after extensive expansion included more than 290 ranks and 19,000 pipes.[117]

While this sort of tradition and history inspired some awe-struck cadets to stay, others remained because Academy life could sometimes be *fun*. Underneath the uniforms and haircuts and hidden below the precision military image projected by most cadets were several thousand regular American college kids. They enjoyed their music, their free time, the occasional date, fast cars, sports, and the other accouterments of American youth culture. Most of all, they relished letting off steam through pranks and assorted unofficial Academy activities. Mooning and flashing, for example, raged among cadets in the 1960s, and streaking became frequent among cadets in 1976 and 1977. On one occasion, a group of exhibitionists even donned masks and sneakers to play nude basketball in a company area.[118] Female cadets played practical jokes on each other as well; in one instance, a women dressed up as a pregnant cadet, complete with a pillow stuffed under her shirt, to the riotous cries of her company.[119] During football season rallies were held before every game to raise Corps spirit, and cadets wearing "togas with sabers, or Full Dress coats with shorts instead of trousers" were not an uncommon sight within the barracks. Cadets were actually encouraged to go crazy from time to time, because it developed esprit de corps and released the pent-up anxiety of the Corps.[120]

Upperclassmen also had the privilege of escaping to New York City on weekends. Only an hour from the monastic confines of the Academy, New York offered limitless opportunities for mayhem, and some cadets snuck off post in illicitly hidden cars (only Firsties were officially permitted to own vehicles) on getaways that became legendary and sometimes increasingly apocryphal as they were recounted over the years. Over Thanksgiving weekend in 1978, for example, cadets from D company, third regiment, took two cars and broke the Academy rule book in half during a trip to the Big Apple. They rented a single room at the Hotel President off of Times Square, got drunk, then dressed in bed linens and shower shoes before assembling in front of the theater at which the film "Animal House" had debuted a few weeks previously. Young, almost naked men cavorted in the snow, drawing a huge crowd. Tourists posed with them for pictures. The evening finally took a bad turn when the aunt of one of the cadets spotted her nephew in the crowd. She had recently arrived on a vacation trip from Florida, no doubt assuming her cadet nephew to be safe and sound at West Point, only to find him freezing and seminude in Times Square. Her presence, and the eventual appearance of the New York Police, heralded the time for the cadets to retreat to more private surroundings, and they did.[121]

This escapade came on the heels of another memorable display of cadet mischief, one that took place during the annual Army-Navy football game in Philadelphia in 1978. With Army losing badly in the fourth quarter to their arch-rivals, men in the Corps of Cadets embraced the futility of further resistance and stripped off their cadet jackets en masse, revealing t-shirts with the number twelve on them that symbolized the role the Corps played as the Army team's twelfth man. Some members of the crowd were dumbstruck by the cadet showstopper, which drew the attention of a national television audience away from the carnage on the field and gave Army fans at least something to smile about. Some older graduates were offended by the breach of decorum, however, and one enraged matron claiming to be the belle of the Class of 1930 wrote, "I couldn't believe it—they took off their shirts! I fainted; thank God the women showed more restraint!"[122] Such incidents, while rarely in public or on so large a scale, were part of Academy lore and often encouraged by the West Point chain of command. Prior to the 1978 Army-Navy game, for example, cadets were *required* to purchase the number twelve t-shirts because tradition dictated that such stunts were a favored method for blowing off steam, relieving stress, and showing spirit.[123]

Yet no amount of ribald antics could hold every cadet at the Academy, and among those who chose to leave, personal reasons were the most common explanation for departing. Some women despised the regimented lifestyle, the lack of privacy, and the Spartan surroundings. One left because cadets were required to stay single, and she "chose marriage over West Point." Ironically, she transferred to a civilian university, entered an Army ROTC program, and was commissioned a Second Lieutenant before the Class of 1980 graduated from West Point.[124]

As Yearling year drew to a close and the Class of 1978 prepared to graduate, other aspects of Academy life tied to the admission of women became more clearly discernible. The women appeared, for instance, to deflect harassment from African Americans and other minorities because they were so deeply despised that they attracted almost all negative cadet attention.[125] Racial bigotry seemed to go increasingly underground while antagonism towards women stayed out in the open, and African-American cadets were generally more sensitive toward women than were whites.[126]

In the classroom, where academics were largely unaffected on the surface by the admission of women, the presence of female cadets still managed to produce discernable patterns of distinctive behavior among the cadets and faculty. Instructors consistently graded women much harder in Military Science classes, to the extent that some female cadets stopped studying because they concluded it was impossible to earn either an A or B in those courses. Some West Point faculty members seem to have assumed women were incapable of understanding military operations, and therefore either consciously or unconsciously gave them low marks.[127] Perhaps this trend stemmed from societal assumptions concerning the proper role of women, or from a conviction that female cadets barred from service in combat units did not need high scores in Military Science anyway. It may also have come from a deep-seated sense of resentment among some members of the faculty and staff, who may have felt angry over the presence of female cadets at the Academy or even threatened because women who earned high marks might challenge male control over combat units.

Female cadets were also "evaluated lower by upperclass cadets" during peer evaluations of leadership, "but [rated] similarly by cadets and officers in the chain of command."[128] This meant that the upperclass generally downgraded the leadership capabilities of women as a *group*, but rated women they *knew* and had seen in action as being equivalent or even superior to their male peers. Like racism, sexism thrived in ignorance; just as many white cadets found it harder to discriminate against black cadets they knew personally, so too did men gradually lessen their antagonism toward women once they had seen the considerable talents of individual female cadets. While encouraging on some levels, the trend meant that women had to win over many male cadets one at a time, a tedious process that left little hope for general acceptance of women by men for many years.

Just as these patterns become discernible among male cadets, so too did women of the Class of 1980 gradually develop some generalized characteristics. Most noticeably, they found common means of adjusting to the overwhelmingly male environment at West Point. They did so because women could not simply blend into the Corps; they had to prove themselves. Some women argued that once they did so most men left them alone, and whether true or not, that conviction empowered those women who believed it with a sense of control over their harassment. It often formed the difference between those who felt their treatment as cadets gradually improved and those who described their time at West Point as four years of hell.

In terms of behavior, female cadets who complained the least generally did better with men but less well with other women, because there was a "thin line between blending in and being one of the guys."[129] Like the men, Academy women ruthlessly evaluated each other, establishing an informal pecking order based on strength, looks, and academics, and these qualities were "graded by everyone."[130] In some cases women turned on other women who were having difficulty as cadets. As one wrote, "if a woman was incompetent we would destroy her—even quicker than the men would—because she threatened all of us."[131] This Darwinian pattern stemmed from the persistent reality that men condemned all women for the performance of even a single average woman, while male cadets who struggled were considered exceptions to the general rule that said men belonged at West Point.

The hyper-competitive atmosphere led women to build their own stereotypes of women outside the Academy too, in part to protect themselves against comparisons with nonmilitary women. Male cadets often said civilian women were "real women," and in contrast some West Point women argued their civilian peers were "air heads" with "no brains."[132] This sort of stereotyping had real implications for those who bought into them most forcefully. For if female cadets at West Point had little in common with civilian women and if they were not fully accepted within the Academy or the Army, then it became a real challenge for them to find a group in which they belonged and were fully accepted.

This sense of isolation and identity crisis may have carried over to the way some women in the Class of 1980 viewed female cadets who followed in their wake. Some women in the Class of 1981, for example, felt deliberately shunned by their female superiors. The distance between women in these two classes may have come from the assumption of many male cadets that Class of 1980 women would become "big sisters" and "mother" the incoming Plebes. To avoid greater harassment, Yearling women "deliberately didn't," and in turn were considered to be "standoffish" and "snobs" by many women in the Class of 1981.[133] This led to a rivalry between women in the two classes, and Class of 1980 women sometimes "dumped" on women subordinates when the latter seemed to be getting favors or were perceived as having things too easy.[134] This rivalry did not exist in every company; where it did, it meant that women continued to endure gendered hardships and isolation even as their absolute numbers at the Academy increased. Female cadets often had trouble helping each other because of the sexism and harassment presented by the system and because of the ever-present fear male cadets would accuse them of playing favorites. Instead of helping each other cope more effectively, they were thus victims in yet another way of the often subtle but effective male resistance that worked against them.

More fundamentally, women in the 1980 class were spread so thinly throughout the Corps that they had very little opportunity to mentor women in the Class of 1981. Unless they were assigned to the same company or platoon, in fact, women in each class could go for days at a time without ever seeing each other; in that environment, the accusation that 1980 women were deliberately cold seems unfair. Like other cadets, they were so isolated within their company or squad and by the demands of their daily routine that they often mailed letters to friends who lived only a few hundred yards away because it represented the only reliable means of contacting them. In the days before e-mail, cadets resorted to attempting to time it right so that they could nudge or exchange glances with passing friends in a stairwell or hallway. This kind of limited contact represented the "highlight of the day" for some cadets and is a measure of the sense of loneliness possible even within a population of more than 4,000 fellow cadets.[135] Given that reality, and given the willingness of male cadets to accuse women in the Class of 1980 of favoritism if they associated with female underlings, it

is little wonder that some outsiders considered the first female cadets cold. Once
rumors regarding their aloofness began, they became an article of faith that no
amount of logical reasoning has ever entirely diminished.

Despite those rumors, the pace of life at West Point remained largely unchanged in 1978. Following June Week and the accompanying graduation festivities,
the Class of 1980 went on leave, then returned for their third summer of training.
As Second Classmen, most attended either Airborne, Flight, Northern Warfare,
Jungle, or Ranger training at various Army posts within the United States. The
majority also participated in Cadet Troop Leader Training (CTLT), which involved assignment for approximately a month to a leadership position with an active Army unit in Germany, Alaska, Panama, Hawaii, or the continental U.S. This
phase of training allowed cadets to gain experience leading enlisted soldiers in the
field and to become better acquainted with life in the "real" Army.[136]

Women who reported to regular Army units throughout the United States and
overseas for CTLT found their trials and tribulations at West Point repeated
again and again; for those who hoped the "real" Army would be a haven from
the sexism of the Academy, the summer of 1978 proved dispiriting. Like the
Academy, the Army fought to adapt its own masculine culture to the growing
number of women in uniform, and every all-male unit erected the same old
hurdles for women cadets to overcome. Men assumed women were either pro-
miscuous, lesbians, or hunting for husbands, and women were routinely held to
higher standards than men. Many posts invested precious little effort in preparing
facilities for the arrival of women. And in a pattern identical to the one at West
Point, the performance of less than superior women reflected on women as a
whole while poorly performing men reflected only on themselves.[137] These patterns and assumptions permeated the Army, making every single day a rigorous
test of each woman's commitment to the service. "Had one guy laugh at me
while I was saluting," noted one cadet in her diary. A day earlier, she wrote
that the cumulative weight of sexism from fellow soldiers made her realize "how
keyed this world is toward suppressing women—how many men do."[138]

In Germany, the same cadet's regular Army commanding officer complained
that his unit had been "hazed" because senior commanders assigned a woman
from West Point to his command. Within the unit, the female cadet saw enlisted
women persecuted and harassed, noting how "chauvinist Pig" comments began
immediately after two new women reported for duty. For herself, rumors about
her alleged affairs with male officers became so rampant she defiantly wrote "I
am NO WHORE" in her diary. This pattern of sexism routinely crossed national
boundaries as well. She described an encounter with English soldiers in Germany this way: "I went outside and some British soldiers whistled. I said 'Gentlemen, I am an officer. That is enough of that. I don't care what they do in
your army.' "[139] Such experiences were common among women from the Class
of 1980, who routinely had male soldiers make passes at them and suggest
sexual liaisons, endured harassment and allegations of sexual promiscuity, and
generally ran the gamut of sexist abuse.[140] Looking back on their time as Year-

lings, from their nightmare at Buckner through the trials of the academic year to the challenges of CTLT, many women marveled at the depth of the entrenched sexism that most had only dimly perceived a few years before. As one put it, "We were just *hated* by some people. And you know, they don't even try to hide it. It really does teach you a lot."[141] That women endured so much speaks volumes about their commitment to the Army and reveals the utter lack of a framework most female cadets had for looking at sexism. They had neither experience nor a suitable vocabulary for defining the scope of their harassment within the Army clearly and put up with unconscionable harassment in large measure because they usually saw it coherently only with hindsight.

As another academic year began anew, the women of the Class of 1980 realized the very worst harassment was slowly subsiding.[142] There were still many male cadets who resented the presence of women within the Corps, yet the overt, physical harassment of years past diminished as the Academy adjusted to integration and women proved themselves. Rank played a prominent role in this process, for hazing almost always rolled downhill. Cow women were typically posted to positions of leadership, normally no lower than squad leaders, and because they outranked the majority of men at West Point, they had more protection. No Plebe man, after all, would consider harassing a ranking woman. The process naturally left Plebe and even Yearling cadets vulnerable, and women in those classes received much of the physical harassment previously focused on the women of the Class of 1980.

Cow year also marked the point at which many of the first female cadets began talking openly about the trials and tribulations of their first two years at the Academy. Rank permitted more open discussions, and for the first time many women realized their experiences had not been unique, that they were not persecuted because of individual flaws, and that their agony stemmed from a kind of institutionalized sexism which affected all of them. The revelation astonished them. The knowledge that so many experiences were shared rather than being isolated to a particular company or regiment became critical in encouraging more women to speak out and in convincing them they were not alone. These discussions also released a great deal of anger, as many female cadets realized they had "suffered in silence for two years really."[143]

Their suffering entered the public realm in the spring of 1979, when the Academy brought in an expert in challenging stereotypes regarding race and sex. In an auditorium filled with cadets, the speaker announced that he would take the place of the regularly scheduled presenter for the day and then began attacking various groups of people en masse. "Women have no business being anywhere near the military," he said, and continued to attack the idea that women should attend West Point to the riotous shouts and cheers of most male cadets. Eventually he shifted his attacks to African Americans, Jews, Hispanic Americans, and so on, and the crowd quieted. Later, cadets were divided into groups to discuss the experience. What stood out for everyone was the malevolent howl that greeted each of the speaker's attacks on women. Resentment against women at West Point, it seemed, penetrated into a very primitive place within many male cadets, and the experience angered and depressed women in the room for years afterward.[144]

Their frustration lingered against the backdrop of an Academy in the midst of almost continuous change, highlighted by the removal of another hallowed West Point tradition when officials did away with the General Order of Merit in 1978. The order of merit began 160 years before, when Sylvanus Thayer introduced the practice of ranking cadets in every subject, every day, and throughout their class based on merit. The order of merit meant everything in terms of opportunities for advancement and rank, and followed West Point graduates informally throughout their lives. By the late 1970s the practice struck Academy officials as anachronistic, however, and quietly and with little fanfare they abolished the practice that began in 1818. Class rank continued to matter when it came to selecting cadets for various branches of the Army, but the overwhelming importance of the order of merit quickly disappeared. The most noticeable casualty of the change was the practice of recognizing the "goat" from each class at graduation. Goats were ranked dead last in their class and over the years were celebrated for their often uncanny ability to teeter on the brink of expulsion without ever committing the final offense which would have sent them packing. Cadets sometimes battled to earn the "honor" of being the goat, reasoning that greater glory attached itself to standing out at the bottom of their class rather than graduating in the anonymous middle. Goats received the loudest cheers from their peers at graduation and a dollar from every other graduate as a token of their narrow triumph over the system. Famous West Point goats included George Armstrong Custer, George E. Pickett, and Rene E. De Russy, but after 1978 the tradition finally ended.[145]

On a more personal and relevant level, Cows became aware of selection of class rings by the Class of 1979. Those rings, which should have been no more than a curiosity to the Class of 1980, soon became a source of controversy because they reflected lingering cadet resentment against the admission of women. Designed by the Balfour class ring company, some cadets alleged that the rings included a very subtle Omega. Others maintained the Omegas were myth, but that the letters "LCWB" were engraved on the inside of individual rings according to the preference of their owner.[146] Both the Omega and LCWB represented a conviction among many members of the 1979 class that they were the last graduates of West Point's glory era. As the last letter in the Greek alphabet, Omega represented an easily recognizable reference to the end of male dominance at West Point. More subtle until explained, LCWB stood for "Last Class With Balls," a phrase that became an unofficial class motto for many 1979 graduates and spoke in an adolescent way for itself. LCWB even showed up on many Class of 1979 t-shirts, prompting the Academy to eventually ban the shirts and make wearing them a serious offense.[147] It was another sign that even in their third year as cadets, women were still despised by many men at West Point.

Ironically, even as some men continued to pressure women to leave the Academy, there were also signs that West Point leaders were using women as public relations tools. In the most famous resignation among the women of the Class of 1980, the ranking female chose to resign in 1979 for personal reasons. Some classmates allege she left after Academy officials offered her a senior leadership position within the Corps of Cadets if she would stay, because her faith in the institution was shattered by what she perceived as a clear case of favoritism. Whatever the case, she left wearing a black leather jacket and riding a BMW motorcycle, to the collective surprise and admiration of her classmates.[148]

As the Class of 1980 moved inexorably towards graduation and senior leadership positions within the Corps, many women approached their Firstie Year with a mixed sense of elation, anxiety, and anticipation. By the summer of 1980, those who graduated would become officers in the United States Army charged with the defense of the nation and free of their arduous life at the Academy. The thought of emancipation, branch selection, and their first duty assignment at Army posts in the United States and overseas filled them with excitement, and they began the mental countdown that led inexorably toward May 28, 1980. Until then, many countered their growing excitement with subdued concern and caution born of their previous three years as cadets, and they reminded themselves that even as Firsties they could still find ways to fail. The odds were against that, of course, but stranger things had happened, and it was important to stay focused.

After all, nothing at West Point ever came easily.

NOTES

1. Thucydides, *The History of the Peloponnesian War*, ed. and trans. Sir Richard Livingstone (1943; reprint, New York: Oxford University Press, 1978), p. 113.

2. EI, 5-1-80, p. 7.

3. LTA, 4-4-2000, p. 3.

4. GEN Andrew J. Goodpaster, IWA, 11-7-95, pp. 1–2.

5. IWA, 5-16-97, author's notes.

6. ETA, 9-26-96, p. 8.

7. GEN Goodpaster, IWA, 11-7-95, p. 3.

8. USMA, *Bugle Notes*, vol. 68 (West Point: USMA, 1976), p. 64. The camp was renamed in 1946.

9. Ibid., pp. 66–67.

10. EI, 5-14-80, p. 17.

11. EI, 5-9-80, p. 29.

12. EI, 5-5-80, p. 13.

13. EI, 5-8-80, p. 19.

14. EI, 4-30-80, p. 30.

15. EI, 4-17-80, p. 18, 20.

16. IWA, 7-28-96, author's notes.

17. IWA, 6-29-98, author's notes.

170 STRONGER THAN CUSTOM

18. EI, 5-5-80, p. 4, 6.

19. EI, 5-80, pp. 11–12.

20. EI, 5-1-80, p. 7.

21. IWA, 2-5-96, p. 9.

22. EI, no date, p. 7.

23. EI, 5-7-80, p. 11.

24. IWA, 2-18-98, author's notes.

25. EI, 5-8-80, pp. 24–25.

26. EI, no date, p. 17.

27. EI, 5-14-80, p. 17, and EI, 5-80, p. 7.

28. IWA, 2-16-96, p. 7, 11.

29. Rick Atkinson, *The Long Gray Line* (Boston: Houghton Mifflin Company, 1989), p. 66.

30. EI, 5-9-80, p. 29.

31. EI, 4-17-80, pp. 20–21.

32. See USMA, "The Superintendent's Annual Historical Review, 1965," USMA files (West Point: USMA, 1965), p. 22.

33. See USMA, "Operations Plan 75–1: Admission of Women Cadets," USMA files (West Point: USMA, September 15, 1975), p. A1.

34. See Captain Jerome Adams, *Report of the Admission of Women to the United States Military Academy (Project Athena III)* (West Point: USMA, 1979), pp. 126–30.

35. Ibid, pp. 128–30.

36. Captain David L. Grosso, "The Dismemberment and Death of RECONDO Training at the United States Military Academy," November 23, 1998, p. 15. Grosso wrote his paper as part of his Tactical Officer Education Program at West Point, and graciously granted permission for me to quote from it here.

37. MAJ Alan G. Vitters and Dr. Nora Scott Kinzer, *Report on the Admission of Women to the United States Military Academy (Project Athena I)* (West Point: BS&L, September, 1977), p. 12.

38. See Colonel D. P. Tillar, Jr., Memorandum for See Distribution, "Doctrine of Comparable Training," June 8, 1981, USMA files.

39. Ibid, p. 16. Grosso cites a memorandum from LTC Donna Alesch Newell, "Cadet Field Training, Summer 1977, Summer 1978, Summer 1997," November 18, 1998.

40. Grosso, "The Dismemberment and Death of RECONDO Training," p. 18.

41. IWA, 9-10-96. Third Regiment's B Company, for example, was considered one of the worst "woman hating" companies in the Corps.

42. The best example from the period was B-3, whose members called themselves the "Bandits" or "The Boys of B-3."

43. IWA, 6-9-96, author's notes.

44. Cadets were expelled very quietly by West Point, especially when homosexuality was an issue. However, five cadets are known to have been expelled in the early 1960s for alleged homosexual behavior. Randy Shilts, *Conduct Unbecoming: Lesbians and Gays in the U.S. Military: Vietnam to the Persian Gulf* (New York: St. Martin's Press, 1993), p. 326.

45. EI, no date, p. 16.

46. EI, 5-80, p. 15.

47. EI, 4-30-80, p. 45, and EI, 5-80, p. 15.

48. EI, no date, p. 14.

49. EI, 5-7-80, p. 14.

50. EI, 5-1-80, p. 9, and LTA, 5-15-96, p. 1.

51. Atkinson, *The Long Gray Line*, p. 123.

52. Carol Barkalow with Andrea Rabb, *In the Men's House: An Inside Account of Life in the Army by One of West Point's First Female Graduates* (New York: Berkeley Books, 1992), pp. 48–49.

53. EI, no date, p. 16.

54. IWA, 5-13-96, p. 12.

55. Ibid.

56. Mike Conrad, "The Adventures of Peter Parsec, Space Cadet," *The Pointer*, October 1977, p. 12. Conrad became a very successful freelance artist after he left the army; among other accomplishments, he is responsible for having Cinderella's castle at Disneyworld painted pink. LTA, 4-4-2000, p. 2.

57. Jamie Mardis, *Memos of a West Point Cadet* (New York: McKay Books, 1976), p. 70.

58. Sidney Forman, *West Point: A History of the United States Military Academy* (New York: Columbia University Press 1950), p. 11.

59. "Ike" Hall, the Cadet Activities Center, opened in May of 1974 and boasted the second largest theater on the East Coast (Radio Center Music Hall was first) as well as ballrooms, snack-bars, and a restaurant.

60. EI, 5-9-80, p. 27, and EI, 5-14-80, p. 27.

61. EI, 5-8-80, p. 18.

62. IWA, 5-16-97, author's notes.

63. BG John C. Bard, Memorandum for Superintendent, "Discussions with Women Cadets," March 1, 1978, p. 4, USMA files. The reference to the "cadet masher" is unclear, though one Academy official said it was a ubiquitous term referring to any male cadet who tried too hard to be attractive to women. IWA, 5-16-97, author's notes.

64. IWA, 6-20-00, side B.

65. "Tiffany Clark" is a pseudonym.

66. LTC Bruzina, Fact Sheet, "Serious Incident Involving Cadets . . . , Class of 1978, and . . . , Class of 1980," April 20, 1978, p. 1. The names of both cadets are omitted for reasons of privacy. The fact sheet did not come from USMA files, though it is an Academy document.

67. Ibid.

68. IWA, 5-16-97, author's notes. Clark's behavior actually fit within established patterns. Many victims of sexual assault do not fight their attackers because they are afraid.

69. EI, 5-7-80, p. 13.

70. EI, 4-30-80, pp. 17–18.

71. EI, 4-22-80, p. 17; and EI, 5-7-80, pp. 8–9. Clark resigned from West Point soon after the incident.

72. EI, 5-5-80, p. 13.

73. EI, 4-22-80, p. 16.

74. IWA, 12-12-95, p. 16, 18.

75. EI, 5-1-80, p. 12.

76. IWA, 12-12-95, p. 16.

77. Ibid., p. 11.

78. EI, no date, p. 15. "Ma'am" refers to Major Irene Evankovich, the Superinten-

dent's Special Advisor on Women's Issues, who conducted some of the exit interviews with Class of 1980 women.

79. EI, 5-9-80, p. 26.

80. EI, 5-7-80, p. 14; EI, 5-9-80, p. 26; EI, 5-5-80, p. 11. Late night visits persisted well into the 1980s, and some women became accustomed to sleeping with empty aluminum cans against their doors to frighten away would-be intruders.

81. IWA, 2-27-96, p. 10.

82. EI, no date, p. 15.

83. Ibid., p. 16.

84. EI, 5-1-80, p. 11.

85. IWA, 3-17-97, author's notes.

86. Quoted in William Manchester, *American Caesar: Douglas MacArthur, 1880–1964* (New York: Dell Publishing Co., 1978), p. 23.

87. Helen Rogan, *Mixed Company: Women in the Modern Army* (Boston: Beacon Press, 1982), p. 186.

88. IWA, 5-16-97, author's notes.

89. IWA, 2-18-98, author's notes.

90. See "Summary Overview of Questions and Responses from Women of the Class of 1980 for the USMA Oral History Program," no date, USMA files.

91. IWA, 7-11-96, side B.

92. IWA, 3-17-97, author's notes. Such denial usually led to anger when the women involved accepted the Academy's complicity.

93. EI, 5-5-80, p. 8.

94. Ibid., p. 11.

95. The problem may have continued well into the 1990s. The Academy installed locks on cadet doors very quietly in 1992, and the Superintendent told one graduate it was because of an outbreak of "thievery and male cadets sneaking into female's rooms after dark and groping them." LTA, 3-28-96, p. 4.

96. Barbara Ehrenreich, *Blood Rites: Origins and History of the Passions of War* (New York: Metropolitan Books, 1997), p. 230.

97. IWA, 5-16-97, author's notes. Several former Academy staff members indicated during interviews that reports detailing the scope of harassment and assaults involving female cadets were prepared for the Commandant's office in the late 1970s and early 1980s. At present, however, no such reports have been seen by the author.

98. IWA, 7-9-96, author's notes.

99. IWA, 7-11-96, side B. Efforts to find a copy of the study have so far met with no success.

100. Geoffrey Perret, *Ulysses S. Grant: Soldier and President* (New York: Random House, 1997), p. 365. Not all graduates agree. As one said succinctly, "I see the injustices as a reason *not* to be deeply attached to the place" (emphasis added). ETA, 7-12-2000, p. 1.

101. IWA, 4-2-96.

102. EI, 5-8-80, p. 20.

103. EI, 5-9-80, p. 38.

104. LTA, 9-2-96, p. 1.

105. ETA, 6-11-96, author's notes.

106. John Alexander Hottell, "A Soldier's Own Obituary," *New York Times*, March 3, 1971, p. 43. Hottell was killed in Vietnam on July 7, 1970, less than a year after his

personally written obituary was published in the West Point Alumni Quarterly, *Assembly*. The *New York Times* republished the piece the following year.

107. ETA, 6-11-96, author's notes.

108. EI, 5-8-80, p. 20.

109. IWA, 2-28-96.

110. EI, 5-8-80, p. 20.

111. IWA, 7-11-96, side A.

112. EI, 5-14-80, p. 27. Also EI, 5-7-80, pp. 4–5.

113. EI, 5-9-80, p. 5.

114. USMA, *Bugle Notes*, p. 120; and Daughters of the United States Army, West Point Chapter, *West Point: The United States Military Academy* (Charlotte, North Carolina: C. Harrison Conroy Co., 1994), p. 18–21.

115. George S. Pappas, *The Cadet Chapel—United States Military Academy* (Providence: Andrew Mowbray, Inc., 1987), pp. 165–66.

116. The bells were put to famous use by H. Ross Perot in 1975. A 1953 Annapolis graduate, Perot provided $25,000 to West Point Chaplain James D. Ford's planned expedition to sail across the Atlantic Ocean in honor of America's bicentennial celebration in 1976. In return, Ford slipped Perot and the Academy bell ringer into the Cadet Chapel prior to the 1975 Army-Navy football game. Perot gleefully played "Anchors Aweigh," the "Marine Corps Hymn," and "Sailing, Sailing" in the middle of the night while hundreds of angry cadets protested. Perot was eventually taken away by military police, and the incident entered Academy lore as one of the many pranks played on both academies by midshipmen and cadets. See Atkinson, *The Long Gray Line*, pp. 393–94.

117. Marie T. Capps, *A Guide to The Cadet Chapel, United States Military Academy, West Point, New York* (West Point: Cadet Chapel Altar and Hospital Guild, n. d.), p. 3; Pappas, *The Cadet Chapel*, p. 165; and USMA, *Bugle Notes*, p. 121.

118. Atkinson, *The Long Gray Line*, pp. 89–90, and EI, 5-80, p. 10.

119. ETA, 7-24-96, p. 1.

120. Barkalow, *In the Men's House*, p. 50–51.

121. ETA, 10-19-2000, p. 1.

122. "Tradition," *The Pointer*, April 1979, p. 32.

123. ETA, 6-13-2000, p. 2. Stealing the Naval Academy's mascot—a goat named Billy—is the classic example of annual cadet pranks over the years. Other famous Academy breakdowns in discipline include the Egg Nog Riot of 1826 and the legendary "Great Mess Hall Riot" of 1963, when 2,000 cadets stacked the giant oak tables in the mess hall and indulged in an enormous food fight. The tactic raised spirits, however, and propelled the Army football team to an upset over Penn State the following weekend. See Theodore J. Crackel, *The Illustrated History of West Point* (New York: Harry N. Abrams, Inc.), pp. 304–5, and Atkinson, *The Long Gray Line*, pp. 85–87.

124. LTA, 9-2-96, p. 1.

125. IWA, 8-14-95, author's notes.

126. EI, 5-14-80, pp. 30–31. The empathy of one oppressed group for another was hardly unique to West Point. Historians have, for example, noted that black soldiers were uniformly more humane in their treatment of German prisoners of war in World War II than were whites.

127. EI, 5-8-80, p. 26.

128. Alan G. Vitters, *Report of the Admission of Women to the United States Military*

Academy (Project Athena II) (West Point: Department of Behavioral Science and Leadership, September 1977), p. xi.

129. EI, 5-7-80, p. 6, and EI, 5-5-80, p. 6.

130. IWA, 7-28-96, author's notes.

131. Barkalow, *In the Men's House*, p. 109.

132. EI, 5-14-80, p. 27.

133. EI, 5-5-80, p. 17; and EI, 4-17-80, p. 22.

134. EI, 5-15-80, p. 22–23. Despite the rivalry, some women argued that women in the Class of 1981 had an even tougher Plebe year than their predecessors.

135. EI, 5-8-80, p. 6.

136. USMA, *Bugle Notes*, pp. 67–68.

137. EI, 5-9-80, p. 30.

138. Cadet Journal, entry dated June 30, 1978, p. 37, and entry dated June 29, 1978, p. 35.

139. Ibid., entries dated 7-11-78, p. 47, 6-11-78, 6-19-78, p. 21, and 6-21-78, p. 25.

140. EI, 5-8-80, p. 23.

141. EI, 4-22-80, p. 4.

142. Ibid., p. 8.

143. EI, 4-22-80, p. 8.

144. IWA, 5-8-00, author's notes; and Barkalow, *In the Men's House*, pp. 123–24.

145. Kenneth W. Rapp, *Whistler in Gray and Other Stories About the United States Military Academy* (Croton-on-Hudson, New York: North River Press, 1978), pp. 80–82, 84, 87. Pickett (USMA 1846) led the famous charge on the third day at Gettysburg which bears his name. De Russy (USMA 1812) later became Superintendent of the Military Academy.

146. LTA, 9-24-96, p. 4, and IWA, 2-18-98, author's notes. The Naval Academy's 1979 graduates held similar views and chose as their class motto the Latin phrase "Omni Vir" (all male). See MG Jeanne Holm (Ret.), *Women in the Military: An Unfinish Revolution*, rev. ed. (Novato, Calif.: Presidio Press, 1992), p. 311.

147. IWA, 2-18-98, author's notes; and ETA, 6-13-2000, p. 2. The first Academy rings were worn by the Class of 1835, and West Point originated the tradition of college graduates wearing class rings in the United States.

148. IWA, 5-11-00, author's notes.

7

★ ★ ★ ★

"All of Our Children"

Long life to the girl cadet! And may she go into the world to prove the benefits of her training and illustrate another phase of the Nineteenth Century Woman!
—Cadet Elsie Fay, Fairfield Seminary and Military College, 1896[1]

As soon as the Class of 1979 tossed their hats into the air at graduation in May, the Class of 1980 became Firsties and rose to the most senior positions within the Corps. They were now the "old" men and women of West Point, serving as leaders from the platoon level up through company, battalion, regiment, and brigade. Aside from placing women in senior leadership posts for the first time at the Academy, the Class of 1980 also enjoyed the distinction of producing the first African-American First Captain, Vincent Keith Brooks.[2]

Most Firsties spent the summer of 1979 accepting new responsibilities, including assignment as a commander, instructor, or staff member within the New Cadet Battalion or out at Camp Buckner. Serving as part of the cadre at Buckner and/or during New Cadet Training involved approximately two weeks of training prior to any actual duty; and once engaged in instructing younger cadets, the Class of 1980 quickly passed on the lessons they learned as Plebes and Yearlings to the classes of 1982 and 1983. This cycle of learning formed part of the symmetry of West Point, of the tradition and the rites of passage that flowed from one class to the next. Every cadet learned from other cadets, each felt the weight of command sooner or later during their four years at the Academy, and West Point tried to make the experience of every cadet as uniform as possible. Those Firsties who for some reason missed Cadet Troup Leader Training (CTLT) during their Second Class summer, for example, were given that duty in addition to or in lieu of regular First Class summer assignments.[3] In that way every member of the Class of 1980 ideally had the same opportunities to train and excel as members of any other class in the Long Gray Line.

The Class of 1980 assumed their new duties wearing the coveted class rings of West Point First Classmen, which they had received the previous April during a banquet and a ceremony in the Mess Hall.[4] Each ring boasted a West Point crest on one side, and the Class of 1980 crest on the other. Prior to graduation, cadets wore the rings with the *class* crest facing inward, toward their heart, to remind them of their responsibility as leaders of the Corps. After graduation the rings were turned so that the *Academy* crest faced the heart, to remind them of their duty as Army officers.[5] The rings visibly signified the power of the Class of 1980 over other cadets, and posed an interesting dilemma for some women. According to Academy regulations cadets could wear only one ring, which put women who were engaged in the awkward position of choosing between wearing a ring which showed their fidelity to West Point and one which showed their devotion to their fiances. The Academy solved the problem by amending regulations to allow cadets one ring per hand.[6]

During the academic year, Firsties moved inexorably toward graduation, counting the days, passing through 100th night celebrations, and planning for their futures in the Army. This process was unique for the first women graduates, who grew increasingly frustrated by the attention showered on them in 1979 and 1980 by the press. As one put it, "Everyone says, 'Do you realize that you are making history?' No, I don't realize that I am making history. I am just doing what everybody else around me is doing."[7] Though true on the surface, the women of the Class of 1980 had to realize at some point that they would always be known first and foremost as the first female graduates of the Academy. For some, this realization became a heavy, almost burdensome title to carry through graduation and into their professional lives and not one whose weight diminished much with time. Women felt the weight of their roles on the stage of history most keenly as members of the press returned to the Academy in droves in the spring of 1980. Men were aghast and jealous once again, just as in 1976, and many women lashed out at the press for ignoring their male peers on the brink of what should have been a triumphant May for all Firsties. As one put it, "our whole class is dreading graduation because they are afraid the only people who are going to graduate are the females in the Class of 80."[8]

Their experiences as cadets also left many women angry and resentful on the eve of graduation. "I have become much more bitter, more cynical," said one, who added that she found the chain of command at the Academy untrustworthy when it came to women.[9] Others said they would tell young women not to come to West Point, that it had been a mistake to open the Academy to women in 1976. "It is good PR for the outside world," one cadet told her exit interviewer in May, "but meanwhile we're suffering."[10] Some women focused their criticism on the men of West Point, whom they argued were never satisfied by the efforts and achievements of ordinary women cadets. "They want the super woman," complained one graduate, "the Raquel Welch Amazon woman."[11] Others railed against reporters and the media, arguing all "the press has done is to cause problems for us."[12]

More than the press and the pressures from outside and more than the frustrations of the past, some women found their final year at West Point filled with disappointment because the lingering resentment of many men toward female cadets refused to die. In fact, it showed few signs of disappearing even in 1980. The most overt forms of harassment had disappeared, of course, but what remained operated underground, beneath the veneer of properly behaved cadets who vented only in private and amongst themselves.[13] Simmering just below the surface of cadet emotions, this subtle and more elusive form of resistance foreshadowed the great difficulty in completely stamping out unequal treatment of women at West Point. As one author put it, "the men (cadets) . . . learned to be evasive, oblique in their comments," and properly supportive in any sort of public discussion concerning the role of women at West Point and within the Army.[14]

This pattern of male behavior existed at the other service academies as well, and obfuscated male resentment that percolated deep inside quite a few cadets and midshipmen. Occasionally, that resentment could break wide open and manifest itself in a public forum. The most famous and revealing incident demonstrating this phenomenon occurred at the Naval Academy when, in November of 1979, Annapolis graduate James Webb wrote an article for *The Washingtonian* entitled "Women Can't Fight." A much decorated veteran of combat with the Marines in Vietnam and a prolific author, Webb savagely attacked the idea that women had any place in the nations' service academies, arguing they destroyed the combat-oriented nature of the institutions, destroyed cohesion, and lowered physical fitness standards. Shortly after the article's publication, a senior admiral visiting the Naval Academy mess hall heard male cadets chanting, "Webb was right! Webb was right! Webb was right!" and one suspects a number of West Pointers would have joined in too.[15]

As graduation neared, time left its mark on surrounding institutions as noticeable as on West Point, and cadets noted with some sadness the closing of nearby Ladycliff College in 1980. A four-year all-women's college situated in neighboring Highland Falls, Ladycliff figured prominently in the social history of West Point, providing female guests for cadet hops and looming as the primary target of many cadet escape fantasies over the years. The irony of Ladycliff closing down during the same year the first women graduated at West Point did not escape notice at the time, and the editors of *The Pointer* penned a fond farewell to the college that had been home to many of the young women who married cadets since the nineteenth century.[16] Ladycliff's demise seemed part of a larger trend noted sadly by many men at West Point, one in which the old familiar landmarks of cadet life were being swept away. As they left, they took some of the old notions about women with them. A few months before, the tradition of electing an Autumn Queen had been eliminated because it seemed overtly sexist in the days of the Equal Rights Amendment (ERA), a fact duly protested by the staff of *The Pointer*.[17] Electing an Autumn Queen without also electing a King *was* sexist, of course, and the Academy hardly needed Ladycliff to keep open its doors solely to furnish dates for male cadets. Yet these arguments missed the larger point that West Point shook off a great many traditions in a very short period of time during the late 1970s, and for those cadets and Old Grads who clung to tradition for its own sake the changes were sometimes deeply disconcerting.

Among those who embraced the changes were the female cadets of the Class of 1980, and in the spring of their final year as cadets, they chose from the gamut of available Army specialty branches in the hopes of being commissioned in their primary field of interest. True to West Point tradition a large number chose service in the combat arms. Infantry and Armor were closed to women by Army policy, but seven chose Field Artillery and eleven selected Air Defense, while the Aviation and Engineer branches received three and six women respectively. Of the remaining women, most went into the Signal Corps, with the rest scattered among Quartermaster, Military Police, Military Intelligence, Transportation, and Ordnance.[18]

They were also the recipients of ornate silver calling card trays presented to them by General Goodpaster and a group of graduates from the Class of 1939 at a reception hosted by the Supe himself. The event, and the silver trays themselves, were meant to commemorate the years which women of the Class of 1980 had spent at West Point. A card accompanying the tray read,

> Congratulations to
> a "First Lady" of West Point
> from some friends
> in the class of 1939
>
> We admire the courage you have demonstrated
> during your four years at the Academy
> We think you are an outstanding example of graduates
> whose good character and achievements in later life
> have made us proud of the school
>
> In the coming years
> we hope you will help us
> encourage young women of your quality
> to enter West Point[19]

While many female cadets viewed the gesture as noble and voiced their appreciation to Goodpaster and his classmates, others felt it signified yet another way women were treated differently by the Academy. After all, very few men were present, and male cadets did not enjoy an intimate reception hosted by the Superintendent.

As the Class of 1980 neared the end of their four years as cadets, it came time for the annual Graduation Parade. Held on May 27, 1980, the day before the receipt of diplomas and graduation exercises, the parade marked the symbolic transfer of command over the Corps of Cadets to the Class of 1981 and an exchange of military honors between the outgoing Firsties and the cadets they were leaving behind. Wearing the distinctive scarlet cummerbunds and plumed shakos that marked them as seniors, members of the Class of 1980 marched on to The Plain to the tune of "Stars and Stripes Forever." The USMA Hellcats slid effortlessly through other music, including "The Dashing White Sergeant" and "Auld Lang Syne," then played "Army Blue" and "Alma Mater" while the First Class formed front and center before the crowd. Forming shoulder to shoulder across The Plain, the Firsties watched as the entire Corps passed in review, mesmerizing the crowd with the seductive rhythms of their concerted efforts. The Hellcats reached a crescendo with the "Official West Point March," and when the last cadet company passed the final First Classmen, cadets exchanged the famous Long Corps yell with the Class of 1980 a final time.[20]

On the following day, graduation ceremonies were held in Michie Stadium. Watching and listening as the USMA Hellcats played "The Star Spangled Banner," the women of the Class of 1980 may have felt a twinge of the emotions which went through Jackie Robinson's mind during in the year he became the first African American to play major league baseball. As he wrote, "At the beginning of the World Series of 1947, I experienced a completely new emotion, when the National Anthem was played. This time, I thought, it is being played for me, as much as for everyone else." For the first time, Robinson felt truly a part of Major League Baseball. "I am standing here with all the others," he said, "and everything that takes place includes me."[21]

Afterward, the Class of 1980 listened to the invocation, the remarks by Superintendent Goodpaster, and the Graduation Address from Secretary of Defense Harold Brown. As the ceremony moved toward its climax, the Combined Chapel Choirs sang "The Corps," one of the Academy's most beloved songs. The final verses implored graduates to "Grip hands—though it be from the shadows— While we swear as you did of yore, Of living, of dying, to honor, The Corps, and the Corps, and the Corps!"[22] When the song concluded, it came time for the presentation of diplomas.

One by one the members of the Class of 1980 crossed the stage, shook hands with the presenting dignitary, and turned to rejoin for the last time the ranks of their fully assembled class. How far they had traveled in only four years. In 1976 they took the oath on The Plain with uncertainty and trepidation. Now they received their diplomas, one of the artifacts of their dreams, with a sense of pride more palpable than words might ever convey.

The Reverend Richard P. Camp, Chaplain of the United States Military Academy, delivered the prayer for the class, then relinquished the podium to Lieutenant General Goodpaster, who administered the oath of office. The Class of 1980 ended their tenure at West Point as they began it, by raising their right hands and vowing to serve the United States. This time, however, they were officers.

Finally, the ceremony drew to a close as the entire Corps of Cadets sang "Alma Mater." The Class of 1980 faced their fellow cadets in the bleachers behind them and sang loudest of all, for the lyrics washing over the assembled crowd in Michie Stadium, so often the brunt of cadet humor and dark sarcasm, suddenly took on new meaning as the Firsties approached their departure from West Point:

> And when our work is done,
> Our course on earth is run,
> May it be said, "Well done;
>   Be thou at peace."
> E'er may that line of gray
> Increase from day to day,
> Live, serve, and die, we pray,
>   West Point, for thee.[23]

Then, after four years of struggle, after all the pain and tears, the stress and the mind-numbing fear mixed with pride and triumph, they were dismissed. The war yells sprang forth, hats flew in the air, and the crowning moment of every cadet's journey on the Hudson came at long last. They were finished.

As the hats rained to the ground in Michie Stadium there were those who wondered how far West Point had moved in the journey towards assimilation of the sexes. To say women achieved complete integration into the Corps of Cadets by 1980 would be inaccurate. To say they found complete acceptance would be an outright lie. Resentment toward women remained a powerful force among some cadet men, and many of the first female graduates argued that during their years as cadets they never even approached full and equal membership in the Corps.[24] Many were fond of citing the unofficial "seven year rule" at West Point, which held that meaningful change at the Academy took a minimum of seven years because enough classes had to graduate so that no one could remember or talk with anyone who remembered a time before the change took place. Others said it would take longer. One instructor said that West Point would not really accept women until the Class of 1980 and below were generals. At that point, he suggested, the Old Grads who remembered an Academy without women would be gone, and the presence of female cadets would seem routine.[25]

What would never seem routine were the sacrifices made by the women of the Class of 1980, each of whom suffered a wide array of harassment and challenge impossible to fully imagine. As one Academy staffer described their experience, "It was well beyond tough. It [Academy life] was tough on the men.

It was absolutely brutal for the women."[26] What the persistent atmosphere of resentment at West Point cost each of them is difficult to gauge, especially since so many West Point women had such differing experiences as cadets. For some, however, and probably for most, the frustration of being in what at times amounted to a despised minority could be overwhelming. "There were times that I absolutely hated being female," said one woman. "I never did before I came here. When I was outside of here I would never want to be a guy. And there were so many times," she added, "that I would curse the fact that I was female and couldn't do what the guys could do. Or that I was blamed for some things simply because I was female, when I had done nothing to deserve it."[27]

Despite this adversity, or perhaps because of it, many women left West Point with a profoundly changed sense of their capabilities and a new sense of how limiting cultural definitions of concepts like "masculinity" and "femininity" could be. One said her concept of femininity shifted from one that emphasized external factors like clothing, hair style, and makeup, to one that became almost exclusively internal.[28] Another expanded this idea by saying, "What I had to learn was that femininity wasn't perfume and little pink dresses. And masculinity isn't pick axes and strong muscles." Instead, "activities like driving a tank, running hard, wallowing in the mud, or crying are not male or female. They are activities. Males do them, and females do them."[29] And despite the notorious mistreatment of some cadet women, there were members of the Class of 1980 who maintained that great progress had been made in gender relations. In the beginning "everyone was tentative and hesitant to make a decision," yet after the polarization of the Corps during the Class of 1980's Yearling year, more and more people were either "for, against, or professional" when it came to their views on the admission of women.[30] The professionals were those who worked to make gender integration work, because that was their duty as cadets and officers, and dealt with their personal feelings privately. By 1980 that group constituted the majority according to some, including one who said she had "no bad feelings" toward West Point because the "Academy was very professional."[31] Other women labeled such positive accounts as "blind."[32] One compromised by saying, "There is definitely a group of guys who have accepted us and there is a group of guys who have not accepted us. And the ones who have not accepted us, I don't think they ever will."[33]

Whether blind, selective, or simply different, these differing recollections symbolized the wide range of experiences within the Class of 1980, for among the sixty-two women who eventually graduated there were sixty-two distinct West Point journeys. Some women adjusted more quickly or more effectively than their peers, or for some reason were the targets of less abuse. Others, no doubt, repressed their most traumatic memories when discussing the Academy with strangers, so that any understanding of what four years at West Point were like for the women of the Class of 1980 remains limited. What seems abundantly clear is that many of the first women cadets found the experience extremely difficult. They had few female role models, no experienced female cadets to look to for support, and no script for how to survive the rigors of Academy life. They were isolated, often alone, and pioneers in an altogether alien environment. They were pathfinders in the very truest sense.

To be fair, the Academy certainly demanded a great deal from men as well, but the rigors they faced were not the same. Even the women who came later, in the Classes of 1981, 1982, and so on, experienced an Academy far more prepared to accept women as members of the Long Gray Line. They hardly experienced an easy time at West Point, for it is fair to say that women have always faced more challenges as cadets than men, but as a group they never experienced the trials and tribulations of women in the Class of 1980. In fact, there is no way they could have, for those first female cadets set the precedent. They alone confronted most dramatically the uncertainty and fear of the early years of sex integration, and the experience cost each of them dearly. "I'm a lot more bitter now," said one, adding, "I think I lost a lot of confidence in myself by coming here. Just as a person."[34] Her feelings were echoed by another graduate who said the women of the Class of 1980 were "a pretty angry lot," because "we were never accepted."[35]

Others spoke of the "cumulative psychological damage"[36] they suffered during their years at West Point and argued forcefully that the Academy badly damaged their self-esteem. "I was told for four years that I was stupid," said one cadet, "that I was incompetent, that I wasn't trying, that I was just the most incompetent boob anybody had ever met, and I was told that by teachers and by upperclassmen. . . ." She added, "I left feeling like I was worthless . . . [and] I resent West Point for doing that to me. . . ."[37] Her views were echoed by other graduates who said that by the time they graduated, a point at which they were supposed to be brimming with self-confidence, they were more uncertain of themselves than at any other point in their lives. As one put it, "I've heard us being referred to as being like battered spouses when we graduated."[38]

Some became more vocal feminists. "If we weren't feminists when we went in," said one, "we were when we came out!"[39] This evolution in some came out of the trauma of their years as cadets and from the visceral knowledge that sexism underpinned many of the assumptions about gender roles prevalent at the Academy and throughout American life. One graduate said, "I think I have learned a lot by being in the first class of women here, in that you really appreciate what it is like to be a minority. It sounds funny, but it is true. You have no idea until you are openly ostracized at times."[40]

In the years following graduation, the issue of whether women belonged at West Point remained a source of considerable frustration and division within the Academy. Though official communiques proclaimed the integration of female cadets a success, there were still those behind the scenes who questioned the role of women at the Academy, in the Army, and in the military in general. While most professionally accepted and often celebrated the achievements of women graduates, a minority felt uncertain or even outraged over the changes which greater female assimilation wrought on military institutions. They argued that a climate of political correctness existed which brooked no criticism or meaningful dialogue over the role of women within the Army. As one graduate put it in 1995: "Those who are still in the Army, of course, will (publicly at least) voice the official 'happy talk' viewpoint on women in the military and at the academies, deviation from which is sure death for prospects of advancement to general officer rank."[41] In such an environment, critics argued, meaningful review of national policy did not exist, and in the event of a prolonged war only the harsh light of experience would determine whether the sweeping changes imposed on the military in the last two decades were truly practical in a national emergency.

On a personal level, some women in the Class of 1980 struggled with their notoriety well into their Army careers. They found they were treated differently, that "the great West Point Protective Society does not exist for women," and that the troubles they experienced as cadets made it difficult to feel good about graduation. They felt, in some cases, "cheated of their feeling of accomplishment."[42] For some, these feelings were never very far below the surface. As a male graduate from the 1960s put it, "Those fault lines in our life [at West Point] are not readily forgotten, and they do leave an indelible mark on our soul."[43] Some women found it impossible to return to the Academy for fear of the memories a trip to West Point might conjure, or confronted those memories forcibly upon assignment to the Academy as members of the faculty or staff.[44] Like all cadets, though to a greater degree than most, the Academy remained a dominant force in their lives, for good or ill, well into adulthood.

Over the years, the Academy has also found it impossible to move completely beyond the struggle with resentment against women, or beyond the pervasive problem of sexual harassment. A General Accounting Office (GAO) report issued in 1994 described an environment at the nation's service academies in which a poor atmosphere for reporting harassment existed because women feared reprisals from male students and commanders. More than sixty percent of the women at West Point said they would hesitate to report harassment and more than eighty percent indicated they experienced at least one of ten forms of sexual harassment listed on a GAO survey on a recurring basis.[45] The report indicated women dealt informally with harassment, for at each of the academies a "long history of silence" surrounded sexual problems of any sort.[46] While it is true that a heightened awareness of what constitutes sexual harassment in the 1990s may have inflated the number of women reporting incidents in the GAO report, it is still a clear indication that the problems first encountered at West Point by the Class of 1980 are in no danger of disappearing anytime soon.

That truth became poignantly clear in the mid 1980s when a female cadet from the Class of 1986 wrote the Superintendent to explain her decision to resign from West Point. After detailing an incident in which a physical education (P.E.) instructor spent more than thirty minutes explaining why the Bible stipulated that women could only be happy as homemakers and mothers, she said her interest in the Army had disappeared and that the Academy seemed "boring."

As a cadet she never reported the incident with her P.E. instructor because she did "not want to make waves," and because she was "taught from the very beginning of my stay at West Point not to question the inconsistencies in the way men treated women."[47]

Yet these lingering ills should not obscure the very real accomplishments of West Point in integrating women into the Corps of Cadets and the Army as a whole. Women have endured and even thrived at the Academy, and to stand and watch cadets on maneuvers or at drill is to see that "women are proving it everyday."[48] They are now part and parcel of the fabric of Academy life, a part of the habit and tradition of the institution. As the Roman poet Ovid wrote, "nothing is stronger than custom,"[49] and the endurance of female cadets year after year ensured that eventually their presence became "business as usual,"while studies showing women can succeed at West Point are now "factual, provable, and empirical."[50] Their contributions, as well as the entrenched male resistance which seeks to lessen the recognition given their importance to the armed forces, demonstrate both how far West Point has come and how far it has to go toward fully assimilating women. Breaking stereotypes and traditions takes time, and lingering sexism should hardly be seen as a reason for permanent despair.

Those stereotypes that endure reflect the notion that gender is a socially or culturally constructed phenomenon, that every society influences its people by articulating in overt and subtle ways the differences between being a man or a woman, a husband or a wife, and a mother or a father. Yet there is more than just gender at work in these constructs. Men and women are not completely the same. They are alike and dissimilar biologically and physiologically at the same time, and thus *sex*, which *Webster's* defines as "either of two divisions of organisms distinguished respectively as male or female," is a scientifically verifiable and predictable description of real distinctions in the human species.[51] The term is often confused or used interchangeably with *gender*, which usually refers to proscribed roles we assign to individuals based on their sex, but they are very different indeed. Gender can be changed, while sex is a biological fact. Yet the considerable overlap between the ways the terms are used creates confusion. What the anthropologist, sociologist, or feminist might see as value-laden social constructs of gender, the biologist might see as a normal turn of the reproductive wheel. When men and women in military units have sex in defiance of regulations and orders, for example, there is often shock and dismay among critics who see gender as an artificial tool of entrenched patriarchy. Such a view holds profound insight, though it cannot erase the simple biological truth that most men and women enjoy sexual intercourse and will indulge in the activity when possible regardless of rank or uniform. Those who are physically fit and young, like the majority of people in the military and especially at West Point, are especially prone to do so. It is that fact which highlights the difficulty inherent in asking men and women to live, work, and train in close proximity to each other and somehow squelch the natural drives their bodies give them. This is not to say the effort to promote and enforce equity and equality among men and women in the armed forces cannot or should not be made. It should, and in the long run it can be successful. As Barbara Ehrenreich put it, "This does not mean that social hierarchies cannot be overthrown, only that those who would overthrow them should be aware of their almost lifelike power to resist."[52]

Attempting to overthrow those hierarchies at West Point involved recognizing that "Men and women can be equally good warriors in modern militaries. However, they remain primates."[53] The latter fact required regulations governing romance and personal behavior and a recognition that proper behavior among all cadets must be rigidly enforced. Lionel Tiger and Robin Fox demonstrated this point when they wrote about efforts to promote equality in other areas in 1971. "Equality and an equal participation of men and women in the political arena . . . must be imposed," they said, and doing so will require saying "no to nature—our own human nature." Given the controversy over expanding opportunities for women in the armed forces, it is safe to say that bringing some measure of equality of opportunity to the military has involved similar obstacles. It is, after all, a daunting if still noteworthy goal to reshape thousands of years of cultural evolution, and society must understand what it has historically been up against. The process, as Tiger and Fox wrote, "may well be possible, but it will not be easy. And it will certainly not be made easier by pretending that all men really want to be equal or that women are simply men who happen occasionally to take time off to have babies."[54]

What really had to change at West Point was the way in which men thought of themselves and the possibilities for their interaction with women. To be a man is first and foremost to not be a woman, and when women entered the Academy and successfully performed traditionally all-male activities, they threatened the image too many men had of their own identity and role in society. Men also had to re-evaluate the way they viewed women and the way they constructed preconceptions governing what women could and could not do. As Joel Barlow wrote in 1792, the most important changes in the world revolve around changes in the way we think. Many "astonishing effects . . . are wrought in the world by the habit of thinking"[55] he said, and nowhere did this point prove more prophetic than at the United States Military Academy. Only with time, as more and more cadets entered the Academy with the knowledge men and women would serve side by side, did the resentment against female cadets begin to forcefully recede. Neither male or female cadets changed during this process. What did change were the assumptions about the parameters within which men and women could comfortably serve, both within the Army and in the larger realm of American life.

The story goes that in 1872 Susan B. Anthony, one of the leaders of the women's rights movement during the nineteenth century, found herself arrested for illegally entering a voting booth. When brought before a judge and fined $100 the fiery Anthony declared, "I will not pay it! Mark my words, the law will be changed," and stormed out of the courtroom. The court clerk turned to the judge and asked, "Shall I follow her and bring her back?"

"No, let her go," the judge said. "I fear that she is right, and that the law will soon be changed."[56]

So it might have gone if Anthony had tried to enlist or enter West Point. Change has a way of seeming inevitable in hindsight; in a hundred years when women are found at every level of the American military fighting and leading alongside their male peers, much of the controversy over the admission of women to West Point will seem quaintly and absurdly anachronistic. Even then, however, the admission of women to the service academies will be seen as one of the most important developments in the enormous expansion of women in the armed services which took place in the 1970s and 1980s. After the end of the draft and the creation of the All Volunteer Force (AVF), gender-integration at the academies became more high-profile proof of a military and social revolution in the United States. It demonstrated that new opportunities for women truly existed throughout the armed services and that women who were part and parcel of our social fabric could be an integral part of the military effort to sustain American life.[57] Perhaps most important, the presence of women at West Point also illustrated the commitment of our society to utilize the talents of everyone—to make this democracy a more just meritocracy.

There are still those who look upon a sex-integrated West Point with sadness or regret. As retired Lieutenant General Harold G. Moore, Jr. put it, "The West Point I graduated from no longer exists."[58] These critics see the presence of women as an intrusive, disruptive force undermining morale, cohesion, and combat effectiveness of the male cadets. They fear a lowering of physical standards and recoil at what they see as the Army's overeagerness to make women seem successful at all costs. Moore, for example, cites an incident at West Point when his escort officer told him officers on instructor duty at the Academy "were under strict orders not to comment (on) or criticize women cadets in any way, shape, or form, whatever."[59] Some argue the Army's fighting effectiveness has been lessened, and point aghast at the deletion of the phrase "and to fight as Infantry if required" from all Army Combat Support and Combat Service Support organizations because women serve in those units and are prohibited from serving in direct combat.[60] If rear-echelon troops cannot be thrown into the breach in times of crisis, they argue, then the Army risks being unable to confront real disaster on the battlefield.

Critics of gender-integration also despise the different standards applied to men and women, which they argue create resentment among men and a feeling of inferiority for some women. Those divergent standards appeared at the Academy in the 1970s, and some Old Grads wish things had been handled differently. As one put it, "If I were King, nothing would have changed, one set of physical standards, single sex bathrooms, any hanky-panky and you are out on your ass . . . whether male or female."[61] So it should have been.

Yet the imperfections embedded in Academy efforts to integrate women should not obscure the fact that West Point weathered the criticisms attending the admission of female cadets and ultimately flourished. It usually does, for at West Point every new and frightening change becomes hallowed tradition in less than a generation. Every new class recreates the Academy with its own perceptions and accomplishments; while rules and regulations come and go, West Point always remains challenging and unique, one part myth and another part reality. The arrangement suits everyone's interests, even America's, and in hindsight, even a monumental change like the admission of women followed the pattern on the surface.

We will never know what women of earlier generations might have accomplished at West Point or in more diverse roles within the Army. Perhaps a female Ridgway, Patton, or MacArthur whose abilities might have swayed the fortunes of our Republic lived and died without utilizing talents America unwisely chose never to harness. We do know, however, about the accomplishments of the women who graduated from West Point in 1980. They proved, for those who needed the lesson, that men have no monopoly on soldierly virtue. Courage, integrity, honesty, and devotion to duty are as readily found among women as men, as are weakness, cowardice, moral corruption, and dishonesty. Certainly the women of the Class of 1980 demonstrated their strengths in a very public, demanding environment, and many continue to do so to this day. What distinguishes West Point cadets regardless of sex is their goal, their conviction that the whole is greater than the sum of its parts—that service still matters.

We also know that gender-integration at West Point and the other service academies accelerated a process of sending women farther into combat than previous regulations allowed. Once given advanced training and graduated from the finest officer training institutions in America, it became impossible in the long run to argue women should not be allowed into combat. Congress had the opportunity to make that decision deliberately on many occasions, especially when debating whether to open the service academies to women in 1975. Senators and Representatives might have considered whether new physical standards were necessary and what it might mean for America when women were taken prisoners of war or killed in large numbers. Rather than embrace that opportunity, however, they skirted it, primarily because it seemed far too controversial. They thus allowed American military policy regarding women to advance one piecemeal, awkward step at a time, never realizing how deeply women might be committed in the event of war.

There have been other opportunities to have such a debate, of course, and it would be inaccurate to claim the lack of comprehensive debate in the 1970s precluded more vigorous and frank discussions in the 1980s or 1990s. The fact remains, however, that there has never been a truly national debate in the United States regarding women in combat. This explains in part the powerful public reaction to the deployment of thousands of women during Operation Desert Storm in 1991. Most Americans had no conception of how dependent the military had become on women, or how vulnerable those women were once the fighting began. This collective ignorance stemmed from a systemic refusal of American leaders to discuss the implications of trying to make the military more truly equal, and that ignorance need not have existed for so long.

Dropping the sex barrier at West Point, Annapolis, and the Air Force Academy formed only one step in the revolution which made women more equal in the military. The admission of women to Air Force Reserve Officer Training Corps (ROTC) programs in 1969 broke critical barriers. So did the removal of ceilings on the number of women allowed to serve in each branch of the armed forces and the expansion of job opportunities in the 1970s. Perhaps most important, the creation of the AVF forced recruiters to realize there could be no effective means of providing for the needs of the armed forces without relying more heavily on women than ever before. Each of these evolutions might have sparked debate aimed at creating a national consensus regarding the role of women in the military, and yet it never took place. America came closest to such a moment when Congress debated opening the service academies to women, and although that moment is one of many opportunities policy makers had to bring such issues dramatically out into the open, it may have been the best.

Even in context as one of many revolutionary changes affecting women in the armed forces, however, admitting women into West Point and the other service academies represents a watershed. Like the drop of rain that finally sends water flowing over a spillway, the arrival of women at the most elite officer training schools in America marked the point beyond which there could be no turning back. Once women were given the leadership skills those institutions impart and sent forth to prove their mettle, it became progressively more difficult to talk of what women could *not* do. Once they graduated from the citadels that produced Eisenhower, Patton, Nimitz, and King, there could be no stopping talk of fuller equality. Ironically, the success of women at these high profile institutions and the attendant publicity grew so great it had repercussions for civilian society too. Once photographs and news stories presented the achievements of women at the academies it was harder for anyone to argue women should not move even farther into formerly all-male domains. Congress sent the service academies to war with American culture in 1976 without fully considering or ever realizing the dramatic consequences of its action, and the academies won.

Yet Congressional failure to discern the future should not obscure the great leap forward the admission of women to West Point represented for the Army and for America, or cloud the enormous contributions women have made to the Academy and by extension to the United States. They did not ask for special treatment, and most have served with quiet distinction and patriotism. It is said the best people give better than they get, and that is certainly true for the women of the Class of 1980, whose accomplishments are too often overlooked. In some measure, that is the fate of all soldiers in a democracy, for as Samuel Bayard said to the Corps of Cadets in 1854, "you will serve a jealous mistress ... Republics *are* ungrateful."[62]

Bayard's words resonate with some members of the Class of 1980, especially those whom time and spending cutbacks have forced from the Army earlier than they hoped. Yet most continue to serve America both in and out of uniform in an unassuming way that is perhaps West Point's most enduring legacy. They are largely forgiving of the mistakes made by the Academy during the integration of women, arguing that West Point leaders were in a "dark room feeling their way along," and that they generally did the best they could.[63]

These convictions were hardened by the experiences of The Citadel and the Virginia Military Institute (VMI) in the mid-1990s, when both military schools opened their doors to female cadets for the first time. Each had historically opposed the entrance of women using arguments similar to those deployed by the federal military academies in 1975, and drew on tradition-rich histories dating to the nineteenth century which honored the service of their graduates and defended the need for all-male military enclaves. Located in the South (The Citadel is in South Carolina, VMI is in Virginia), neither school served as a federal institution, and in the end both were forced to admit women by a suit brought against The Citadel by Shannon Faulkner, who applied for admission and was accepted because Citadel officials believed her to be male. When they realized their mistake, they rejected her application and she sued. Faulkner eventually won and entered The Citadel in 1995, only to be forced out by harassment within two weeks. The incident drew national attention and considerable television coverage, and prompted Phyllis Schlafly to write a letter to VMI begging them to continue the fight. "You've lost a major battle," she wrote. "Are you going to be survivors, or are you going to let the enemy wipe you and your kind from the face of the earth . . . ?"[64] Her rhetoric failed to sway VMI, which admitted women the following year with considerable success, and that failure demonstrated how much America had changed in the two decades following the admission of women to West Point. The experience, especially at The Citadel, also demonstrated how much West Point had done right when they admitted women. As one Class of 1980 woman put it later, her experience "was never in its worst hour as bad as anything I've seen on television at VMI or The Citadel."[65] The Academy, after all, had no mobs openly celebrating the departure of women cadets and graduated just under half of the women who arrived as New Cadets in 1976. Whatever the faults of the West Point attempt to fully integrate women in the 1970s, the Academy effort, unlike those of The Citadel and VMI, must always be judged with the caveat that it was first.

The success of West Point in the long run can be measured in many ways. One is in the service of some Class of 1980 women on the Academy staff, where they trained cadets to follow in their footsteps. "I want them [cadets] to be able to be courageous and make the right decisions," said one staffer, who hoped the young men and women she trained would "protect the sons and daughters of America in the future."[66] She noted, along with others, the considerable amazement she felt upon her return to West Point when she saw the progress made in gender relations. Today, she said, "There is absolutely an institutional norm that says, 'This is a co-ed institution.' "[67]

As a co-ed institution, West Point produced 2,092 female graduates between 1980 and 2000, and those women have largely served with distinction.[68] Between 1993 and 2000, 10.1 percent were recognized as Distinguished Cadets (compared to 9.5 percent of male cadets), while 25.5 percent received the Superintendent's Award (versus 22.1 percent for men), which is awarded to cadets who excel in academic, military, and physical programs at the Academy. Since 1980, fourteen women have earned postgraduate academic scholarships, including Rhodes Scholar Andrea Hollen, who graduated in 1980. Kristin Baker became the first female Cadet First Captain in 1989, Rebecca Marier became the first woman ranked at the top of her class in 1993, and Leticia Gasdick earned distinction as the first "Queen of Beast" in 1996. In fact, women have now served in every high-level cadet position at West Point. It remains only for female graduates to become Commandant and Superintendent for the litany of firsts to come to a close.

Women have generally left the Academy at a higher rate than men over the years, with attrition accounting for 34.2 percent of female and 27 percent of male cadets since 1980. Given the lack of societal encouragement for women desiring military careers, perhaps it is amazing the attrition rates are not more divergent. Despite the attrition rate, women are slightly more likely to receive promotion than their male peers, and slightly more likely to remain in the Army on active duty.[69] They are also attending West Point in larger numbers than ever before. Between 1997 and 2000, the number of female New Cadets reporting on R-Day has averaged 16 percent, a far cry from the days when the Academy had to scramble to find the 119 women who paved the way for others to follow in 1976.[70]

Of the sixty-two women who graduated in 1980, twelve remained on active service as of the summer of 2000, with a handful of that number likely to receive promotion to Brigadier General and perhaps beyond. By any standard these women have made valuable contributions to the Army, to West Point, and to the nation. The Army is now a better organization—more inclusive, more representative, and more talented—for opening its ranks to women and forcefully expanding the struggle against stereotypes about gender and sex. In the end the issue is not whether women belong in the Army or at West Point. They do. Instead, the central question is how long our culture will struggle to reconcile itself with the truth that the profound consequences of sex integration are worth the cost, that on a balance sheet comparing gains versus losses the military and America have prospered since expanding opportunities for women and allowing them to showcase their talents in the profession of arms. It is a simple truth, expressed well in 1978 by a thirty-five year old soldier with sixteen years of service in the Army. Responding to questions concerning the impact women were having on the service he said, "The only real limiting factor is our crippling perceptions of what a woman can and cannot do, and these perceptions are not only those which the men have, but the self-perceptions women have. Overcome this," he wrote, "and they *can do anything* (emphasis in original)."[71] A former West Point cadet echoed this sentiment years later, saying that associating with the women of the Class of 1980 turned him into an ardent feminist. As he put it, "I have never underestimated women since."[72]

Such a view highlights the impact the first female graduates had on the Army as a whole and on the men they have served with in particular. Many men were forced to examine their views regarding women when they served with or dated them, and some found the experience humbling. One whose views changed after befriending a female cadet during Cow year realized he had been "the most narrow-minded s.o.b. on the planet."[73] Another recounted his transformation from a "knuckle-dragger" phase toward a realization that leading women sometimes required different strategies than he used for men. That realization made him a better leader, he said, in the Regular Army and in civilian life.[74]

Though unrealized by 1980, the vision of an Academy open to the talents of every American and providing the finest leaders regardless of their race, ethnicity, or gender persisted. It is an enduring vision, dating at least to the late nineteenth century when Cadet Henry Ossian Flipper described the promise of West Point to America. As the Academy's first African American graduate, Flipper knew a great deal about discrimination, harassment, and abuse. Despite the harshness of his cadet years, or perhaps because of it, he held great hope for the Long Gray Line. "No college in the country has such a 'heterogeneous conglomeration'—to quote Dr. Johnson—of classes," he wrote in 1878. "The highest and lowest are represented. The glory of free America, her recognition of equality of all men, is not so apparent anywhere else as at West Point." With great optimism, Flipper added, "the day is not far distant when West Point will stand forth as the proud exponent of absolute social equality. Prejudice weakens, and ere long will fail completely. The advent of general education," he said, "sounds its death knell. And may the day not be far off when America shall proclaim her emancipation from the basest of all servitudes, the subservience to prejudice."[75] While Flipper referred to racial prejudice, his optimism and faith are equally relevant to the enduring problem of sexism, and his faith remains a clarion call for the Academy and the Army to strive more forcefully to become the beacon of which he dreamed.

That West Point might be a place where the nation made known a desire to promote equality and open up the Army to the talents of all Americans was an idea on which Flipper had no monopoly. In a 1975 letter to Lieutenant General Berry, a Columbia University professor noted that the admission of women to West Point signified yet another occasion where the Academy could adapt itself to the changing needs of the nation. Such adaptation formed a vital part of West Point's role in America, and the admission of women could be viewed as a positive development because "resorting to an ideology of sexism, . . . neglecting any resource which may contribute to our military posture," in short, by continuing to keep women out "[is] to disarm ourselves in the face of the enemy."

Further, he noted that the admission of women was a challenge well suited to the "tradition of flexibility and responsiveness to national needs" that characterized the Academy. "This change," he wrote, "which will bring all of our children into the officer corps is in the best tradition of West Point and our democratic society."[76]

The truth of that statement can be measured many ways, but none is so compelling as the story of one of the many accomplished graduates of the Class of 1980. Her story began on the island of Malta in the 1960s, carried her through the ordeal of her father's loss at sea and her subsequent journey to America, and on to the banks of the Hudson River and a place in the Long Gray Line. After graduating in 1980 she attended medical school, won the World Powerlifting Title in 1988, and served with U.N. forces in Somalia. Yet of all those moments, she said, receiving her diploma at West Point was among the proudest of her life. It demonstrated forcefully for her that "America has been the land of opportunity, for there is no other country in the world which would have offered me, a penniless immigrant, the opportunities I have had." Like others, she started off to West Point for the free education. And like so many before her, she soon recognized that her service to her adopted country, like the service of all men and women in uniform, "guarantees opportunities for others."[77] So it does.

The United States Military Academy remains an imperfect institution, struggling to produce hardened warriors in a rapidly changing society drunk with affluence, and it has not yet solved the problem of sexual harassment in the Army. In time, perhaps the Academy will help make certain that the accomplishments and sacrifices of military women will garner as many accolades as those of men and that women will serve their country without ever fearing their male peers in uniform. If that time arrives, West Point will be a step closer to becoming both a true meritocracy and an even more meaningful ideal to which our fractured society can look for inspiration. That would be a remarkable achievement for the Army, for the Academy, and for all of us as Americans. No one deserves to see that time arrive more than the women of the West Point Class of 1980.

For now, we may yet find ourselves closer to that goal than we sometimes realize. One promising event took place long ago, when the cadet from England attended her first Founders Day celebration in March of 1981. Hosted by West Point societies all over the world and attended by legions of faithful graduates, Founders Day ceremonies are held in March of each year to commemorate the founding of West Point in 1802. In 1981, the cadet in question found herself attending the celebration in Washington, D.C. As she nervously approached the ballroom to sign the guest register and enter, a graduate stopped her and said, "I'm sorry ma'am, this gathering is for West Point graduates only."

"I know," she replied. "I did graduate from West Point."

After signing in she slowly entered the ballroom, full of apprehension after four tumultuous years at the Academy. How, she wondered, would the other graduates receive her? As she walked into the room, the hundreds of male graduates inside slowly went silent and turned to stare. One heartbeat passed and then another, until the silence finally ended, broken by a steady wave of applause that began in the back of the room and slowly washed forward toward the doorway. Quickly it became a crescendo.

West Pointers had welcomed one of their own.

NOTES

1. Susan Finlay Watkins, "It is No Longer a Matter of Comment to See a Body of Young Ladies under Military Training," *Assembly* June 1980 p. 27.

2. Kristin Baker became the first woman to serve as First Captain at West Point in 1989. She graduated in 1990. See Theodore J. Crackel, *The Illustrated History of West Point* (New York: Harry N. Abrams, Inc., 1991), p. 290.

3. USMA, *Bugle Notes*, vol. 68 (West Point: USMA, 1976), p. 68.

4. Class rings are now received in August of the Firstie year at Battle Monument.

5. *Assembly*, September 1994, p. 20.

6. LTA, 5-15-96, p. 1.

7. EI, 4-17-80, p. 35.

8. Ibid., p. 33.

9. EI, 5-5-80, p. 24, 22.

10. Ibid., pp. 26–27.

11. EI, April/May 1980, p. 15.

12. EI, 5-14-80, p. 26.

13. EI, April/May 1980, p. 7.

14. Helen Rogan, *Mixed Company: Women in the Modern Army* (Boston: Beacon Press, 1982), p. 18.

15. Robert Timburg, *The Nightingale's Song* (New York: Simon and Schuster, 1995), p. 262. See also James Webb, "Women Can't Fight," *The Washingtonian*, November 1979, pp. 144–48, 273–82. Webb eventually became Secretary of the Navy during Ronald Reagan's administration and was the author of *Fields of Fire*, an influential novel dealing with the war in Vietnam.

16. *The Pointer*, May 1980, p. 9. The Academy eventually bought Ladycliff, using the grounds as a site for the West Point Museum and the official USMA Visitor Center.

17. *The Pointer*, September 1979, p. 3.

18. MAJ Jerome Adams, *Report of the Admission of Women to the United States Military Academy (Project Athena IV)* (West Point: Department of Behavioral Sciences and Leadership, 1980), p. 39.

19. Noted during an IWA on 4-13-96.

20. Crackel, *The Illustrated History of West Point*, pp. 306–7; and USMA, *Bugle Notes*, p. 199.

21. Jackie Robinson, *This I Believe*, cited in *Pegs to Hang Ideas On*, ed. Marjorie P. Katz and Jean S. Arbeiter (New York: M. Evans and Company, 1973), p. 101. Graduation ceremonies are unrelated to formally becoming officers in the United States Army; cadets are commissioned before graduation, usually by members of their family. See LTA, 4-4-2000, pp. 2–3.

22. "Lyrics to The Corps" was written by Bishop H.S. Shipman, USMA Chaplain,

around 1902, and was put to music composed by W. Franke Harling in 1910. See USMA, *Bugle Notes*, p. 206–7. MacArthur's allusion to "the Corps, and the Corps, and the Corps" in his famous 1962 address was taken from the song.

23. "Alma Mater" was written by Cadet P. S. Reinecke in the fall of 1908 while he walked a punishment tour. The lyrics were put to a tune called "Treuebeliebe," which dated to 1827, and became an Academy favorite after 1912. See USMA, *Bugle Notes*, p. 204–5.

24. EI, 4-30-80, p. 35; and EI, 5-8-80, p. 23.

25. EI, 5-14-80, p. 31.

26 IWA, 11-8-95, p. 11.

27. EI, 5-5-80, p. 26.

28. EI, 5-9-80, p. 31.

29. EI, no date, p. 8.

30. EI, 5-9-80, p. 32.

31. IWA, 7-19-96, author's notes.

32. EI, 5-9-80, p. 32. One graduate complained the Commandant and West Point Tactical Officers (TACs) had a group of women cadets they went to in the early years to get "good answers to assimilation questions." See EI, 5-5-80, p. 25.

33. EI, 4-17-80, p. 13.

34. EI, 5-14-80, p. 35

35. IWA, 6-5-96, author's notes.

36. IWA, 6-20-00, side B,

37. IWA, 5-13-96, p. 15.

38. IWA, 2-28-96, p. 7.

39. Ginny Carroll, "Women Have What It Takes," *Newsweek*, August 5, 1991, p. 30.

40. EI, 4-22-80, p. 4.

41. LTA, 6-13-95.

42. IWA, 6-20-00, side B.

43. ETA, 6-28-96, p. 1.

44. IWA, 2-16-96, p. 15, and IWA, 4-13-96, side A.

45. Eric Schmitt, "Study Says Sexual Harassment Persists at Military Academies," *New York Times*, April 5, 1995, p. A14. The forms of sexual harassment listed on the survey ranged from derogatory comments to assault.

46. U.S. General Accounting Office, "DOD Service Academies: Further Efforts Needed to Eradicate Sexual Harassment," Statement by Mark E. Gebicke, Director, Military Operations and Capabilities Issues, National Security and International Affairs Division, in Testimony Before the Subcommittee on Force Requirements and Personnel, Committee on Armed Services, U.S. Senate (GAO/T-NSIAD-94-11, February 3, 1994), p. 4.

47. Letter from T.B. to unknown West Point recipient, undated, pp. 1–3. USMA files. "T.B." was a member of the Class of 1986. Her letter was included with other letters to the Superintendent from the 1980s, so I surmise it was to him as well.

48. IWA, 11-3-95, author's notes.

49. Graves Haydon Thompson, *Selections from the Ars Armaatoria and Remedia Amoris of Ovid, with Introduction, Notes, and Vocabulary* (Hampden-Sydney, Va.: published by the Author, 1953), p. 63. The original Latin phrase is "nil adsuetudine maius."

50. IWA, 5-16-97, author's notes.

51. See *Webster's Ninth New Collegiate Dictionary* (Springfield, Mass.: Merriam-Webster, Inc., 1991), p. 1078.

52. Barbara Ehrenreich, *Blood Rites: Origins and History of the Passions of War* (New York: Metropolitan Books, 1997), p. 236.

53. Lionel Tiger, "Durkheim, Sociology, and the Science of Bodies in Conflict," paper presented at the Interdisciplinary Summary Conference of the Study of War Project, Triangle Institute of Security Studies, June 1997, p. 17.

54. Lionel Tiger and Robin Fox, *The Imperial Animal* (New York: Holt, Rinehart, and Winston, 1971), p. 101.

55. Joel Barlow, *Advice to the Privileged Orders in the Several States of Europe, Resulting from the Necessity and Propriety of a General Revolution in the Principle of Government* (London: J. Johnson, 1792 and 1795; reprint, Ithaca, N.Y.: Cornell University Press, 1956), pp. 14–15.

56. Joanna Strong and Tom B. Leonard, "Susan B. Anthony," in *The Book of Virtues for Young People*, ed. William J. Bennett (Parsippany, N.J.: Silver Burdett Press, 1996), p. 211.

57. Carolyn Becraft, *Women in the Military* (Washington, D.C.: Women's Research and Education Institute, 1990), pp. 9–11. The number of women in uniform grew from less than 2 percent of total armed forces personnel in 1972 to 13.7 percent in 1997. In that same year, Army women accounted for 15.1 percent of enlisted personnel and 13.1 percent of officers. See Lory Manning and Jennifer E. Griffith, "Women in the Military: Where They Stand," 2nd ed., A Women in the Military Project Report Prepared for the Women's Research and Education Institute, 1998, p. 10.

58. LTG Harold G. Moore, Jr., IWA, 9-30-95, p. 11.

59. Ibid., 9-30-95, p. 11.

60. LTA, 3-28-96, p. 2.

61. Ibid., p. 3.

62. The Honorable Samuel J. Bayard, Address Delivered Before the Graduating Class of Cadets, June 16, 1854 (Camden: Office of the *Camden Democrat*, 1854), p. 3.

63. IWA, 7-11-96, side A.

64. Phyllis Schlafly, "Open Letter to VMI Alumni," *The Eagle Forum*, Alton, Ill., June 11, 1996.

65. IWA, 6-20-00, side A.

66. IWA, 7-11-96, side A.

67. Ibid.

68. USMA Public Affairs Office, telephone interview, 9-22-00, author's notes. Between 1980 and 2000 the Academy graduated 20,348 total graduates; since 1802 it has graduated 57,518.

69. Karen Fralen, "20th Anniversay of the First Women West Point Graduates: Part II," *Gray Matter E-Mail Newsletter*, June 16, 2000, pp. 4–5.

70. USMA, Public Affairs Office, telephone interview, 11-20-00, author's notes.

71. United States Army, "Final Report: Evaluation of Women in the Army" (Washington, D.C.: U.S. Army Administrative Center, March 1978), p. A-4–2-15.

72. IWA, 3-26-97, author's notes.

73. IWA, 2-18-98, author's notes.

74. IWA, 5-11-00, author's notes.

75. LT Henry Ossian Flipper, *The Colored Cadet at West Point: Autobiography of Lieut. Henry Ossian Flipper, U.S.A., First Graduate of Color From the U.S. Military*

Academy (New York: Homer Lee and Co., 1878), p. 147. The "Johnson" referred to in Flipper's remarks was the famous Samuel Johnson.

   76. S.F. to LTG Sidney B. Berry, July 22, 1975, USMA files, p. 2.
   77. ETA, 7-26-00, pp. 1–2.

Epilogue

Yet it no longer falls to me to bear arms in my country's defense. It falls to you. I pray that if the time comes for you to answer the call to arms the battle will be necessary and the field well chosen. But that is not your responsibility. Your honor is in your answer, not your summons.

—Senator John McCain[1]

Sunsets come slowly at West Point, as if golden shafts of light dread leaving the hallowed grounds of the fortress on the Hudson. They linger, reluctantly pulling away from the river as El Sol descends westward behind the mountains, leaving long shadows in their wake. Beams recede past the timeless statues of George S. Patton and Dwight D. Eisenhower, shower through the barracks windows of a thousand cadets, and dance across the weathered visages of Sylvanus Thayer and Douglas MacArthur standing eternal watch over The Plain. Rays glint from the peak of Battle Monument and retreat painfully from the shaded sanctuary of the post cemetery. Like the rearguard of a withdrawing column, one last glittering sliver of light pauses atop the mountains to the west. Desperate to stave off nightfall, it darts brilliantly through the stained glass of the Cadet Chapel, glides across the dusk-shrouded ruins of Fort Putnam, and kindles the clouding eyes of an Old Grad lost in memory along Trophy Point. In an instant, the brightness is gone, abandoning the United States Military Academy to sable night, yet promising to lead the minions of Apollo back from the east in the morning.

It has been that way as long as anyone can remember, or at least as long as

The King of Beast and his staff lead the men and women of the Class of 2000 in an evening salute during Beast Barracks, 1995. Illustration by Pamela Lenck Bradford. Copyright © 2001 by Pamela Lenck Bradford.

there have been people to stand on The Plain at West Point and notice. The sun rises across the majestic river and sets behind tree-covered mountains, and in summer, as it has every year since 1802, the United States Military Academy receives a new class of cadets.

One such class arrived on June 29, 2000. One thousand one hundred and ninety strong, it represented every state in the Union, several foreign countries, and the promise of a generation eager to take its place in the Long Gray Line. During a summer when the Academy noted the twentieth anniversary of the graduation of the first female cadets, the New Cadets of the Class of 2004 began a new phase of their lives with a personal commitment to public service.

Gathering in the Holleder Center, many New Cadets were accompanied by friends and family during their welcome from Academy officials.[2] They were told what to expect from life at West Point and encouraged to keep a sense of humor during the weeks ahead. Finally it came time for separation. New Cadets went one way; family and friends went another. Young men and women hugged their families, gathered their belongings, and were gone. It was a moment of extraordinary poignancy. Parents wanted it to linger; their children wanted it to end. One group fought back tears and faced a tour of the Academy and a long drive home to a world less full than before. The other stood on the threshold of admission to the society of warriors, at the beginning of the most challenging journey of their lives.

All too quickly the moment vanished. New Cadets moved from a world with precious few rites of passage to one with a dazzling array of hurdles, each linking them more closely to the Corps of Cadets. They left a world of individuality where little was expected, failure was commonplace, and the emphasis was on choice, to join a world where the group mattered most, a great deal was expected, failure was unthinkable, and the emphasis was on obligation.

After several hours and a dazzling array of in-processing formalities including haircuts, uniform issue, and instruction in the timeless art of the military salute, New Cadets formed up for the afternoon parade which signaled the beginning of Cadet Basic Training. Known as "Beast Barracks," the training consisted of a six-week program of instruction focusing on physical fitness, military protocol, and weapons proficiency roughly analogous to basic training for Army enlisted personnel. The Cadet Captain in charge of the first half of this training period was a First classman traditionally known and feared as the "King of Beast," and in June of 2000 the King was Charleston, South Carolina native David Uthlaut.

As the Cadet Training Battalion Commander, Uthlaut led the New Cadets and their company commanders onto the historic Plain at West Point. After taking their oath to "support the Constitution of the United States, and bear true allegiance to the National Government . . . ," the New Cadets formed by company behind the famous "Hellcats," the drum and bugle detachment of the United States Military Academy Band. After aligning their ranks, they began to pass in review before the spectators gathered in the surrounding bleachers to celebrate their first steps on the long road to graduation.

The Hellcats, smartly in step and immaculately attired in Army dress blues, passed first playing the "West Point March." They were followed by the Academy color guard carrying the Stars and Stripes and the colors of the United States Army. Atop the Army's flag were battle streamers commemorating the 173 campaigns and major engagements fought by the Army since the American Revolution. Saratoga mingled in the breeze with the Argonne, Gettysburg with Normandy and Bataan, and Chosin Reservoir with the Ia Drang Valley, Grenada, and Desert Storm. Behind the colors came the New Cadets, arranged into eight companies and struggling to maintain their newly-received places in the Long Gray Line.

Parents and friends strained to recognize their New Cadet in the sea of identical uniforms and closely cropped hair. They cheered en masse as the long column passed in review, letting out isolated bursts of joy when a solemn face became suddenly familiar. They hardly noticed the ragged marching, the awkward attempts to keep in step, or the grimaces stress was already placing on the faces of their loved ones. Caught up in the emotion of the moment, they would have forgiven these incongruities anyway. After all, their willing young soldiers were neophytes, not the disciplined formations of precision marchers that would astound crowds at weekend parades in the fall.

In many ways, this rite of passage resembled so many others in the Academy's long history. It represented the first step in a metamorphosis through which civilians became soldiers, young people shouldered the burden of citizenship, and West Point unobtrusively accepted another class of young people and began preparing them for careers in the service of their country.

In fact, very little seemed unique about the class destined to take the Academy and the Army into the next millennium. Press reports noted in passing that 199 women reported on R-Day in 2000, and that the first women admitted as cadets had arrived at West Point on July 7, 1976. Twenty-four years and another America had come and gone in the interim, and no one in the Class of 2004 seemed to notice.

The Long Gray Line marched on.

NOTES

1. Robert Timburg, *The Nightingale's Song* (New York: Simon and Schuster, 1995), p. 462. McCain's words come from a June 1994 speech given at the Marine Corps Command and Staff College.

2. Opened in 1985, the Holleder Center is home to the Army basketball and hockey teams, and named after MAJ Donald W. Holleder, USMA Class of 1956, who was killed in Vietnam in 1967.

Appendix

FEMALE GRADUATES
UNITED STATES MILITARY ACADEMY CLASS OF 1980

Name	Company	Hometown
Donna Sue Alesch	A-3	Albuquerque, New Mexico
Ann Shelley Ashworth	D-3	Greensboro, North Carolina
Carol Anne Barkalow	A-3	Laurel, Maryland
Brigid Benya	G-1	Fremont, California
Rebecca Ambrose Blyth	F-1	York, Pennsylvania
Diane Bracey	F-1	Woodridge, New Jersey
Janis Marie Calhoon	G-2	Cheektowaga, New York
Karen Ann Cicchini	D-1	Bay City, Michigan
Ruth Ann Colister	G-4	College Park, Maryland
Joy Suzanne Dallas	G-3	Fairborn, Ohio
Denise Irene Dawson	A-2	Woodbridge, Virginia
Robin Fennessy	E-2	Dyersville, Iowa
Bobbi Lynn Fiedler	D-2	Vienna, Virginia
Anne Walker Fields	G-4	Fort Knox, Kentucky
Mary Elizabeth Flynn	A-4	North Caldwell, New Jersey
Brenda Sue Fulton	E-4	Jensen Beach, Florida

Kathleen Mary Gerard	D-4	Carlisle Barracks, Pennsylvania
Katharine Goodland	E-2	Ames, Iowa
Mary Ellen Gridley	D-3	Dixon, Illinois
Eleanor Ruth Griffin	D-1	Fort Sill, Oklahoma
Nancy Lorraine Gucwa	E-3	Staten Island, New York
Janet Jane Harrington	B-3	Moore, Oklahoma
Karen Jayne Hinsey	G-2	Packer, Colorado
Andrea Lee Hollen	D-3	Altoona, Pennsylvania
Ann Marie Hughes	G-4	Garden City, Michigan
Debra Ann Johnson	A-4	Poughkeepsie, New York
Tamara C. Kaseman	A-3	Fargo, North Dakota
Susan Puanani Kellett	A-1	Kaneohe, Hawaii
Karen Louise Kelly	A-3	Naperville, Illinois
Karen Mary Kinzler	D-4	Aiea, Hawaii
Clare Kirby	I-4	West Point, New York
Debra Malvene Lewis	D-2	Strafford, New Hampshire
Danna Maller	G-2	Cockeysville, Maryland
Vicki Louise Martin	E-3	Fenton, Michigan
Debra Lynn McCarthy	G-1	Grass Valley, California
Jane Mary McEntee	D-4	New Braunfels, Texas
Sylvia Thorpe Moran	I-4	Homewood, Illinois
Amy Jane Muir	G-1	Greenwich, Connecticut
Sonya Elich Nikituk	A-4	South Saint Paul, Minnesota
Rita Annette Null	E-4	Kennett, Missouri
Marene Nyberg	B-2	Halifax, Massachusetts
Erin Marie O'Connor	B-2	Bordentown, New Jersey
Jane Hunter Perkins	D-2	Ridgewood, New Jersey
Lillian Ann Pfluke	G-1	Palo Alto, California
Susanne Patricia Reichelt	E-2	Panama City, Florida
Mary Grace Rosinski	E-2	St. Joseph, Michigan
Brynnen Gayle Sheets	D-1	Edmond, Oklahoma
Kathleen Silvia	B-3	North Reading, Massachusetts
Joan Mary Smith	I-4	Tenafly, New Jersey
Christi Lynn Stevens	G-2	Jacksonville Beach, Florida

Dianne Louise Stoddard	A-1	South Kent, Connecticut
Terry Jane Tepper	B-2	Elmsford, New York
Regina Claire Todd	E-4	Peekskill, New York
Barbara Lynn Treharne	A-4	Livonia, Michigan
Doris Ann Turner	D-3	Lyndhurst, Ohio
Priscilla Marie Walker	A-2	Detroit, Michigan
Kathleen Ann Wheless	G-4	Clearwater, Florida
Kathryn Annette Wildey	D-2	Spokane, Washington
Donna Marie Wright	A-2	Merrick, New York
Carol Ann Young	G-3	Fairport, New York
Kelly Lynn Zachgo	F-1	San Antonio, Texas
Joan Marie Zech	E-4	Enumchaw, Washington

Bibliography

PRIMARY SOURCES

Barkalow, Carol, with Andrea Raab. *In the Men's House: An Inside Account of Life in the Army by One of West Point's First Female Graduates*. New York: Berkeley Books, 1992.

Berard, Augusta B. *Reminiscences of West Point in the Olden Time*. East Saginaw, Mich.: n.p., 1886.

Blaik, Earl H. *The Red Blaik Story*. New Rochelle, N.Y.: Arlington House, 1974.

Dickens, Charles. *American Notes*. Boston: Dana Estes and Company, 1868.

Flipper, Lieutenant Henry Ossian. *The Colored Cadet at West Point: Autobiography of Lieut. Henry Ossian Flipper, U.S.A., First Graduate of Color From the U.S. Military Academy*. New York: Homer Lee and Co., 1878.

Kinzler, Karen, as told to Valerie Eads. "West Point Woman." *Seventeen* 36 (April 1977): 74–76.

Mardis, Jamie. *Memos of a West Point Cadet*. New York: McKay Books, 1976.

Peterson, Donna. *Dress Gray: A Woman at West Point*. Austin, Tex.: Eakin Press, 1990.

Schwartzkopf, H. Norman. *It Doesn't Take a Hero: General H. Norman Schwartzkopf: The Autobiography*. New York: Bantam Books, 1992.

Smith, Dale O. *Cradle of Valor: The Intimate Letters of a Plebe at West Point Between the Wars*. Chapel Hill, N.C.: Algonquin Books, 1988.

SECONDARY SOURCES

Books

Ambrose, Stephen E. *Duty, Honor, Country: A History of West Point*. Rev. ed. Baltimore: The Johns Hopkins University Press, 1999.

Atkinson, Rick. *The Long Gray Line*. Boston: Houghton Mifflin Company, 1989.

Babbie, Earl. *Survey Research Methods*. Belmont, Calif.: Wadsworth Publishing Company, 1973.

Bach J., Shirley, and Martin Binkin. *Women in the Military*. Washington, D.C.: The Brookings Institute, 1977.

Bachman, J., J. D. Blair, and D. R. Segal. *Ideology and the All-Volunteer Force*. Ann Arbor: University of Michigan Press, 1977.

Barlow, Joel. *Advice to the Privileged Orders of the Several States of Europe, Resulting from the Necessity and Propriety of a General Revolution in the Principle of Government*. London: J. Johnson, 1792 and 1795. Reprint. Ithaca, N.Y.: Cornell University Press, 1956.

Bartlett, John. *Familiar Quotations: A Collection of Passages, Phrases, and Proverbs Traced to Their Sources in Ancient and Modern Literature*. Edited by Justin Kaplan. Boston: Little, Brown and Company, 1992.

Baskir, Lawrence M., and Willaim A. Strauss. *Chance and Circumstance: The Draft, the War and the Vietnam Generation*. New York: Vintage Books, 1978.

Baynes, John Christopher Malcom. *Morale: A Study of Men and Courage; the Second Scottish Rifles at the Battle of Neuve Chapelle, 1915*. New York: Praeger, 1967.

Becraft, Carolyn. *Women in the Military*. Washington D.C.: Women's Research and Education Institute, 1990.

Blacksmith, E. A., ed. *Women in the Military*. New York: The H.W. Wilson Company, 1992.

Bowden, Mark. *Black Hawk Down: A Story of Modern War*. New York: Atlantic Monthly Press, 1999.

Brenton, Myron. *The American Male*. Greenwich, Conn.: Fawcett Publications, 1970.

Brodie, Laura Fairchild. *Breaking Out: VMI and the Coming of Women*. New York: Pantheon Books, 2000.

Cameron, Craig. *American Samurai: Myth, Imagination, and the Conduct of Battle in the First Marine Division 1941–1951*. New York: Cambridge University Press, 1994.

Cavalli-Sforza, L. L., P. Menozzi, and A. Piazza. *The History and Geography of Human Genes*. Princeton, N.J.: Princeton University Press, 1994.

Cincinnatus. *Self-Destruction: The Disintegration and Decay of the United States Army During the Vietnam Era*. New York: W. W. Norton and Company, 1981.

Coffman, Edward M. *The Old Army: A Portrait of the American Army in Peacetime, 1784–1898*. New York: Oxford University Press, 1986.

Connell, R. W. *Masculinities*. Berkeley, Calif.: University of California Press, 1995.

Cooke, Miriam, and Angela Woollacott, eds. *Gendering War Talk*. Princeton: Princeton University Press, 1993.

Cortwright, David. *Soldiers in Revolt*. New York: Anchor Press/Doubleday, 1975.

Crackel, Theodore J. *The Illustrated History of West Point*. New York: Harry N. Abrams Inc., 1991.

Dean, Donna M. *Warriors Without Weapons: The Victimization of Military Women*. Pasadena, Md.: The Minerva Center, 1997.

Dinsmore, John C. *Women as Cadets: An Analysis of the Issue*. Maxwell Air Force Base, Ala.: Air University Press, 1974.

Dupuy, R. Ernest. *Men of West Point*. New York: William Sloane Associates, 1951.

Ehrenreich, Barbara. *Blood Rites: Origins and History of the Passions of War*. New York: Metropolitan Books, 1997.

Ellis, Joseph, and Robert Moore. *School for Soldiers: West Point and the Profession of Arms*. New York: Oxford University Press, 1974.

Endler, James R. *Other Leaders, Other Heroes: West Point's Legacy to America Beyond the Field of Battle*. Westport, Conn.: Praeger Publishers, 1998.

Evans, Sara M. *Born for Liberty: A History of Women in America*. Rev. ed. New York: Free Press, 1997.

Ewing, Elizabeth. *Women in Uniform*. Totowa, N.J.: Rowman and Littlefield, 1975.

Fallows, James. *National Defense*. New York: Random House, 1981.

Fleming, Thomas. *West Point: The Men and Times of the United States Military Academy*. New York: William Morrow, 1969.

Forman, Sidney. *West Point: A History of the United States Military Academy*. New York: Columbia University Press, 1950.

Freedman, Lawrence, ed. *War*. New York: Oxford University Press, 1994.

Gabriel, Richard A., and Paul L. Savage. *Crisis in Command: Mismanagement in the Army*. New York: Hill and Wang, 1978.

Galbraith, John Kenneth. *The Affluent Society*. New York: Mentor Books, 1958.

Galloway, K. Bruce, and Robert Bowie Johnson, Jr. *West Point: America's Power Fraternity*. New York: Simon and Schuster, 1973.

Gilligan, Carol. *In a Different Voice: Psychological Theory and Women's Development*. Cambridge, Mass.: Harvard University Press, 1982.

Ginzberg, Eli. *The Lost Divisions*. New York: Columbia University Press, 1959.

Gitlin, Todd. *The Sixties: Years of Hope, Days of Rage*. New York: Bantam Books, 1987.

Goldman, Nancy L., and David R. Segal, eds. *The Social Psychology of Military Service*. Sage Research Progress Series on War, Revolution, and Peacekeeping. Vol. 6. Beverly Hills: Sage Publications, 1976.

Gray, J. Glenn. *The Warriors*. New York: Harper and Row, 1959.

Green, Jane. *Powder, Paper and Lace: An Anecdotal Herstory of Women at West Point*. Charlottesville, Va.: Priority Press, 1988.

Gutmann, Stephanie. *The Kinder, Gentler Military: Can America's Gender-Neutral Fighting Force Still Win Wars?* New York: Charles Scribner, 2000.

Hackworth, David H., with Julie Sherman. *About Face: The Odyssey of an American Warrior*. New York: Simon and Schuster, 1989.

Hauser, William L. *America's Army in Crisis: A Study in Civil-Military Relations*. Baltimore: The Johns Hopkins University Press, 1973.

Heise, J. Arthur. *The Brass Factories*. Washington, D.C.: Public Affairs Press, 1969.

Holm, Major General Jeanne (Ret). *Women in the Military: An Unfinished Revolution*. Rev. ed. Novato, Calif.: Presidio Press, 1992.

Huntington, Samuel P. *The Soldier and the State*. New York: Vintage Books, 1957.

Janowitz, Morris. *The Professional Soldier*. New York: The Free Press, 1960.

———. *The U.S. Forces and the Zero Draft*. Adelphi Papers, No. 94. Washington, D.C.: International Institute for Strategic Studies, 1973.

———, ed. *The New Military*. New York: W. W. Norton, 1969.

Johnson, Haynes, and George C. Wilson, et al. *Army in Anguish*. New York: Pocket Books, 1972.

Just, Ward. "Introduction." In *About Face: The Odyssey of an American Warrior*, by David H. Hackworth and Julie Sherman, p. 14. New York: Simon and Schuster, 1989.

Katz, Marjorie P., and Jean S. Arbeiter, ed. *Pegs to Hang Ideas On*. New York: M. Evans and Company, 1973.

Katzenstein, Mary. *Faithful and Fearless: Moving Feminist Protest Inside the Church and Military*. Princeton, N.J.: Princeton University Press, 1998.

Keegan, John. *Fields of Battle: The Wars for North America*. New York: Alfred A. Knopf, 1996.

————. *The Mask of Command*. London: Jonathan Cape, 1987.

————. *A History of Warfare*. New York: Alfred A. Knopf, 1993.

Kemble, Charles Robert. *The Image of the Army Officer in America: Background for Current Views*. Westport, Conn.: Greenwood Press, 1973.

Kemp, Peter, ed. *The Oxford Dictionary of Literary Quotations*. New York: Oxford University Press, 1997.

Kimmel, Michael. *Manhood in America: A Cultural History*. New York: The Free Press, 1996.

King, Edward. *The Death of the Army: A Pre-Mortem*. New York: Saturday Review Press, 1972.

Kinzer, Nora Scott. *Stress and the American Woman*. New York: Anchor Press/Doubleday, 1979.

Kitfield, James. *Prodigal Soldiers: How the Generation of Vietnam Revolutionized the American Style of War*. New York: Simon and Schuster, 1995.

Lang, Kurt. *Military Institutions and the Sociology of War*. Sage Series on Armed Forces and Society. Beverly Hills: Sage Publications, 1972.

Lefkowitz, Bernard. *Our Guys: The Glen Ridge Rape and the Secret Life of the Perfect Suburb*. Berkeley: University of California Press, 1997.

Lenney, John J. *Caste System in the American Army: A Study of the Corps of Engineers and Their West Point System*. New York: Greenburg Publishers, 1949.

Lever, Janet, and Pepper Schwartz. *Women at Yale: Liberating a College Campus*. Indianapolis: The Bobbs-Merrill Company, Inc., 1971.

Lovell, John. *Neither Athens Nor Sparta? The American Service Academies in Transition*. Bloomington, Ind.: Indiana University Press, 1979.

Manchester, William. *American Caesar: Douglas MacArthur, 1880–1964*. New York: Dell Publishing Co., 1978.

————. *Goodbye, Darkness: A Memoir of the Pacific War*. Boston: Little, Brown and Company, 1979.

Manegold, Catherine. *In Glory's Shadow: Shannon Faulkner, the Citadel and a Changing America*. New York: Alfred A. Knopf, 2000.

Margiotta, Franklin D., ed. *The Changing World of the American Military*. Boulder, Col. Westview Press, 1979.

Marshall, S. L. A. *Men Against Fire*. New York: William Morrow Co., 1947.

Mathews, Donal G., and Jane Sherron De Hart. *Sex, Gender, and the Politics of ERA: A State and the Nation*. New York: Oxford University Press, 1990.

Mead, Margaret. *Male and Female: A Study of the Sexes in a Changing World*. New York: William Morrow and Company, 1949.

Millett, Kate. *Sexual Politics*. Garden City, N.Y.: Doubleday, 1970.

Moran, Lord. *The Anatomy of Courage*. Boston: Houghton Mifflin Company, 1967.

Morgan, Robin, ed. *Sisterhood Is Powerful: An Anthology of Writings from the Women's Liberation Movement*. New York: Vintage Books, 1970.

Morrison, James L., Jr. *The Best School in the World: West Point: The Pre-Civil War Years, 1833–1866*. Kent, Oh.: The Kent State University Press, 1986.

Moskos, Charles C., and John Sibley Butler. *All That We Can Be: Black Leadership and Racial Integration the Army Way*. New York: Basic Books, 1996.

Nelson, Daniel J. *A History of U.S. Military Forces in Germany*. Boulder, Col.: Westview Press, 1987.

Nelson, Mariah Burton. *The Stronger Women Get the More Men Love Football: Sexism and the American Culture of Sports*. New York: Harcourt Brace, 1994.

Nite, Norm N. *Rock On Almanac: The First Four Decades of Rock n' Roll: A Chronology*. New York: Harper and Row, 1989.

Nixon, Richard. *Leaders*. New York: Warner Books, 1982.

Nye, Robert A. *Masculinity and Male Codes of Honor in Modern France*. New York: Oxford University Press, 1993.

Palmer, Dave Richard. *The River and the Rock: The History of Fortress West Point, 1775–1783*. West Point, New York: Association of Graduates, USMA, in association with Hippocrene Books, 1991.

Pappas, George S. *The Cadet Chapel—United States Military Academy*. Providence. R.I.: Andrew Mowbray, Inc., 1987.

Perret, Geoffrey. *Old Soldiers Never Die: The Life of Douglas MacArthur*. New York: Random House, 1996.

————. *Ulysses S. Grant: Soldier and President*. New York: Random House, 1997.

Peterson, Susan Goldner. *Self-Defense for Women: The West Point Way*. New York: Simon and Schuster, 1979.

Plato, *The Republic of Plato*. Translated by Francis MacDonald Cornford. New York: Oxford University Press, 1968.

Rapp, Kenneth W. *West Point: Whistler in Cadet Gray and Other Stories About the United States Military Academy*. Croton-on-Hudson, N.Y.: North River Press, 1978.

Reeder, Red, and Nardi Reeder Campion. *The West Point Story*. New York: Random House, 1956.

Ricks, Thomas E. *Making the Corps*. New York: Scribner, 1997.

Robarchek, Clayton A., and Carol J. Robarchek. "Cultures of War and Peace: A Comparative Study of Waorani and Semai." In *Aggression and Peacefulness in Humans and Other Primates*, edited by James Silverberg and Patrick Gray, pp. 189–213. New York: Oxford University Press, 1992.

Rogan, Helen. *Mixed Company: Women in the Modern Army*. Boston: Beacon Press, 1982.

Rotundo, E. Anthony. *American Manhood: Transformations in Masculinity from the Revolution to the Modern Era*. New York: Basic Books, 1993.

Sarkesian, Sam C. *The Professional Army Officer in a Changing Society*. Chicago: Nelson-Hall Publishers, 1975.

Savage, William W., Jr. *The Cowboy Hero: His Image in American History and Culture*. Norman: University of Oklahoma Press, 1979.

Schlesinger, Arthur M., Jr. *The Crisis of the Old Order: 1919–1933*. Boston: Houghton Mifflin, Company, 1957.

Shilts, Randy. *Conduct Unbecoming: Lesbians and Gays in the U.S. Military: Vietnam to the Persian Gulf.* New York: St. Martin's Press, 1993.

Simpson, Jeffrey. *Officers and Gentlemen: Historic West Point in Photographs.* Tarrytown, N.Y.: Sleepy Hollow Press, 1982.

Spurling, Kathryn, and Elizabeth Greenhalgh. *Women in Uniform: Perceptions and Pathways.* School of History, University College, UNSW: Australian Defense Force Academy, 2000.

Stewart, Robert, and Edward C. Meyer. *The Corps of Cadets: A Year at West Point.* Annapolis: United States Naval Institute Press, 1996.

Stiehm, Judith Hicks. *Bring Me Men and Women: Mandated Change at the U.S. Air Force Academy.* Berkeley: University of California Press, 1981.

Teitelbaum, Michael S., ed. *Sex Differences: Social and Biological Perspectives.* Garden City, N.J.: Anchor Press/Doubleday, 1976.

Thompson, Graves Haydon. *Selections from the Ars Amatoria and Remedia Amoris of Ovid.* Hampden-Sydney, Va.: By the Author, 1952.

Thucydides. *The History of the Peloponnesian War.* Ed. and trans. Sir Richard Livingstone. 1943. Reprint. New York: Oxford University Press, 1978.

Tiger, Lionel. *Men in Groups.* 2nd ed. New York: Marion Boyars, 1984.

Tiger, Lionel, and Robin Fox. *The Imperial Animal.* New York: Holt, Rinehart, and Winston, 1971.

Timburg, Robert. *The Nightingale's Song.* New York: Simon and Schuster, 1995.

Todd, Frederick P. *Cadet Gray.* New York: Sterling Publishing Company, 1955.

Treadwell, Mattie. *U.S. Army in World War II: Special Studies—The Women's Army Corps.* Washington, D.C.: Department of the Army, 1954.

U'Ren, Richard C., M.D. *Ivory Fortress: A Psychiatrist Looks at West Point.* Indianapolis: Bobbs-Merrill, 1974.

Van Creveld, Martin. *The Transformation of War.* New York: The Free Press, 1991.

Walton, George H. *The Tarnished Shield: A Report on Today's Army.* New York: Dodd/Mead, 1973.

Weed, Elizabeth, ed. *Coming to Terms: Feminism, Theory, Practice.* New York: Routledge, 1989.

Weigley, Russell F. *History of the United States Army.* Bloomington: Indiana University Press, 1984.

Weisman, Leslie Kanes. *Discrimination by Design: A Feminist Critique of the Man-Made Environment.* Chicago: University of Chicago Press, 1992.

Wheelright, Julie. *Amazons and Military Maids: Women Who Dressed as Men in the Pursuit of Life, Liberty and Happiness.* London: Pandora Press, 1989.

Whyte, William F. *The Organizational Man.* New York: Simon and Schuster, 1956.

Wicks, Stephen. *Warriors and Wildmen: Men, Masculinity, and Gender.* Westport, Conn.: Bergin and Garvey, 1996.

Williams, Christine L. *Gender Differences at Work: Women and Men in Nontraditional Occupations.* Berkeley: University of California Press, 1989.

Zeiger, Susan. *In Uncle Sam's Service: Women Workers with the American Expeditionary Force, 1917–1919.* Ithaca, New York: Cornell University Press, 1999.

Zimmerman, Jean. *Tailspin: Women at War in the Wake of Tailhook.* New York: Doubleday and Company, 1995.

Zinn, Howard. *A People's History of the United States: 1492–Present.* Rev. and updated ed. New York: HarperCollins, 1995.

Journals

Adams, Jerome. "Group Performance at West Point: Relationships with Intelligence and Attitudes Toward Sex Roles." *Armed Forces and Society Journal* 7 (Winter 1981): 246–55.

———. "Attitudinal Studies on the Integration of Women at West Point." *International Journal of Women's Studies* 5, No. 1 (January/February 1982): 22–28.

———. "Women at West Point: A Three-Year Perspective." *Sex Roles* 11, No. 5–6 (September 1984): 525–41.

Adams, Jerome, Howard T. Prince II, Robert F. Priest, and Robert W. Rice. "Personality Characteristics of Male and Female Leaders at the U.S. Military Academy." *Journal of Political and Military Sociology* (Spring 1980): 99–105.

Adams, Jerome, Howard T. Prince II, Debra Instone, and Robert W. Rice. "West Point: Critical Incidents of Leadership." *Armed Forces and Society Journal* 10 (Winter 1984): 597–611.

Adams, Jerome, Robert W. Rice, and Debra Instone. "Follower Attitudes Toward Women and Judgements Concerning Performance by Female and Male Leaders." *Academy of Management Journal* 27, No. 3 (September 1984): 636–43.

Adams, Jerome, Howard T. Prince II, Jan D. Yoder, and Robert W. Rice. "Group Performance at West Point: Relationships with Intelligence and Attitudes Toward Sex Roles." *Armed Forces and Society Journal* 7, No. 2 (Winter 1981): 246–55.

Boening, Suzanne S. "Women Soldier, Quo Vadis?" *Parameters: The Journal of the Army War College* 13, No. 2 (1983): 58–64.

Braty, Howard, and Everett Wilson. "Characteristics of Military Society." *American Journal of Sociology* 51 (March 1946): 371–75.

Browne, Kingsley R. "Biology, Equality, and the Law: The Legal Significance of Biological Sex Differences." *Southwestern Law Journal* 38, No. 2 (June 1984): 24–91.

———. "An Evolutionary Perspective on Sexual Harassment: Seeking Roots in Biology Rather than Ideology." *Journal of Contemporary Legal Issues* 8 (Spring 1997): 5–78.

Campbell, D'Ann. "Servicewomen and the Academies: The Football Cordon and Pep Rally as a Case Study of the Status of Female Cadets at the United States Military Academy." *Minerva: Quarterly Report on Women and the Military* 13, No. 1 (Spring 1995):1–14.

Clark, Albert P. "Women at the Service Academies and Combat Leadership." *Strategic Review* 5 (Fall 1977): 64–73.

Corbitt, Richard W., Donald L. Cooper, Donald J. Erickson, Frederick C. Kriss, Melvin L. Thornton, and Timothy T. Craig. "Female Athletics." *Journal of the American Medical Association* 228, No.10 (June 3, 1974): 1266–67.

Cross, William M., and James J. Cortez. "A Comparative Personality Study of Resignees at the United States Military Academy." *Proceedings of the Second Symposium of Psychology in the Air Force* (April 1971): 245–54.

DeFleur, Lois B., David Gillman, and William Marshal. "Sex Integration of the U.S. Air Force Academy." *Armed Forces and Society* 4, No. 4 (August 1978): 607–22.

Durning, Kathleen P. "Women at the Naval Academy." *Armed Forces and Society Journal* 4, No. 4 (August 1978): 569–88.

Feld, M.D. "Arms and the Woman: Some General Considerations." *Armed Forces and Society Journal* 4, No. 4 (August 1978): 557–67.

Franke, Volker C. "Warriors for Peace: The Next Generation of Military Leaders." *Armed Forces and Society Journal* 24, No. 2 (Winter 1997): 33–59.

———. "Duty, Honor, Country: The Social Identity of West Point Cadets." *Armed Forces and Society Journal* 26, No. 2 (Winter 2000): 175–202.

Galluscio, Eugene H. "The Effect of Combat Oriented Training on the Perception of Femininity of Women Cadets." *Journal of the Colorado-Wyoming Academy of Sciences* (April 1977):141–72.

Gillman, David C. "Patterns of Accommodation for Female Cadets of the U.S. Air Force Academy." *Journal of the Colorado-Wyoming Academy of Sciences* (April 1977).

Goldman, Nancy. "The Utilization of Women in the Armed Forces of Industrialized Nations." *Sociological Symposium* (Spring 1977): 12–24.

Gruner, Elliott G. "Merging Fear and Fantasy: Early Images of Women at West Point." *American Transcendental Quarterly* 7, No. 3 (September 1993): 271–84.

Gunderson, E. K. Eric. "Body Size, Self-Evaluation, and Military Effectiveness." *Journal of Personality and Social Psychology* 2 (1965): 902–6.

Hansen, Richard P. "The Crisis of the West Point Honor Code." *Military Affairs* (April 1985): 57–62.

Hester, DeLacie Caroline. "The Quiet Battle: An Integration of Men and Women in State Military Academies." *Law and Psychology Review* 21 (Spring 1997): 221-EOA.

Mazur, Allan, Julie Mazur, and Caroline Keating. "Military Rank Attainment of a West Point Class: Effects of Cadets' Physical Features." *American Journal of Sociology* 90, No. 1 (July 1984): 125–50.

Ponte, Lucille M. "Waldie (Waldie v. Schlesinger, 509 F.2d 508) Answered: Equal Protection and the Admission of Women to Military Colleges and Academies." *New England Law Review* 25 (Summer 1991): 1137–60.

Priest Robert. "Personality and Value Changes in West Point Cadets." *Armed Forces and Society Journal* 8 (Summer 1982): 629–42.

Priest, Robert, Alan Vitters, and Howard T. Prince. "Coeducation at West Point." *Armed Forces and Society Journal* 4, No. 4 (August 1978): 589–605.

Priest, Robert, Howard T. Prince, and Alan G. Vitters. "The First Coed Class at West Point: Performance and Attitudes." *Youth and Society* 10, No. 2 (December 1978): 205–24.

Rice, Robert W., and Alan G. Vitters. "Leader Sex, Follower Attitudes Toward Women and Leadership Effectiveness: An Experimental Study." *Journal of Organizational Behavior and Human Performance* 25 (1980): 46–78.

Rice, Robert W., Debra Instone, and Jerome Adams. "Leader Sex, Leader Success, and Leadership Process: Two Field Studies." *Journal of Applied Psychology* 69, No. 1 (February 1984): 12–31.

Rice, Robert W., Jan D. Yoder, Jerome Adams, Robert F. Priest, and Howard T. Prince II. "Leadership Ratings for Male and Female Military Cadets." *Sex Roles* 10, No. 11–12 (June 1984): 885–901.

Schreiber, E. M., and John C. Woelfel. "Effects of Women on Group Performance in a Traditionally Male Occupation: The Case of the U.S. Army." *Journal of Political and Military Sociology* 7 (1979): 121–34.

Segal, David R., Nora Scott Kinzer, and John Woelfel. "The Concept of Citizenship and Attitudes Toward Women in Combat." *Sex Roles* 3 (1977): 469–77.

Segal, Mady Welchsler. "Women in the Military: Research and Policy Issues." *Youth and Society* 10, No. 2, (December 1978): 101–26.

Segal, Mady Welchsler, and David R. Segal. "Social Change and the Participation of Women in the American Military." *Research in Social Movements, Conflicts, and Change* 5 (1983): 235–58.

Stiehm, Judith Hicks. "Women and the Combat Exemption." *Parameters: The Journal of the Army War College* 10 (1980): 51–59.

Stockdale, Rear Admiral James B. "Experience as a POW in Vietnam." *Naval War College Review* (January-February 1974): 2–6.

Tiger, Lionel. "Are the Harassers in Charge?" *Journal of Contemporary Legal Issues* 8 (Spring 1997): 79–86.

U'Ren, Richard C. "West Point: Cadets, Codes, and Careers." *Society* 12, No. 4 (May/June 1975): 23–29, 36.

Van Creveld, Martin. "Why Israel Doesn't Send Women Into Combat." *Parameters: The Journal of the Army War College* (Spring 1993): 5–9.

Vaugh, William P. "West Point and the First Negro Cadet." *Military Affairs* 35, No. 3 (October 1971): 100–102.

Willard, Charity Cannon. "Early Images of The Female Warrior: Minerva, the Amazons, Joan of Arc." *Minerva* 6, No. 3 (Fall 1988): 1–11.

Yoder, Janice D., Jerome Adams, and Howard T. Prince. "The Price of a Token." *Journal of Political and Military Sociology* 11 (Fall 1983): 325–37.

Yoder, Janice D., Jerome Adams, Stephen Grove, and Robert F. Priest. "To Teach Is to Learn: Overcoming Tokenism with Mentors." *Psychology of Women Quarterly* 9, No. 1 (March 1985): 119–31.

Yoder, Janice D., and Jerome Adams. "Women Entering Nontraditional Roles: When Work Demands and Sex-Roles Conflict: The Case of West Point." *International Journal of Women's Studies* 7, No. 3 (May/June 1984): 260–72.

Welch, Michael J. "Women in the Military Academies: U.S. Army (Part 3 of 3)." *Physician and Sportsmedicine* 17, No. 4 (April 1989): 89–92, 95–96.

Government and Military Publications

Adams, Jerome. *Report of the Admission of Women to the United States Military Academy (Project Athena III)*. West Point: USMA Department of Behavioral Sciences and Leadership (BS&L), June 1979.

———. *Report of the Admission of Women to the United States Military Academy (Project Athena IV)*. West Point: BS&L, June 1980.

———. *Early Career Preparation, Experiences, and Commitment of Female and Male West Point Graduates*. West Point: USMA Office of Institutional Research (OIR), 1983.

———. *Project Proteus: Early Career Preparation, Experiences, and Commitment of Female and Male West Point Graduates*. 3 vols. West Point: Science Research Lab, USMA, 1984–85.

Adams, Jerome, Howard T. Prince II, Robert F. Priest, Janice Yoder, and Robert W. Rice. "Predicting Institutional Ratings of Leadership Ability for Male and Female Cadets." Research Note 79–17. Alexandria, Va.: U.S. Army Research Institute for the Behavioral and Social Sciences, July 1979.

Adams, Jerome, Robert W. Rice, Debra Instone, and Jack M. Hicks. *Follower Attributional Biases and Assessments of Female and Male Leaders' Performance*. Alexandria, Va.: Army Research Institute for the Behavioral and Social Sciences, 1981.

Borman, Frank, et al. "Report of the Special Commission on the United States Military Academy (The Borman Commission), December 15, 1976." *Assembly* 35, No. 4 (March 1977): 2–29.

Bridges, Claude, and Robert F. Priest. "Development of Values and Moral Judgment of West Point Cadets." West Point: OIR, August 1983.

Chapel Board, United States Military Academy. *The West Point Prayer Book*. West Point, NY.: Macmillan Co. for the USMA, 1948.

Congressional Record. 94th Cong., 1st sess., House, 1975, pp. 15449, 15452–54.

Davenport, J., Robert W. Stauffer, and R. de Moya. "Profile of United States Military Academy Women's Physical Education Program." West Point: Department of Physical Education, October 1979.

Davidson, Ted G. "Analysis of PAE Admission Standards." West Point: OIR Report 78–020, September 1978.

Devilbiss, M.C. *Women and Military Service: A History, Analysis, and Overview of Key Issues*. Maxwell Air Force Base, Ala.: Air University Press, 1990.

de Moya, R., Robert W. Stauffer, and J. Davenport. "Profile of United States Military Academy Men's Physical Education Program." West Point: Department of Physical Education, October 1979.

Dickinson, Hillman, Jack V. Mackmull, and Jack N. Merritt. "Final Report of the West Point Study Group." Washington, D.C.: Department of the Army, July 1977.

Foley, Captain Mark. "Leadership and Women in the Army." In "Final Report: Evaluation of Women in the Army." Washington, D.C.: Directorate for the Evaluation of Women in the Army, U.S. Army Administration Center, March 1978.

Hoffman, T., and Robert W. Stauffer. "Sex Differences in Strength." West Point: Department of Physical Education, May 1979.

Houston, John W. "Admission Scores of the USMA Class of 1980." West Point: OIR Report 77–001, October 1976.

———. "Trends in Admission Variables Through the Class of 1980." West Point: OIR Report 77–008, January 1977.

———. "Trends in Admission Variables Through the Class of 1981." West Point: OIR Report 78–008, January 1978.

———. "The First Class Questionnaire, Class of 1981." West Point: OIR Report 81–012, June 1981.

———. "The First Class Questionnaire, Class of 1982." West Point: OIR Report 82–008, June 1982.

Laird, Melvin P. *Final Report to the Congress of Secretary of Defense Melvin R. Laird before the House Armed Services Committee*, 93rd Cong., 1st sess., January 8, 1973.

Leider, Robert. "Why They Leave: Resignations from the USMA Class of 1966." Washington, D.C.: Department of the Army, July 1970.

Military Service Publishing Company. *The Officer's Guide: A Ready Reference on Customs and Correct Procedures Followed Within the Army Which Pertain to Commissioned Officers*. 4th ed. Harrisburg, Penn.: Military Service Publishing Company, 1941.

Peterson, James A., James A. Vogel, Dennis M. Koval, and Louis F. Tomasi. "Summary Report, Project 60: A Comparison of Two Types of Physical Training Programs on the Performance of 16–18 Year Old Women." West Point: Office of Physical Education (OPE), May 1976.

Priest, Robert F. "Cadet Attitudes Toward Women—1975." West Point: OIR Report 76–015, May 1976.

———. "A Comparison of Faculty and Cadet Attitudes Toward Women." West Point: OIR Report 76–017, May 1976.

———. "Changes in Cadet Attitude Toward the Admission of Women to USMA." West Point: OIR Report 76–018, June 1976.

———. "The Effect of Company and CBT Testing Day on New Cadet Attitudes—Class of 1980." West Point: OIR Report 7T-008, September 1976.

———. "Content of Cadet Comments on the Integration of Women." West Point: OIR, 1977.

———. "Cadet Perceptions of Inequitable Treatment During CBT 1976." West Point: OIR Report 77–012, March 1977.

———. "The Intergroup Contact Hypothesis As Applied to Women at West Point." West Point: OIR Report 77–015, June 1977.

———. "Group Membership, Status, and Contact Effects on Male Sex-Role Attitudes." West Point: OIR Report 78–011, March 1978.

Priest, Robert F., and John W. Houston. "Analysis of Spontaneous Cadet Comments on the Admission of Women." West Point: OIR Report 76–014, May 1976.

Priest, Robert F., and J. W. Houston. "New Cadets and Other College Freshmen—Class of 1980." West Point: OIR Report 77–013, March 1977.

Priest, Robert F., Howard T. Prince, Teresa Rhone, and Alan G. Vitters. "Differences Between Characteristics of Men and Women New Cadets, Class of 1980." West Point: OIR Report 77–010, March 1977.

Priest, Robert F., Howard T. Prince, and Alan G. Vitters. "Women Cadets at the United States Military Academy." West Point: OIR Report 78–002, October 1977.

Priest, Robert F., and Howard T. Prince. "Women at West Point: Their Performance and Adjustment." West Point: OIR Report 79–004, February 1979.

"Report to the Secretary of the Army by the Special Commission on the United States Military Academy (Borman Commission)." Washington, D.C.: Department of the Army, December 1976.

Rice, Richer, and Alan G. Vitters. "The Impact of Male and Female Leaders on the Group Performance, Morale and Perceptions of West Point Cadets." Washington, D.C.: Army Research Institute Technical Report, October 1977.

Stauffer, Robert M. "Comparison of United States Military Academy Men and Women on Selected Physical Performance Measures . . . Project Summertime." West Point: Office of Physical Education (OPE), October 1976.

———. "The Prediction of Selected Body Composition Measures of United States Military Academy Men and Women . . . Project Body Composition, Part I." West Point: OPE, August 1977.

———. "Comparison of U.S. Military Academy Men and Women on Selected Anthropometric and Body Composition Measures . . . Project Body Composition, Part II." West Point: OPE, December 1977.

———. "Anthropometrical Assessment of USMA Men and Women . . . Project Body Composition, Part III." West Point: OPE, March 1978.

Stauffer, Robert M., and Richard M. Hayford, Jr. "Comparison of U.S. Military Academy Men and Women on Selected Pulmonary Function Tests." West Point: Department of Physical Education, May 1979.

United States of America v. Commonwealth of Virginia, Lawrence Douglas Wilder, Governor of the Commonwealth of Virginia; Virginia Military Institute, et al., "Transcript of Proceedings Before The Honorable Jackson L. Kiser, Roanoke, Virginia, on the 8th Day of April, 1991." U.S. District Court for the Western District of Virginia, Roanoke Division, 1991.

U.S. Air Force. "Women in the Military." Special Bibliography Series. Colorado Springs: U.S. Air Force, November 1975.

United States Army. "Final Report: Evaluation of Women in the Army." Washington, D.C.: U.S. Army Administration Center, March 1978.

U.S. Congress. House. *Authorization Appropriations for Fiscal Year 1976 and the Period Beginning July 1, 1976 and Ending September 30, 1976 for Military Procurement, Research and Development, Active Duty, Reserve, and Civilian Personnel Strength Levels, Military Training Student Loads, and for Other Purposes.* Report 413, 94th Cong., 1st sess., 26 July 1975, pp. 9, 63–64.

U.S. Congress. House. Committee on Armed Services. *Hearings on Military Posture and H.R. 12564, Department of Defense Authorization for Appropriations for FY75.* 93rd Cong., 2nd sess., January 30, February 25, March 5–7, 12–14, 20–22, 25–28, April 2–4, 8, 23, 1974, pp. 3057–3141.

————. Committee on Armed Services. *Hearings on Military Posture and H.R. 3689 (H.R. 6674), Department of Defense Appropriations for Fiscal Year 1976.* 94th Cong., 1st sess., February 18, 19, 21, 24, 26, March 3, 10, 11, 13, 19, 20, April 14, 17, 21, 22 and May 6, 1975, pp. 1905–8.

U.S. Congress. House. Committee on Armed Services. Subcommittee No. 2. *Hearings on H.R. 9832, To Eliminate Discrimination Based on Sex with Respect to the Appointment and Admission of Persons to the Service Academies and H.R. 10705, H.R. 11267, H.R. 11268, H.R. 11711, and H.R. 13729, To Insure that Each Admission to the Service Academies Shall be Made Without Regard to a Candidate's Sex, Race, Color, or Religious Beliefs.* 93rd Cong., 2nd sess., May 29–August 8, 1974.

————. Subcommittee No. 2, Committee on Armed Services. "Statement of Martin R. Hoffman." *Congressional Quarterly*, July 13, 1974, pp. 1818–21.

U.S. Congress. Senate. "Admission of Women Would Change Primary Mission of Service Academies to Prepare Combat Officers." Statement by Senator B. Goldwater. 94th Cong., 1st sess., August 1, 1975. *Congressional Record*, vol. 121, no. 126, p. S14748.

————. Statement by Senator Goldwater. *Congressional Record.* Vol. 121, no. 143, 94th Cong., 1st sess., September 26, 1975, pp. 16923–24.

————. *Public Laws, 94th Congress, H.R. 6674, Authorizing Funds for Military Procurement for Fiscal Year 1976.* Approved October 7, 1975. Public Law 106. 94th Cong., 1st sess., 1975.

U.S. General Accounting Office. "DOD Service Academies: Further Efforts Needed to Eradicate Sexual Harassment." Statement by Mark E. Gebicke, Director, Military Operations and Capabilities Issues, National Security and International Affairs Division. Testimony Before the Subcommittee on Force Requirements and Personnel, Committee on Armed Services. U.S. Senate. GAO/T-NSIAD-94-111, February 3, 1994.

————. "Military Academy: Gender and Racial Disparities." GAO/NSIAD-94-95, March, 1994.

————. "DOD Service Academies—Update on Extent of Sexual Harassment." Report to Congressional Requesters. GAO/NSIAD-95-98, March 1995.

U.S. Government Printing Office. *Public Papers of the Presidents of the United States: Gerald R. Ford—1975.* 2 books. *Book I : January 1 to July 17, 1975.* Washington, D.C.: GPO, 1977, 1975.

United States Military Academy (USMA) "The Annual Report of the Superintendent, 1980." West Point: USMA, 1980.

————. *Bugle Notes.* vol. 68. West Point: USMA, 1976.

————. "The Fourth Class System 1976–1977." West Point: USMA, 1976.

————. "Four Year Changes in Cadet Personal Values: Class of 1981." West Point: ODIR Report 82-002, April 1982.

————. "Information for Women Cadets." Booklet. West Point: USMA, November 1975.

————. "Operations Plan 75-1: Admission of Women Cadets." West Point: USMA, September 15, 1975.

————. "Report of the Senior Management Conference on Leadership of an Integrated Army." West Point: USMA, April 1978.

————. *The Howitzer: The Annual of the United States Corps of Cadets.* West Point: USMA, 1980 and 1900.

————. "The Superintendent's Annual Historical Review, 1965." West Point: USMA 1965.

————. "Trends in Admission Variables Through the Class of 1982." West Point: ODIR Report 79-001, October 1978.

————. "Trends in Admission Variables Through the Class of 1984." West Point: ODIR Report 81-006, January 1981.

————. "Trends in Admission Variables Through the Class of 1986." West Point: ODIR Report 82-014, October 1982.

Vitters, Alan G. *Report of the Admission of Women to the United States Military Academy (Project Athena II).* West Point: BS&L, June 1978.

Vitters, Alan G., and Nora Scott. Kinzer, *Report of the Admission of Women to the United States Military Academy (Project Athena I).* West Point: BS&L, September, 1977.

Vitters, Alan G., and Howard T. Prince. "Women at West Point: Non-Traditional Roles in a Traditional Setting." West Point: BS&L, April 1977.

White, Jerry, Mary Willis, John Kuspa, and John Adams. "Study of the Integrated Services of Men and Women Within the Corps of Cadets." USMA Report, 15 November 1978.

Wright, Jack B. "Trends in Admission Variables Through the Class of 1989." West Point: OIR Report 86-003, March 1986.

Yoder, Jan, Robert W Rice, Jerome Adams, Howard T. Prince, and Robert F. Priest. "Predicting Institutional Ratings of Leadership Ability for Male and Female Cadets." Alexandria, Va.: U.S. Army Research Institute for the Behavioral and Social Sciences, July 1979.

Newspaper and Magazine Articles

Air Force Times. "Academy Idea Gains Strength: DACOWITS Wants Women Admitted." November 27, 1974, p. 26.

————. "Females in Academy Backed: Stratton Raps Hazing." June 12, 1974, p. 2.

————. "Women in Academies: House Votes Big Yes." June 4, 1975, p. 22.

————. "Jacqueline Cochran Tells Why She Can't Back Female Cadets." December 4, 1974, pp. 13, 48.

————. "Only 1 of 15 Females Quits at Kings Point." August 28, 1974, p. 28.

————. "Women Cadets: Up to the Courts to Decide." March 13, 1974, p. 6.

Army Navy Air Force Journal. "Senator Chavez Seeks 'West Point' for Women." February 26, 1955, p. 754.

————. "A Women's Academy Suggested." January 23, 1954, p. 623.

Army Navy Air Force Register. "Women's Armed Services Academy." February 26, 1955, p. 3.

Assembly. "Report of the West Point Study Group." December 1977, pp. 5–12.

————. "Graduation 1980." September 1980, pp. 18–19, 38.

Bernstein, Amy. "Shannon Faulkner Should Have Come Here." *U.S. News and World Report*, August 22, 1994, p. 16.

Brantley, James. "Dereliction of Duty: Compromising Our Armed Forces for Political Correctness." *Soldier of Fortune*, January 1993, pp. 30–35.

Broder, Jonathan. "The Army of the Right." *Salon Magazine*, January 12, 1998, pp. 1–10.

Brower, J. Michael. "Undermining Old Taboos: U.S., U.K. Studies Say Women Can Meet Physical Demands of Combat." *Armed Forces Journal*, May 1996, p. 13.

Buckley Jr., William F. "Women's Place: In the Foxhole." *Los Angeles Times*, March 20, 1978.

Bunting, Josiah III. "West Point Counterpoint." *Esquire*, November 1976, pp. 67–70.

Butler, Richard P. "Graduates' Image of the U.S. Military Academy." *Assembly*, September 1979, pp. 34–35, 127.

Callender, Bruce, et al. "The Unseen Force Theory: What Caused the Pentagon's Turnaround on Women's Rights?" *Air Force Times*, April 10, 1974, p. 13.

Carroll, Ginny. "Women Have What It Takes." *Newsweek*, August 5, 1991, pp. 118, 130.

Clark, Albert P. "Women at the Service Academies and Combat Leadership." *Assembly*, June 1978, pp. 12–14, 28–30.

Cohen, Martin. "The West Point Diet and Exercise Program for Women." *Ladies Home Journal*, May 1976, p. 60.

Conroy, Pat. "Conroy's Complaint." *Atlanta Magazine*, January 2000, pp. 64–71, 129.

Cousins, Norman. "Cheaters Unlimited." *Saturday Review*, October 16, 1976, p. 4.

Dolan, B. "West Point: The Coed Class of 1980." *Time*, May 19, 1980, pp. 6–8.

DuPont, Nicholas. "The Military Husband." *The Times Magazine*, November 1, 1976, pp. 16, 32.

Ettlinger, Catherine. "Skiing With the Guys: A Parable for Women of West Point, Wall Street, and Other Formerly All-Male Territory." *Working Woman*, February 1987, pp. 76–80.

Evans, David. "The Navy's Blues." *New York Times*, June 8, 1996, p. 19.

Famiglietti, Len. "Combat Role Not Settled; Coed Academy Now in Works." *Air Force Times*, June 25, 1975, p. 2.

Fein, Esther. "The Choice: Women Officers Decide to Stay In or Leave." *New York Times Magazine*, May 3, 1985, pp. 32–37.

Feron, James. "Change Marches Through West Point." *Colorado Springs Sun*, September 29, 1975, p. 3.

Fleming, Thomas. "West Point Cadets Now Say, Why, Sir?' " *New York Times Maga-zine*, July 5, 1970, pp. 14–20.

Foster, George. " 'Men Only' Academy Fight Nears." *Air Force Times*, January 2, 1974, p. 13.

Fraker, Susan, and Eric Gelman. "The Army: A Point of Honor." *Newsweek*, May 24, 1976, p. 29.

Hackworth, David H. "Soldier's Disgust." *Harper's Magazine*, July, 1972, pp. 74–78.

Hansen, Richard P. "The Crisis of the West Point Honor Code." *Military Affairs*, April, 1985, pp. 57–62.

Hasenauer, Heike. "Women at West Point." *Soldiers*, July 1991, pp. 42–44.

Heffernan, C. F. "Look, the Mate's a Girl!: Women in the Merchant Marine." *Seventeen*, February, 1976, p. 160.

Holmes, Steven A. "Time and Money Producing Racial Harmony in Military." *New York Times*, April 5, 1995, pp. A1, A14.

Hottell, John Alexander. "A Soldier's Obituary." *New York Times*, March 3, 1971, p. 43.

Hoy, Pat C. III. "Soldiers and Scholars." *Harvard Magazine*, May/June 1996, pp. 65–70.

Jastrzemski, W. M. "Women's Liberation and the Service Academies." *Armed Forces Journal International*, March 1974, p. 29.

Johnson, Tom. "Cadet Edgar Allan Poe." *American Heritage*, June 1976, pp. 60–63, 87–88.

Just, Ward. "West Point Rendezvous: Notes on the 'Vietnam Class.' " *Atlantic*, January 1975, pp. 44–47.

Keerdoja, Eileen. "Second Chance" and "Silent Treatment." *Newsweek*, August 8, 1977, p. 11.

Kinzer, Stephen. "West Point Faces Life." *New Republic*, December 3, 1977, pp. 14–17.

Lichtenstein, Grace. "Kill, Hate, Mutilate." *New York Times Magazine*, September 5, 1976, pp. 10–11, 37–42.

———. "A Year Later: How Women Are Faring at the Air Academy." *New York Times Magazine*, September 11, 1977, p. 107.

McEwen, Darryl D. "Women at West Point." *Soldiers*, June 1976, pp. 28–31.

Moore, Robert, and Joseph Ellis. "The (Latest) West Point Cheating Scandal: Obeisance to an Ideal." *New Republic*, June 12, 1976, pp. 15–17.

Morganthau, Tom, et al. "The Military Fights the Gender Wars." *Newsweek*, November 14, 1994, pp. 35–37.

Myers, Steven Lee. "To Sex-Segregated Training, the Marines Remain Semper Fi." *New York Times*, December 26, 1997, p. A1.

National Review. "I'm No Angel." June 25, 1976, pp. 662, 664.

Newsweek. "The New Gray Line." December 1, 1975, p. 65.

———. "West Point: Braced For Reform." September 24, 1973, p. 36.

———. "West Point: The Silencing." June 18, 1973, p. 42.

Newton, Helen. "Women at West Point." *Ladies Home Journal*, May 1976, p. 59.

Nichols, Claudia. "An Officer and a Gentlewoman." *The Times Magazine*, June 3, 1985, pp. 4–6, 10–12, 25–27.

Officer. "Rep. DuPont Pushing for Women in Service Academies." December 1973, p. 8.

Pappas, George. "What if the Academy Had Been Abolished in 1830?" *Assembly*, May 1995, pp. 12, 14, 16, 18.

Rapp, Kenneth. "The Legend of Fanny Elssler's Pirouette by Moonlight." *Dance Magazine*, July 1975, pp. 41–42.

Rayner, Richard. "Women as Warriors." *New York Times Magazine*, June 22, 1997, pp. 25–29, 40, 49, 53, 55–56.

Ropp, Theodore. "A Visitor at West Point: Some Mostly Academic Impressions." *Assembly*, June 1978, pp. 8–9, 27–28.

Rowes, Barbara. "Cadets Were Skeptical at First, but Now Bonnie Bennett Has 'Em Doing Handstands at West Point." *People*, June 3, 1985, pp. 86–87.

———. "Fighting Chance." *Omni*, November 1984, pp. 81–84.

Rozen, Leah, and Barbara Rowes. "West Pointers Flip and Fall for Marian Rockwell." *People*, March 23, 1987, pp. 65–68.

Ryan, D. M. "Women and the Service Academies: Introduction." *High School News Service Report* 19, No. 7 (April 1976): 3.

Salter, James. "It's Not the Old Point." *Life Magazine*, May 1980, pp. 70–79.

Schmitt, Eric. "Study Says Sexual Harassment Persists at Military Academies." *New York Times*, April 5, 1995, p. A14.

Senior Scholastic. "Does the Honor Code Make Super-Soldiers or Sneaks?" September 9, 1976, p. 15.

Shaw, C. Dennis. "Deployment Criteria—Who Stays and Who Stays Behind?" *Army Magazine*, December 1995, pp. 13–15.

Simons, Anna. "In War, Let Men be Men: Why Combat Units Should Remain Male." *New York Times*, April 23, 1997, p. A15.

Stamell, Marcia. "The Basic Training of Joan Smith." *Ms.*, August 1977, pp. 48–51, 98–99.

Stevens, Phil. "Women at Academies: Navy Also Stresses Combat Role." *Air Force Times*, June 26, 1974, p. 3.

———. "Women in Combat Key Issue of Bill." *Air Force Times*, June 19, 1974, p. 19.

Tausch, Egon R. "Should West Point Survive?" *National Review*, March 15, 1974, p. 318.

Thompson, Mark. "Academies Out of Line." *New York Times*, April 18, 1994, pp. 37–38.

Tiger, Lionel. "Trump the Race Card." *Wall Street Journal*, February 23, 1996, p. A12.

Time. "Return of The EE 304's." September 19, 1977, p. 29.

———. "Dating at West Point." November 19, 1979, p. 43.

———. "Flourishing Academies." August 26, 1974, p. 73.

———. "An End to Silence." June 18, 1973, pp. 24–25.

———. "Long Gray Hemline." February 9, 1976, p. 29.

———. "The Faltering Gray Line." May 10, 1976, p. 88.

———. "What Price Honor?" June 7, 1976, pp. 18–29.

———. "Upstaging the Goat." June 14, 1976, p. 18.

———. "Beauties and the Beast." July 19, 1976, p. 74.

———. "A Barrage Hits West Point's Code." December 27, 1976, p. 16.

U.S. News and World Report. "When Women Enter the Service Academies." August 18, 1975, p. 25.

———. "Women at Military Academies: Not Much of a Problem." October 20, 1975, p. 64.

———. "So Far, So Good: A Report Card on Coed Military Academies." July 11, 1977, pp. 26–31.

Vitters, Alan G. "A Preliminary Report on Women Cadets at the US Military Academy." *Assembly*, December 1976, p. 15–18.

———. "Down the Trail—Women at West Point." *Assembly*, December 1977, p. ?.

Vitters, Alan G., and Nora Scott Kinzer. "Woman at West Point: Change Within Tradition." *Military Review*, March 1978, pp. 20–28.

Wansley, J. "First Women Graduates of West Point Say with Pride: It Was Tough but We Survived." *People*, April 21, 1980, pp. 28–31.

Washington Post. "Women Sue Service Academies." September 27, 1973, p. A34.

Watkins, Susan Finlay. "It is No Longer a Matter of Comment to See a Body of Young Ladies under Military Training." *Assembly*, June 1980, pp. 6–7, 26–27.

Webb, James. "Women Can't Fight." *The Washingtonian*, November 1979, pp. 144–148, 273–282.

Unpublished Sources

[Author's note: *Cadet letters, journals, and correspondence would fit into this category. They are not listed, however, because they cannot be referenced without compromising the author's identity*.]

Columbia Pictures Television. "Women at West Point." Script dated August 1, 1978.

Crowley, Eileen Mary. "Physical Education Program Modifications at the United States Military Academies to Accommodate Women." M.A. thesis, University of Maryland, 1978.

Dean, Donna Margaret. "Warriors Without Weapons: The Victimization of Military Women." Ph.D. dissertation, The Union Institute, 1993.

Fincher, Michele Sakuyako. "Gender-Role Orientation of Female Cadets at the United States Air Force Academy." M.S. thesis, Auburn University, 1993.

Friedman, Stanford B. "Long Term Stress and Illness Project: Fourth In-Progress Review, March 1994 to April 1995." Montefiore Medical Center/Albert Einstein College of Medicine, Department of Pediatrics, Division of Adolescent Medicine, 1995.

———. "Third In Process Review: Long Term Stress and Illness Project." Montefiore Medical Center/Albert Einstein College of Medicine, March 1994.

Galloway, Judith M. "The Impact of the Admission of Women to the Service Academies on the Role of the Woman Line Officer." A paper prepared for the 10th Annual Inter-University Seminar on the Armed Forces and Society, October 17, 1975.

Goldstein Sayre, Bette Ruth. "Analysis of Selected Physical Performance and Psychological Factors Related to Achievement of Women Cadets at the United States Coast Guard Academy." Ph.D. dissertation, New York University, 1984.

Gould, Jay W. III. "Education and Training of Women in the United States Military: A Study of Primary Leadership Institutions." Paper prepared for a seminar within the University of Southern California Department of Public Administration and reproduced by the Defense Systems Management College, 1992.

Hancock, Cynthia Riffe. "Women Officers at the United States Military Academy: A Study of Acceptance Patterns and Coping Mechanisms." Ph.D. dissertation, University of North Carolina at Chapel Hill, 1991.

Harris, Major Boyd. "West Point Journal." West Point, New York: United States Military Academy Library—Special Collections, 1976.

Heinzman, Richard R. "A Policy Analysis of the Admission of Women by the U.S. Military Academies." Maxwell Air Force Base, Ala.: Air War College, Air University, 1986.

Hillman, Elizabeth Lutes. "Uniform Identities: Women, Gender, and Images at the United States Service Academies." M.A. thesis, University of Pennsylvania, 1994.

Kowal, Dennis M. "Physical Fitness in the Army." Paper prepared for the U.S. Army Research Institute of Environmental Medicine, March 1977.

Manning, Lory and Jennifer E. Griffith. "Women in the Military: Where They Stand." 2nd ed. A Women in the Military Project Report Prepared for the Women's Research and Education Institute, 1998.

McBrier, Debra Branch. "Gender Equality and Perspectives Toward Women in the Military: The Effects of Politics, Religion, and Gender Roles on Attitudes Towards Women in Combat." M.A. thesis, University of Oklahoma, 1994.

McKeon, Jane Perkins. "Predicting Attrition for Women at West Point: Is It a Function of Adopting the Male Dominant Culture?" M.A. thesis, University of Richmond, 1990.

O'Neal, James P. "Female Cadet Attrition at the United States Military Academy." M.S. thesis, University of Tennessee, Knoxville, 1978.

Priest, Robert F., Stephen B. Grove, and Jerome Adams. "Institutional and Historical Perspectives on Women in Military Academy Roles." Paper Delivered at the American Psychological Association Annual Meeting, September 1980.

Remley, Mary L. "Physical Education at the United States Military Academy, 1966–1992." Paper prepared for the Department of Physical Education, 1992.

Schoonmaker, Linda Lee. "The History and Development of the Programs of Physical Education, Intercollegiate Athletics, Intramurals and Recreational Sports for Women at the United States Military Academies." Ph.D. dissertation, Ohio State University, 1983.

Sands, Gene Cameron. "An Administrative History of the U.S. Air Force Academy, 1954–1979." Ph.D. dissertation, Catholic University of America, 1982.

Tiger, Lionel. "Durkheim, Sociology, and the Science of Bodies in Conflict." Paper presented at the Interdisciplinary Summary Conference of the Study of War Project, Triangle Institute of Security Studies, June 1997.

Yoder, Janice D., and Jerome Adams. "A Report on Women West Point Graduates Assuming Nontraditional Roles." Paper presented at the 56th Annual Meeting of the Midwestern Psychological Association, Chicago, May 3–5, 1984.

Fiction

Bunting, Josiah. *The Lionheads*. New York: George Braziller, Inc., 1972.

Efaw, Amy. *Battle Dress*. New York: Harper Collins Juvenile Books, 2000.

Ruggero, Ed. *The Academy*. New York: Pocket Books, 1997.

Spiller, Benjamin A. *Indomitable*. Colorado Springs: Pike's Peak Publishing, 1989.

Truscott, Lucian K. IV. *Dress Gray*. Garden City, N.Y.: Doubleday, 1979.

———. *Full Dress Gray*. New York: William Morrow and Company, 1998.

Vakkur, Mark. *A Matter of Trust*. New York: Harper Paperbacks, 1990.

Index

About the Author

LANCE JANDA is an assistant professor of history at Cameron University in Lawton, Oklahoma. He earned his Ph.D. from the University of Oklahoma in 1998, and serves as the book review editor of *Minerva: Quarterly Journal of Women in the Military*. His articles and book reviews have appeared in *The Journal of Military History* and *Magill's Guide to Military History*, among others, and he recently published a chapter on the admission of women to West Point in *A Soldier and a Woman: Sexual Integration in the Military*.